INNOCENT IN A REVOLUTION

INNOCENT IN A REVOLUTION

Colin D. Forbes

The Book Guild Ltd
Sussex, England

The Book Guild Ltd.
25 High Street,
Lewes, Sussex

First published 1999
© Colin D. Forbes, 1999

Set in Times
Typesetting by
SetSystems Ltd, Saffron Walden, Essex

Printed in Great Britain by
Antony Rowe Ltd, Chippenham, Wiltshire

A catalogue record for this book is
available from the British Library

ISBN 1 85776 308 4

To my Father –
We've made it!

CONTENTS

PREFACE

Early in 1958, I went to Iraq as export representative for Colgate Palmolive UK. Increasing business meant encouraging the Iraqis to wash and clean their teeth more – what could be more interesting?

My stay in Iraq was cut short after three and a half months by the Bloody Revolution of 14 July 1958, which resulted in the murder of the King, his uncle and the Prime Minister. After skirmishes with the mobs I managed to get away, but had to destroy all my papers and notes.

People have been amused and interested in my experiences, so I started to jot them down on paper. These jottings were read by a friend one day, who suggested that they might make a book. Enlarging on the Revolution, the story you are about to read covers my whole stay in Iraq – my first venture overseas, and then ventures into the Far East.

Within two weeks of my escape and return to a hero's welcome at Colgate UK's London office, I was on my way to Singapore with the new territories of Afghanistan, East and West Pakistan, Portuguese Goa, Ceylon, Burma, Malaya and the Borneo Territories.

Just four months after escaping Baghdad, I was in Rangoon for another major revolution – an army coup. Could I survive two in one year? Read on!

ACKNOWLEDGEMENTS

The point is reached when you think you have the ms how you want it and hypermania prevails. You look about the full range of friends and acquaintances to see which might read the thing for you and make honest noises back. Erstwhile work-place colleague like Keith Boyall – an avid reader and prone to say his piece, whatever. John Bell, who would not only say his piece, whatever, but did a fantastic proof read too. Terry Cubbin from boyhood days who now takes me flying in his Grumman A–5. Bob Fowler (best man); Paul Gibbs-Pancheri – old Far East hand; Prof Rees Jones ex UEA historian; Keith Eastman – fellow churchman; Trevor and Penny Robinson – erstwhile clients.

When into the offering about and rejection phase, other help and encouragement is needed and much is owed to the likes of Dr John Humphreys, the book gnome of Mattishall and old Borneo hand; Lesley Higgenbotham of BDH Printers; Tim Williamson – of Norfolk Club fame; the late Dr Ann Reader; Stephanie Zarach of Book Production Consultants; Anthony Tuffin, fellow worker at Inchcape who was at Habaniyah in 1958 via RAF National Service, with Paul Girling, and the likes of Margaret Boepple and John and Anne Steel in New York.

While the chapters on the bloody experiences of 14th July 1958 and the wonders of the land between the two great rivers that is Iraq were written down almost 40 years ago and reflect attitudes and languages of that time, there was always the prospect of writing up on similar experiences in Rangoon at October 1958 Coup and Vietnam and Cambodia later.

This was given a kick start by encouraging words from John Simpson after getting sight of my record of Baghdad 1958 while he was reporting from there for BBC at time of Gulf crisis. So, once the tranquil waters of retirement came to pass the taping on Tubby in the Far East began and dear Sheron Harley of WORDPRO, here in Norwich, became a most helpful guiding hand.

Finally, my dear wife and Penelope of 40 years – come the Millenium – bonded in our abiding christian faith. Thankfully, she retired first to be my full-time shrink and with her organ playing, fuchsias, horto society, choirs etc., has understood my retreats to the upper den to be at the Words!

Colin D. Forbes

P.S. Join good old Colgate-Palmolive Company and see the world!

INTRODUCTION

Have you ever stood opposite the top of the escalators in the London Underground at rush hour and watched the endless stream of humanity spouting up from the trains below? Numbed by the humdrum and routine of life people automatically go their various ways with mask-like expressions. I am one of this stream, in spite of grand ideas after the war to do something different. Now that is many years ago, and I am well and truly a suburban troglodyte, entrenched in the routine of 'to and from' the big city.

I work for a large, international company and, what with work and odd jobs to be done at home, I hardly read beyond the headlines in my daily paper. Luckily, however, I work in the export department and meet our overseas operators when they come back from trips. These fellows are a breath of fresh air in my small sphere of existence, especially one fellow, whom we call Tubby. He is not fat, as the name might imply, but tall and well-covered, which is not surprising as he really enjoys good food. This we know because we often have him round to dinner when he is home, and this was how I was able to hear so much about his last trip, though the whole story was spread over several visits.

Tubby is quite a character and how much extra of his own humour he has thrown in as his story-teller's licence I don't know; but it was all good listening for home dwellers like myself and it threw much light on certain headlines which shook up even us on 15 July 1958.

1

AWAY TO BAGHDAD

Starting at the huge BOAC international terminus building at Victoria in London, Tubby began relating the things which happened on his latest trip. He was there for one of the numerous injections one needs before going overseas. How amused he had been to find some benevolent medico seated, resplendent, behind a big desk in all his glory, with pen in one hand, rubber stamp in the other, waiting to perform the necessary paperwork once the pretty nurse had performed the medical side. He smiled as he returned Tubby's little yellow health book and said, 'Don't come in before 10.30 a.m. next time – save you waiting around.'

Good grief, thought Tubby, he probably goes home each day to write fiery articles in *The Lancet* condemning the iniquitous health scheme. On reflection though, Tubby thought all medicos deserved some return for their early years in penury and toil even after six years of sweat and study. Tubby was always going off the rails and airing his views on various subjects in this round-about sort of way, but he always managed to mount the rails again before we lost interest or arguments broke out.

He continued with a description of the great hall of the Victoria air terminal on his departure day – the eye catching posters; the prim and efficient uniformed staff attending to the numerous needs of the ever-changing cosmopolitan crowd. The sound of the bagpipes outside drew the waiting travellers to the swing doors to watch a platoon of Scots Guards pass along the road. All the types and nations were there to be seen; fussy Americans demanding the attention of at least five officials; various African and Asian students going home with mementos of their stay in Britain; families on the move surrounded by

1

children and baggage and Lord knows what; and the seasoned business travellers, arrival timed nicely, the right documents all at hand and in order, and dressed ready for the journey and the climate to which they were heading.

One can never fail to stand in awe of the place, or be carried away by the romance and excitement of travel as the numerous flights are announced.

'BOAC announce the departure of flight BA226, calling at Rome, Beirut, Damascus, Baghdad, Kuwait and Bahrain. Will all passengers please assemble at the South end of the hall where a bus is waiting to take them to the airport.'

This is mine, thought Tubby, as he knocked out his pipe and moved off.

A last look at London as the bus passed through Chelsea. The boat race came to mind as they drove through Putney, Chiswick, Mortlake. How amazing to think that one can fly from London to Paris in the same time it takes to travel from the Victoria terminal to London Airport. Oh, for the advent of helicopters! At last the beautiful sight of the sleek monsters of the air lined up and ready to go to the four corners of the globe. Off the bus into the wartime Nissen huts – which still served as departure buildings. Here again the cross section of the peoples of the world was being ushered toward their respective coloured lights by the staff of the various airlines.

Tubby had just unloaded his bag and portable typewriter and was contemplating a smoke before the second phase of formalities started, when he heard his name announced over the loudspeaker system. Without more ado he picked up his bits and pieces again and started for the fairest looking wench at the desk, but was swept down upon by a magnificently-uniformed character with gold braid up to his elbows. No less than the senior captain of the airline himself, thought Tubby, turning to this gentleman and giving his puckered-eyebrow question-mark look. Mr Gold Braid just steered him into the VIP lounge with a smile and some gracious remark about BOAC hospitality. Tubby was seated in a plush chair, plied with smokes and drinks, relieved of his passport, informed that all details would be attended to, and that he would be called when it was time for take-off.

Nothing like this had ever happened before and he was convinced he had been mistaken for Robin Douglas Home, or some other leftover from Debrett, fleeing from the press after a love affair. His mind was put at ease when some arch character, dressed in sporting civvies, bounced through the door, introduced himself as Spring-heeled Jack of the West End Travel Agency, and explained that all this was just part of the service. Tubby then remembered that the various secretaries who attended to his tickets at Head Office had their own pet agencies and obviously he had never had this one before. He made a mental note of the name so that he could ask for it specifically next time he was home. And so Spring-heeled Jack once more demonstrated the immeasurable value of the representative. A gesture here, a remark there, passed unnoticed by the untrained eye, and yet paying such dividends.

Finally, the call to the plane. Jack saw him right to the door, dismissing Customs with a sweep of the arm. Passing Tubby safely into the tender care of the hostess, Jack bowed out, his mission accomplished.

The bus trundled out from the airport building and weaved in and out among the graceful ships of the air. They always reminded Tubby of huge queen ants with their busy little attendants fussing round them; the fire extinguishers, the baggage trolleys, the generators, the maintenance ladders, the fuel tenders. It was fascinating how they all appeared on cue at each airport as soon as the little man with the bats had directed the big plane into its exact allotted square footage. The bus passed along the rows of Super Constellations, Boeing Strato Cruisers, Britannias, DC6s and 7Bs, and eventually stopped by a rather faded Connie – the Lockheed Constellation, which preceded the Super Connie. Well that's torn it, thought Tubby. Royalty must be on the move somewhere and taken one of the Britannias, so they had to bring this old bus out of semi-retirement. What a pity the Comet had been set back several years.

It was a first-class-only plane, and there were only enough

3

passengers to fill half of it, so all and sundry were able to stretch out their legs and spread their bits and pieces over two seats. One picked out the seasoned travellers immediately by the way they set about making themselves comfortable. Jackets came off, ties came off, old slippers were produced and shoes replaced, and reading matter was placed within reach before the seat was finally adjusted. They really looked as though they were settling down for the generation and first timers always just sat and stared with open-mouthed wonder.

The stewardess gave her little speech of welcome and assured them that they would lack nothing till the journey's end. A steward then appeared and they both did their regulation demonstration of how to blow up the old life jacket in case the plane crashed in the drink. The final check-through at the start of the runway began and the captain put each engine through its paces, which forcibly reminded Tubby that he was in an old 'Connie'. The engine noise and vibration made the old wings flap so much that one thought she was actually going to propel herself by this means. Finally, gaining speed every second, she started down the runway and after what seemed an age she pulled herself clear and started the long laborious climb towards the grey ceiling of an overcast sky. To think that those big roaring monsters of engines outside the window would keep it up like that for hours and hours. Tubby resigned himself to the prospect of a sleepless trip.

The plane was halfway across the channel and still climbing when it finally broke into the sunshine. Tubby looked back at the vast grey mantle covering the old country and noticed the thin, almost silver, vapour trail of a jet bomber flying in the dark blue cold of the high heavens. Shortly after the French coast, clouds began to speckle the earth away below and by the time they were over Paris, the ground was obscured. The cloud remained even over the Alps and all that could be seen were a few of the highest peaks which broke through the white shroud. It made one wonder how the crews took these big planes down into Switzerland in such conditions.

Shortly after take off, the first class treatment had started. The drinks, the smokes (no pipes allowed), the aperitifs, the umpteen course meals, and back to the drinks and smokes again – all on the house, of course. This was well and truly impressed upon Tubby by the character sitting on the opposite side of the plane. Employed by the airline as a resident overseas ground mechanic, he was on his way to Bahrain to look after all planes passing through there. He had been waiting in London for several days, ready to move at a moment's notice on the first plane heading in that direction which had empty seats. How these characters can liven up one's journey. He was most proud of his employers and their service, so much so that whenever Tubby looked as though he were about to reach for his own cigarettes his mate would shout to the stewardess, 'Miss! Miss! Cigarette for the gentleman – and a whisky for me while you're at it.' He would then nudge Tubby in the ribs and confidentially stage-whisper: 'Wonderful service, ain't it?'

At the sight of a uniformed figure appearing from up front, he immediately asked Tubby if he had ever been 'up front.' Before an answer could be given, Matey had collared the uniform and fixed everything up. Tubby didn't mind as it always interested him to see the array of equipment crammed in the cockpit, and the view from the driver's seat, as it were. Before returning to his seat he vociferously explained to the flying crew that his intrusion was really none of his doing.

Of the rest of the passengers, there were only two of interest. One was an elderly gent, with pallid complexion, thin wispy grey hair, an elongated, tired face – half spaniel – half bloodhound, who wore a pair of wire-framed bifocal glasses. He had the rather wandered air of a professor about him, and appeared at the airport in a high-crowned grey felt hat, navy blue suit, knitted cardigan, wrongly buttoned down the front, and an old raincoat over his arm. One would expect, by his appearance, that he was going home to his little greenhouse in suburbia to potter with his plants, and not going on a plane to some hot place in the Middle East. It transpired that he was a back room boffin of some sort and had held a professorship at some time. He turned up in Baghdad at the same hotel as Tubby – as did the other interesting party on the plane. He was a young Italian who came aboard at Rome. He looked more like a Frenchman, really, with a longish toothbrush moustache which stuck straight out. He stared at the world through a pair or enormous black-framed spectacles which, when seen head on, looked like the observation windows in the side of a big aquarium. While at Rome, a Britannia which had left London well after the Connie caught up with them. Down she came like a sleek arrow with her great propeller blades thrashing the air as they changed pitch once she was on the ground. It made Tubby realise just how long it had taken the old Connie to get to Rome. Darkness began to close in as the hoard of attendant vehicles gathered round the Brit.

Night had descended when the plane took off on the next stage, and out of the window Tubby could see only the small green light on the wing tip and the spitting, roaring flames of the engine exhausts, making the metal glow red hot. After more food, more drinks, and more smokes, some put their seats right back and pulled blankets over them in an effort to sleep. Eventually they descended into Beirut, gradually dropping below the tops of the mountains, only discernible by the myriad lights shining from them.

Beirut sported a very swish and modern airport building which accentuated the extreme grubbiness of Damascus, where they landed in the dead of night. Here they were really getting away from accepted standards. This was dear Uncle Nasser's United Arab Republic and everywhere his 'Punch' face stared down like a World War One poster. The air of suspicion and hatred started at the airport building – 'Surrender your passports for inspection,' said the armed guard at the door. Tubby wondered if it was going to be like Indonesia, where in similar circumstances one's passport has a habit of getting lost until a handsome sum is paid over to an official who miraculously finds it again. Dirty little lads followed the passengers round like evil spirits. Three little boys in dirty shimmies swarmed into the gents to assist Tubby in the act of relieving himself. All with one accord pointed to the largest silver coins in his hand when the time came to try and get out of the gents again. It was also here that Tubby first came in contact with that ever present facet of life in the Arab world – the smells; but more of this later.

All the passengers couldn't get back to the plane quickly enough and were soon bedded down again as the plane climbed up into the black velvet of night sky over the desert, speckled with twinkling stars. The few who did manage to drop off into a deep sleep lost the chance to witness one of the wonders of this world we live on, which began after an hour or so – dawn over the desert. It is one of those experiences which makes one think deeply about a lot of things: life, the world, mankind, why we are here, the One who is behind it and where and what it is all leading up to. A sailor once told Tubby of feeling this same way when alone on the bridge of his ship at night in the middle of some ocean with nothing but the stars in the heavens and the noise of the sea all around him.

Dawn was a very slow process but ever changing. First the slightest trace of light turned all outside into an unreal steel-grey colour. There appeared to be clouds everywhere and even the desert appeared grey, and yet alive with faint light. The grey slowly turned to white; what had seemed to be cloud became semi-transparent and the true sand colour began to assert itself below. The whole great scene seemed to glow, intensify and take shape like a huge backcloth at the theatre when the lights are gradually brought up. At one stage it seemed cold, clear and white like the Arctic wastes until, almost imperceptibly, one became aware of a slight yellowness coming into the vast scene and one realised that the sun still had not arrived.

When it did appear it was like a Jack-in-the-Box in its suddenness. Not much of it, only the top curve of an orange ball, but not the slightest indication was given at which point it would appear. Like the beams from a searchlight one could almost see the first rays which shot across the scene when the sun did make its entrance. The semi-transparency of cloud just dissolved and there was suddenly a blue tinge in the heavens. The desert below was immediately turned into relief as the rays of sunlight sped across it, revealing ripples, dunes and gullies which were not visible before, giving the ground a deep sandy colour. The sun became a pale butter colour as it rose, the heavens became bluer, the desert less intense and more even in colour as the higher angle of the sun's rays reduced the shadows. Another day in this earth's long history had begun and few are those who witness it from such a grandstand seat.

On over the endless wastes the Connie droned, until suddenly the earth below became green. How long those two great rivers have brought life to the desert. What history lies between the Tigris and the Euphrates as they wind their way to the Persian Gulf, some places so near, others far apart. Oh, that they could speak and tell mankind more about the ruins that abound along their banks. Babylon the Great and Nineveh, the centres of the ancient world. How obvious it all was from the air, that civilisation should flourish in these great areas of green among these endless wastes. And so Tubby arrived in romantic and mysterious Baghdad, the scene of his adventures to come; thank goodness the future is withheld from mankind. The sun was bright, it was still early, and the place looked fairly clean.

2

THE HOTEL KHAYAM

Out across the tarmac in the fresh of the morning in a new land, such is the magic carpet of air travel. How wonderful it is during the first hours of day in any climate or part of the world. All seems clear, bright and peaceful before man begins to walk the face of the earth again. Well has it been said, 'Man loves darkness rather than light because his deeds are evil.' Tubby couldn't make out who the people supposed to be meeting him were, as all the people in the public enclosure seemed to be viewing the passengers with the same quizzical look. Although numerous forms had been filled in on the plane – in Arabic and French of all things – there were still more to be filled in once inside the airport building. Thankfully there were no pictures of Uncle Nasser leering from the walls – Iraq was well and truly pro-British, thanks to the Baghdad Pact, Nuri-el-Said and the ex-Regent, Prince Abdul Illah.

Having at last completed all the formalities required, and having convinced the Customs and the powers-that-be that he had not come to Iraq for subversive activities, Tubby emerged into the entrance hall of the airport building. He was approached by two characters who looked like ex-Chicago gangsters of Sicilian origin. They led Tubby to a large American car which all but convinced him that he was being taken for the 'long ride'. The hoodlums turned out to be the son-in-law and nephew of the old man whose company acted as agents for Tubby's company. He was soon to realise that all Iraqis tended to look this way when dressed in European clothes but the majority of the people wore long, flowing Arab dress. As it happened, one of the two boys had been in America for at least three years and had an American university degree.

9

Strangely enough, the whole place reeked of American influence, though the country was tied so closely to Britain; all traffic drove on the right and virtually all the cars were of American origin. Later Tubby was to discover that there were few tarred roads and, let's face it, American cars are about the only ones which can stand up to dirt tracks.

Their departure from the airport was delayed due to the discovery that the nice shiny hub-caps had disappeared from the car. Seeing their sad plight a small Arab boy said he could sell them a new set. After some bargaining he shot off and returned with the originals, or another set taken from another car. The drive from the airport was quite impressive considering the mental picture one builds up from tales of old Baghdad and the romance of the East and all that. Tubby used to work with an old sweat who had ended up in Baghdad, as a grand finale to his episodes in France during World War One. He could tell some tales of sheikhs and dancing girls, and maintained that one would flake out in the evening, when the sun went to rest and the cold came down from the mountains of the north, unless one had a double Scotch to replace the warmth of the day.

Certainly everything was most impressive that morning: the large modern building of the railway station, the new National Museum under construction, the palm trees and greenery down the centre of the dual carriageway roads. The only things which somewhat disturbed Tubby were the horse drawn taxis and the flocks of sheep and goats which often blocked the roads causing even more hooting from the traffic than the permanent din. The taxis were all right – rather nice black open landaus, but the horses were pathetic. They were nothing but skin and bone and had great bald patches where the harness and tack rubbed their skins; some were even lame with ancient bandages tied round their legs. The car crossed the Tigris via the Queen Aliyah Bridge, a rather magnificent new structure of German construction, and they drove into old Baghdad.

All and sundry in the London office had assured him that the hotel was the best and most expensive in town, but Tubby had his doubts when the car turned off Rashid Street into a small side street. 'This is it,' his two friends announced in triumph. They must have read the misgivings on his face as he surveyed the small entrance between four shops. A cinema was joined on, and opposite there was an empty area of ground strewn with rubble, which at home would be called a 'bombed patch'. An old Arab had the carcass of a sheep strung up by its rear legs on the lattice type steel gate of the cinema. He had already split it open from bottom to top and he was in the process of disembowelling it, eagerly watched by a pack of dogs and other human scavengers. All this was bad enough, but the smell of human excreta was positively overpowering. Hastily he ascended the carpeted stairway, adorned with the usual airline posters, and rose from the realms of heat smells to the realms of air-conditioning.

So this was the Hotel Khayam; this was to be Tubby's home for the next three and a half months. They say that an Englishman's home is his castle, but this hotel was indeed to become his castle, his fortress, his refuge from the mob. The Khayam had been planned as an office block but halfway through construction the westernised Iraqi tycoon who was financing the set up realised that Baghdad did not possess a first class hotel run in true European style. So he decided he would provide one instead of a block of offices – hence the Hotel Khayam.

Well-covered with flesh through years of good living, the tycoon always dressed in expensive suits. Of medium height, he had a bullet head topped with a semi-crewcut, and his hook nose stuck out between dark horn-rimmed specs. He looked like a cross between Alfred Hitchcock, a vulture, and a boxing promoter. Never obviously interfering in the running of the hotel, he was always to be seen at least twice a day in the reception lounge. This lounge was situated at the top of the entrance stairs and had the reception desk recessed on the right. Straight ahead was the dining room at the rear of the building and in the far left hand corner was the entrance to the bar. Padded leather seating lined the left wall opposite reception and circled a large pillar in the centre. Small coffee tables and chairs were dotted round the rest of the lounge.

Next to the entrance stairs was a lift and staircase to the floors above, while to the left was the main lounge at the front of the building, and to the right the first floor rooms. Tubby's room was the third along to the right. The Khayam was air-conditioned throughout.

The majority of the staff were Europeans and the tone of the place stemmed from Hans, the manager. A graduate of the hard school of European hotel management, it was said that he had gravitated to the lucrative profession of pimp attached to one or several of the Baghdad night clubs. One never knew whether the tycoon had seen in Hans a manager for his office block, now hotel, or whether Hans had landed the job during one of the tycoon's many midnight visits to the night clubs.

Hans was the matron's dream of the continental charmer. Tall and fair, he dressed well, had a mischievous face and just the right amount of accent to his voice. He called himself Austrian, but judging by his almost brotherly attitude to German guests and the ruthlessly efficient manner in which he ran the Khayam, one suspected that he was actually German. People who didn't like him used to spread tales that he was a Nazi or SS man. Be that as it may, it was so much nicer to be Austrian; it went down better with those who were touchy about Germans.

The manager's rooms were just off the reception lounge so he could step right out into the hub of things and know all that was going on. Hans had one aversion, stray women from outside in his hotel rooms. Maybe a strange attitude from a former pimp, perhaps it was a case of 'set a thief to catch a thief'. Having his room where it was, he could keep an eye on both stairs and lift so Tubby would tease him about this and offer to be Purity Patrol on his nights off.

With siesta from 1 till 4 p.m. work would go on till 7.30 p.m. by which time it was dark. Each night Tubby would shower, change, then relax in the lounge or wash the sand out of his gills in the bar. About this hour Hans would sweep out of his room immaculate in Italian suit and shoes for his evening round of the guests. It never failed to fascinate; the full bow and kiss on the hand for '*Bonsoir, Madame,*' the half bow and hand-shake for '*Bonsoir, Monsieur*'. Invariably Madame's hand was half way there in anticipation, head coyly half-turned and eyelids fluttering. Often on completing his round of the tables in the dining room Hans would sit with Tubby and a few others for dinner, mumbling some unrepeatable remarks about the guests. There was the night a couple entered with their rather sweet teenage daughter. Hans rose and graciously bowed. As he sat down again he turned and said, 'Gentlemen, what you say in English? Beddable, huh? They asked that zee girl be in zee next room, but I say the only other room is at the other end of the hotel. I could tell the vay she looked at me – she did not want to be in zee next room to Mummy and Daddy.'

Service in the dining room was good – anything amiss would bring a snap of the fingers and a cry of '*Maitre*' from Hans. Karl, the *Maitre*, would rush over in consternation. He was a short, round jovial Swiss, but on these occasions he would disappear in the direction of the kitchen shouting in German as he went through the door threatening to beat the head of the waiter in question. Two at least needed beating over the head. Luigi, a young Italian, and Louis, a French Lebanese, a man of moods who would sulk on his off-days and do nothing right. He was suspected of leanings for his own sex rather than the opposite which could have accounted for the trouble. Luigi was just juvenile, he would always rush up for an order, pad and pencil in hand. He always scribbled something down, but one never knew what was really going to come unless one spoke in Italian. One night when an American woman with a voice like Claudette Colbert in *The Egg and I* asked for a steak – 'medium rare – real rare!' his face became a pattern of question marks and he furiously scratched the top of his head with his pencil.

The others were Emile, a quiet young Lebanese with a dry sense of humour, but most efficient; Mario, a typical black wavy-haired womanising Italian – very smarmy; Franz, the assistant head waiter who spent most of his time away at the Royal Palace organising banquets. He looked like a Frenchman but was actually German, wore rimless glasses and had an elongated crew cut which was not short enough for bristles but

13

just long enough not to stand up quite straight. Though he had never been to the UK his English was magnificent. These were the food waiters. The fetchers and carriers were an amusing bunch of Armenian and Persian boys.

There was one other vital member of the staff, Charlie the barman, but more of him anon.

3

THE NIGHT LIFE

Life was rather strange at first in Baghdad. Days off were
Friday and Saturday, work on Sundays. Hours of work were 8
a.m. to 1 p.m. and 4 p.m. to 7.30 p.m. Tubby never quite got
used to this long siesta period, whereas the locals would be off
to sleep at the stroke of one, and return half-awake at 4 o'clock
and become fully awake by 7.30 p.m. for the night life. Actually, rules and regulations in Iraq were very puritanical so the
main night clubs were very orderly indeed. In this respect
Baghdad just did not compare with the big bad city of Beirut.

The majority of the show girls were European doing a three
month spell before moving off to another place. They could be
entertained at the rear of the night club after the show, which
was usually about 1 a.m. For the privilege, one bought a bottle
of fantastically highly priced 'champagne' which was watered-
down cider. After a while one found out that the girls gathered
in a certain bar in the night club area before their shows at
11 p.m. Here at least one didn't need to buy champagne as a
preliminary. Wherever it was, the girls were generally obtain-
able and there were umpteen hotels where rooms could be
booked up by the hour. The show girls would appear some
nights with black and blue marks in the most peculiar places.

As can be expected, there was one real dive in Baghdad, and
as was often the case it was run by a shady Greek. Up an alley
in a dubious district of Baghdad, it was the sort of place one
did not visit alone, not for the first time anyway. Who else
could organise a visit other than Charlie, the barman at the
Khayam. Charlie was one of those international characters.
Born in Gibraltar, he was a British citizen, spoke French,
Spanish and Greek after a spell in Cyprus, and had served

many years in the British Army. His long service, he would explain, was due to a mistake at the recruiting office. They had said to him: 'Two/six or six/nine?'

'Naturally I wanted to earn 6/9d per day and not 2/6d, but I found myself in for nine years with an option to go at six years.'

It was rumoured that when a sergeant during the war in the Canal Zone, he owned two night clubs. When court martialled for some reason or another he flew his own barrister out from the UK. Charlie was a real character who knew his way round and could lay-on almost anything.

On their first visit to the dive things went wrong. As they approached up the alley, the police emerged with a body hanging by feet and hands from a pole carried by two police-men. Charlie suggested that this was not quite the right time to pay a visit so they beat a hasty retreat. On the next occasion they were not met by a body but they were frisked for weapons on entry by the strong-arm doormen.

Once inside Tubby could understand why – he had never seen quite such a collection of characters. What a place, and what filthy old whores; enough to make anyone sign the pledge of celibacy. However, the joker on the door could not have done a very good job because a fracas broke out in one corner and some wild boy pulled a gun. What a hoot! Before the man even fired it, all and sundry started to heave things at him. Bottles, glasses, lamps, knives, forks and even chairs and tables. Tubby had only seen the like of this before in films. As soon as the fellow was safely buried under a pile of bottles and furni-ture, Charlie and Tubby left via a way he knew through the gents as the police arrived with the pole again at the front. From then on wanderings were restricted to the conventional night clubs along the river.

The waters of the Tigris were dropping each day as the summer progressed and the heat grew more intense. After siesta at 4 p.m., leaving the hotel was like entering a blast furnace, but the nights, thankfully, were always magnificent; hot but very clear with every star a brilliant jewel twinkling in the heavens. It was interesting to walk along Rashid Street

16

after dinner and on along the road which ran beside the river, after passing under the arch of the new Queen Aliyah Bridge, which smelt like a urinal. All the eating stalls with sizzling Khebab were on the banks of the river at pavement level, but as the level of the river dropped the proprietors moved their tables and chairs down to the water's edge. Along the water's edge the fires of the masquf sellers flickered. The masquf is a large fish like a pike only larger. In the UK one looks on white fish as light invalid food, but the masquf, though beautifully white, turned out to be extremely heavy and greasy. The amount of whisky one would consume at a masquf party was fantastic. Each fisherman had the masquf in a big water tank. Once a fish had been selected he would hack it open from tail to head with a big chopper. After cleaning and gutting, the fish would be flattened out like a huge kipper and staked out horizontal to the ground near the wood fire. The flames from the wood and dried reeds were blown by the wind to cook the greasy masquf. Crude in preparation but wonderful in taste.

All the main night clubs were within a few blocks of one another and the floor shows were all about the same mediocre standard. There was one favourite, but it wasn't a case of its show being better, but the others being worse. The last item in all the clubs was the belly dancer. The others had European girls trying to belly dance, but this club had a lithe, willowy Egyptian girl and a proper string band. Tubby called them the 'Deadpans' because they sat poker-faced and motionless except for their arms, playing the instruments which produced the weird music for the dance.

The final performer at this club was Affifa, the wife of the proprietor. She would sing Iraqi songs with such zest and animation the whole crowd would join in and even the Deadpans would liven up and smile. Though he did not understand a word, Tubby enjoyed Affifa most of all.

On the walk back after taking in a night club, the pastime was to throw stones and bark at the many dogs. In a few seconds the whole large army of stray dogs would bark and howl all over Baghdad. These poor mange-ridden creatures with virtually no hair slept all day under cars or in any shade they could find, and roamed about at night when it was cooler. Tubby could never understand in a Muslim country how they were never shot and cleared off the streets.

4

BUSINESS IN BAGHDAD

Tubby's agents in Iraq were Christians, which was unusual for a Muslim country. An old family business, they also had a large department store in Baghdad. However, over the years they had won honour and respect through their honest and straight dealings. Most of their staff too were Christians, from round Mosul in the North. Most departments were run by sons, nephews, or sons-in-law, and it was one or the latter named Wahdib who looked after Tubby's products.

The store was a big square building with a second floor round the edges only, so that light from the glass roof could light the whole place. With the weather so hot and dry the floor of the place had to be washed twice a day to keep the dust down. Some mornings, after a great dust storm had started to blow in from the desert during the night, the whole sky would be sand coloured. People who slept on the roofs at this time of the year would come to work with mouth, eyes, hair, ears – the lot – full of sand, having been covered by the storm before they could retreat below. Everything in the store on these mornings would be covered with a layer of sand in spite of the place having been all shut up. Even in Tubby's air-conditioned hotel room, clothes in the wardrobe would have a fine film of dust on them. It was fantastic every time these storms would sweep in from the desert. Sand and dust would get in everywhere and anything.

The store manager had his desk just to the left of the main door and the senior members of the company had desks behind a partition further along on the left. One of the wireless and gramophone salesmen on the far right of the top floor would go to the racecourse and gamble on the horses during the siesta time. It was easy to tell when things had not gone so well or when he was upset. He would lean over the rail up on the right and begin to hold forth across the store in the direction of the manager's desk like a Hyde Park orator. It was a priceless performance and always he would end his harangue with Oliver Cromwell's famous speech:

'It is high time for me to put an end to your sitting in this place which you have dishonoured by your contempt of all virtue and defiled by your practice of every vice. Ye are a factious crew and enemies to all good governement; ye are a pack of mercenary wretches, and would, like Esau sell your country for a mess of Pottage, and like Judas betray your God for a few pieces of money. Is there now a single virtue remaining amongst you? Is there one vice you do not possess, ye have no more religion than a horse; gold is your God. Which of you have not bartered your conscience for bribes? Is there a man amongst you who has the least care for the good commonwealth? Ye sordid prostitutes have ye not defiled this sacred place, and turned Lord's temple into a den of thieves by your immoral principles and wicked practices? Ye are grown intolerably odious to the whole nation. Were Ye deputed to let grievance be redressed; and now you yourselves become greater grievance? Your country therefore calls upon me to cleanse this Augean stable by putting a final period to your iniquitous proceedings in this house, and which by God's help, and the strength he has given me, I am now come to do. I command ye therefore upon the peril of your lives to depart immediately out of this place. Go, get out, make haste, ye venal slaves, begone; so take away that shining Bauble there, and lock up the doors.'

To hear this Iraqi, foaming at the mouth, arms flailing, rendering this speech to his bosses in his broken English always sent Tubby into hysterics. Louis, this was the salesman's name, told Tubby how he had learnt it at school and with great ceremony presented him with a typed copy of the speech.

One day Tubby walked out of his office on the second floor to find an old school friend wandering round the store. They both just stood and stared at one another in disbelief. Tom Kendall was his name and many a game of rugger they had played together. Tom was working for a seismograph oil exploration company under contract to Iraq Petroleum Co. His wife and child were coming out and he was buying things for the house which he had just rented. Working up in the deserts away to the north-west for three weeks at a stretch, Tubby saw more of him later on, during his weeks in town at the end of each three week period. It is amazing how one bumps into people from home in the most unexpected places when abroad.

The first few weeks were spent in Baghdad getting things organized and getting the feel of the market. When one is a new arrival all sorts of smart characters get in touch trying to work something before one can get the hang of things. One such character rang Tubby from the American PX stores. There were a surprisingly large number of Americans in Iraq working on various projects. Many were retired people who had been induced by fantastic financial rewards to come out to Iraq and lend their expert advice and years of experience to the railways, etc.

One of the failings of Americans abroad is that they tend to isolate themselves from the local community. In Baghdad, instead of patronising the local shops, which in the European areas were first class, they bought at their PX store. This place was really swish, air-conditioned and sold almost everything; but the man in charge was the smoothest Iraqi in town. Tubby saw him in his office and talked prices and quantities. He was assured that fantastic quantities would be sold, but special arrangements and prices would have to be made in this case because Mr Smoothy could get his goods in without duties under Diplomatic Immunity. A few discreet enquiries round and about soon convinced Tubby that Mr Smoothy would soon have his cut-price, Diplomatically Immune goods moving out of the side door of the PX store and into the market, upsetting Tubby's whole marketing operation.

On his first time out with a salesman in the old part of

21

Baghdad, Tubby had to give up after an hour and a half. They had gone up an alley off Rashid Street which started with half canvas awnings across it. There was a gutter down the centre with foul matter of doubtful origin trickling down it. Every hole in the wall was a shop, and other traders squatted on the floor. The male population seemed to just stand around doing nothing other than watch what was going on. The salesman was always surrounded by a gallery of these fellows in the long dirty shimmies and Arab head-dress. They pressed forward to see what was going on – hands behind back ceaselessly flicking through their string of yellow or white beads. Invariably they had a week's growth on their faces, some had teeth missing, some were blind in one eye with cataracts and they all smelt to high heaven.

Moving further in, the alley became completely closed over, darker, more oppressive and more smelly. Rounding a corner, Tubby ducked in a reflex action as a black cloud shot past his head and back again. On recovering he found that they were by a butcher's shop. The hunks of meat hung along the front, and the black cloud had been a swarm of flies. The flies had been driven off by a small boy in a dirty striped shimmy. He held a large piece of bloody sackcloth in his hands and his job was to swipe at the meat every so often to keep the flies off. At that moment it was the lull between swipes and the flies were all back on the meat. Tubby assumed there was meat there, as it couldn't be seen for flies. The stench was appalling, pigeons in the awnings above were dropping things and the curious gallery of males who followed them were spitting. Tubby felt ill and reckoned this was enough for one day and returned to the office.

The next outing in Baghdad was to the biggest market – the Shorgah Bazaar. The size and shape of the buildings it occupied could not be measured. It was a veritable labyrinth of passages and alleyways and it took several visits before one could dispense with a compass or trail of cotton thread, and manage to emerge into the daylight again.

One entered through several half covered alleys and immedi-ately plunged into a hive of activity and noise, shouts of stallholders and shouts of coolies staggering along bent double under huge loads. Once Tubby actually saw one of these coolies carry a large size, double-door refrigerator up a flight of stairs. Avoiding donkeys, swishing horse tails which hit one across the face, and slipping in the sludge of droppings down the centre of the alleys, Tubby and Wahdib made their way deeper into the bazaar.

The main part in the centre was divided into areas specializing in different goods, and eventually they reached the main dealer of their goods – Mosche the Jew. One of the few Jews to avoid being strung up during the Arab-Israeli war, it looked as though he had had his nose altered. It certainly did not resemble the noses of his Israeli brethren. Here he was, operating from a little hole deep in the bazaar with a stranglehold on several big selling commodities. A few weeks later Mosche went off to the States to engineer American citizenship for himself. Tubby took the opportunity of breaking the stranglehold on his products, much to the pleasure of the other dealers in the bazaar. However, Mosche was not one to give up without a fight and it was a month or so later before it came to light what little underhand tricks he organised in retaliation.

After a month or so, tubby had four vans covering Baghdad and a chief salesman concentrating on the big dealers in the Shorgah Bazaar. The hard work put into the establishment of the beginnings of a future sound marketing organisation was paying off and stocks were running low. In his first week Tubby had laid down his plans, won the co-operation of the agents, and orders for large quantities had been placed. In the weeks that followed, more and more orders had gone off to London as the result of approaches to the oil companies and other big accounts, but no goods seemed to be forthcoming. Not even the first shipments had arrived in Baghdad though they had had shipping documents for their arrival in Basrah.

Through Wahdib's influence they had obtained the use of a school hall under his house for a godown – warehouse – in anticipation of the goods arriving. Previous to that, the goods had been mixed up with all other products carried by the agent, at the back of the store in Rashid Street. The poor loading facilities and the traffic problems made it impossible to service the vans properly, so now the new place across the river was a great improvement, and Wahdib found a very keen and capable young Iraqi called Sammy as storekeeper. He was keen and sharp with a tremendous thirst for knowledge. All his spare time was spent studying and listening to broadcasts from other nations. Many an hour Tubby spent with him at the end of a day answering questions about all sorts of things. The big thing was that he was scrupulously honest and determined to be able to account for every single item of stock under his care.

Tubby had been chasing the agent's customs and shipping clerk about the delays but he always got the same poker-faced reply that he was doing his best. Pressed harder he admitted that some goods were in the customs godown in the railway yard, and at long last a lorry arrived with a load of goods.

Actually two lorries came on the first day and the cases were all counted and signed for without any trouble. The next day many more came and Sammy got quite excited and worked up when the supervisor of the lorry company complained that his lorries were being delayed unnecessarily. Sammy, however, was on the ball and told them to unload the lorries outside if they were in a hurry so that he could count the cases against the documents before receiving them into the godown. The supervisor was annoyed at this and became positively jumpy when Sammy found shortages.

Thoughts began to trouble Tubby's mind when he saw so much arriving after so long and he sensed trouble. On the third day they had trouble with a capital 'T'. The lorries came one after the other in an attempt to swamp Sammy, but he stuck to his checking until mid-morning when he burst in on Wahdib and Tubby in the office. He was white with rage and babbling incoherently in Arabic at the top of his voice. Tubby had never seen anything quite like it before and was positively alarmed while Wahdib sat open-mouthed with eyes rolling round in consternation. Somehow they calmed Sammy enough to get the gist of what he was saying.

Evidently the lorry men had planned and had started to shanghai large quantities of the goods en route from the railway yard to the godown. By bringing so much all at once they thought nothing would be counted and the quantities on the delivery notes would be accepted, but they had not reckoned on Sammy. After he had found the shortages on the second day and insisted on counting again on the third day the supervisor approached him and offered him a share of the proceeds if he would only stop counting. This is what had sent him rushing into the office.

When Tubby went storming out he found the lorry supervisor looking a sickly pale green colour under his Arabic tan. Even the tan all but turned white when Tubby lifted him up off the ground by his shirt front and pinned him against the wall to shake the truth out of him. It came out too, in all its sordid details, and dear old Mosche was at the bottom of it. The supervisor was put down again and told that no lorry was getting away until every single item had been counted, checked and all shortages noted down. He was also told that Mosche would be dealt with later.

Back at the store Wahdib and Tubby went through everything with the old man, Basheer, Wahdib's Uncle). How Mosche had worked to ruin their whole operation by leaving them with no stocks to honour orders from the trade. He had bribed officials all the way down the line – even the agent's customs and shipping clerk – but he had just not been able to hold it long enough, so he decided to help himself. Tubby was really looking forward to laying his hands on little Mosche, but alas, the Revolution broke out and the pleasure was gone. Often he wondered if Mosche had engineered that too, but in the light of later events he doubted if Mosche even survived when the mobs ran amok.

5

NAJAF – THE HOLY CITY

One of the first trips Tubby took outside Baghdad was to the Holy City of Najaf, about 80 miles to the south. The road was paved and very good so the journey didn't take too long. Once outside the city of Baghdad the way of life was still many centuries behind the times. Veiled women in black abas, coffee shops full of idle males sucking their hookah pipes and preserving their energy for the night's activities.

At El Hillah the road crossed the Euphrates, so Wahdib and Tubby stopped for some refreshment. All was very peaceful by the river as they watched a man having his head shaved by a travelling barber who carried all his gear in a little case. They both sat cross-legged opposite one another while the barber patted water on the fellow's head and deftly scraped off a portion of hair with a vicious looking cut-throat razor.

The scene did not remain peaceful for long. Down the street came a rather wild procession of musicians and coloured banners – the lot. In the centre of the throng were a jubilant bunch of males carrying on high an Arab boy. Just behind them followed a rather dignified little man, like the proverbial family doctor back home, carrying a wee black bag. Wahdib explained that the boy had attained or was about to attain manhood and was going to be circumcised as a sign thereof. The little man with the black bag was the honoured gent who travelled round the area performing the ceremony with his Nasset (Gillette Export) razor blades, carried in the wee black bag. Having been made a true Israelite himself at the age of 11, the thought of it and the pain in store for the lad made Tubby sink at the knees so they proceeded on their way south with all haste.

Driving at a good speed they suddenly realised that for once the moving patterns in the road ahead were not heat mirages but a herd of camels moving across the road. Tubby threw out the drag chairs but even so only just missed a big fellow. On the hard surface of the road camels are unsteady on their feet and can slip easily and split their big hanging bellies. This was a particularly large herd stretching away from left to right and the beasts appeared to be moulting as large patches of their winter coats were missing or half hanging off.

After that episode Tubby was more careful not to let the heat and glare dull his senses. He saw away ahead what appeared to be the Eiffel Tower in the desert. It turned out to be about the biggest oil derrick he had ever seen. In the distance, shimmering in the heat it had seemed extremely high, but even so it actually was pretty big. They turned off up the small metal road to have a closer look. Rounding a sand dune they found that even a small airstrip had been laid nearby. The crew must have had the head up to fit a new drill. To one side within the frame-work of the derrick were lengths of piping, which reached from the base to the top platform which was about three-quarters of the way up.

What was simply amazing was the speed with which the crew were getting the drill back down into the earth. The enormous pulley block was moving up and down almost non-stop. As it was rising the top crew would bring out the top of the next length. This would be clamped into the block as it went past, pulling the bottom clear for the base crew to slip it into the previous length as the block started down again. The only pause was as the block spun to screw home the new length and then the plunge down thrusting the new length into the ground. The whole operation of picking up a length, screwing it home and driving it down took about 50 seconds. On the way back in the late afternoon Tubby noticed that two thirds of the lengths had been put back into the earth.

The first sight of Najaf was the glint of the golden dome of the great mosque of the Shi'as flashing brilliantly in the sunlight. This flashing could be seen for many miles away, before one could even make out the form of the mosque itself and the huge gold crescent moon on top. The mosque was Najaf – the Holy of Holies for all Shi'ite Moslems. Back in the early days of Islam, the sons of Ishmael had warred among themselves. The Father of the Shi'as had been slain in treacherous circumstances for which his followers had never forgiven themselves and once a year they showed their feelings by walking through the streets cutting themselves. On this day they are also liable to cut up any unfortunate infidel who happened to get in their way. Most Iraqis were Shi'a and to them Najaf ranked with Mecca for sanctity. All the Shi'as from Persia, Pakistan and further east tried to journey to Mecca via the holy places of Iraq – especially Najaf. It was interesting to see people in Najaf with Asian or Mongol features.

Since arriving, Tubby had seen taxis and cars leaving Baghdad with coffins tied on the top and always the explanation was 'going to the holy city of Najaf for burial'. Now that he was in the town he realised just how holy and organised it was. Life in the town evolved round the mosque. A tannoy system covered every street in the town right to the outskirts so that the Muezzin could whip in all loiterers before each prayer time. At midday the whole town shut up shop and set off with their prayer mats under their arms.

The store they were visiting in Najaf was run by one Haji Abood and his brother. Abood was a tall graceful Arab, who always wore a Haji hat and suit. This is what Tubby called the white Arab hat and flowing robes. His brother was a short jovial fellow who always wore a western style suit. The mosque was roughly the shape of St Paul's, only scaled down somewhat. In the afternoon, Wahdib went through the mosque with Haji Abood. Tubby was warned off, so after looking into the outer court through one of the beautiful ornate doorways, he went round the outside with the brother to meet Wahdib at the other side. In the part that Tubby could see from the gate there appeared to be humanity everywhere wailing or bowing and scraping on prayer mats. The walls of the main building were covered and decorated with the most fantastic mosaic and inlaid gold workings that Tubby had ever seen.

Wahdib emerged relieved and rather shaken. His pockets

were also a lot lighter after keeping the multitudinous beggars at bay. Most large mosques in Baghdad allowed infidels in to look around, but he reckoned that Tubby would have been torn apart in five minutes if he had entered this one in Najaf. Never had he seen such emotion and fanaticism inside as the pilgrims hung to the gold railings round the tomb weeping, wailing and gnashing their teeth. It would be like throwing a lamb to the wolves to allow an unsuspecting infidel among that lot. Though an Iraqi himself, Wahdib feared that they would smell that he was a Christian and was most relieved to be outside again. Having an American university degree after several years in the States he had one exclamation when he was really overawed as in this case. 'Wow!'

At lunch time Haji Abood had announced with great pride that the visitors would dine with him at his new home. The house turned out to be a new European type bungalow on the edge of town. The road wasn't finished nor was the house for that matter, but water and electricity were laid on, so what more could one ask for. All the hangers-on came along too in the convoy of cars, but the meal was so long in coming, Tubby soon used all the Arabic words he had learned so far. However, if one laughs at jokes and appears to be having a good time, they are all happy even though they haven't a clue what you are talking about.

After over an hour the gathering was ushered into the next room where a huge table occupied most of the space. The table was simply laden with all manner of food. Haji, Wahdib and Tubby were given chairs, the other principal guests stood round the table. Behind them the minor minions watched eagerly waiting for their turn once the honoured front ranks retired. Whatever food remained after the second sitting had gorged themselves was thrown out the back to the women who were never allowed to appear.

Wahdib and Tubby were the only ones with spoons and plates, the others ate off huge flat grey/brown objects like asbestos door mats which were issued out by a boy who had a number of them draped over his arm. The mats must have been some sort of dhal-cum-chapatti, as the others would tear

29

lumps off and eat them with the other food. The other food consisted of a whole sheep (no eyes luckily), chickens prepared umpteen different ways, eggs the same, various types of extremely rich and greasy sweet breads, masquf, bowls of thick yoghurt and literally heaps of rice, both yellow and white.

The brother parked himself with the sole object of looking after Tubby, and feeding himself, of course. His first act was to pick up Tubby's plate, thrust it into a heap of rice and pull the stuff on to the plate with the right hand. He then got stuck in, as did the others, pushing one fist full after the other into his mouth and washing it down with yoghurt, or leban, as it was called in Iraq. He was having a great time laughing and joking and gorging. Each laugh usually resulted in half the previous mouthful coming back out again to be caught halfway down his chin and pushed back in again. It was just after one of these push backs that he noticed Tubby pause for a minute. His hand went straight from his mouth, tore off a handful of the masquf and deposited it on to Tubby's plate, with a flourish worthy of the best head waiter.

They had waited a long time for this meal and, being held in high regard in the UK as a big eater, Tubby really put a lot of food down, with the able assistance of the brother. He was up and over the plimsoll line when he eventually crawled away to the other room. To his amazement these skinny Arabs, only half his size, just went on and on. This became the pattern at all subsequent feasts in Iraq, even when Tubby began to starve the day before in preparation. Flat out and feeling like Henry VIII he was summoned back to the room to find the table had been relaid with all manner of fruit. It was fantastic, but he simply had to eat an Iraqi orange. Whatever people and advertisements may say about other oranges from South Africa or anywhere, there is nothing to touch an Iraqi orange.

There is little to comment on about the drive back from Najaf that evening except that the old digestive system was working overtime and some good work had been done to expand business beyond Baghdad.

As a follow up to this visit, a van was sent the next week with a team of Arab boys to do some promotional work. The salesman in charge of this van was called Yelda. He was not the brightest of characters but all the same he went to great lengths to impress how superior he was to his fellow men.

Yelda set off for Najaf with great pomp and ceremony for he was the first salesman to go out of Baghdad. He climbed up into the van, waved to those watching and ordered his driver to be off and away. Later, a phone call came through from a remote town 40 miles away reporting that the van had killed an old man and the driver was being held in prison. Wahdib immediately called the lawyers and then drove off south to see what he could do.

That night he returned with the news that the driver had been released, the van only had one headlamp damaged and they had proceeded to Najaf as planned. The other salesmen were there and he began to tell them the tale in Arabic. As the tale unfolded Wahdib waxed more lyrical and began to mime in order to illustrate his story. Tubby watched, fascinated and heard Yelda's name mentioned frequently. When the tale ended with them all hysterical with laughter he was almost mad with curiosity.

It took Wahdib some minutes to return to normal and wipe the tears of laughter from his eyes while the others kept repeating a certain phrase in Arabic, with a dramatic gesture, followed by uproarious laughter. It seemed that the old man was a vagrant whose identity could not be established. He had been standing by the side of the road and had jumped in front of the van in a sudden and deliberate attempt to end his life. This was tragic but the funny side of the episode came at the police station.

When the officer in charge had asked for their version of the accident, Yelda had dismissed the others with a sweep of his hand and stepped forward as the self appointed spokesman. His profile resembled a wall carving of Darius the Mede and he assumed a similar dramatic pose in front of the policeman's desk. Then, with gestures befitting a Greek orator, he related his experience in flowing, archaic, classical Arabic, which was the equivalent of a man in modern Italy giving his evidence in Latin.

31

Tubby just could not grasp the full humour of it all but apparently Yelda ended his long oration thus: 'And so the aged patriarch did mount up on winged feet as Mercury of old, and did swoop with the speed of the lightning in the heavens, before our onrushing chariot.' Poor Yelda!

6

ANCIENT BABYLON

Tubby was convinced that nothing could quite surpass the feast at Najaf, but on the way home from a trip to Babylon he ended up at a feast to end all feasts.

One Saturday he and two others from the hotel decided to go to the site of ancient Babylon the Great, which was also south of Baghdad on the Najaf Road near El Hillah. Leaving in the morning they arrived about midday. One has to look carefully for the turning off which is only marked by a rather small wooden signpost. A short drive along a dirt road took them to a small building known as the Babylon Museum, and a nearby police hut. An old Arab in flowing robes sat at the door but inside was very little to see: a few showcases of articles which had been unearthed, and plans and drawings on the walls showing the layout of ancient Babylon at various stages of its history as revealed by various archeological digging sessions.

Behind the so-called museum, they climbed up a dry barren mound, and on reaching the top they realised that this was one of the many mounds that were once a great city – centre of the known world of years ago. The scene vividly brought to mind the words written by Jeremiah the prophet thousands of years ago (chapter 51, verse 37): 'And Babylon shall become heaps, a dwelling place for dragons, an astonishment and an hissing, without an inhabitant.'

It was indeed astonishing to look upon these barren heaps stretching away to the fringe of palms in the distance on the banks of the Euphrates, and to realise what little remained of Babylon the Great. This was the place where Nebuchadnezzar held sway over most of the known world. The capital of the fertile land between the rivers with its hanging gardens – one of the seven wonders of the ancient world. Daniel upheld the honour of his Lord here and saw his prophetic visions. Belshazzar's Feast; how the scenes of the Old Testament flooded the mind.

One of the mounds had been excavated to about two-thirds the depth of one main street to reveal the towering walls of the buildings with the outlines of various beasts embossed on the brickwork. One could almost hear the rumble of chariots and horsemen as one imagined a triumphal march down this street, and longed to be carried back through the ages to witness the scene and Babylon as it was before its fall.

There was little else to see save recent excavations served by small tracks and hopper trucks for carrying the earth away. For a tourist attraction there was a huge stone Lion of Babylon between two of the mounds on which visitors usually sat for a photograph, to be shown at home with the comment 'This is me at Babylon'. The other attraction for photographers were the very smart police who patrolled the area on magnificent Arab horses. A remarkable sight after the rather tatty police to be seen in Baghdad.

After eating a packed lunch, Tubby and his friends started the drive back to Baghdad. On these long drives in Iraq with no change in the dry colourless scenery, things can get rather boring, so they sat up and took notice when they saw a great throng on the road ahead. The throng turned out to be a sheikh and his entourage returning home after a Saturday outing. There are many of these sheikhs in the south of Iraq, especially in the marsh and swamp areas of the deep south. They still lived as feudal lords with their slaves and private mercenaries.

This fellow stopped the car and after much sign language and broken Arabic, Tubby and co gathered that El Sheikh desired to proffer his hospitality upon them. As the day was fairly far spent, they were inclined to push on and refuse the kind offer, besides some of his boys were a pretty evil looking lot and well-nigh armed to the teeth. However, they decided to stay as the old sheikh was most insistent. They also thought that there was an element of doubt as to whether they could have pushed on if his boys had got nasty with them for refusing the old boy's generous hospitality.

The sheikh's entourage mounted their horses and arranged themselves fore and aft of the car, and the procession left the road and headed for the wilderness. After several miles, which seemed very long miles to Tubby and co, the procession stopped. By this time the sun had gone down, but they could see the outline of tents about, and the smell of camels filled the air.

They were ushered into a large tent and seated on the floor in a semi-circle. One of the chaps with Tubby spoke a bit of Arabic and was busy talking away trying to find out what the actual form was. Judging by the space on the floor in front of them and the minor vassals behind them in the second tier, as it were, Tubby gathered that another Najaf-style feast was on the way. Soon enough the dishes started to arrive. He shuddered at the thought of the sheep's eyes, because this would be one occasion when he would not be able to refuse this great delicacy customarily offered to guests. All the usual stuff came in, masquf, leban, sweet meats, olives, and many more things, but still no sheep. Suddenly four men staggered in carrying the most enormous dish, and plonked it down in the middle of the gathering. There was the usual covering of rice over the dish, but instead of a sheep there was a whole young camel. It had been so dressed and prepared that sitting there all brown and cooked it looked almost like a huge turkey. What a Christmas dinner for the folks back home!

What to do with it or how to start eating it was the problem, but a quick look round the Arab boys gave the answer. With the hands and arms bared to the elbows, they all had an eager hungry look and were obviously waiting for the word go. Before giving the word the sheikh explained to the visitors that inside the camel was a sheep, inside the sheep was a turkey, inside the turkey was a chicken and inside the chicken was a mouse, and first to the mouse was champion of the feast.

They looked at one another, then at the camel, and then at each other again with incredulity. Before they had a chance to work it all out, the others had started. Never had they seen

35

such frenzied eating before. These small wiry fellows were thrusting great lumps of flesh into their mouths with fistfuls of rice, and washing the lot down with yoghurt. A great shriek would go up as each new layer of flesh was pulled out by eager hands.

The visitors could not hope to compete with this lot, besides they were too fascinated by the whole scene to think of eating. Finally one fellow leapt to his feet in triumph holding up the mouse by the tail for all to see, before popping it in his mouth. Tubby was glad he had not won. The very thought of popping a whole mouse down his throat was positively emetic.

After such a climax, other events were insignificant. All had eaten so much they could scarcely move. The fruit was brought in, while the second string started on the remains of the meat. So in great discomfort, they all but crawled to the car taking leave of their host with many *salaams* all round.

A squad of the sheikh's household cavalry escorted them to the road again and they drove to Baghdad with enough food inside them for a week. Tubby, reclining in the back, dozed feeling like Falstaff of old with his hands clasped across his belly.

7

TUBBY GETS A CAR

Shortly after this Tubby was joined by a colleague from London who was to spend some time in Iraq before going off to another part of the world. Dick Malyon was quite a character. Taller and thinner than Tubby, he had a rather medieval appearance, resembling an illustration of the Reeve in a copy of Chaucer's *Canterbury Tales*, which Tubby had studied at school. He could also tell similar stories to the one related by the Reeve in the celebrated *Tales*, so for the purpose of this tale he shall be known as the Reeve.

On Saturday they both set off in a newly acquired second-hand American station wagon which after being used to British cars was like a bus. What with its size, left-hand drive, and driving on the 'wrong side' of the road in Iraq, it took some getting used to.

Tubby and the Reeve decided to go to Habaniyah Lake for a swim one Saturday, so they filled up with petrol before heading out of Baghdad. Though the country flows with oil, the only filling stations were those of the government's Khanaquin Oil Company. No refinements like super grades, just two manual pumps, one diesel fuel, one low-grade petrol. The hoses from the pumps in most cases had bandages round them to stop up leaks, so the place reeked of petrol. For this reason the Reeve and Tubby didn't realise that something was amiss until they saw petrol spreading out from under the car.

There was a hole in the upper third of the tank, but never having filled right up before, the hole had never been revealed. They had to laugh as they remembered the jovial fat Iraqi from whom they had purchased it. He was the main agent for these particular cars, a millionaire of course, and he could be always found in the night clubs or the bar of the Khayam in the evenings. During the day he sat in his air conditioned office wiping the perspiration from his fat jowls and bemoaning his lot. His doctor said he was too fat and must drink less or go to the UK for medical treatment, but who was going to look after his wonderful business?

He had assured Tubby that the station wagon had been stripped down, overhauled and rebuilt under his own personal supervision. What a joke; still they wanted their swim, so there was nothing for it but to jump in and drive off as fast as possible for Habaniyah and at least use some of the petrol before it ran out of the hole. Away they went across the river past the railway station and the airport, non-stop for Fallujah.

The paved road ended at the single line bridge over the river at Fallujah and they pulled up behind two huge desert trucks which were waiting to cross. Tubby half opened the door and leant out to see across the bridge. The man at the far end waved them through and the first truck crawled forward as Tubby put his wagon into gear. The second truck in front moved back slightly as heavy trucks often do before moving off, but suddenly it was evident that for some reason it was reversing. Tubby pushed on the horn and flung his wagon into reverse, but too late. On it came like a bulldozer, snapping off the chrome ornament on the front of the bonnet; the two great chassis girders started to gouge out parallel grooves up the bonnet and the great trailer hook slowly and inevitably came nearer and nearer their windscreen. With about a foot to go the Reeve made his getaway out of the other door, while Tubby just sat with his hand on the horn. This obviously was just not their day except that the truck did stop short of the windscreen. After exhausting their combined meagre vocabulary of Arabic words without any results they took down the number of the truck and drove on with gouged bonnet and minus one chrome ornament.

The road after the bridge was a mixture of ancient broken-up surfacing, dirt, gravel and potholes which one avoided or fell into after much braking to soften the blow. The soft suspension of the American car bounced it out of the potholes which helped no end.

Eventually they reached the great RAF base at Habaniyah which was the centre of so much activity in World War Two. In fact it had been the centre of most British activities in the Middle East and had now developed into a self-contained township with shops, houses, a swimming pool, cinemas, the lot. Throughout Iraq's turbulent history of ups and downs, the RAF had sat them out in splendid isolation in the desert at Habaniyah. After passing the gates and the huge broad runway they turned off left and climbed up to a plateau where there was a smaller dirt landing strip and a huge flashing direction beacon.

At the edge of the plateau they stopped before driving down to take in the wonderful view of this huge inland sea, Habaniyah Lake. With water stretching as far as the eye could see, it was indeed a wonderful sight in such a barren area of brown hills and one could imagine they were on the shores of the open sea. This was the landing place for the great Imperial Airways flying boats (the fore-runners of the wartime Sunderlands) on their way out east to Singapore pre-war. It must have been a wonderful sight to see those great silver birds come in over the dry hills and skim to a halt on the waters of this lake.

Now it was a peaceful scene with the yachts moored at the RAF Sailing Club. Here one would often meet King Feisal sailing or swimming. How tragic that this quiet, young unassuming king was to be killed so soon by the mob.

Tubby and the Reeve parked the car right by the water's edge and plunged into the cool waters of the lake. It was worth all that they had gone through to get there. While drying off in the sun they witnessed a sight which always intrigues newcomers to the desert. They saw a small figure appear from nowhere among the brown hills and descend to the water's edge some hundred yards away. The Arab boy squatted there and splashed water over his face and finally drank the water of the lake from his cupped hands. His wash and drink finished, he arose and went off again to disappear in the barren wastes of the surrounding country.

On another occasion, Tubby had seen two Arabs appear out of nowhere in the desert, climb into a Cadillac and go off until they tore the bottom out on a boulder. They climbed out, walked round it once, kicked it and walked off again into the wilderness. From this habit of appearing and disappearing out of the ground, as it were, Tubby called the desert folk termites.

In the late afternoon they were witnesses of a scene which made them wonder if they had travelled back through time into the days of John the Baptist. People began to arrive in cars and buses until quite a throng had gathered on the water's edge. The newcomers began to sing hymns as one of their number entered the water fully clothed. After he had preached from the water for some minutes two came forward in flowing robes to be baptised by total immersion in the waters of the lake. It was a very moving experience in this a setting so similar to those far off hills of Galilee – a public profession of Christian faith in a country which was virtually 100% Muslim.

Tubby and Reeve sat in silence as the sun went down and darkness descended on them.

On the return journey they twice had to go through the nerve-racking experience of overtaking a desert truck in the dark before they reached the bridge at Fallujah and the paved road. Though they batted along at a merry 40 mph in spite of the potholes, they had to overtake these trucks because of the blinding cloud of dust they throw up. Coming up behind them is like driving into a London fog. Tubby flicked the head lamps up and down repeatedly to get some idea of distance when suddenly the rear of the truck appeared towering over them. The truck drivers were either unaware of anything behind or determined not to notice the flashing lights behind and the frantic hooting. With the rear of the truck about ten feet in front, Tubby stamped on the accelerator and pulled out through the stream and sand alongside the desert monster, praying that nothing was coming the other way or any huge potholes in his path.

At Fallujah they filled up with petrol again till it came out of the hole in the tank and the Reeve drove back to Baghdad like Stirling Moss in spite of the fact that one of the gears ceased to function. When they parked outside the hotel and removed the hub caps (to prevent them disappearing in the night) they found that half the exhaust had dropped off. What a day! Oh, the pleasure to come in the morning when they were going to take the car back to their fat Iraqi friend, who had personally supervised its assembly.

Early next morning Tubby and the Reeve fitted the hub caps on again, and set off for the workshop of Damerji, the car agent. They drove off in the clear morning sunlight to the big circle roundabout below the Queen Aliyah Bridge, passed the Armenia Church and left, down past the Baghdad Pact headquarters, and on towards the growing industrial area where most motor companies had the big repair workshops.

There was Demerji – lord of all he surveyed – hiding his dismay on seeing them behind a big smile and an outstretched hand of welcome. 'Gentlemen, what can I do?' he said, when he heard the tale of the first trip out of town in the station wagon. 'Just look what I have to deal with – these people – what to do?' He was pointing to the entrance of his depot where two of his mechanics were being searched for tools before they went out. They were facing the wall with hands raised while the gateman frisked them like a Chicago cop, looking for concealed weapons.

The main trouble was that Tubby and the Reeve had planned to go on a trip north in the car, so Demerji assured them that he personally would see that the wagon was ready in time. True to form it was not ready, but as a big gesture of his goodwill he lent them a big saloon he had available, which was in good order. The Reeve reckoned it was bound to be better than going north in the old station wagon. Little did he know what lay in store for them.

8

THE 'ROAD' TO THE NORTH

It was June and the temperatures in Iraq were reaching over a hundred in the shade during the day. Wahdib (son-in-law of the old man) was to come north with them to introduce, guide, and also inspect his company's other retail stores in Kirkuk and Mosul. Wahdib, like most of the others in the company, hailed from Mosul and he was quite looking forward to seeing his old father again there, and the other members of his family. Many times he had made this journey north and his advice was: 'Start in the middle of the night when it is cool and get to Kirkuk before lunch.'

Sometime between 3 a.m. and 5 a.m. Tubby and the Reeve crawled out of their pits in the Khayam and found Wahdib as large as life in the hotel lobby. Demerji's trustworthy car was loaded up and Wahdib drove off through the black of night with two somewhat sleepy characters in the car. Tubby soon freshened to the cool of the night and began to wake up and take note of things. How fantastic are the nights in Iraq, and the cool seems to sharpen one's senses. The stars seem to have extra voltage of light power in the desert sky; they all sparkle, great and small, like a myriad diamonds on black velvet. De Beers, with all their dazzling diamonds, could not compare with this.

Wahdib said he would drive as far as the town of Baquba, by which time it should be daylight, then Tubby could take over while he got some sleep in the back. They sped along the road away from Baghdad until the red glow from the kilns of the numerous brickworks beyond the outskirts grew less and less and they were away from everything. In no time they turned off the Khanaquin Road and headed North-north-east,

42

Again Tubby was awed by the wonder of dawn in these desert regions – this time he witnessed it from ground level instead of 20,000 feet up. The barely discernible weakening in the twinkle of the stars as the black velvet they shone from turned gradually grey. How gradually the stages of dawn changed from one to another and yet too quickly to ponder the wonder of each stage to the full. One could almost see the rays from the yet unrisen sun darting upwards from beyond the horizon to light the heavens, while the ground remained dismal and dark. Not the friendly dark of night under a myriad stars but a dense muddled dark full of peculiar shadows and shapes, as it sought to cling and hang on in spite of the inevitability of another day. The sun thrust its head above the black line of the desert horizon in all its golden glory, sweeping as though it were a brush the last vestiges of darkness from the face of the earth.

They reached Baquba just after the dawn when one could say that the new day had established itself. All was cool and fresh and clean, one couldn't help but feel that all was well with the world. The petrol tank was filled to the top as this was the last petrol station for many miles. A quick stretch of the legs and they all piled into the car and set off. Tubby was at the wheel with the Reeve up front too, while Wahdib curled up in the back for some sleep. After years of training and experience in gaining the maximum number of minutes sleep during siesta time in the afternoons, Wahdib went out like a light. Before performing this trick he mumbled vaguely that to arrive safely in Kirkuk, one just drove north and followed one's nose.

The railway from Baghdad to the north did not touch Kirkuk, but went due north to Mosul following the River Tigris. There were plans for a road too, but it only reached as far as Samarra. Actually it wasn't a road at all but a track which had come into being during the construction of the big new dam on the River Tigris at Samarra.

However, wanting to study and assess the country of Iraq business-wise, Tubby and the Reeve had decided to do their trip north by road rather than rail. The maps showed a good road going north-east to Kirkuk, which they heard had been

43

built by a French company, or at least French engineers, though there had been some financial difficulties regarding the project. With minds at ease and full of the spirit of adventure they drove merrily along the road, but before long they began to wonder if they should have gone by rail after all.

The town limits of Baquba ended with the last vestige of greenery and so did the road. At least what was there did resemble the rough foundation of a road, so they pressed on thinking it was just a short stretch and the surface would start again. What a hope! After some miles the rough foundation gave way to dirt and stones. The change was not sudden but crept up on one gradually, but at least there was still something to follow. Soon they were driving on sand – plain sand – but as yet there were numerous tracks left by other vehicles going in the same direction. The vastness of the desert increased as they pressed on, while the tracks left in the sand by other vehicles got fewer and fewer.

Away ahead a small dust storm turned out to be a desert bus. Not one of the big Pukka Baghdad-Teheran air-conditioned jobs, but a small local one. An old Ford or General Motors chassis and engine, on which a bulbous brightly-coloured body had been built with bright shiny chrome screwed all over it for decoration. There it was bouncing along with its passengers' baggage on top; earthenware water bottles hanging out of the windows and huge poles tied along both sides, for levering it out when it got stuck in the sand.

Tubby and the Reeve got quite attached to the old bus as they followed it along at a safe distance to keep out of the miniature sand storm it created, but true to form it stopped. Miles and miles from anywhere and anything, and not a living soul or tent to be seen from one horizon to the other. They watched a passenger get off the bus, pull his bundle of belongings down from the roof, throw it over his shoulder and set off walking away into the wilderness. This took them ahead of the bus and out of sight of it before they realised. All they had to guide them was a small ridge of sand left by the double rear wheels of a desert truck, though its actual tyre tracks had been smoothed over by blown sand.

On they pressed, even though the ridge had gone – searching the way ahead for anything in the sand resembling a track or the remains of one. Where was the road shown on the maps which the French had built? The Reeve shouted and pointed to the left. About a mile away, a big desert truck was rolling along on a parallel course. Another mile or so on it was obvious that the truck was getting further away. The truck driver is bound to be right – maybe we should change on to his course, they thought. Then they saw a car half a mile to the right on a parallel course, but going in the opposite direction. They wondered then if they should go right and find the tracks of the car and follow them.

Years before Tubby had read about long range desert warfare in *Popski's Private Army* so he tried desperately to remember what it had said in the book about desert navigation. He remembered being told when young about Eskimos and trappers in the north of Canada getting lost in the snow and walking in huge circles instead of going straight on. So, he and the Reeve began to study carefully the tracks of their own car in the mirror in case they showed a slight curve to the right or left.

Eventually, feeling very much like the disciples of old in their storm-tossed boat on the Sea of Galilee, the pair wondered if the time had come to arouse Wahdib from his slumbers in the back of the car. After many many miles of doubt, and wondering, they were relieved to see a new track on the left sweeping in towards the direction in which they were travelling. Tubby and the Reeve felt quite chuffed as the tracks became more numerous until they saw something far away in front which finally removed the last fearful doubts about being lost. In this wilderness any structure or truck, once spotted, can be seen from a great distance. It was therefore quite some time before they arrived at what they had seen and found it to be a coffee shop, duly decorated with gaudy Sinalco, Coca Cola, and Pepsi signs. Several big desert trucks were parked by the coffee shop as tracks seem to converge on the place from several directions. Whether the meeting of the tracks brought the coffee shop or it brought them to it was not clear, but

Wahdib seemed to know the place when he woke up and found they had stopped – much to the relief of Tubby and the Reeve, though they were ashamed to admit it.

The journey continued with all three duly refreshed. The sun was really and truly up now in full charge of the day and its glare and heat was intense. Speed was necessary to keep a good breeze blowing through the car, but that was not to be. The surface had changed from desert sand to loose stones like a dried river bed which necessitated slower driving. Soon they were actually finding gullies or wadis, which Wahdib said flowed with water during the rains in winter. What interested Tubby and the Reeve more were the concrete ramps-cum-bridges built across some of the wadis and soon they came on stretches of road. The road at last, they thought. Abandoned half-way through construction, it certainly looked a mighty and worthwhile project. Some stretches went for miles, others were quite short with only the sides or rough foundations completed.

The surface now changed to sharp stones as they approached a low escarpment running from north-west to south-east across their path. Though low, the track over it was twisty and steep with deep potholes among the loose jagged stones, which were only avoided after much braking and frantic turning. Those which were just impossible to avoid were bounced through on the suspension after violent braking. Handling the big car was like riding a bucking bronco at a rodeo, so it was not surprising that they blew a tyre on the way down the other side of the escarpment.

The wheel change didn't delay them too long and thankfully the stretches of the new road appeared again. After some miles they came to a good motorable surface compared with what they had come to expect.

Soon they began to notice signs of habitation again, but more intriguing was the blackness of the sky above the horizon. Wahdib enlightened his two friends. Kirkuk is oil and oil is Kirkuk, and this was their first smell of Kirkuk, as it were. The darkness in the sky was the black smoke rising from the flaming torches of waste gas burning away at the great oilfields.

Before long they reached the first petrol station since

Baquba and filled up the tank. From there on the road was a real road in the full meaning of the word, and they relaxed blissfully as they sped along at top speed fascinated by the sight of the great blackness of the smoke in the sky and the lines of concrete-capped drills with their 'Christmas tree' valves which made the scene resemble a plantation. The nearer they got, the more intense the blackness became, until at last they saw the flaming torches themselves leaping many feet in the air from pipes sticking out of the ground, sending great dense columns of black smoke ever upwards to join with similar columns, to form the one big pall of smoke which hung high over the town before drifting off westwards.

9

NINEVEH AND THE WALLED CITY OF ERBIL

There wasn't much to Kirkuk except the great oil fields to the west. It was hot and dusty so the three stayed just long enough for lunch and a look round the market after calling in on their agent's big store. Some weeks earlier, Tubby and the Reeve had seen a government film about the mountains in the north of Iraq showing a fabulous government rest house situated in beautiful surroundings with a swimming pool. Though this particular place was north of Mosul, Wahdib said there was a similar rest house in Shaqlawa in the mountains north-north-east of Erbil, so they had planned to spend the night there on the way north. Little did the pair realise how fabulous it was going to be.

The north of Iraq bordering on Iran and Turkey is very mountainous, and the north-east portion peopled by the Kurds. Tubby was fascinated when he first saw several Kurds in Kirkuk, they were so different from the Iraqis of the south. They were much cleaner, wore peculiar baggy pants and jackets made of coarse heavy cloth, and had a turbaned head-dress. Strong-featured and bearded, the Kurds were mountain people and appeared to be very similar to Afghans. In fact, further north in the mountains, Tubby saw many Kurds with long rifles and leather bullet holders over each shoulder, which reminded him of his schoolboy adventure stories of the north west frontier and the Khyber Pass.

Driving out of Kirkuk they were surprised how few oil derricks there were, but as they left the town and climbed another escarpment they noticed very many more wells which

48

had been tapped with 'Christmas tree' valves once their derricks were removed. No need for pumps here, the pipes from the drill holes being drawn off came straight up from the ground in a big loop and off in the direction of the main oilfield. There the big main pipeline started, which carried the flow of black gold across the miles of desert to Jordan and then the Mediterranean coast.

The escarpment immediately north of Kirkuk was as jagged and barren as the one they had crossed before, but larger and higher, stretching as far as they could see from east to west. The difference this time was the good road and surface to drive on. This was the case from Kirkuk onwards except that the road did follow the contours right to the bottom of each gully. Why the builders had not tried to even things out was hard to understand, but Tubby would just work up to a real good speed when he would find the car heading straight down the side of a V-shaped gully with road going straight up the other side. The first few times he braked hard but still thumped the bottom point of the 'V' with the front wheels. The suspension would hit rock bottom and bounce the bonnet out again up the other side. To try and ease this bounce and shock on the suspension they took to rocking the car through the bottom of the 'V's' one front wheel just ahead of the other, by flicking the steering wheel sharp left and right just as the car hit.

Wahdib said nothing as they wound their way up and over the escarpment, he just waited for Tubby and the Reeve to react to the view before them. He was not disappointed, initially they were both struck dumb in amazement. To the left and to the right the jagged top of the escarpment stretched as far as the eye could see; nature's wall between the barren, dry, and dust regions they had just left and the garden of Eden to the north. The scene before them as they looked north was almost similar to the prairies of Canada at harvest time. Before them stretched yellow ripe crops for miles and miles dotted with spiral columns of dust rising in swirling heat thermals to disappear in the blue sky.

After the barren dusty land they had driven through south of Kirkuk, the contrast had to be seen to be believed, and, as they drove on to Erbil, Wahdib told them that the view from the escarpment was even more breathtaking in March and April when the crops were still green. The thermals of dust were a constant fascination. Some were huge and seemed permanent and awesome, slowly drawing a great column of dust ever upwards. Tubby could not help thinking of the Children of Israel following 'the Cloudy Pillar by day and the Fire by night'. Others were small and broke up on reaching the road. Several of them all but hit the car, and it was amazing to see how fast they moved when close, and feel the car rock with the impact of the swirling mass of air and dirt. The approach of one of the 'swirligigs', as they were christened, meant a hasty winding up of the car windows. Wahdib said it was nothing compared to running into a swarm of locusts or hoppers, as they call the young ones before their wings have developed. Iraq was not too bad for locusts due to tracing and poison-laying along the Saudi Arabian border where they come from. Still, swarms did get through, and one just had to drive on through the solid mass of locusts, crushing them and skidding on them until the car got through the swarm.

Here and there in this wonderland, the twentieth century took the form of an occasional tractor pulling a harvester, but on the whole it was like a drive through biblical times.

... and became like the chaff of the summer threshing floors; and the wind carried them away, that no place was found for them. (Daniel, chapter 3, verse 35)]

Behold I will make thee a new sharp threshing instrument having teeth. (Isaiah, chapter 41, verse 15)

These words of the prophets of old came alive to Tubby as they passed labourers in the fields tossing the wheat into the air while the chaff was carried away by the wind, and donkeys pulling the ancient threshing instruments round and round the grain piled on the threshing floors. Later in Erbil, Tubby examined one of these threshers in a shop: great heavy wooden sides like a giant lawn mower without wheels, having numerous axles inside bristling with blades of iron which spun and threshed the grain as the instrument was dragged round.

The journey seemed short through this wonderland of the ancient world, there was so much to see. The workers busy with the harvest; the whirlwinds of dust and the great storks high above in the blue sky with wings outspread and long legs trailing as they turned and wheeled effortlessly, riding the invisible heat thermals that rose from the sun-baked earth. Their interest turned from these things as Wahdib pointed to a mound or single hill which had come into view miles ahead of them. It was the only high ground to be seen in this great plain; it was Erbil.

Tubby knew that Erbil was a very old city and he had been told that Alexander the Great fought a great battle near this place. He watched with interest the mound ahead and the details of it which became clearer as they approached, until at last they stood before it.

Erbil was unbelievable – a walled city standing on a hill dominating the great plain. One of the oldest inhabited cities in the world, it had grown over the years and modern Erbil clung round the bottom of the hill in a network of streets and houses, but the old walled city on the top was very much the centre of things. Tubby's eyes followed the upsweep of the sides of the hill from the roofs of the houses at the bottom, to the mighty ancient walls at the top. The years had rounded the bold defensive squareness of the ancient ramparts and now storks' nests decorated the battlements, but on the whole, all was pretty well preserved.

Never in this day and age did Tubby think he would see in reality the illustrations from the family bible and his history books, but here they were as large as life. Through half closed eyes he gazed at this place while his mind wandered over the sands of time: was Jericho like this when the Israelites marched round and round till the great walls came tumbling down? Was Saul of Tarsus lowered down in a basket from a window in walls like these, at Damascus?

Once in the city they parked the car and called on their main dealer, who sold practically everything. He was moderately fat and with a week's growth on his face, quite jovial, though there was something shifty about him. It turned out that there were some shadows in his past and he had been a jailbird at some time. His term as a jailbird had been somewhat shorter and less severe than it should have been and for this he was forever indebted to a certain lawyer who actually owned the shop.

After Wahdib had talked to their fat friend, they all went off in the car to see the said lawyer at his office. They joined a ragged bunch of vagrants in the waiting room for a few minutes before they were ushered into the inner office. Our lawyer friend was quite a big wheel in Erbil, and even beyond, which was evident from the western suit he was wearing. Most of the people were Kurds and western dress was not a common sight in the streets. Tubby and the Reeve christened him the 'Crooked Lawyer', not because of any reflections on his legal dealings, but because of his appearance. He looked as though the mob had got hold of him at some time and left him somewhat lopsided and deformed. After a short discussion about developing business in the Erbil area, the three took their leave, promising to call again on the way back from Mosul.

With petrol tank full again, they headed north-east along the road to Mahabad in Northern Iran. The countryside was dry and barren, but soon they turned off left and started to wind through the foothills of the northern mountains, passing several armed Kurds watching over their goats and sheep. Here the donkey was the standard means of transport.

The climb through the foothills was mild compared with the final hair-raising climb to the top. The road climbed thousands of feet in a series of quarter-mile stretches, with a hairpin bend on each end. Tubby started in grand style, keeping in top gear by swinging the car wide just before each hairpin, clipping the inside corner and winging out wide into the next upward stretch. This was possible because each stretch was visible from the previous one and in the whole ascent they only passed one bus going the other way. It was a weird ramshackle bus with no cover on the engine at all and coachwork like a London single decker in the 1920s. After the twentieth hairpin, Tubby wondered how much longer he could keep it up. The low gear ratio on the steering meant about two revolutions out followed by about ten back again to get the car through the bend, and then a frantic unwind into the next straight. The gradients got steeper and there were still more hairpins, till he had to start changing down, wishing he had four gears to play with. The engine got so hot it slowed down, but just in time they reached the top and the rest house at Shaqlawa.

The signing-in duly completed, they dumped their stuff in their rooms and went off to the swimming pool which was about half a mile away. The tiredness of the long day vanished with the first plunge and they sat at the side of the pool relaxing and enjoying the fresh mountain air.

Back at the rest house they changed and went out on the terrace to watch the sun go down. With rushing off to the swimming pool Tubby had had no time to study the situation of the rest house. Now on the terrace he just stood simply enthralled by the panorama. Facing south he felt like God on high as he looked down at the great plain stretching from below his feet, as it were, to the jagged escarpment dividing it from the deserts beyond. Turning to the north he became a humble man again awed by the majesty of the great mountains. Ridge after ridge to the Turkish border seemed to be peeping over the one in front to catch a final glimpse of the setting sun, which painted each gold and then glowing red as a last flourish before yielding to the night.

Sitting in the dusk Tubby relived the day from its dawning in Baghdad to its ending here in the mountains at Shaqlawa. He was rudely startled from his reverie by something racing down the road below the terrace, resembling a powerboat at 42 knots with its great bow waves bursting from its sides. It was a government lorry on its dusk patrol spraying DDT. Without more ado the three of them retreated inside for dinner, and so to bed. Sleep came easily that night.

It was a glorious morning, and the mountains to the north were sharp and clear but the plain below to the south was shrouded in haze. Soon they were swinging down through the hairpins on their way back to Erbil. No stopping this time, but

53

quickly through the new town at the foot of the ancient walls and away to Mosul.

This stretch of the journey was not so interesting except for the occasional steep dips down dried valleys and gullies. Water did flow down these valleys at some time of the year, as witnessed by a narrow bridge at the bottom. At one of these gullies they were on the way down as a lorry was coming down the other side. Both reached the point of wondering who was going to slow for the other, when the lorry's headlights flicked on and off. That was all Tubby needed and he stamped on the accelerator, but the lorry driver must have done the same. Somehow he managed to get the car over the bridge and yanked out of the way a fraction before the lorry hurtled past them on to the bridge. Fighting to hold the car on the road as it zoomed up from the bridge, Tubby muttered something about lorry and bus drivers at home flicking headlights when they intended to hold back, and leaving them on full beam when they intended to come straight on. He suddenly noticed that Wahdib had a peculiar blanched look and his eyes seemed stuck in a wide-open position. The Reeve in the back seat was gibbering. On recovering, Wahdib explained that flicking of headlights meant the opposite in Iraq, as had just been demonstrated.

The Kurds were left behind as they approached the regions which were once ancient Assyria. There was a strong Christian heritage among the Iraqis there, which could be felt in various ways. Time had not stood still as in the south where small towns, villages and the way of life was the same as centuries ago, except for the modern roads through them. Here in the north as they drew nearer to Mosul, it was noticeable that the villages were more modern and orderly; streets were clean and had some pavements; and the majority of people wore western style clothes. Iraq, however, is a land of contrasts, and as they passed a turning off to the right Wahdib told them that this road went to a village whose inhabitants worshipped the Devil himself. Once a year these people had a procession through the streets, headed by a brazen cockerel held on high.

Mosul was indeed clean and relatively modern compared

with other towns they had passed through and the people were different too. Perhaps the memory of Jonah the Prophet still echoed down the centuries because this was the site of Nineveh of old. They crossed the River Tigris by a large and beautiful suspension bridge to the main city. Who would have believed that in the not too distant future this city would be the scene of bloody riots and this very bridge would be strung with bodies from end to end. The sight from the bridge was of a sprawling city dominated by a great mound. The mound was all that remained of Nineveh after years of digging and investigation by archaeologists.

On the mound stood a mosque, beneath which no tunnelling was allowed, though it was believed many interesting treasures lay hidden there. This mosque at Mosul was said to have adorning one of its walls the bones of the great fish, claimed to be those of none other than the fish which the Lord prepared for Jonah when he tried to escape from going to Nineveh. They passed on through the city and across the plaza to a big imposing building of the railway station and hotel where they were to stay. Wahdib went off with the car to stay with his own relations and look up old friends.

After dinner, Tubby and the Reeve wandered down into the station itself. The whole place was in a fever of activity prior to the departure of the night train for Baghdad. Judging by the numbers of people about, it was a busy train, but on reflection Tubby thought it was probably much cooler and more comfortable to make this train journey at night. The desert wastes to the south got mighty hot through the day. Slowly they walked the length of the platform observing the different classes of coaches. The luxury first class, with sleepers; the second class with padded seats; and the third – well, it did have seats! The old, the lame and the blind, whole families with all their possessions including sheep, goats, poultry, the lot! Hanging out of each window for refrigeration were earthenware water pots of all shapes, sizes and descriptions. This was a far cry from British Rail and Tubby was rather glad that they had come by road. Eventually everyone was squeezed on and the train pulled away into the night.

For all its great past Tubby was disappointed with Nineveh; perhaps he had expected too much, especially after Erbil; perhaps it was having no time to explore the place properly.

Mosul rated about third in Iraq after Baghdad and Basrah. It was a military centre of sorts and sported an airfield. During the many changes of allegiance and the involved operations in the Middle East in the World War Two, the Germans actually landed in Mosul, but didn't stay long. The three didn't stay long either and in two days they were off south again.

10

THE DESPERATE DRIVE BACK

Starting the long steady run from Mosul to Baghdad straight after breakfast, Tubby took the wheel for the first stage to Erbil. It was a clear day as they sped away across the river and out of the town. Soon they were past the turning off to the village of Devil worshippers and well on the way to Erbil. This was going to be a good run in spite of the heat, thought Tubby, settling back comfortably behind the wheel; then it happened – bump! bump! He sat up and got a good hold on the wheel as he slowed the big car down and pulled it into the side. Little did they know that this was just puncture number one.

The spare wheel was fitted on without much trouble except that they were all dripping with perspiration and glad to be moving again to get some breeze through the car. Tubby began to feel better as he dried out, but then he felt the first twinge of pain in his lower regions. The dreaded Baghdad Belly, one of the many plagues one has to accept as part of one's existence in the Middle East, especially in the heat of the mid-year. In their first week both Tubby and the Reeve had suffered a peculiar nausea for several days, when the very sight of food made one want to vomit. Tubby had just slept for the first day and for the next three days Hans had made him eat only plain boiled rice and drink only mint tea. The diet was unbearable by the third day, but it did the trick.

The Baghdad Belly, however, was a different kettle of fish. One day most of the residents in the hotel had been struck down before it was discovered that the refrigerator in the kitchen had broken down and someone had bought ice from a local factory. Another time, Tubby had gone to the cinema with the Reeve – they stayed for the whole show, but just got back to the hotel in time after a wild dash in a taxi down Rashid Street, doubled with pain.

Here it was again, only this time it was a mad dash for Erbil as Tubby's foot stamped harder on the accelerator with each twinge of pain in his guts. The car screeched to a halt outside the dealer's shop and they jumped out. After a hasty, vociferous, animated exchange of words with the dealer, Wahdib told Tubby to follow a little Arab boy in a striped shimmy. He was past caring as he staggered down the street after the boy but when they turned down an alley, through a doorway, down steps and on through a veritable labyrinth of back cracks, Tubby began to think of all the tales he had read about the Casbah in Algiers, and wondered if his body would end up in an alley, duly knifed. He wished he had a reel of cotton to find his way out of this labyrinth, as Theseus did after slaying the Minotaur in ancient Crete.

Finally they mounted a flight of five stone steps to a small courtyard. The boy stopped at the top of the steps and pointed sheepishly. Tubby looked at the circular stone pool in the centre with water pouring into it from pipes round the side. Oh, no, he thought, not out in the open! Then he saw a Kurd appear from a hole in the wall on the right, tying the waist cord of his baggy pants. There were a row of these holes in the wall resembling the entrances to railway tunnels, but these were only about four and a half feet high. He staggered into the first one and before closing the heavy wooden door he saw a hole at the back and a tall brass water pot behind the door. Any port of call in a storm, thought Tubby as he slammed the door. It was as black as pitch except for the thin line of light under the door and the heat was appalling. He felt like a Communist political prisoner in solitary confinement; thank goodness he didn't suffer from claustrophobia.

To his great relief when he finally emerged, he saw the little boy in the striped shimmy waiting for him. In no time he was back at the shop where Wahdib and the Reeve were loading great tins of peculiar greyish-white stuff into the back of the car. The smell of it was really horrible and strong and it lay in the tins heaving and wobbling as though it were alive. Wahdib apologetically explained that it was Erbil leban (yoghurt) which would be diluted down into gallons of the stuff and shared out among his relations. This yoghurt was a favourite drink to the Iraqis and the mention of 'Erbil leban' usually made them drool at the mouth and roll their eyes. Evidently Wahdib had been threatened by his clan not to come back unless he brought a good supply of Erbil leban concentrate. With the precious load safely in the boot they went off to get the tyre repaired.

The tyre shop was in a building right under the ancient walls of Erbil. The damage to the tyre was much worse than they realised so Tubby had a wander round while they worked on it. He went round the back and stood on the rubble at the base of the ancient walls, staring up at the old ramparts and the storks' nests on the top. Oh, that these walls could speak! It was while he was wandering around to fill in time that Tubby found a workshop which made the threshing instruments they had seen on the way to Erbil earlier, so he inspected them carefully.

Soon they were off again heading for Kirkuk, but poor Tubby was bad again and they had to hastily pull off the road while he ran off behind a sand dune. As soon as he staggered back, the Reeve really set off at a cracking speed to make up time to Kirkuk. Luckily puncture number two was the same as the one before Erbil and not a blow out. They were about halfway to Kirkuk when the Reeve felt the bump and quickly pulled the car to a halt.

This journey was becoming a proper nightmare to Tubby. He felt weak and limp as he lay in the back of the car while they changed the wheel, and once they were going again it seemed an eternity before they reached Kirkuk. He could not face any food when they got there, but spent most of the time in the primitive gents at the back of the shop while the others ate.

The second puncture repair further delayed them, but they made good time down the stretch of good road from Kirkuk to the last petrol station before the roadless desert. By this time Tubby was feeling weak and thoroughly miserable. He was soaked in perspiration and his clothes stuck to him, and he was covered with a layer of dust. He just lay in the back watching the black clouds of smoke over Kirkuk fade into the distance as they sped south.

Time was getting short and the thought uppermost in their minds was whether they would get across the desert and on to the road at Baquba before darkness fell. Before they reached the jagged escarpment Tubby had to stop them again and disappear under one of the unfinished bridges for the new road. Thankfully this was the last bout of his Baghdad Belly because there was virtually no cover from then on, and once they were over the escarpment they began to meet a steady stream of cars heading north from Baghdad which would have made things difficult. There was to be a public holiday the next day giving a good long weekend, so many people were driving north for the break.

Another worry they had was the state of the car's tyres, and sure enough on the jagged escarpment another tyre went bang. As it was impossible to drive fast on this dreadful track there was no danger from going off the road with a blow out and really wrecking the car.

Tubby began to recover somewhat as the cool of evening approached. When they stopped for a quick drink at the desert coffee shop, he took over the wheel as the others too had really been bounced about keeping up a high speed on the bad surface. There was no fear of losing the track now with a steady stream of cars coming the other way. Their main aim was to get back on the road before dark, but the sun was rapidly descending to the horizon. A slight wind helped by blowing away to the left the churned up sand from the other vehicles.

In spite of his almost reckless speed across the sandy wastes, darkness caught them in its grip obscuring the firm sand from the soft. They could see the headlights of on-coming cars and the following dust necessitated constant flicking of the headlights. Straining his eyes to pick up every detail in the headlight beams Tubby noticed that the dust was thickening. It was similar to the cloud of dust one met when approaching a big desert truck from behind, but it was too widespread and not turbulent enough. Caution made him slow down when suddenly the head and neck of a camel materialised out of the murk almost above the front of the radiator. He just saw for an instant the huge load on its back, its tassled reins and its terrified eyes bulging and white in the glare of the headlights as he frantically took avoiding action. His sharp left turn brought him on another, there seemed to be camels everywhere in the churning dust, until they suddenly came out of it with the car slithering and wallowing in the sand like a ship in a heavy sea. Tubby stopped the car and just sat with the visions of the last few seconds still swirling before him as in a kaleidoscope, wondering how on earth he had managed to avoid hitting a camel.

Wahdib had jumped out when the car stopped and he came back to announce that they had just come through a camel caravan which in the darkness had got strung out, line abreast instead of line astern. Wahdib also announced that one of the tyres had gone as a result of the violent manoeuvering. The three of them got out and stood looking at the car. Miles out in the desert, the spare already flat and now another flat. Tubby didn't know whether to laugh or cry. Surely nothing else could happen now.

The first thing was to get the car off the tracks before a big truck came along. This was duly done and the wheel removed. It was beyond repair so the spare was taken out and Wahdib said he would get a lift into Baquba on the next truck, heading south and get it repaired. The first truck to appear was actually heading north and the driver pulled up and jumped down to see if he could help. He said that we were quite near to Baquba and promptly offered to go back with Wahdib there and then. The truck turned and headed off and the silence of the desert settled round them. The Reeve remembered that they still had some cans of beer in a portable ice box. The stars twinkled in the heavens, and after the day they had had, it was cool and quiet as they supped ice cool beer from the cans – how could they fail to relax, unwind and laugh about all that had happened to them.

It seemed no time until the truck was back. Wahdib jumped down with the spare wheel and with a cheery shout from the driver the truck was off again. He wouldn't hear of payment for helping us, a real gentleman of the desert tracks. Wahdib was in high spirits as they were really quite close to Baquba and there was a man next to the tyre shop who had killed a sheep and was cooking fresh khebab for them. Tubby was ready for a good meal by now, in fact they all were, so the wheel was fitted without more ado and soon they were in Baquba.

The owner of the food stall was a fat jovial man in a long white shimmy, somewhat bloodstained and smeared with grease from his sizzling khebab. The smell of the cooking khebab was wonderful and the taste even better. Before long there was quite a crowd around to see the sight of two somewhat travel-worn Britishers guzzling khebab and hunks of bread at a local food stall. Tubby and the Reeve must have really looked as though they were enjoying themselves and the food because many of the crowd started to buy too, which made their fat friend even more jovial. The whole thing developed into quite a hilarious feast until the whole sheep was finished. The fat stall holder was quite delighted over the whole affair and obviously considered himself the uncrowned King of Khebab. He personally saw them to the car shaking them all by the hand after he had wiped his own hand on the front of his shimmy.

Partly because of their full tummies and partly because of fatigue after a long eventful ride, the rest of the journey was made in silence. Before long the myriad twinkling lights which were Baghdad became visible away ahead. As they drew nearer the form of the city became clearer and soon they drew up outside the hotel. Unloading their bits and pieces they bid good night to Wahdib and crawled upstairs. No need for dinner after all that khebab; a hot bath and a nice bed was all they wanted.

11

THE QUEEN'S BIRTHDAY

Back to routine the next morning Tubby set off on his usual morning walk. Out on to Rashid Street, across the Queen Aliyah Bridge, past the British Consulate, over the road, round the corner of the beautifully gardened Iranian Embassy and down to the school they were using for a godown under Wahdib's house. In the early morning it was a pleasant walk and Tubby liked the exercise each morning. Often on the bridge he would meet flocks of sheep being led to market. In true biblical style the shepherd would stride out in front and all the funny long eared sheep would follow after. Sometimes another man would bring up the rear dragging a sheep by its back feet while blood ran from its recently slit throat. Tubby could only assume, as he followed the red trail, that they wanted fresh meat ready for sale as soon as they reached market.

The aftermath of a trip away is usually a pile of letters on one's desk. One large white envelope stood out among the others, so it was investigated first. On the back was the lion and the unicorn heavily embossed in gold. The envelope contained an impressive card, also embossed with a gold lion and unicorn, inviting Tubby to attend a reception at the British Embassy in honour of the official birthday of her Majesty the Queen. The Reeve had also received an invitation and later at the hotel they found that Charlie, the barman from Gibraltar, also had his. In fact this reception was quite an event overseas for Britishers and all others in any way associated, past or present, with Britain and her far flung dominions.

On the evening of the reception all cars seemed to be heading across the river to the British Embassy. Though the

Embassy was situated near a rather terrible part of Baghdad, known as the Showakah, it was isolated off in spacious grounds guarded by huge walls and majestic gates. Tubby and the Reeve walked up the palm lined main drive and nearing the main building they joined the end of a long snake of guests which wound its way up the rest of the drive along by the terrace and down to the lawn where the ambassador and his wife were greeting the guests.

As they moved slowly along Tubby studied the beautiful and impressive embassy. The building backed on to the river while the pillared front looked down majestically on to the rolling lawns, trees, and palms from a terrace boldly lined with shining cannons. The trees and gardens were gaily decorated with flags and bunting. A pipe band marched to and fro on the spacious lawn and another band at the far side took over when the pipes stopped. Just before they reached the ambassador, a very smooth young Foreign Office type asked for their names and formally introduced Tubby and the Reeve to Sir Michael and Lady Wright. How they kept up the hand shaking with so many people was quite miraculous.

The lawns were obscured as more and more guests filled the gardens, sipping away at their drinks. As day gave way to night a myriad lights came on, twinkling in the trees to transform the grounds into a veritable fairy land.

Eventually all had arrived and the climax of the evening reached: the toasts to King Feisal, followed by the Iraqi national anthem, and to the Queen, followed by the National Anthem. Away in a foreign land everything seemed to take on a new significance and a great feeling of patriotism welled up inside at the sound of the National Anthem. The homeland and all it stood for seemed very near and Tubby felt very proud of being British. No-one present that night could possibly think or even remotely imagine the beautiful grounds and embassy as the scene of mob violence in the near future.

From the embassy, Tubby and the Reeve moved off to another place which was destined to see the violence of the mob – the new Baghdad Hotel. For the capital of a country so steeped in ancient history and with such a tremendous potential tourist industry, Baghdad was lacking in big first class hotels. The one Tubby was staying in was top quality and, fully air-conditioned, etc., but it was originally built as an office block with a cinema, and at the last minute it was changed into an hotel. Every now and then half the staff used to be shanghaied to the Royal Palace to cater for large banquets and dinners during Baghdad Pact Council meetings. These meals were usually served on the lawns under the starlit skies and Hans used to tell Tubby that the biggest problem was to stop the Iraqi boys from tipping whole trays of food and drink to their families hiding in the shadows among the flowerbeds and hedges.

Ever since his arrival Tubby had been watching the growth of the big new seven-storey Baghdad Hotel along the road to the Alwiyah Club. One day he had been taken all over it by one of the proud owners. They were brothers who had started as waiters, it was said, and for several years they had owned one of the smaller older hotels in Rashid Street. The brothers had certainly gone to town with Persian carpets and marble, and it was all very modern. Now it was open and Tubby and Reeve went there after the reception to see how things were doing. No parking problems here as the hotel was well back from the road with grounds and a forecourt. Boys in Kurdish dress opened the doors as they went in and upstairs to the lounge. Everyone seemed to have had the same idea as themselves, even Hans was there spying out the opposition, as it were. Demerji, their car friend, was there too and swept Tubby and Reeve into his party in an attempt to appease their wrath after the terrible trip north they had had in his special car.

It had been a long time in the making but the new Baghdad Hotel had opened its doors at last. Little did Tubby and Reeve realise how glad they were going to be that this hotel had not been delayed further.

12

BRIAN BORU TO THE RESCUE

Ever since his arrival in Baghdad, Tubby had been searching for a house to live in. Hotels, however luxurious, are alright for short spells, but certainly not for permanent residence. Like all capital cities of fast developing countries, houses were hard to come by. Compared with its Arab neighbours, Iraq was indeed way ahead in its progress and the many projects afoot had brought in the usual high quota of foreign technicians. Baghdad also housed the headquarters of the Baghdad Pact.

One day Tubby heard of a certain doctor who was going to London for several years' specialised research, so he and the Reeve drove out to see him at his house. It was way out in the Hindiyah area of Baghdad, near the US Embassy. They found that it was a bungalow with a well kept garden and large hedges all round. As they were trying to find out how to open the gate there was a loud scuffling noise and down towards them came a bundle of snarling fury in the form of a great dog. They managed to close the gate, with themselves on the outside, as the great beast hit the inside of the gate at head height barking vociferously. Satisfied that the dog could not get at them they stayed and soon the doctor appeared out of the house.

He was a short, jovial, mustachioed Iraqi and he assured them that once they were inside the dog would be their friend. Nevertheless the Reeve and Tubby were on their marks ready to leap to the top of the gate posts as the doctor unlocked the gate and the dog ran straight past them intent on having a good sniff in the road before being dragged in again.

The doctor's wife and family had already gone to the UK, so the place looked more like a bachelor flat as he was doing his final packing and cleaning up. All was satisfactory, so it was agreed that they would rent the place from the next Monday as the doctor was leaving by Iraqi Airways Viscount on the Sunday night. As they left, the doctor warned that if the telephone rang on or about midnight it would probably be one of the girls from the cabarets. This bungalow did indeed have all mod cons!

Highly pleased with their negotiations and the prospect of having a house to live in, Tubby and the Reeve made plans for a final thrash with their friends in the hotel. With Friday being the Holy Day in Iraq, Sunday was a working day, so a quiet but special dinner was arranged at the hotel for the Sunday night. However, these things can get out of hand and the dinner was followed by a crawl round the night clubs of Baghdad. They walked back to the hotel in the early hours of the morning exchanging salutations with the ragged night guards who patrolled the various areas carrying bent rifles which couldn't fire a bullet if they wanted to. They talked to a baker and his men preparing their bread for the morrow and bought a loaf straight out of the oven. They stoned the usual packs of dogs that roamed the streets. All was normal in the streets of Baghdad that night as they finally returned to the hotel.

Monday 14th July – Bastille Day, thought Tubby, as he crawled along to the dining room for his usual scrambled eggs done shish-khebab style. Emile, the faithful Lebanese waiter, came solemnly to attention at his table: 'Good morning, sir. There has been a revolution.' With the newspapers having been full of the trouble in the Lebanon for the last few weeks, Tubby mumbled something about Emile going back to Beirut and blowing up a few more buses if that was how he felt.

Breakfast finished, Tubby was joined by the Reeve at the last minute as usual. Discussing what was to be done that day, the pair shouted 'Ashlonak' to the doorman as they left the air-conditioned atmosphere of the hotel and stepped into the dry heat and ever-present smells of the street. Still talking away, they soon covered the short distance to Rashid Street and crossed to the far side to hail a passing taxi. Usually they were hooted at by about five taxis before they got across the stream of traffic. Their conversation came to an abrupt halt as simultaneously they realised that this morning Rashid Street was not the same as usual.

The atmosphere was positively electric, especially compared with the usual state of lethargy. Tubby could almost feel it in his hair like a cat in a thunderstorm. The traffic was not as heavy as usual, people waved and shouted from the buses and what taxis there were didn't seem interested in fares. People were excitedly rushing in all directions at once, apparently to no purpose, and, let's face it the Iraqis never rush at the best of times!

'It must be a holiday we haven't been told about,' thought the Reeve aloud. 'Perhaps they do celebrate Bastille Day here after all.' Just then they noticed that the heavy steel shutters, which the shops rolled down each night to protect the windows, were still very securely locked down.

Feeling somewhat conspicuous standing in the middle of Rashid Street among all the excitement they tried to pin-point the significance of the steel shutters being down. Their deliberations were somewhat rudely interrupted by a terrifying noise and clatter about 100 yards down the street. To their horror they saw two huge Centurion tanks come trundling round the corner from the Queen Aliyah Bridge and head towards them. It wasn't the tanks which horrified them but the mob that rode on them and ran with them, all chanting wild slogans and carrying large pictures of dear old Colonel Nasser!

Now, Tubby had often read about Arab mobs, especially at the time of the dreadful Cairo riots in 1952. He also knew that Baghdad had quite a good reputation for this sort of thing, but one never considers for a minute that one day one might have to face a real mob. This one coming towards them was definitely the genuine article. These boys weren't just excited, one look at the faces and eyes was enough to see that they were worked up to a frenzy. With two tanks to back them up what could they fear? They had reached the pitch of excitement and only the slightest provocation was needed to turn these men, these human beings, into ferocious blind beasts capable of far

68

more destruction and killing with their bare hands and weight of numbers alone than anything in the jungle.

Stunned momentarily by the suddenness of it all, the Reeve eventually exclaimed, 'Colonel Nasser's boys!' The big game hunters say, 'Wait till you see the whites of the eyes,' but Tubby and the Reeve were the hunted in this case and self preservation was uttermost in their minds. Wyatt Earp once said, 'A sawn-off shotgun is the only weapon for facing a leaderless mob,' but this was no ordinary mob. Their first impulsive reaction was to make a beeline for the hotel, but this meant crossing Rashid Street in front of the advancing mob. The sight of two hated Britishers running like scared rabbits would just be about the right provocation for the mob to indulge in the favourite sport of lynching. The obvious thing was to take off sunglasses, pull out shirt tails and retreat into a building under construction just behind them and look as inconspicuous as possible.

Flattened against a wall inside this building they both rubbed dirt off the walls on to their exposed skin and watched the mob go by chanting good Egyptian anti-British slogans, which were being shouted by a cheerleader riding on the first tank. Tubby produced a green Irish passport, which he carried for such occasions, and assuming the character of Brian Boru he prepared to shout in his best Dublin brogue to any who came near that the decent Irish had been fighting the British far longer than any of the Arabs.

After what seemed an eternity the mob and the tanks passed down Rashid Street and Tubby and the Reeve, feeling a bit sick and weak at the knees, made their way as inconspicuously as possible across Rashid Street. They met their agent's storekeeper on the pavement and asked him what was going on. He was a pasty-faced character with thick glasses which were steamed up. Even paler than usual he blubbered something about a radio broadcast in the morning which said that the army had overthrown the government and had declared a holiday to celebrate their revolution. They could not get any more sense out of Sami so they made their way back to the hotel.

People huddled in small groups in the reception lounge at

the top of the stairs talking in muffled tones. Looks of apprehension all round greeted the besmirched pair as they staggered up the stairs, but the apprehension turned to relief as they were recognised. They then formed another group as several others gathered round to hear of their experience. So it went on as each person who had gone out to business as usual returned with another hair raising story to add to the confusion.

Little fat Yussof, their chief salesman, appeared, so Tubby pulled him over to the secretary's office behind the reception desk where someone had a radio. Yussof began to mutter odd snatches of translation out the corner of his mouth as he strained to catch the stream of excited Arabic which came from the radio.

'Early this morning . . .. at the palace .. . . . King abdicated .. . . . the corrupt government of Nuri-el-Said and Prince Regent Abdul Illah overthrown by the army . . .. keep calm . . . . . . curfew . . . . . . the army is in control . . . . . . revolution complete . . . . . . return to work as usual tomorrow .. . . . blah, blah, blah . . .' and so it went on.

The tales from the street, however, were far from reassuring. 'The palace has been ransacked . . . the British Embassy burnt down and people killed . . . the mob have torn Abdul Illah to pieces . . . The British Consulate burnt down and ransacked . . . the King is dead . . . the mob have started down Rashid Street as usual smashing in shops and looting . . .' With each new arrival the events of the morning became more gory. Fear began to take over and reveal itself in people's faces and reactions. Twitches developed and the odd voice rose to make some rash pronouncement when suddenly the mob arrived up the stairs from the street. With great presence of mind, someone offered them the pictures of the King and the Prince Regent which hung on the wall above the lift gates. Apparently appeased they went off in great glee to smash both the pictures in the street before moving off to the next building.

There was silence for a minute before guests appeared from under tables and chairs. Suddenly all spoke at once and the lounge was filled with suggestions and counter-suggestions in various languages. It was like the Tower of Babel all over again as the volume rose egged on by fear and excitement, until a voice of utter calm and authority broke through the hubbub.

'We'll be alright you know! Us British have been through revolutions before you know. We've had our embassies burned over our heads before! Of course, in the old days we used to send a gun boat and it was all over!'

The owner of the voice was Colonel Nimmo, ex-Governor of Tobruk, Foreign Office retired. Short of stature and somewhat stooped with the years, his trousers started just below his armpits. However, he had a young complexion, sandy hair flecked with grey, and he wore a truly Churchillian bow tie, spotted of course.

'I remember Cairo '52,' he continued, 'the mob were only interested in the first three floors of the hotels.' An American secretly began counting the floors of the Hotel Khayam on his fingers and visibly paled when he realised three fingers had been used up.

By this time Colonel Nimmo was the centre of attention, though he was scarcely visible relaxed in a large lounge chair. He carried on quite unmoved, his booming British Civil Service accent filling the whole lounge.

'Mainly young fellas, the mob. Students, you know. Parents didn't know what they were up to, so we cracked a few skulls, then their parents knew what they were up to and kept 'em home out of trouble!'

With these and other rugged assurances from this obvious veteran of the mobs, a semblance of calm spread through the ranks of the guests and they drifted to their rooms to draft cables or think out what to do next. Before Tubby and the Reeve could decide what to do several of their young salesmen appeared up the stairs, their eyes bright with excitement as they related all the goings-on in gory detail. Arms flailed about showing how places had been wrecked, old statues toppled and bodies strung up. They eventually left, warning Tubby that it was not safe to go out again into the streets that day.

As soon as the boys had gone, several of the guests pounced on Tubby and Reeve asking if they were in league with the revolutionaries and if their friends who had just left had been investigating the interior of the hotel and noting who was in it. These guests took some reassuring, but they eagerly lapped up the news from outside that the King and Crown Prince were dead, and the British Embassy and Consulate had been looted and burned.

Knowing young Farid, his salesman, as he did, Tubby wondered how much had been added to their tales for effect. He went to his room and opened the window on to his balcony, because he could see from this vantage point a small part of Rashid Street and catch a glimpse of anything that passed along it. Things had certainly warmed up since he and the Reeve had returned to the hotel at 8.30 a.m. after their brush with the tank mob. The air was more electric and frightening as people seemed to be everywhere, restlessly moving about looking for trouble. Feeling conspicuous out on the small balcony, he went up on the roof via a door he had found to the air conditioning equipment.

Much less visible but with wider vision through gaps between buildings Tubby saw that in Rashid Street people lined each floor of the half finished five storey building where they had retreated to on the riverside opposite the road of Tubby's hotel. By now the buses had all gone and just cars and lorries passed, loaded with people and cheered on by the crowds on the sidewalk. Tubby began to hear a faint chanting and as it grew louder he noticed that the people on the building were pointing down Rashid Street. As the noise increased so did the feverish excitement of the onlookers.

There was obviously a large mob coming along and Tubby felt his stomach tightening as he wondered if it was the wreckers and looters this far down Rashid Street already. The forerunners of the mob appeared at the end of the street and as the shrieks and the excitement of the onlookers reached fever pitch, the mob passed the end of the street.

Tubby's hair prickled and his flesh goose-pimpled when he saw that they carried the mutilated body of Abdul Illah, the Crown Prince. The face was half-gone, one leg was half-off and the penis had been cut off and stuck up the rear. The mob

72

carried its prize on high with great relish, turning it over for all to see.

The events of the day suddenly became sickeningly sinister and for the first time in his life Tubby experienced sheer unadulterated fear.

> . . . and behold a pale horse: and his name that sat on him was Death, and Hell followed with him. (Revelation, chapter 6, verse 8)

It certainly seemed true that Death and Hell were stalking the streets of Baghdad.

13

REVOLUTION – THE FIRST DAY

The best thing to do at a time like this is to work rather than brood, so Tubby put some records on the gramophone he had in his room and started to review his plans in the light of what had happened. About half an hour later his room door burst open and in came an American named Hank who had the next room. Things were obviously getting him down.

'For Pete's sake, must you play that gramophone? Of all things to play at a time like this!'

Before Tubby could think of a suitable reply Hank had gone as quickly as he had arrived. Up till then the records had been just background noise to Tubby, but he now listened to the record – Eartha Kitt at her most tantalising best. Poor Hank – Eartha and revolutions just didn't mix.

Hank was based in Teheran and the thought of the borders of Iran being only about 100 miles away beyond Khanaquin at the end of a good road made him dream up the most weird escape ideas ever heard of. Firstly he was all for taking over an armoured car and making off. When asked about the problem of road blocks he said they would just rush them. Later he found that one of the guests named Rudi had just come up from Kuwait in his Mercedes saloon. Hank began to give Rudi the hard sell on the idea of putting a false body on his car to make it look like an armoured car. Rudi was a short jovial German with laughing eyes and a comic opera accent and giggle. He entered into the fun of the idea with great gusto, until Hank said they must make the dash at night so that in the event of trouble they could just turn the car off the road and take to the ditches. At this point Rudi began to babble incoherently in German and the frustrated Hank had to give up yet

74

another idea, but his fertile mind was later to produce the most fantastic idea yet.

Lunchtime came and Tubby and Reeve joined a session in the bar presided over by the self styled 'Vice'-Consul for Spain, Charlie the barman. After Colonel Nimmo's remark about the first three floors of hotels being mobbed in Cairo and the Khayam only having three floors, the topic of conversation was 'where to go if and when the mob comes in'. All nooks and crannies and other 'mob-proof' hidey-holes had been booked, but Charlie reckoned the best bet was out of a top floor window on to the high wall of an open air cinema which backed on to the hotel, and thence along the top of it to another building. The fact that the wall was extremely high and only about one foot thick did not seem to deter Charlie in spite of his fat and well covered mid-regions. Still, thought Tubby, with a screaming mob after one, bent on tearing limb from limb, it would probably be possible to find hidden talents for tightrope walking and mountaineering.

'Foul rumour, painted with tongues' had really been running amok that morning, so at the lunch table, Tubby, the Reeve and some others tried to fit everything into a picture as follows: At 6 a.m. the army had taken over the radio station, placed tanks at all strategic road and rail positions and surrounded the RAF base at Habaniyah. The leaders had then gone out to the palace to obtain the abdication of King Feisal. They had met with the King in the Royal Palace and everything was going smoothly, when the power behind the throne – Uncle Abdul Illah – had interrupted the proceedings, armed with a sten gun. After a sharp exchange of words, uncle decided to enforce his objections with his sten gun. The military boys answered back with their guns and what had started as a gentlemanly coup between Sandhurst graduates degenerated into a shooting match.

The arrival of the mob at this point took the whole affair a step further and turned the proceedings into a bloody Middle East Revolution. Unknown, or underestimated by the military coup boys, dear Colonel Nasser had also been preparing for this day. His Baghdad Embassy was chock-a-block with big posters of himself with his best anti-British smile, and his agitators had been liberally spread about in various jobs and positions, just waiting for the day. As soon as the Iraqi military had taken over the radio station and gone off to the palace, one of these Nasser boys had started to shout real rip-roaring agitation over the air.

After working up to a screaming pitch of excitement, he had shouted that the leaders had gone to the palace and the people must follow. And so the mob arrived at the palace in buses, on lorries, anything they could lay their hands on – raring to go, out for blood, and led by Nasser agitators. It was bad enough for the leaders having their quiet coup with the King degenerate into a shooting match, but the mob was another matter. Already the mob had started to ransack the palace, so they tossed out uncle's body to appease them.

What happened to the King, how he died or when and where he was buried, no-one seemed to know. His body was never desecrated, never seen. In the days that followed the feeling among the people was of deep sorrow that the young, quiet King Feisal had been killed, and many openly wore black armbands in the streets.

Not a tear was shed for Uncle Abdul, and Prime Minister Nuri Said was nowhere to be found. It was said that an armoured car or tank had pulled up at his house, swung its turret round, fired, and blown its own turret off. This failure to blast open Nuri's house mattered little because the mob later tore the place apart.

After looting and ransacking the palace, the mob moved back to Baghdad with their chief trophy – Uncle Abdul's body – carried on high. The road from the palace enters Baghdad proper through the Showakah, a filthy old area of Baghdad – a labyrinth of back alleys and dingy passages, grossly over-populated and a breeding ground for mobsters. Those who had been too lazy to go to the palace now joined the returning mob, swelling the ranks to frightening proportions. Also with daylight news was getting about, and the mud hut dwellers soon realised that this was a day when law and order had collapsed.

Herded in the awful mud hut colonies beyond the long mound of earth which protected the city from floods before the Samarra Dam was built, these people lived for such a day as this. They were not concerned with the purpose or meaning of the revolution – this was their day. Anarchy reigned and under its cover they started to loot at will. The enlarged mob passed through the Showakah and came face to face with the large impressive gates of the British Embassy. What Egyptian agitator could resist such an opportunity? All the mob required was a few hysterically screamed words about filthy Imperialistic British, and in they went, taking the gates with them. In the fracas of looting and pillage that followed, the British Military Attaché was shot through the head.

On the radio, the early morning fanaticism gave way to more serious calls for calm. The revolution was complete; people were to return to their homes as the army was going to enforce a curfew from 1 p.m. Tomorrow it must be back to work as normal. Some hope, thought Tubby, as he left his room after lunch and went up the back stairs to the roof again. His flesh went all goose-pimply for the second time that day and the hair on his neck seemed to crinkle. The streets were empty and the utter silence after the morning was weird and unbelievable. Tubby wondered which was more frightening – the noise and mob violence of the morning or this weird and unreal silence of the curfew. Was he in a dream? Had time itself stopped? A cheer, like that from a football crowd, brought Tubby back to his senses. He took his hat off to General Kassim and his fellow revolutionaries in the military. They had said a curfew from 1 p.m. and there jolly well was a curfew after 1 p.m. – mob or no mob, gippo agitators or no gippo agitators. From his vantage point on the hotel roof he could feel and see just how complete the curfew was.

The sun was high in the empty sky and the whole of Baghdad lay shimmering and silent under its tremendous heat. In spite of the heat Tubby stayed well over an hour on that roof. One could live a lifetime and never have an experience like this. One of the world's greatest and oldest cities suddenly still and utterly silent in the middle of a day. Tubby lived every minute and every second of this experience, walking round and round the hotel roof looking across the shimmering roofs of Baghdad in every direction.

How the news wires and teleprinters all round the world would be jumping with the news of the morning's events. He could see in his mind's eye the headlines of the next day: 'Mobs roam streets of Baghdad.' 'Bloody revolution erupts in Iraq.' Would his cable saying he was safe reach his parents? In the chaos of the morning he felt sure it was never sent off. These were his thoughts as he stood alone on the roof of the Hotel Khayam on that 14th July 1958.

The earlier cheer he had heard had come from the rows of people now standing on the floors of the unfinished building in Rashid Street where he and Reeve had withdrawn to first thing. They cheered every military jeep or lorry which passed because those were the only things moving in the streets. Soldiers with rifles and bayonets stood on the street corners and through a gap between two buildings Tubby could see the tanks on the Queen Aliyah roundabout at the bridge. The only other noise to break the silence was made by the aeroplanes which buzzed the city at roof top height, at first a lumbering Bristol Freighter and then several Hunter Jets.

The first tremendous reaction to the silence of the city was that it was too unreal to be true and something unearthly must happen any minute to shatter it. This feeling was still with Tubby when he eventually descended from the roof, convinced that the curfew was indeed complete and well-enforced.

The only viewing to be had that night on Baghdad TV was an Egyptian film entitled *The Retreat of the French and British from Suez*. Over and over again they were shown from all conceivable angles but never a film of the landing and the advance of the Israeli Army! Tubby and the Reeve therefore dined early. While having coffee in the reception lounge they noticed a man come up the stairs from the street and go into the dining room. Tubby recognised him as a Dr Safi, director of the Khanaquin Oil Company. A month or so previously, Tubby had been introduced to Dr Safi by Wani, his advertising agent from Beirut, who had been at University with the doctor.

Safi was a PhD (Chemistry) and he and Wani had talked over old days. How many of their old cronies were now politicians holding influential ministerial posts, while he, Dr Safi was away from the bright lights in a backwater job at Khanaquin? What was the doctor doing in Baghdad after dark during a curfew? Surely he didn't come all the way from Khanaquin for dinner at the Khayam at a time like this.

As soon as Dr Safi came out to the lounge for coffee Tubby went over and re-introduced himself. Safi remembered him and immediately they both started talking about the morning's events. Not knowing exactly where the fellow stood, Tubby led off by expressing in most guarded terms how alarmed and shocked he was at the morning's events, and how impressed he was at the way in which the leaders of the revolution had restored order and imposed the curfew.

He didn't need to try any further to find out where Dr Safi stood. It was almost as though the doctor had come to the hotel in the hope of telling somebody just how important he was, and just how much better he had done than his old college cronies: 'I have just told the other leaders that the King should not have been killed. They should not have let these things happen. We have just finished our first meeting reviewing what we have accomplished and planning our next moves.' As though to prove his statement he then proudly produced a photograph of himself with General Kassim and three others. 'This was one of our final meetings the other week. You see, I am the only civilian amongst them.' There he was, the only one in a smart city suit, all the others in military uniform. He obviously wanted to ensure that Tubby got the point that he was the brains, he was the crafty one. 'I am away out at Khanaquin you know, and I must get back there tonight. They keep in constant touch with me but I don't want to come into Baghdad until things have settled down.' Before he left he did throw some light on the suddenness of the morning's coup. Evidently their date had been fixed for later, but the order had come to move two armoured divisions to the Jordanian border, a part of Baghdad Pact, in case King Hussein should be attacked from the west by Colonel Nasser's United Arab Republic.

The revolutionaries realised that they could be stuck for some time in the barren wastes near the border, miles and miles away from Baghdad. Also the thought of losing their precious tanks, so necessary for a coup d'état, in defending King Hussein made them decide it was now or never. So, in the middle of Sunday night one division rumbled through Baghdad en route for the border and headed off west. The second division rumbled into Baghdad in the early hours of Monday morning, but it did not head off west! It took over the city and signalled the first division to turn round and come back to consolidate the position.

Dr Safi had said enough. He looked at his watch, bade Tubby farewell, asked to tell the outside world that the death of the King had not been their intention and off he went. Tubby stood at the top of the stairs as the roar of Safi's car and escort faded into the distance.

'Well, well, well!' mused Tubby to himself. 'So that's why old Nuri-el-Said got caught on the wrong foot!' The deposed Prime Minister was a wily old fox, who had survived this sort of thing over and over again. He always kept his ear to the ground and had his men planted everywhere, he was probably all organised to lock this lot of revolutionaries away, but for their spot decision to change the date. Even so, it was said that the last Iraqi Airways Viscount to leave was held back several hours waiting for a VIP. This was probably Nuri but he didn't make it so the plane took off – the last scheduled flight to leave Baghdad before the revolution.

Tubby was wondering just where old Nuri-el-Said was at the moment, when his thoughts were interrupted by someone calling from the main lounge. Someone had produced a very sensitive radio with a long antenna aerial and a German chap was trying to pick up some news from the outside world, under the direction of Colonel Nimmo. Tubby felt quite ashamed as the German translated Hungarian, Russian, Polish and Norwegian broadcasts but nearly collapsed when he turned and asked: 'Anyone speak French?' This fellow had been caught in Egypt during the Suez fiasco and had got away in a bus which just headed off into the desert. After that experience he was determined to sit this one out right here in the hotel.

Eventually he got the BBC. The Iraq revolution seemed about to trigger off the whole of the Middle East, so it was a great relief to hear that Cyprus was bulging with troops and the whole of RAF Transport Command was ready to lift troops anywhere. The biggest cheer came with the news that British Paratroops had landed in force in Amman, the capital of Jordan. That night the guests in the Khayam dreamt of little men floating down on parachutes, and that in the morning the Red Berets might be on guard in the streets and not Iraqi troops.

14

REVOLUTION – THE SECOND DAY

The second day dawned and no British Paratroops were in the streets. Still, all seemed fairly normal and General Kassim had said over the radio that it was to be back to work. Tubby and the Reeve hailed a taxi in Rashid Street as usual and went away across the bridge to the godown. Tanks were positioned on the roundabouts at each end of the bridge, but the sight of the British Consulate really brought back with a jolt the events of the previous morning. The windows and doors were just empty holes, charred black with fire. The surrounding walls and iron railings, which had held the showcases of photographs and posters, had just disappeared. The looters were methodically carrying out furniture, filing cabinets and anything that took their fancy. A coffee vendor had set up his stall in a hole in the wall of the consulate and above it was a poster showing a man who had been chained, but whose bonds were now broken, and he was free. Words were written in Arabic to the effect that the British would enslave them no longer.

After seeing all this Tubby and the Reeve felt less assured, but their greeting at the godown made them positively frightened. Wahdib was quite horrified to see them and asked how they had come down. When they said by taxi he asked if they were mad. The taxi driver could have driven them anywhere and handed them over to the mob. The whole place was still seething and would be until old Nuri-el-Said was found. The mob were still out for blood and already that morning there had been shooting only 50 yards away which had convinced him not to send the salesmen out in the vans.

They went inside and held a council of war. Wahdib told them how the looters had been roaming the streets the day before completely unconcerned with the revolution or what it was about, they were out for their fun – blood and pillage. There was an ugly, tense atmosphere which would remain until Nuri-el-Said was found. The wisest thing was to suspend operation for the time being and for Tubby and the Reeve to stay in the hotel contacting no-one outside. This was safer not only for themselves but for their Iraqi friends, as telephones were being tapped.

It was 10.30 a.m. when they finished and Wahdib said he would take them back to the hotel in his Volkswagen. What a change from when they had come down first thing in the morning. The streets were now crowded and approaching mob proportions by the bridge. They all had a crazed, wild animal look about them ready to burst into blind violence at the slightest provocation.

Tubby and the Reeve huddled in the back of the car with half their faces covered, praying that the car would not have to stop long enough for some termite to take a good look at them and shout: 'They're British.' Already this had happened to two Germans. A dirty little urchin in striped shimmy had pointed at them and shouted: 'Filthy British' and they were set upon from all sides.

Across the bridge they went round the tanks and through the mob of people standing watching and waiting until at last they reached the hotel cul-de-sac entrance on Rashid Street Wahdib sped off as they ran up along to the hotel door, ever so glad to be back. Others who had been out had the same tale to tell which was far from reassuring for those who had not left the apparent safety of the hotel. Once again, however, Colonel Nimmo came to the rescue and revived their flagging spirits.

The conversation in the lounge had once again got round to escape routes. An American slamming his fist down on the arm of his chair shouted: 'I'm just pissed off, sitting around here contemplating my navel. Why can't we get some camels and get the hell out of here?' There was silence for a moment before a little grey-haired American spinster called Miss Robens spoke. She was doing a Sociology study of the Iraqis when the Revolution broke and now she just sat and watched Colonel Nimmo with starry-eyed wonder.

'Have you ever ridden a camel, Mr Nimmo?'

'Gad,' he replied. 'I remember once with Glub Pasha, you remember old Glubby? Well, Glubby and I were on one of Lawrence's operations, on a camel for 40 days, was having a shower at the end of it when I felt me backside. Thought it was a piece of leather! By the way Miss Robens; do you play the piano?' asked the Colonel.

'Gee no Mr Nimmo, I only majored in Sociology.'

'Pity,' he went on, 'we might have had a jolly old sing-song! Nothing like it at a time like this! I remember Cairo '52,' he continued.

At this point Tubby and the Reeve retired to the bar to hear what latest news their 'Vice'-Consul had. Charlie, like Karl the Maitre, had brought his wife and family into the hotel, which rather confirmed Tubby's feelings that something was afoot out in the streets. He and the Reeve decided to send more cables in case those of the day before had not been wired off.

On his way back to his room just before lunch, Tubby was halted in his tracks by a loud 'Phst!' which came from behind him. Turning round he saw Hank peeping out of his room and beckoning frantically. Inside the room Tubby found that a small hard core of the guests had been summoned to hear Hank's latest escape idea. Among those present were Graham Smith and 'Batch' Bachelor, who hailed from Vitafoam Ltd., Manchester. Batch was a rotund, buoyant character, rather like Robert Morley in manner, but not appearance. Graham Smith was taller, lean, with the skin on his face tightly drawn over a strong bone structure. He had an accent as Lancashire as they come, and one eye off-centre, which seemed to give extra significance to his dry humour. Batch always had a good tale to tell, especially about his experiences in West Africa before and including the early years when he became an officer in the forces there, responsible for recruitment and training the bush natives to be soldiers. He always punctuated these tales with passages in the pidgen English they use on the Gold Coast, and one particular tale always had Tubby in hysterics. It concerned a real wild native with sawn off teeth, who got so enthused with the soldiering game that one day when Batch and his party were mock ambushed during training, this fellow disappeared in the bush and came out carrying four of the ambush party, disarmed, battered, and bloody about the heads.

One just took Batch to be the leader, but it turned out that Graham Smith was the managing director of their company, and Batch was his sales manager. As Tubby got to know them better it was not hard to believe this – Graham was a very shrewd man and Tubby watched him as he listened to Hank's latest escape plan. Hank claimed to be in touch with an Iraqi Airways pilot who was willing to fly them out if they could get one of the Viscounts out of the hangar. They were to slip out of the hotel in the dead of night and make their way to the airport. Once there, they were going to trundle the Viscount silently to the end of the runway and the pilot would fly it straight off. Someone asked how they were to pull it quietly from the hangar and Hank enthusiastically replied: 'Donkeys.' There was silence for a moment, then, staring earnestly and straight at Hank with his good eye, and with a twinkle in his off-centre eye, Graham said: 'Eh lad! How many quiet donkeys d'ye think it will take to tow t'Viscount t'end o'runway?' With that Hank's gathering just fell apart, the sentiments of all those present having been expressed. Poor Hank had to think again.

When they went in for lunch, another American called Schroeder was trying to sell his escape idea. A quiet bald-headed chap, about 50, with glasses, moustache and bow tie, he always smoked his cigarettes through a peculiar holder which contained a cigarette to act as a filter. He was one of a group of guests who all sold locomotives. The Iraqi Railways had called for tenders but the behind-the-scenes offerings of bribes and counter bribes had reached such proportions that the government had stepped in and called for new tenders.

Schroeder's scheme was not really an escape idea, it was just that he said he had located a Pan Am DC7 in Kuwait which was available provided he could get enough people to fill it – at a price. The price was high, but nevertheless one Canadian eagerly put his name down at the top of the list. He was a freelance something or other, operating from an apartment in Toronto, and resembled Charlton Heston in appearance. However, far from being a courageous Moses or Ben Hur, he was downright scared and jumpy about something, which made him take to the bottle from 5 p.m. each night. Hence his desperate eagerness to get on any plane out of Baghdad. This joker was one of a quartet who kept very much together at meal times, all the time virtually.

Number two of this quartet was a red-haired American woman in her late thirties who, it was said, was the wife of an American serviceman somewhere. She was en route to or from her husband when the revolution broke. Number three was an elderly gent with a white fringe of hair round a bald pate. He would pass for a TV gardening expert or a benevolent bank manager, who would smile at you paternally while refusing an overdraft. Number four was a Turkish prince, so enormously fat that Tubby and the Reeve christened him the walking Bell Tent. Viewed from behind, his lower portions were just like an elephant and as he walked each leg would swing out in an arc to get round and past the fat folds of the other leg. When one met him head on in a corridor one just had to stand in a doorway out of the way so that he could pass.

Bell Tent could only sit on the edge of even the large armchairs in the lounge as the arms were not far enough apart to allow him to slide back into the body of the chair. When seated on an armless chair he spread all over it and hung down the sides. The story went that he was a close relative of the princess to whom King Feisal had just become engaged. This close association with the late deceased monarch was probably the reason for old Bell Tent's fear, because he really was scared. He would go and sit with anyone who voiced the opinion that everything would turn out alright, seeking assurance that the British Paratroops would come from Jordan or even the American Marines might come up the Tigris. Later events were to throw more light on this quartet.

After lunch the same weird silence fell over the city with the curfew, but somehow the quiet seemed more electric, more tinglingly tense than the day before. Something is going to happen, thought Tubby, as he came in from the balcony outside his room. Almost an hour later he heard machine gun fire and dashed from his room up the back stairs and on to the roof in the blinding heat.

As soon as Tubby stepped out on to the roof the noise of the mob came in great waves over the roof tops, and then he saw them through the gaps between buildings. Purposely keeping back from the edge of the roof half hidden behind the cooling units of the air conditioners lest someone take a shot at him from the streets, he watched with fascinated horror. Curfew or no curfew, something had roused the mob and the streets over the back from Rashid Street were filled with humanity. Just as the smoke from a pile of smouldering leaves swirls in an autumn breeze so these people moved and swept in a mass to and fro following the noise of gunfire. First away to the right; and then the rat! tat! tat! of machine gun fire brought them back and had them running away towards the Armenia Church. Relentlessly and blindly they moved, through or over anything in their way, be it tank or lorry. Another burst of fire from the direction of the Alwiyah Road brought them all back swarming over the Queen Aliyah roundabout and away to the right.

Whatever happened there must have satisfied their wild madness because they began to spread throughout the streets in triumphal processions, anything that moved being commandeered for transport. All that could be seen of the open landau taxis were the two bony horses pulling a pile of humanity. They must have caught Nuri-el-Said, their joy seemed so complete; even the soldiers were firing their guns into the air. Watching all this going on – humanity gone mad – Tubby, for the second time in two days felt cold and utter fear seep through his very bones. Were these people now going to celebrate with a looting and burning session of shops and hotels such as the Khayam – renowned for its western and capitalist clientele? Had he lived this long to be torn in pieces at the whim of a street mob. Tubby just stayed there up on the roof praying that the mob would keep their distance, and wondering just what he would do if they came down the street to the hotel. His prayer was answered for the main body of the rabble moved along the big street away over from the rear, probably heading to the Ministry of Defence in the north end of Baghdad without touching Rashid Street. For the rest of that day everyone had one ear trained to pick up any noise from outside which sounded like the mob trying to enter, even after dark when all was really quiet and the card games had started in the big lounge.

The guest-staff relationship had all but disappeared. The European members of the staff had their wives and children in the hotel from their homes outside and all in the Khayam were united by the fear of the common threat outside – the mob. Tubby had brought his records and player into the lounge; the Reeve and Peter the Dane laughing and puffing on cigars; Batch and Graham Smith were engaged in a game of cards; others read or talked quietly in small groups. As it was nearly 7 p.m., Tubby fiddled with the radio to see what stations he could find. All at once out came the BBC, loud and clear, which brought Nimmo over at the double. This was Tubby's folly. From then on for the rest of the siege of the Khayam, whether he was deep in a game of chess with Coello, or wherever he was, the voice of Nimmo would shout each night, 'Tubby! The radio. It's seven o'clock!'

The games of chess with Coello became a nightly exercise too. He was a Chilean employed by one of the big American car companies. He had been a long time away from his own country, working in many countries. To Tubby, he was the first Latin American he had met who had some understanding of British traditions and humour.

One of his sojourns had been in Calcutta where he had been the first non-Britisher to be admitted as a club member to the very ancient and venerable Light Horse. It seemed that the only words uttered by some of the older members were: 'Bearer! Whisky!'. But one day he had heard two of them complaining bitterly that the bearers now wore shoes: 'Never have happened in the old days.' A very sacred and greatly revered relic of this club was a great horn which adorned one of the walls in the bar. One night Coello and several other of the more rowdy young members had arrived at the club rather high, and one of their party took the sacred horn down and actually blew it. Nothing was said at the time, but the next day a whole page of the complaints book was filled with a horrific description of how some of the irresponsible younger element in the club had taken down the sacred and beloved relic and played upon it.

Another time, in the Caribbean, Coello had booked on a local airline from Trinidad to British Guyana. The plane was an old wartime Walrus amphibian bi-plane with pusher engine. The pilot landed on a river just above a waterfall, which just about scared the life out of the passengers. As they disembarked, the pilot cheerily remarked that he had to land here as the only way he could get airborne for the return journey was by shooting over the edge of the falls.

True or false, Tubby could not say, but Coello's tales were good for laughs and helped to take one's mind off the events of the days they were living through. After being kept eight weeks in Saudi Arabia before clinching a lorry contract, friend Coello could face anything. There had been no night clubs, no drinks, nothing. He and his friend had got so bored, they used to open the room windows and let the flies in. Once a goodly number were in they would shut the windows and attack with swatters till they were all dead and then open up and start all over again.

Thus ended the second day with the ranks of the Hotel Khayam closed even tighter.

15

REVOLUTION – THE THIRD DAY

As usual before breakfast, Tubby went out on his balcony to study the form. Certainly things seemed to be more back to normal than the last two days, but groups of people were still loitering at the street corners looking for trouble. One could still not be sure.

The guests seemed to grow more restless as the morning wore on. Colonel Nimmo was mumbling something about looking up an old associate whom he heard had been in the consulate. 'Remember him as a young fella in Cairo '52. Didn't think much of him then, goodness knows what he's like in this!'

Inwardly everyone was wondering if it was safe to go out, yet no one would make the move. Suddenly Nimmo arose, his mind made up. 'Well! There's nothing for it. I'll have to go out and speak to them in me best Egyptian Arabic!' To the other Arabs, the Egyptians spoke the lowest form of Arabic, but with so many pictures of Colonel Nasser about in Baghdad, Nimmo must have reckoned the locals would be most impressed to hear him speaking Egyptian. He went off to his room and soon reappeared in his best white jacket, carrying his walking stick, and with his spotted bow tie at a rakish angle he set off down the stairs and into the street.

After an hour or so he appeared again, still alive much to the surprise of some of the guests. Eagerly they gathered round him in the reception lounge as he leaned back in an armchair, but he had only one brief comment to make: 'The natives are friendly today!' General confusion broke out, but nothing more could be got out of him. He was satisfied that he had expressed his feelings concisely, and that was enough.

On the strength of this, Tubby decided to go out for a

haircut, but not a shave. A bit of stubble about the face helped at this time and besides it would be somewhat foolhardy to let an Iraqi work on one with a cut-throat razor two days after a bloody revolution. Things definitely were more relaxed in the streets. One thing was immediately noticeable. Colonel Nasser's pictures were not nearly so much in evidence and they were being replaced by bigger and better photos of General Kassim. It was being put abroad, quietly but firmly, that it was not really the done thing to display Nasser's picture. He might fancy himself as the champion of Arab nationalism, but this revolution was the doing of General Kassim & Co., not any old disorganised and uncontrolled riot set in motion by the pressing of a button in Cairo.

In contrast to this influence being exercised by the new leaders, Tubby found the Iraqis in the barber's shop expressing feelings and opinions similar to his own. Admittedly they were middle class compared to the rabble from the mud hut colonies, and one was bordering on being wealthy, but these fellows were not antagonistic towards Tubby, in fact they were friendly and communicative.

Firstly they filled Tubby in on the events of the previous day. Nuri-el-Said had been caught on the wrong foot, had tried to get on the last Viscount to fly out of Baghdad, failed and gone underground. He was a wily old fox who had survived in Middle East politics for a long time by building up his own underground system, but the suddenness of this coup had caused such an upheaval that he must have been literally thrown back on his own personal resources to survive. Nevertheless, the new boys just could not afford to underestimate old Nuri, he was an old pro at this game, hence the unease which prevailed from Kassim at the top, through to the mobs in the streets, until he was caught. Nuri was getting a bit old for this sort of thing and on the previous afternoon, by a flower shop in the Alwiyah Road, he had been recognised and shot, even though he was disguised as an Arab woman.

This had been the gun fire which had sent Tubby dashing to the roof of the hotel, and the commotion which followed was as Nuri was dragged through the streets behind a motor cycle before being hung from a lamp post with Abdul Illah outside the Ministry of Defence. The attitude of the men in the barber's shop was that he had lived by intrigue and mobs, and thus he perished. Abdul Illah, the King's uncle, they said, deserved all he got. He had had people shot at his whim and now life had caught up with him. The death of the King, however, was a much different matter, the matter on which they were most anti the new leaders, and a matter on which they expressed themselves with a strange depth of feeling. Divine right of kings, or whatever it was, Tubby was moved by the intensity of their feelings, especially in contrast with the death of the other two.

Though only a tiny cross-section of the population, perhaps not even a proper sample or opinion by Gallup Poll standards, Tubby found them utterly interesting. These men went on to express their feelings about the country as a whole and how the turn of events might affect it. Compared with most of their Arab brethren round about, Iraq had come on quite well. There was a healthy, modernised middle class developing with TV sets, and in some cases motor cars. Dams had been completed, others were being built, and vast road and other projects were afoot. Though still far behind in development and progress by most standards, they felt that Nuri, for all his faults, given another few years, might have seen Iraq over the worst uphill stage and finally on the road to booming prosperity. Now things would grind to a halt they said, and it would be many a long day before things would be cranked up to the same rate of progress. This was food for thought indeed, and Tubby returned for lunch thinking perhaps all was not lost if men in Iraq could still think and speak as these had done.

At lunch Colonel Nimmo was in good form gibbering away in Italian to Mario and Luigi who thought he was quite wonderful. It was about the first time Tubby and the Reeve had received from Luigi exactly what they had ordered, so Nimmo's Italian must have been good. He related how once in the Western Desert campaign he had addressed a whole gathering of Italian POWs. Before he had started he had heard one of the prisoners in the front rank say something ribald about his toothbrush moustache. 'When I finished me lecture in Italian, I looked down at the fella in the front rank and asked him pointedly what he thought of me speech! The fella didn't know what to say.' Tubby asked Nimmo if he had ever come across Popski during the North African campaign. 'Of course – I remember Popski. Burst into me office one day with an Italian general by the ear. Asked me what I wanted doing with the B——!'

The afternoon quiet had settled again and Tubby was deep in a book when he was summoned by Big Mac to meet a man from the embassy in the main lounge. Big Mac was another who emerged from the ranks of guests as a leader. Some mumbled that he was an old woman and a busy-body, but generally he was accepted and liked. A big bluff Scot, he kept spirits high when they could have dropped dangerously low, partly by his enormous presence alone, but mainly by his loud vociferous assurances that all would be well, and his sense of humour. He needed a sense of humour to accept his own position, as he and his wife had just packed up home, settled their affairs and everything else after some years in Iraq and had just come to sleep in the hotel for one night before flying off on Monday. A brewer by profession, he had lived in many parts of the world, where he had bought interests in local breweries, built them up with his brewing know-how for several years and then sold out and moved on.

One night he had been amusing everyone with an experience he had had in the West Indies with a representative of one of the two big cola companies in America. This fellow, who had flown down from New York, proved to be a right screwball, entering clubs and complaining at the lack of mammoth displays of his Pepsi drinks and repacking refrigerators behind bars so that his drinks would be on the right hand side and therefore the first thing the barman would get hold of when he thrust his hand in. All this was rather embarrassing for Mac, whose company produced this Pepsi drink under licence. Things finally came to a head when his friend, the Chief of Police, rang him and asked if he was aware that Mr Pepsi from New York was ringing people at random from the telephone directory at 2.30 a.m. in the morning to ask them if they had tried his Pepsi and if not, would they please try one the next day. Needless to say Mr Pepsi was put on the next plane back to the States before he could be prosecuted for causing a public nuisance.

That night Tubby, the Reeve and another American guest recorded on Tubby's pocket tape recorder, a somewhat amateurish but catchy Pepsi jingle. At 2.30 a.m. they had dialled Big Mac on the hotel intercom and played back the jingle. At breakfast Big Mac lost some of his sense of humour, but admitted that he had rather left himself wide open for such a thing.

On entering the lounge, Tubby found all the British and Commonwealth guests sitting round the visitor. Big Mac sat on his right and introduced him as the warden. However, the visitor was not from the embassy, but worked at the YMCA, which was up the Alwiyah Road. Due to his work at the YMCA he was accepted and respected by the locals and thus could move about the streets at this time with less risk than other Britishers. He confirmed that the UK Embassy and Consulate had been sacked, and that it was the Master of the Household, Lt. Col. Wright who had been shot, and not the Military Attaché. The ambassador and all others were safe and were now operating from the new Baghdad Hotel.

Being newly opened primarily for western visitors, patronised by the filthy rich, and now the new home for the hated British Embassy, the new Baghdad Hotel had become, as it were, the very centre of bourgeois influence in the eyes of the mob and its agitators. This was no doubt the saving of Tubby and co in the Hotel Khayam, because the warden told them that the mob had clamoured to get at the new place and only a solid front of tanks and soldiers had kept them at bay. The military had entered and taken away a number of Jordanian officials who were staying there and some other nationals who were sitting with them. These unfortunate souls had nearly been lynched in front of the hotel when being put in a lorry, and the mob all but went mad with frustration. However, at the Ministry of Defence, when the lorry halted for a few seconds while the gates were being opened, the mob there pounced on them before the lorry could move through the gates and tore them limb from limb.

The procedure at a time like this was to locate all British passport holders and divide them into groups or blocks and delegate a warden to each group. Any trouble would then be reported to the warden, who was in direct contact with the embassy staff. After he had explained things in more detail, answered queries and given more information on what was going on outside, all and sundry felt much more relieved and hopeful. He left instructions for a list to be prepared showing which guests were going to stay, which ones wanted to go as soon as possible, and where they wanted to go. The list was to be collected the next day so that the embassy could get cracking on arrangements for getting people away.

Ever since the Monday morning when all hell had broken loose, Tubby had been worried about the wife and baby of his friend Tom Kendall from home. He knew that Tom was working on his oil exploration miles out in the desert west of Kirkuk so he had been ringing the house every day without getting a reply. At last he found out to his relief that Jane and the baby had been taken from the house and grouped with other families for safety. Not getting an answer from the phone had made him imagine the worst, as Tom's house was near the Alwiyah Club, which was a centre of attraction to any anti-British mob.

The visit gave food for conversation till dinner, after which the usual evening activities got going, Tubby working the radio for Colonel Nimmo.

16

THE GUN-RUNNERS

Next morning Tubby phoned the house of his friend Tom and was overjoyed to hear Tom himself answer. However, he did not sound like the usual old Tom, so Tubby went out and borrowed Wahdib's car to run out to Tom's house. On the way out to the Alwiyah Club, he passed the spot where Nuri-el-Said had been recognised and shot.

Tom was united again with his wife and baby and the deep relief and joy of their union filled the home, but the strain of the last few days had left its mark, she with the baby, knowing her husband was in the same country and yet so far away, he trying desperately to get to them to protect them, fearing the worst. Knowing Tom as a 'hard citizen' from rugger club days back home, Tubby was quite shaken to see him jumpy, and realised he must have had a rough time.

Tom was on his second tour in Iraq and knew only too well how the locals reacted in times like these. Working away in the desert west of Kirkuk, he heard the news over the radio and, though things were quiet up there in the north, he knew only too well what was happening in Baghdad. Having a wife and child brings out one's basic protective animal instincts and his only concern was to be with them when he knew that the mobs were out in the streets.

He had jumped in his Land Rover and set off for Baghdad hell for leather, and had got half way when the military had stopped him and tossed him into jail. For three long days and nights he had been kept there haunted with visions of the mob fiendishly working their way through the European quarter after ransacking the Alwiyah Club – enough to turn any man round the bend.

Though united again in their home with no harm done, the visions still haunted them. The termites had been making minor sorties into their area from over the great mud-wall which separated the mud hut colonies beyond from the houses of the European quarter. The walls and streets had been painted with filthy anti-British slogans and any noise resembling the arrival of mobs or military set Tom and Jane on edge.

Across from their house was a private hospital and one of the nurses was a dark colleen from Southern Ireland. How this lass came to be working in a private hospital in Baghdad could only be explained by the fact that she came from the country of the wee folk. She had been befriended by the Kendalls and spent many an off-duty hour in their home, but now this friendship had its doubts and fears. The girl was engaged to a Sandhurst-trained Iraqi Officer. He was not in favour with what was happening and wanted to clear out with his beloved, but he was scared to see her. She was scared to see him. She didn't want to drag the Kendalls into her affairs. They didn't want to be dragged in. This is what happens when anarchy erupts and the powers of revolution take over. Mobs and violence can be seen and possibly avoided and survived, but fear creeps unseen into the minds of men. Doubts arise and friendships become suspect as in self-preservation one seeks to avoid anything that might bring down the wrath of the new powers at their slightest whim.

This bloody revolution started on the same fateful day as the Bastille day of 14 July centuries before and Tubby had a deep understanding of the weeks of terror and suspicion that followed in Paris. He asked the Kendalls if he could help by spending a night with them and his offer was accepted, so he went off back to the hotel to collect some of his things, feeling somewhat heroic. During the night that followed he lost all his ideas of heroism.

Tubby had lunch with the Reeve and the others in the hotel and then went out to the Kendalls before the curfew came down later in the afternoon. They talked of the past, the present, and the future, ate a good meal, and played records until Tom and Jane retired to bed.

Having decided to be on guard, as it were, by staying downstairs, Tubby settled in a comfortable chair but the noises of the night began to assail him. These noises and the heat made him think of the hotel. The little community would all be enjoying themselves free from fear in the safety of their numbers and sure of a good sleep in their air-conditioned bastion with only one small door on to the street. Was he mad to be sitting here in a house with umpteen flimsy doors and windows when he could be back in the dear old Hotel Khayam?

The doors and windows downstairs were duly locked and bolted and Tubby retreated to a bedroom upstairs. Perhaps it was the fears of the Kendalls which had washed off on to him, or just the fact that he was out of the hotel for the first time at night. Whatever it was, he found himself jumping at every sound and listening carefully to every truck which went down the main road 50 yards away in case one stopped and he heard the tramp of many feet.

The next day eventually dawned on a rather haggard Tubby, completely disillusioned as to grand ideas of helping the Kendalls. To his great surprise, however, he found them much better at breakfast and they claimed they had had the first reasonable night's sleep. They certainly devoured more breakfast than Tubby could face. In the days that followed he saw them several times and each time they had more and more of their old bounce and zest for life.

Back at the hotel Tubby was greeted by a rather excited Reeve who dragged him to his room to tell him the news. Evidently things at the Hotel Khayam had not been as idyllic as Tubby thought as he lay on his sleepless couch. All the guests had been settling down to their chosen nightly activities after dinner, when a great knock had come on the door of the hotel and much noise from the street. An armed guard had appeared and marched off with old Bell Tent, the Turkish Prince, after sealing his room.

The plot thickened. Was it Bell Tent's matrimonial tie-up with the late King or was it something else? The other members of the quartet reacted in various ways. The Red Head retired to her room, the old gent with the bald pate took it upon himself to carry food from the hotel on his daily visits to Bell Tent in prison, while Charlton Heston, the Canadian, doubled his consumption of the bottle, if that were possible. This worsened till a few days later, in desperation, he broke into Bell Tent's sealed room somehow, and removed certain papers bearing his name. The tale got around that they were up to their necks in arms dealing with the previous regime. This could have been so, as many months later, via London and the Reeve, who had been back briefly from Athens for a meeting on the Middle East, Tubby heard that old Bell Tent had been shot by the revolutionaries shortly after they had got away from Baghdad.

17

DEPARTURE FEVER

As the days went by, the tension decreased and more of the guests made sorties out into the streets. There was one character who had been going out almost every day since the start of the whole affair. Tubby and the Reeve called him the Secret Drinker and believed that he would not have been out if he had been fully aware of what was going on. He was an American who was reputed to own an island in the States, a villa in Casablanca, and have vast interests in several big construction contracts in Iraq. Ever since Tubby arrived he had been staying in the Khayam except for an odd day when he would charter an Iraqi Airways Viscount to fly down to Basrah or some other place where construction was in progress.

Through the day he would sail out, half stupefied but always well dressed as befitted a Scarsdale or Long Island business tycoon. In the evening, however, when his rather severe wife would appear, bejewelled and with blonde hair up-swept, he would sit quietly sipping soft drinks and making small talk with selected guests. The old Secret Drinker would stand this for so long and then, on the pretext of going to the gents, he would dart into the bar. His very appearance at the bar would prompt Charlie to plonk one or two double pink gins on the counter. These would be down in a gulp and the Secret Drinker would be off out again to the lounge stuffing chewing gum into his mouth. He had almost become part of the Hotel Khayam, was not roused when the departure fever started, and he was still there carrying on as usual when Tubby and the Reeve eventually got away.

The departure fever started towards the end of the first week when the airport was eventually opened for charter planes sent in by the governments of the various nationals caught in Iraq. Every nation seemed to treat the situation as an emergency, except dear old Britain whose Embassy and Consulate had been burned down and ransacked by the mob. In came Al Italia, and all the Italians went. In came SAS and all the Scandinavians left. In came Pan Am and all the Americans left. In came Lufthansa, and all the Germans left. All these were emergency flights and passengers were allowed only 27 pounds of baggage, but still the Americans staggered to the Pan Am planes loaded with their loot – Persian carpets, the lot – and all had to be left at the airport. The only scheduled flights allowed into Baghdad Airport were those from the United Arab Republic – Damascus and Cairo. These brought in hordes of Egyptian and East European Communist press reporters who began to fill the hotel; so the British and Commonwealth guests had to close the ranks.

One interesting aside to the Lufthansa flight was the fact that one of the German guests smuggled out photos of the mutilated bodies which had appeared for sale on the streets until General Kassim had ordered them off, and the firing squad for anyone caught selling or possessing them. All people departing were ruthlessly and thoroughly searched at the airport, so this German placed the photos at the back of a portrait of General Kassim which he had framed. Tubby had heard that the portrait was openly laid on the Customs counter during the searching, and the German had walked off to the plane deliberately leaving it behind. An Iraqi official had run after him with it, shouting: 'You've forgotten your portrait of our beloved General Kassim.' With profuse thanks to the official, he took the portrait, clicked his heels, bowed, and entered the plane. The door was shut and the plane roared off carrying the bloody photographs to the free press of the world.

Tubby and Reeve had heard nothing since they had given their names to the YMCA warden from the embassy. They had been round the various government ministries and been told that all imports would be stopped temporarily and reviewed, with the accent on Eastern European goods. This and other facts convinced the pair that business from their point of view was going to be at a standstill, and besides they were an embarrassment to Wahdib and the others at their agents, so they decided to leave as soon as possible. A year or so later this decision was vindicated when Tubby met a chap in Penang who had stayed on in Iraq. He had gained nothing by staying and suddenly one day he had been presented with an ultimatum to be away in 48 hours, or else!

During the evacuation of all the other nationals, Nimmo, Big Mac, Tubby, Reeve and the others had naturally separated out 27 pounds of their luggage and made plans for the rest. However, nothing seemed to be forthcoming from the embassy so they started to peddle their names round all the airline offices. Tubby also realised that his visa should have been renewed on the 14th July so he went off to the immigration offices away up the north end of the city beyond the Defence Ministry. He was going to make sure that they could not pick him up on the pretext of not having a visa.

It took almost a whole day to work one's way through from desk to desk, as being British no longer helped with the officials. In fact it had the opposite effect – especially for members of the western press who were there on the same day. The *Daily Express*, *Daily Mail*, and the *Mirror* were all there, a photographer too, all being chased from pillar to post by the un-co-operative officials. It amazed Tubby to see what utter fools some of them were. Especially with the stupid, bullheaded attitude they adopted, they deserved to be treated with scant respect and even disdain. Later when Tubby eventually got home he was highly amused to see photos of some of them in their respective papers alongside their daring dramatic reports: 'I was first reporter to get through to besieged Habaniyah RAF base, surrounded by Iraqi army tanks.' Not only had they arrived far too late when everything had been cleared up, but Colonel Nimmo found out that they had all been taken together in one bus on a carefully planned restricted tour, conducted by the Iraqi army. One press report he read was from Beirut by a chap who claimed to have flown in and out of Baghdad in one day and he was sending his 'eye witness' account of the scene just after the revolution. With only

Egyptian airlines allowed in from Damascus and Cairo, Tubby reckoned this character must have written the 'eye witness' account in a Beirut night club from the numerous tales which had filtered through to there from Baghdad.

Eventually news came through that some British wives and children had been flown out and finally all in the Hotel Khayam were told to be ready on 28th July. Tubby and the Reeve went out to see the Kendalls and were horrified to discover that they had not yet received instructions for leaving – not even Jane and the baby. So much for the mothers and children story. Tubby and the Reeve offered their seats but the Kendalls had had enough and were not going to be parted again. Tom had arranged for them all to go north by train and live with the oil community in Kirkuk. Things were a lot quieter up there, and besides the revolutionary powers were well aware of the steady revenue from Iraq Petroleum Company and would make sure that the mobs did not do any wrecking there. So the pair took their leave and wished the Kendalls God's speed.

Back at the hotel, Colonel Nimmo was just back from visiting the officer in charge of security. Nimmo, like the rest of them, had lots of business papers and was perturbed by the tales that had filtered back of how the boys at the airport were tearing into people's bags and briefcases. It turned out that the officer knew Nimmo from way back in his military days and his reflex action on Nimmo's appearance was to stand up out of respect. The Colonel had arranged for himself and any others who wanted to go to the Security Office the next morning to have their papers inspected and their briefcases sealed. The Reeve went with him the next morning and told Tubby that it had been a great lark. Old Nimmo had taken over and nearly caused an uproar shouting at them in Arabic and talking over old times with the officer. This officer must have been of high standing because when they got to the airport on the day of departure the boys there positively avoided their briefcases like the plague when they saw his seal on them.

18

THE JOURNEY HOME

The 29th July was the big day when they made their fond
farewells at the Hotel Khayam. On the way to the airport they
dumped all but their 27 pounds of luggage at Wahdib's house
as he had kindly offered to keep them. After milling about for
half an hour at the airport they were finally informed that it
was no emergency flight, but a Middle East Airways official
flight. They must pay, or give an official guarantee of payment
before they could board and they were entitled to the normal
baggage allowance of 44 pounds. The payment was no problem
as it helped to clear their Iraqi money but Wahdib tore off at
the double to bring back as much of their other clothes as he
could. Tubby was just about liquid in the 120° temperature
because he had put on two UK suits to save as much as he
could on the 27 pounds emergency allowance. The others were
fuming because they had no Wahdib to send and had just had
to leave their other baggage and proceed with only 27 pounds.

The second shock at the airport was the news that Middle
East Airways could only take them as far as Cyprus and from
there they would have to see what the RAF could do. After
two weeks of revolution and mobs, the thought of being
dumped with Makarios and his Eoka gunmen was just about
the end, except for the Canadian who was only too glad to be
going anywhere other than Baghdad.

It was afternoon before the Viscount arrived, but it was a
welcome sight. The boys had gone over them and their baggage
very thoroughly indeed. They listened to all Tubby's tapes on
his recorder, even the blank ones. He had had his monthly
report recorded but had rubbed off the paragraph on the
political situation of the country!

Soon they were flying west over the arid wastes of Iraq and Jordan. Over Beirut they could see way below the ships which had landed the US Marines there. As they circled before landing at Cyprus, Tubby could not believe so many planes could be concentrated in one place. True, the Middle East was seething, but the whole of RAF Transport Command must have been at Akrotiri as hardly a blade of grass could be seen for aircraft. The place was a hive of activity with great Beverleys trundling off the runway and jets zooming overhead.

They staggered off the plane and were escorted to a waiting room, where an RAF officer was changing Iraqi money for Sterling. If only they had been told in Baghdad they need not have worried about getting rid of their Iraqi Dinars. While walking from the plane Tubby and Reeve overheard a young Flight Lieutenant confidentially informing a WRAF officer that they were refugees, so they both dragged one foot behind them and limped on scratching at their sticking clothing.

Here they bid a tearful and fond farewell to their erstwhile leader Colonel Nimmo. His home was in Beirut so he was staying on the Viscount; the Aussie too was going with him to pick up a through flight to Sydney from Beirut. And so they were all breaking up and going their various ways to the four corners of the globe. In the bar they charged their glasses and drank a solemn toast to Colonel Nimmo and the gunboat.

The man behind the bar was a real Greek with big black moustache – and could have been Grivas himself. This thought brought them back to earth as they wondered how long they would be on the troubled island. They went off in a bus which had wire over all the windows to stop hand grenades from being lobbed in. Reaching a rest centre place some miles from the airport they all made themselves comfortable and awaited further developments.

Were they to be stuck here for some days? After an hour or so, much to their relief, they were taken back to the airport and led out to a battered old DC4 or 6. It was cramped and it creaked and groaned but it was heading for dear old England non-stop though not fast. Sleep was impossible to Tubby in his two UK suits and perspiration which lay on him in layers now

105

that he had cooled off, but he found solace in thoughts of home and comfort. These thoughts were rudely shattered when the voice of the captain crackled over the intercom saying he had received instructions to divert to Malta. This would have been wonderful any other time, but right then Mr Dom Mintoff was creating riots and strife. Baghdad, Cyprus and now Malta. Was there any other trouble spot they could call on? Perhaps they might make Algiers on the way.

Thankfully it was only a stop of an hour and a half in the middle of the night to pick up some RAF personnel from Tunisia or somewhere. The dread of what it could have been, and the extra hours the diversion added to the journey, drained that much more vitality from the weary Baghdadites.

On reaching the journey's end at last in Southend-on-Sea, some passengers were so ill and green at the gills with the fumes and the rattles that they crawled into the first hotel to sleep for the rest of the day. Sunny Southend was not sunny that day even though it was almost August, but oh, how wonderfully green everything looked after the burning sands and dust of Iraq.

Tubby, the Reeve, Batch and Graham Smith got the train into Liverpool Street where they parted company. Dirty and grubby, tired and weary, Tubby and the Reeve staggered into their London Office looking as though they literally had just fled the mob.

And that was the end of Tubby's Iraqi adventure.

19

THE HOME-COMING AND
THE TURN ABOUT

After causing a sensation in the Oxford Street head office of
Colgate UK by bursting into the office of the export department still wearing the two suits each had escaped in and still
with the dust of Baghdad amongst several days growth, Tubby
and the Reeve were ushered into the presence of their ultimate
boss, the export manager.

Since they had virtually been lost with all communications
broken for two weeks, their boss listened to their tale in awe,
and after hearing them out decided that they had better get
back to their next of kin, who had equally been out of touch
because of the breakdown of communications and the way in
which Colonel Nasser and the United Arab Republic had
sealed off the whole area from Damascus to Cairo.

Tubby and Dick Malyan went their separate ways and since
Tubby was not from the London area he headed for Euston
Station and took the train north to Liverpool and across to
Birkenhead, in that most beautiful part of the county of
Cheshire known as the Wirral.

Although it was only April when he had left home for his
first overseas adventure, with all that had happened since then
and with the vision of the land of the dead – Hades – itself in
the terrible sights which he had witnessed in Baghdad, he felt
very much like Odysseus, in the great Greek epic, *The Odyssey*
by the blind poet Homer.

Like Odysseus, he was looking forward to meeting with his
Penelope since she had been busy too, but not doing her
needlework like the Penelope in the epic poem – she had been

deeply occupied completing her medical studies and getting her final qualifications. Alas, he found that she had gone off on a previously booked holiday to Switzerland with her sister in reward for her success in her medical examinations, and like Tubby's parents, had been completely unaware of what had happened to him in Baghdad since the terrible events of 14th July.

After the news of the shattering events had come through there had been a complete blackout of communications, both inwards and outwards, since none of the cables which Tubby and the Reeve had sent out had got through. In the end, he met up with his Penelope on Euston Station when he had been up to London office again after a week's break. He appeared before the two sisters like some ghost from the dead on the Euston platform as they were about to board their train for Liverpool after coming across London from the ferry train after their trip to the continent.

Tubby and the Reeve had some hilarious times meeting up again in London and frequented Wheelers and other bars along Fleet Street which in those days used to be the hub of the news activities in London and for the rest of the country. However, the interest and attention of the media had moved on and other happenings had taken over from the momentous events of the 14th July. Besides – they had to find out where they were off to next since the Reeve had only been in Baghdad with Tubby before posting to other parts, whereas Tubby had been meant to stay in Iraq for two years. Within a week or so, the Reeve was on his way to Athens to be based there with the object of working towards a Greek subsidiary operation, while Tubby was summoned into the presence of the export manager to find out where he was going to end up next.

John Steel was an Aussie, well rounded both in shape and personality. He informed Tubby that with his sudden and unexpected arrival back again from Baghdad, where operations with the Hasso Brothers were not likely to revive for many years, he was to be their man in the Far East.

Tubby had met Smudgy Smith when in Baghdad since he had been made into a sort of overseer of Middle East activities after having been in Singapore some years previously. He was the chap who was notorious for having had two years in Singapore and never indulged in the marvellous opportunity for Chinese food and all other types of wonderful food of the Orient! The second dubious accolade to Smudgy Smith was the fact that he had, at great expense, brought the famous bubble machine to Iraq from the Far East to help sell detergent, not appreciating that the Middle East had very dry hot air with no tropical humidity, so no bubbles came out of it.

Fortunately, he had been succeeded in the Singapore and Malaysian territories by a South African called Abe le Roux and since his two years were coming to an end Tubby was to go out there as soon as possible to take over from him. However, it was not to be a simple matter of taking over the running of an existing and very important UK Export territory. The international company operating out of New York was actively adding three more subsidiaries to the 44 already round the world and Tubby was to be the final UK export rep for Singapore-Malaya and to hand over to international management to be appointed by New York for establishment of Colgate Palmolive (Malaya) Ltd, while two other general managers were setting up Colgate Palmolive (Hong Kong) Ltd, and Colgate Palmolive (Thailand) Ltd.

Since it was felt that this might be a case of simply handing over, Tubby was taken aback to find that from a central base of Singapore he was to look after all other remaining territories of UK export in the Far East. Afghanistan, East and West Pakistan, Portuguese Goa, Ceylon (now Sri Lanka) and the Borneo Territories of the old East Indies which were Sarawak, North Borneo and Brunei.

As a symbol of UK exports great trust and confidence in him, John Steel handed over to Tubby an open plastic IATA card which he was to guard with his life since it allowed him the complete freedom to book any flight to anywhere from anywhere thus giving him no excuse for not getting around his new vast export territory.

John Steel had had in the past a posting in Singapore and mentioned that his white dinner jacket remained in the wardrobe of the apartments of the current UK rep in the Far East – to be collected by himself some day! In the years since, John has ended up as boss of Colgate Australia, then New York, so Tubby, as the last UK rep in Singapore Malaya, still had the jacket, until assigned to him after the re-union meeting with John Steel in New York in 1996.

Before parting for some brief leave prior to his new Far East adventure, John Steel, with a wry smile, touched upon another item which gave Tubby an inkling of the certain attitudes he might come across when he was later to get involved with the high-powered types from New York. Tubby had what in those days might have been referred to as an RAF moustache above his top lip and John Steel mentioned that he had noticed that certain American top brass within the company seemed to have an aversion towards people from the UK with this sort of appendage. However, Tubby remembered that the UK subsidiary had once had a very high-powered American general manager called Bill Miller who was now a Vice President of the international operation, and he too had a moustache and had done all right thank you, so the whiskers were to stay.

At the age of 27, Tubby was finding it difficult being seen as a folk hero of export at the Oxford Street head office, particularly now that the Reeve had gone off to Athens. He was positively tingling with excitement and apprehension at the scope of his new responsibilities as he went through the details on the Singapore-Malaysia scene and all the other scattered domains he was to get round.

Back home amongst family and friends, he was very much the centre of attention and particularly filled with wonder all those at the Old Boys Rugby Club with his tales of playing an odd game for the Casuals on the banks of the Tigris River in Baghdad. However, Tubby was somewhat sobered to hear what it had been like for loved ones to have one of the family disappear from all types of communication in a part of the world which had gone very much on the boil. Apparently his Penelope and his parents would see one another across the street and both would look at one another in anticipation and then shake heads at one another to indicate that neither had received any communication as yet from Baghdad.

Once more he felt a very close affinity with Odysseus from the ancient Greek epic in that he had had delays in meeting up with his Penelope again and was about to set off once more on another venture! She had her two years of pre-reg and intern medical work to do which would keep her occupied while her Odysseus set off with a toothpaste tube on his shoulder instead of the oar from his ship which the epic Odysseus carried. The only real difference was that their adventures were reversed – Odysseus had had his epic experiences almost totally within the realm of the sea on his boat and then was to head off with his oar into lands where people knew not of the sea and described his oar as a winnowing-fan. In Northern Iraq, Tubby had actually seen farmers using the winnowing-fan with their grain harvest, so he was doing the reverse in that he had come back from trying to bring his toothpaste to Iraqis in a barren dry land where people were not quite inclined to use the product, while now he was going out to the Far East where there were legions of fastidious Chinese who well knew what a tube of toothpaste was and indeed readily made lots of imitations of his beloved Colgate tubes and red cartons. In under four weeks from his escape from Baghdad, Tubby was to be on his way again for his next big adventures in the Far East. After fond farewells he was glad in a way to be back into the excitement of the London scene and getting himself geared up again with the adrenalin pumped up.

It was high summer and this time Tubby was equipped with light clothing, having been kitted out in Baghdad at the Hasso Brothers department store. With his flight out with Qantas in the early evening he bid a fond farewell to the London scene by walking from the City down to the Embankment, taking in the scenes of the Thames and those buildings across the river, one with the big Oxo sign on the chimney and the other which used continually to spew out white steam – Tubby never ever found out which building emitted the steam which he always used to see from that part of London looking south. Whether or not it was the prospect of being away for a number of years

111

once again, the scenes along the Thames and past Parliament and into Chelsea and to BOAC House in Victoria were particularly attractive. He even took a quick look in at the Tate Gallery for a cultural intake to keep him going overseas.

This time his plane was the improved version of the wartime Constellation known as the Super Constellation, with those huge streamlined wing tip fuel tanks. It seemed no time until they were touching down in Rome as their first stop, with Athens next where he was looking forward to seeing the Reeve if possible at Athens airport, having sent messages ahead of his flight details and estimated passing-through time.

They all boarded the Super Conni once again on schedule for departure at Rome, but after a brief moment there was a polite cough on the intercom from the captain to announce that the baggage taken aboard with the intake at Rome had not been loaded properly for the trim of the aircraft and they would have to wait while it was all taken out and re-loaded. Tubby was annoyed at the prospect of the delay throwing out the timings at Athens and not meeting up, but he did enjoy being able to sit out in the open at Rome airport as it went dark on that summer's evening over the Eternal City.

The delay meant that they did at least arrive in Athens in daylight and Tubby was delighted to see that Dick Malyan, the Reeve, was on a public gallery up above and within earshot from where they approached the buildings for the stopover. He was most surprised to see that alongside the Reeve was none other than Smudgy Smith. This meant that he was able to tell Smudgy Smith person to person that he had brought back from Baghdad some odd records and other bits and pieces that Smudgy Smith had left in the Khayam Hotel off Rashid Street, and had deposited them back at the export department with Deirdre for him to pick up when he was back there again.

As regards the Reeve, his dear partner in revolution, they never met again, though he did hear through the company grapevines that he had married into a Greek family in Athens and had become general manager of the new Greek subsidiary which was set up by Colgate, as yet another international operation.

112

The next stop by the Super Conni was Cairo which again was a part of the world new to Tubby and he was a little apprehensive since this was home country of Colonel Nasser, who was now very much in ascendence since the revolution in Baghdad and all the other eruptions. Having remembered his rather creepy feelings in Damascus on the way out to Baghdad even before the revolution, when they confiscated all the passports of the passengers, he was keen to fly off again. Damascus and Syria were, of course, the other end of the United Arab Republic, which was then very much the centre of things until it all split up later when Baath Socialism resulted in bitter rivalry between those in Damascus and those in Baghdad, post the revolution.

As they flew in and out of Cairo, Tubby was able to catch a glimpse of the Sphinx and the incredible pyramids, but he was more impressed at the vision from the air of the vital role that the Mother Nile plays in the life of Egypt. He had remembered seeing these very small fork wheels of green from small oases as he crossed the barren wastes from Damascus to Baghdad, but here in Egypt the scale of influence of Mother Nile was tremendous in terms of green cultivation. But yet again it was very soon cut short and turned back to desert once they were beyond the limits of practical irrigation from the river water.

The vast wastes of the southern Arabian desert passed beneath as they headed for Karachi, and Tubby noticed the great and remarkable edifice of the huge hangar at the airport, which had been built for the air ships such as the R101, which had never actually reached Karachi and used it. There were stories in abundance of mad fighter pilots in the area during the war having great fun flying in and out and through the big hanger when the doors were open at either end. It was a mirror image of one that stands near Cardington in England, which was the base from which the air ships departed.

The scenes at Athens, and indeed Egypt, and then on to Karachi were still not dissimilar to the dry environment he had been in since April, but the landing at Calcutta gave him his first taste of the humidity which was to be his environment from here on. The other item of tremendous impact were the legions of humanity in white dhotis which seemed to make black skins of Bengalis even more intense, and everybody was covered in perspiration from the humidity.

This reminded Tubby of the tales of his Chilean friend Coello, in the Khayam Hotel in Baghdad during the revolution, who related how he was the first Latin American ever to be admitted into membership of the Light Horse Club in Calcutta. This had been very much the centre of the influence of the Raj in the old days and Tubby could understand why it was the way of life then for ex-pats to send their wives and youngsters away up to the hills in Darjeeling during the heat of the monsoon season and the humidity in Calcutta.

With further delays along the line Tubby ended up very tired and weary in the middle of the night in Singapore which has the ultimate in humidity, being surrounded by sea and virtually touching the very equator itself. In spite of the late hour, Abe le Roux was there to meet him at the airport, and the journey in from the airport in the taxi was like an unreal dream. He seemed to be seeing out of the window big concrete troughs on either side of the road backed by a raised pavement area which was partly within the buildings and had bodies lying all the way along, which were actually people who slept the night out in this way because of the heat. Those which had string beds were usually the Jagas, who were indeed the watchmen of the buildings and had their beds across the entrances. They were almost always big Sikhs with turbans and whiskers, and they were the money lenders to the poor serfs who worked in the buildings and could be seen collecting their usury on pay day at the end of each month.

The hotel was not the celebrated Raffles, for sure, but he did take in that it was colonial and oriental as anticipated, as he bade Abe farewell. Very readily he hit the sack in the very welcome cool of the air-conditioned room.

114

20

SO THIS IS SINGAPORE

Tubby was always an early riser and could exist on about five hours sleep, therefore it was much to his consternation to become awake to the vision of Abe le Roux standing at the bottom of his bed in the Adelphi Hotel. He had slept and slept through jet lag and it was approaching lunch time. Abe said he would meet him over at the Harper Gilfillan office, so Tubby roused himself and got organised.

After a light lunch he set off on the short walk from the Adelphi Hotel which was in Colman Street near to the cathedral and the legislative buildings, and therefore within a short walk across the footbridge over the Singapore River to the Bank of China, and on to the Harper Gilfillan offices in the building on the corner of Collyer Quay. St Andrew's Cathedral was a magnificent building with a great spire and indeed a reduced version of a cathedral back at home. City Hall and the Supreme Court were magnificent too and, being along St Andrews Road, overlooked the great Padang which is the green area near to the esplanade on the waterfront, which had the Singapore Cricket Club at one end and the Eurasian Club at the other end with tennis courts, bowling greens and of course the rugby pitches.

It was more like being in a well appointed place back in UK, and Tubby set off at great speed to walk to the office but soon realised the humidity did not allow walking at UK pace, because he very rapidly became like a wet rag and had to slow down to a snail's pace.

There was always a breeze towards the seafront and he was enthralled with the Singapore River which he crossed by footbridge since it was cram-jammed with junks and motorised sampans coming to and fro carrying merchandise, and being unloaded by teams of coolies who carried the big loads off up and down precarious planks and on to the warehouses, handing in their little tags to the counter as they went by bent under their loads of rice or whatever.

Facing one across the bridge was the huge edifice of the Bank of China. There never seemed to be much activity of customers going in and out, but it was a rather sombre presence dominating the office area like a great statue of Chairman Mao in his plain worker's tunic.

Harper Gilfillan and Company were Colgate's agents, and they were a typical overseas agency house in this colonial situation, and a cog in the great commercial machine which was the British Empire. They were part of a bigger organisation called Blyth Green and Jourdain, which had its main offices in Plantation House in the City of London and had a large operation by that name in Mauritius and in other parts of the world including Hong Kong.

He entered the building and found to his relief that it was air-conditioned, and up on the second floor he found rather palatial offices with a row of individual offices down one side, which were the domain of the various representatives of the major companies with whom they had agencies. There was an office for Abe le Roux of Colgate Palmolive, and then the man from Reckitt and Colman, and then the man from Heinz, then the drinks – Courvoisier VSOP and VAT 69 Scotch, before the offices of the engineering types who related to that part of the Harper's agencies which covered heavy plant and machinery for the tin mining industry up-country and warehousing facilities.

As he entered Abe's office, le Roux was talking away in Afrikaans with a friend from the Dutch community, which is numerous in Singapore, as a result of the big import/export houses and plantations of the old Dutch regime in the East Indies, mainly Sumatra and Java, following the take-over by the dictator Sukarno.

In those days, Indonesia was not a place one wanted to visit particularly and the Dutch back home had to cope with a large influx of natives from the East Indies who were opposed to Sukarno, similar to the waves of ex-colonial immigrants who had come into Britain from the West Indies. In time Tubby was to hear of great pogroms going on in Indonesia against the Chinese community, which often happens in these countries during the convulsions which follow independence and he was to get a closer feel for the situation once he came to visit Sarawak, Brunei and the Borneo Territories.

Abe le Roux's name indicated that he was probably descended from Huguenots who had moved away to various parts of the world from persecutions in Europe, since he was very cultured in his manners and appearance with an old fashioned centre or high parting in the hair. He was certainly not the huge rather fierce neanderthal man you could meet on the front row of a South African rugby scrum of white Dutch ancestry. Nevertheless he did go to the Afrikaaner Stellenbosch University in Cape Town and he was a very dyed in the wool Afrikaaner in attitudes.

He had worked for Colgate in South Africa but got itchy feet to see something of the world and particularly to visit the UK, which was quite a regular thing to do for most young whites growing up around the world in colonial territories. He had his own little plane which was a single engine Air-Coup with fixed tricycle undercarriage and twin tails. He had with him a friend who had no flying experience and there was just about space for their meagre luggage, with no spare capacity for even a radio!

They had worked out the flight up the great Rift Valley of Africa and on into Egypt to cross into Europe via Athens, but early on in their journey through the Transvaal they had run into a very fierce electrical storm which meant that Abe simply had to pull back the stick and let the plane hang on the prop as the only way to be sure of direction, while his non-flying friend sat beside blissfully unaware of Abe's dilemma. Once they came out of the storm, Abe decided to land on the first strip he could see which was a private strip at the back of a large citrus farm in the Transvaal. After quick check of the plane, they took off again. Many months later when he was relating this experience in the London office, one of the typists, who was also a colonial doing a stint in London, listened for a while and then announced that it was her father's airstrip at the back of the home farm!

The journey north had gone according to schedule until Khartoum in the Sudan when they had their passports stolen and had to reorganise things. This meant that they took off later than their early morning take off time which was chosen to get up height before the heat of the day when the engine got too hot. This meant that as they were heading for Luxor, in the Valley of the Kings, the engine began to splutter and they had no option but to glide down in a decreasing spiral towards an Egyptian Air Force base which had rows of MIG fighters and Russian Illusyn Bombers. Having no radio communication they began to have angry red flares coming up at them which was the signal to clear off; however, Abe had no alternative but to taxi down along with his momentum and eventually came to rest under the wing of an Illusyn Bomber with two armoured cars following them along with guns trained on them.

They received a very hostile reception and were put under close guard. Their story about missing passports and engine problems seemed much too implausible and they were kept in close guard until a red-haired Egyptian pilot came down from Cairo, who was obviously in the intelligence branch. He was to go up with Abe in the little Air-Coup to prove their story about the overheating, while the friend was kept under guard.

Abe took off with his Egyptian pilot alongside and pulled the plane into vertical, hanging on the propeller and praying to goodness that the engine would eventually splutter, stall with drop of its nose immediately. However, our Egyptian pilot from Cairo had only experience of high performance jets and other military aircraft and was totally unaware of the fact that this small Air-coup with the twin tails and fixed wheels would not simply flip over and head straight for mother earth, but would do a series of even loops, or half loops, until its nose dropped again and then loop up again and then drop again. When eventually this did happen, with the engine spluttering to a stop, the poor man blanched and his knuckles went white as he gripped the rail, the seat, or anything possible, waiting for the straight descent as a stone to the ground.

When he opened his eyes and realised what was happening he began to enjoy the whole scene and they floated on down in the same large spiral until they came down again on to the runway and taxied along to the building. From that moment onwards, all changed completely and they were taken into the officers' mess and treated as fellow aviators and had a great party.

The next day they were able to get off in the Air-coup in the early hours of the morning as was their normal practice for good height while the engine was still at a reasonable temperature. They had an open invitation to the Cairo Flying Club and on arrival there were again met and entertained royally. While enjoying their brief stop over in Cairo they were quietly visited by the British Air Attaché who didn't exactly incriminate them by asking them direct questions, but in their earshot rhymed off the exact numbers of the Russian Bombers and MIG fighters which were down at the airstrip in lower Egypt near to Luxor.

The two intrepid flyers reluctantly bid their farewell to the Cairo Flying Club because they needed to get across to Athens while the weather was good and eventually they arrived in airspace over Athens and began to circle amongst the other commercial planes until a green flare came shooting up towards them from the ground once the controllers realised they had no means of communication in order to get them out of the way.

The next morning at breakfast they picked up the papers and were chilled to their very marrow at the headlines which heralded in bold print the start of the 1956 attack by the British and French on Egypt at the canal. The details described how British and French jets had zoomed down through Egypt smashing up all the planes lined up on the runways at Luxor. They decided that was one country they had better not go back to, and shuddered at the thought of still being in Cairo as guests of the Flying Club just as the Fleet Air Arm and other jets went zooming down on their friends at Luxor. No one in Egypt would believe that they were two innocent young colonials from South Africa passing through on a personal venture to the UK in their own plane.

Once landed in Britain, Abe had stowed his plane and walked into Colgate office in London asking if they had any temporary vacancies. As luck would have it, the export department wanted an experienced and more mature person for Singapore after Smudgy Smith, so here was Abe enjoying himself in this marvellous place of Singapore with the Borneo territories to look after as well.

Abe took Tubby for a walk round the Harper offices which were pretty palatial and air-conditioned throughout. There was a main office area of open-plan style with desks occupied by Chinese, Eurasian and Indian staff, reflecting the ethnic breakdown of the population of Singapore which was around 1.5 million in those days, predominantly Chinese, with some 10% of Indians and a few Eurasians and the ex-patriates from Europe, who were generally referred to in conversation as *putehs*, the Malay word for white.

The directors had offices on the other side of the main office which were very well appointed, since the directors of these colonial British import/export companies lived like lords. Many of them were ex-prisoners of war under the Japanese and many had come out of their terrible experiences with health handicaps, so, one was very glad to acknowledge that these ex-pats deserved some good years now. A most likeable director called Charlie Fell particularly fitted into this category since it was generally agreed that his main claim to fame was that he played off at four at the golf club. Bill Bailey, who was the big chief, had a palatial dwelling with chauffeur driven Humber and Princess limousines akin to those brought out for Royalty on overseas visits.

The main director dealing with their Colgate agency was Desmond Brown, who had a great sense of humour, but could become very sharp and edgy once the chips were down on negotiations and business matters. These shrewd observations came from Abe and it was acknowledge that he represented an

American multi-national and took hard-nosed attitudes when it came to sales and profitability.

Desmond Brown was a keen horseman and actually rode in amateur races, and was also a keen skier. He loved to tell of his first six month leave, lodging with a favourite landlady in Kitzbühel over the whole skiing season. However, he did not take into account that most of the other skiers changed week by week and lived it up accordingly during their week. Desmond, being in permanent residence for the skiing season found he was living it up almost permanently and ended up in collapse, sitting up in bed in hospital beaming in apparent bronzed good health from his daily runs on the ski slopes.

Going back to the matter of hard-nosed attitudes, Tubby had come from UK where the Heinz company was known as one of the most vicious sales organisations with a very regimented sales force of ex-guardsmen who had to attend Saturday morning rallies of exultation every two weeks. These were for indoctrination into the belief that the shop keepers and the trade were just necessary evils between the consumer and their glorious Heinz beans, soups, baby foods, etc.

It came as a great shock to Tubby to be introduced to Howard Frey in the most luxurious and well appointed of the representative's offices, because he was the rep in Singapore, Malaya and Hong Kong for the H. J. Heinz Company of the USA. He was an idle, patrician Californian who played his big car and expense accounts to the maximum and moved between Hong Kong and Singapore-Malaya according to the monsoon seasons and social events. Tubby found it impossible to credit that the Heinz Company in the States was regarded as an archaic family concern where the walls of the various offices and reception areas were adorned with their own Monets, Dalis and other original priceless works of art.

The rep from the UK Reckitt and Colman organisation was of an older generation who obviously found life in Singapore very much to his liking compared with anything he might aspire to in the UK at a similar status. Therefore he had made sure that things kept ticking along and that he did not create any

121

situation that might give cause to move him on from this wonderful posting in Singapore.

When they had finished certain of the niceties and introductions, they stepped out into the heavy humidity and the bright sunshine to walk across Collyer Quay to where Abe's car was parked along with many others along the waterfront. The parking area was highly organised by young Indian Boys who 'adopted' drivers not only for washing the car, but for ensuring a parking space on arrival in the morning and safety while there – all for a weekly fee!

As they came out of the car park and along Collyer Quay, Tubby noticed the tourists off the cruise boats beset by the many money changers who frequented the pavement along this stretch of the seafront. As the car swung over the Anderson Bridge across the entrance to Singapore River, Abe turned the car into the great edifice of colonialism which was the Singapore Cricket Club, saying that they must get their priorities right and fix up Tubby's membership of this celebrated club. After the formalities with the club secretary, they strode into the long bar which almost stretched along the width of the building once inside. Abe shouted 'Boy! Two sa-tengahs,' and turned and asked Tubby if this was to his liking. When Tubby said that he didn't know what on earth had been ordered, it was explained to him that Scotch in this part of the world was served in double portions by UK standards, so it had become the custom to use the Malay word for 'half' to order a normal measure of Scotch, hence the call for two 'sa-tengahs'. Instead of paying the Chinese barman, the 'boy' pushed over a bar chit which Abe duly signed indicating that this would go on his 'slate' for monthly settlement with his account.

As he sat on the stool at the bar, Tubby took in all the trappings of colonialism and Stamford Raffles since 1819 which lay before him across the tables and chairs of the great room. The leather seats at the side walls and then the view out into the great green stretch of the Padang in the bright sunshine beyond the bowling greens, and the tennis courts which were nearer to the Clubhouse. Two arms of the horseshoe stretched out on either side with great green roller blinds (chicks) which were let down when the torrential tropical rain came on, or in the heat of lunchtime when they were usually half down to shelter from the glare of the noonday sun.

From the rubber plantations and the old colonial beginnings, the Malay words of *tuan*, which means the boss or the owner, and *besar*, which means big, the colonial whites became generally known as *tuan besars*. They would come into the club at lunch times and have an afternoon or post-lunch nap on the marvellous big seats which were out on this extended verandah part of the club. These chairs were canvas recliners with very long arms across which a canvas band could be looped for putting feet up and really it was then very difficult not to have a post-lunch snooze in the shade of half rolled green blinds – away from the midday sun. Who said it was just not British to indulge in a siesta?

Tubby just sat with Abe at the bar and watched in wonder as the end of day pattern unfolded with the young blades from the other big colonial business houses of Henderson-Crossfields, Sime-Derby and Bousteds, together with those from the rubber broking concerns and the shipping boys from the Ben Line and the Straits Steam Ship Company. The general rig out for the young blade at that time in Singapore was light coloured slacks, partly rolled-up sleeves, the tie possibly undone at that time of the day, and invariably clutching in one hand a round tin of 50 cigarettes. The cry of 'Boy!' could be heard as they came up to the bar and signed their chits for their beers and gathered in groups, or played with sets of liar-dice from behind the bar.

Tubby's experience of running a car was primarily during the six months' sales training spell as a soap salesman, on joining Colgate. The cars issued to salesmen were standard Ford Populars of the very upright variety available in 1956 with the enormously long gear handles, but here there were gungho blades of the same age arriving in their flashy cars at their own exclusive colonial drinking and sports club.

The image of Singapore he had grown up with from school geography lessons was of a steamy, insect-ridden place on the equator full of undesirable Chinese, and here he was now in this throbbing, commercial centre, the crossroads of many great sea lanes from west to east, with buildings which would grace any capital city of the world.

Abe explained how all these young fellows with the shipping lines and import houses lived in big houses which were known affectionately as the 'mess', with Chinese cookie boys in attendance who fed them and kept their laundry up to scratch and their places in order. Tubby thought to himself if he had only known what the place was like, he would have been out there years ago by fair means or foul.

However, the shrewd le Roux brought him down to earth again by explaining that many of them were probably in debt, or lived to the limit, wondering at the end of each of their two to three year stints (before six months leave) whether they would be coming back to promotion, or back at all. The chaps with the big import houses were particularly vulnerable in that they were really locked into a Far East situation, whereas company people like Tubby, with big American multi-national company, and even those with the big shipping lines, had the prospect of moving elsewhere in the world. Although the boys in Harper Gilfillan and the likes had alternative branches at Hong Kong and all round the territories of the Malay States and Singapore, they were still 'overseas wallahs' who in no way could expect to come back to the UK and find a job which would give them the level of lifestyle they were enjoying here in Singapore and the east.

Being almost on the equator, Singapore did not have clear-cut seasons, therefore the sporting calendars and events seemed to follow those of the UK, and it being late August the rugger season was coming on.

With games on Monday evenings, Wednesday evenings and a big game on Saturday being the order for the rugby season, it was little wonder that this became the place into which Tubby's car seemed automatically to turn into on his way from the Collyer Quay at the end of a work day, before the dark which descended rapidly and early on the equator.

21

SIGNS OF THINGS TO COME
FROM NEW YORK

September was rapidly approaching and things were beginning to hot up on the commercial side with regard to the new subsidiary operation to be established from Singapore and Malaya operations, because Frank Hill was well on his way with the Hong Kong subsidiary and Ken Page had his toothpaste factory up and running in Colgate-Palmolive (Thailand) Ltd.

It appeared that the up and coming prospective general managers for overseas subsidiaries came up through the ranks in an office in the New York Headquarters known as 'the second floor' and the new general manager to come to the Malayan subsidiary, anticipated mid-September, was named Jimmy Kevlin. He was coming from his first overseas charge which was the Colgate subsidiary in Panama.

It appeared that the set up in New York was that the patrician, Ed Little, dominated the scene, holding the positions of chairman, president and chief executive officer. With many stories prevailing about the demise of any who had looked like getting near to one of these three posts, it was not surprising that he had become somewhat autocratic after twenty-odd years. He had no family, and he and his wife lived along Fifth Avenue within walking distance of the Colgate building, and the immediate threat seemed to be that Colgate International, currently under Bill Miller, was rapidly coming to the point where it might well overtake the domestic Colgate company of America on billings and profitability, which are the factors which count with shareholders.

There were tales that the three new subsidiaries in this corner of the Far East were to be the responsibility of one Sears Wilson-Ingraham, who had come up through the 'second floor' system too, but he came from an up-market place called Darien in Connecticut and could trace his ancestry back to the pilgrim fathers! The snide remarks had it that he was able to 'arrange' entry introductions to those special inner 'status' clubs round New York for the rough-and-tumble types who attained high office in Colgate but did not have the 'founding fathers' background needed to be really acceptable for these 'status' clubs.

Harper Gilfillan were Colgate agents for UK export, providing the valuable facility of their offices and godowns throughout eight major towns of Singapore and Malaya. 'Godown' is common parlance throughout the Far East for a warehouse, and all the major import houses had godowns at the docks and in the main commercial centres, from which distribution was made to the wholesale and retail trades.

There was talk that the new subsidiary would continue to use the Harper Gilfillan network of godown facilities and management throughout their branches. Nevertheless, a developing heightened feeling of agitation prevailed amongst their top management until this should be resolved, so the pending visit of Sears Wilson-Ingraham was to be the next high point.

As the final UK export incumbent, Abe le Roux was to be around for the visit of Sears Wilson-Ingraham and the coming of the new general manager, but before their arrival Abe had ideas of doing a farewell sentimental journey across to those old colonial places in the East Indies called Sarawak, Brunei and British North Borneo. His excuse was that he simply had to introduce Tubby to these far away remnants of the empire.

In the short time before they were to turn their attention to this trip to the Borneo Territories, Tubby did get a taste of promotional and marketing activities which took place in these outposts. Abe's final flourish was a Colgate trade stand in the big exhibition and trade fair on the old Kallang Airport, as a joint venture with Harper Gilfillan.

Palmolive soap and the Colgate toothpaste were established

leaders throughout the world, but back in the UK, Colgate had simply not got a footing into the lucrative detergent market against Proctor and Gamble and Unilever. In early fifties they had rushed in with a product called FAB via chemical company Marchons in Cumberland, but the product had not been quite proven, and powder began to expand in the cartons. Apparently the same thing had happened to Proctor's and Unilever's early detergents, but with their own manufacturing facilities they were able to replace the dud stock in the shops so that the consumer never really experienced the funny swelling product which took in damp and made the cartons all gooey. Poor Colgate with sub-contract and manufacture and no flexibility just simply lost out. When Tubby did his stint as a salesman on the road in the UK in the backwoods of Cheshire and North Wales, he had found two hardware shops which for some reason or another still kept new improved and stable FAB in stock and placed regular orders to satisfy demand.

Therefore, he was astounded to find that in Singapore and Malaya, USA produced FAB was the absolute winner and dominated the detergent scene, with the added plus that 'FAB' translated into Chinese as everything wonderful, good, bubbly and foamy, which was ideal for a detergent cleaner. Additionally, the formula in the packs they brought in from the States had an A.I. (active ingredient) of some 70%, and in the lovely soft water of the tropics it really did foam and bubble – even for those upcountry washing in rivers, beating their clothes against the rocks. The fastidious Chinese, who made up virtually all the population in Singapore and 50% of the population in the Federation, were chief devotees of FAB.

The old Kallang Airport had runways right down to the sea so that in the wonderful high days of the Imperial Flying Boats, the lovely big planes could come right in across the water and into the landing jetties. With the demise of the flying boats and the increasing size of aircraft – particularly through the war – Singapore airport had been moved to Paya Lebar which is more inland towards Changi, and has one huge runway. The large Nicoll Highway had been then built along the front of Singapore Bay from the end of the Esplanade, out to Geylang, and across the front of Kallang Airport, which was turned into a modern industrial park. Hitherto promotion efforts and trade fairs had been held in one of the wonderful great fun/amusement parks in Singapore affectionately known as the 'Happy World', the 'New World' and the 'Great World'. If you were to ask any who had been in the armed forces out in Singapore in those days, you would see their faces light up at the memory of wild nights out in the 'Worlds' fun centres of Singapore.

Singapore was thick with armed forces establishments, with the huge naval base at the back of the island to the east near the Causeway, RAF Seletar, which still had some Sunderland flying boats, and RAF Changi, the great air base on the eastern corner which became notorious to those taken prisoner by the Japanese after the fall of Singapore. There were numerous army establishments, with the main one at Alexandra Barracks and finally a New Zealand squadron with Canberras at a place called Tengah, which was out in the *ulu* in the western interior of Singapore island beyond the Chinese University. *Ulu* is the Malay word used for the jungle or up-country parts, which was what it was like – with swamps too.

22

THE BORNEO TERRITORIES – THE RAJ STILL LIVES

In the autumn of 1958, the mainland parts of Malaya across the causeway were still very much in the grip of the Communist insurgents, and the armed conflict against them used the 'new village' technique which General Templer made to work. However, the old hands from before the war, and the high days of Raffles Hotel and the author Somerset Maugham, would say that the state of affairs over in the colonies of Sarawak, Brunei and North Borneo was 'as it used to be'. As preparations went ahead for the trip to these places on 2nd September 1958, Tubby could feel a certain excitement with Abe le Roux, for this would be his final visit.

In those days Malayan Airways operated a two way 'bus' service with Douglas DC3 Dakotas. Each morning at 6 a.m. one took off from Singapore heading east while one took off from Sandakan on the far side of North Borneo facing the Philippines, and they used to pass one another over Sarawak somewhere near Sibu on the great Rajang River. It took the old Dakota about four hours hard slog across that open stretch of the South China Sea with its tanks pretty empty by the time it flew into Kuching from the sea, avoiding the 3,000 ft Mount Serapi to the west.

While this 50,000 odd square miles of jungle-clad mountains and swamps became a Crown colony in 1946, it was still being run on the lines evolved by the Rajah Brooke family since 1839 when the first Rajah Brooke devoted himself to the suppression of piracy and head-hunting. Sir Charles Vyner Brooke succeeded his father in 1917, but following the centenary of the

Brooke family's rule in 1941, the country was devastated by the Japanese occupation. In order to facilitate the restoration of Sarawak to its former prosperity, it became a Crown colony by Order in Council on 1st July 1946.

The Brooke family and now the governor ruled this outpost of empire from the *Istana* (the Malay word for palace) across the river in Kuching, and they would be transported across in a special launch to meet with 'the people' in the town and beyond. While the currency was the same Straits Dollar as in Malaya and Singapore, the notes for these colonial territories were printed by and with the name of the Borneo Company.

The chain of command went through district officers who were responsible for order in the five separate divisions, with the first centred on Kuching and the others ranging eastwards until the fifth division which was the mountainous area surrounding the Sultanate of Brunei. Kuching was quite a well-appointed place and Tubby was surprised that it actually had a cathedral. The largest segment of the 600,000 or so, population of Sarawak were the *Sea Dyaks*, or *Ibans*, and as the most prominent of the native population they really did look quite primitive. The Chinese were next in population and were usually to be found as shopkeepers, or involved in anything which was commercial – mining, rubber, peppers, shipping or whatever.

Tubby's agents were again Harper Gilfillan for the mainland of Sarawak, and after spending a day in the office going over the figures etc. with the local manager, Tubby and Abe were taken to their accommodation for the night which was the government rest house. After the air-conditioned hotels and pseudo-westernisation of Singapore, this really was a step back into the days of the empire. Tubby was to find that throughout the East where British empire had reigned, there were government rest houses. They were set up to accommodate civil servants and district officers as they moved around visiting the outposts of empire, and if they were not full up with their bookings, then commercials like Tubby and Abe were able to enjoy the old world comforts of the rest house.

The standard roofing material throughout these parts of the

world were nipah palms which grew along the rivers and swamps. They were harvested and then cut down the middle line of the branch so that the two halves were able then to be suspended like a long row of tiling, and with each overlapping the other they formed a good rainproof wall or roof, as required. Buildings made and roofed from the materials of the jungle were usually called *atap*, and these rest houses were most often in this part of the world made of timber, and roofed in this way.

The grounds were well-kept with Union Jack aloft the flag pole at the front, and moving through the entrance one stepped back into almost Victoriana, or most certainly the later days of the Empire. Furniture was large and grand and of the period, with a reception desk on which lay a leather-bound book for signing-in, and often there was a gong for meal time, and in the corner a walking stick holder, for Malacca canes, or whatever.

There was no air-conditioning in these places and the bed-rooms were dominated by what appeared to be a four-poster bed, but transpired to be designed to hold the hanging mosquito nets under which one could retreat for a peaceful night's sleep. The dining room would be furnished with the essential, but again very substantial, furniture and dazzling white linen cloths on the tables. A stay in a government rest house was pure Somerset Maugham.

In this part of the world roads were very minimal, though where they existed they were well surfaced. The numerous rivers were the prime arteries and veins as demonstrated after flight from Kuching. Progressing onwards to the east, the next stop was at the other main town, Sibu, in the third Division, on the great Rejang river which reached 150 miles right up into central Sarawak and the jungle clad mountains on the Indonesian border. There was a saying that the Rejang was the backside of the empire and Sibu was halfway up it. Certainly it was a town which had to be seen to be believed.

Harpers again had an office here, the man in charge being a huge, red headed chap called Frank Burke-Gaffney. Frank was the only *puteh* (white) in the Harper set up there. Much of

Frank's time was spent on shipping, which sounded ridiculous in a place which was so far up the river, but indeed there were 90 miles of navigable river yet to go above Sibu. It was quite a 'frontier town', with much of the commerce coming from transport of natural resources from up-country down through to this place for on-shipment.

At that time the cutting of timber was very controlled and involved small teams going out into the jungle for the specialist timbers like meranti. There was a team of Aussies operating on the timber at that time and when they hit town things tended to get a bit wild. Most of the places in the town centre, where the eating houses were congregated, were raised above ground level indicating that the river could flood, which was not difficult to understand considering the volume and the distance that the water travelled down from the high mountains of the interior.

Shortly after six it can suddenly go dark in the tropics, and they were not long into their meal when Tubby began to realise that there were lots of women on bicycles going round and round and round the streets outside. It transpired that this was the custom of the local 'ladies', Abe's abiding Achilles' heel. Later on in the evening after the meal he simply had to go out and see what he could find. It was difficult to understand in one so educated and cultured, particularly when he had complained about ending up with a touch of 'the dreaded' via a Eurasian girl in Singapore whom he regarded his exclusive.

The next day they were to head ninety miles up the Rejang River to Kapit, beyond which navigation was impossible because of the extensive rapids. Their means of transport was a large dug out canoe with a length of corrugated roofing in the middle on four posts at each corner, under which they could sit shaded from the blazing sun. Tubby felt like an old-time explorer except that the means of power was a huge Evinrude outboard strapped on the side towards the rear.

It was utterly hair-raising at first because they were soon up to 30 knots or so, against the current of the river, so that the speed impression was tremendous. This was particularly heightened when a large log, or piece of jungle tree was avoided due to the skill of the driver with his hand on the throttle arm of the powerful outboard. After rounding a prolonged bend in the river they passed Kenowit, the first major place on the river going up the third Division, and soon after that they pulled in at the small landing of an Iban long house which was known to their Iban driver. Up a steep bank there were two crudely-carved wooden figures to ward off the evil spirits on the path to the long house. Soon laughing, smiling little Iban children were arriving to greet the white people coming up to see them. Since it was Abe's last trip through these idyllic parts, he had arranged with Frank Burke-Gaffney for a landing at this Iban long house.

While many long roofs of *atap* had been seen sticking up above the jungle canopy at intervals along the river bank, one cannot believe the size and stilt construction of a long house until actually there on the main platform stretching the full length of the building. Each part of the family appears to have a room off this main platform, and in spite of the timber and *atap* construction of these amazing buildings for communal living, they each have their fires for cooking. Tubby noticed at intervals that there were nets hanging from the rafters containing many skulls and he remembered that this was where the Iban chief Temenggong Koh held sway who had restarted the old Iban sport of head hunting during the Japanese occupation in the name of the Rajah Brookes and the empire.

The Iban hospitality is legendary and before departure they had pressed upon them a dram of Iban's powerful local brew, while the old head man and his son adorned themselves with monkey skins and feathers and performed a few gyrations brandishing favourite *pangahs* (jungle swords). All the little ones came running down to see them off and soon they were speeding on their way again.

Tubby had remembered his geography lessons about the mighty Amazon and the jungle of Brazil. Here he was entering a similar vast, empty, green world with only the occasional dug-out boat seen with a family of Ibans, and they flashed past before he could even get a proper shot with his cine-camera.

The camera had been bought at the insistence of Abe who took him into Change Alley off Collyer Quay in Singapore, which was the main bargaining centre, and Abe had helped haggle for an American cine-camera with a turret lens. This proved to be a most valuable piece of equipment indeed, since Tubby was starting to record sights which he might never see again. They were soon hurtling along past the next small concentration of dwellings at a place called Song, where another tributary of the Rejang River flowed in. It was recognisable by the twin towers of a Methodist Mission Church which could be seen sticking above the green jungle canopy.

As they sped along upstream towards Kapit, Tubby noticed things going past in the water which looked like half-peeled dried-out bananas, but they were obviously smaller and were more like nuts from which the outer shell had broken back to reveal the kernel. On arrival in Sibu he had felt a current of excitement in the place, and Frank told him that these objects floating past were illipe nuts, which he had never ever heard of before.

These nuts were collected from throughout the high jungle areas by the Dyaks and lesser known tribes people from the higher plateaus – the Kelabits and Muruts, Kayans, Kenyahs, Kejamans, and even the secretive jungle dwelling nomads, the Penans.

The illipe nuts are a variable crop, and they are a much valued ingredient for production of chocolate and cocoa, so that when there is a bumper year, as was becoming obvious in 1958 in contrast with the poor year of 1957, there was much excitement in these upper regions. This would mean that an ocean-going tramp steamer would sail all the way up the navigable Rejang River to the bazaar centre of Kapit to take on board the big crop of these unique nuts, collected into large storage bins or cages set up along the river bank for this big event. When they reached Kapit the excitement was tremendous and the big storage pens were filling up with illipe nuts in anticipation of the 'big' boat coming all this way upstream to take them away.

The rapids which ended navigation at Kapit were indeed

spectacular; however, the most memorable part of this experience was to witness a bumper illipe nut season and to have sight of so many of the very elusive and little seen native peoples who have inhabited the remote upper areas of the third division of this equatorial wonderland for centuries. They were in Kapit to deliver illipe nuts which they had collected from the abundant crop out in their isolated jungle dwelling areas that year.

These native peoples make elaborate carvings on burial posts and have incredible tattoo patterns on themselves and on their shields. The skins of the Kayans and Kejamans are most peculiarly smooth with wide oriental faces and elongated ears, particularly the women who have many rings in these extended ear lobes. The Kelabits were quite wild and powerful looking, with black hair cropped with a fringe right round. Many had animal fangs through the earflesh, and had bands above the elbows and just below the knees as their only dress additions to a tight waist band with straight drape down their fronts – they were very primitive indeed when seen face to face that day at Kapit. Tubby had never met so many strange people all at once or seen so many bare bosoms in his life!

A bumper crop of illipe nuts is a bonanza time for these primitive natives, and the river dwelling Dyaks sometimes made enough to invest in an outboard motor and perhaps a rifle. Unfortunately the schedule on this final trip for Abe was tight, and soon they were back in their dug-out boat heading non-stop for Sibu at even more hair-raising speed, going with flow of river water.

The internal flights throughout Sarawak, into Brunei and on to North Borneo were via the local airline called Borneo Airways, recently equipped with twin-engined high-wing fixed-wheel multi-seater planes called Scottish Aviation Twin Pioneers. These planes were quite squat with high triple tails, a deep body and fixed undercarriage stretching down from the high wing engine mountings, and in flight their prime advantage was that they could operate from runways little longer than a cricket pitch.

The only crew was the pilot, and all the pilots were ex-

Bomber Command, since Robbie, the chief pilot with a huge handle bar moustache, held that only they had the experience needed for the specialised flying in these parts. There was a story that when the first Scottish Aviation Twin Pioneer was delivered, the Mayor of Kuching and various dignitaries were to go up on the first flight for a demonstration of the short take-off ability of these planes. Robbie did this by taking off across the runway straight from the airport building and into the sky without having to taxi out and up the runway!

From Sibu they flew across towards Bintulu and up the coast over the Miri oilfields, set for Kuala Belait in the sultanate of Brunei, but the landing place was the Shell oil strip at Anduki which was a stretch of grass 1080 feet long and 150 feet wide, just above the sea shore. The Sultan of Brunei is one of the richest men in the world from his oil revenues, since part of the oilfield extends into Brunei at Seria from Miri, which is in the fourth division of Sarawak. North Borneo Trading were agents here, and after one night in the rest house in Kuala Belait they flew on to Brunei Town airport, which was properly tarmacked and had a small building with a glass control tower on the roof.

Brunei Town was located at the north of a wide, sheltered lagoon with at least half the town dwellings situated out in the water on stilts. On a long arm at the end of the lagoon was the first of the many buildings to be provided from Brunei's the oil revenue, which was of course the mosque. As one flew in, one could see the newly completed gold dome glistening in the sunshine and the beautiful, tall, square minaret alongside for the muezzin to call the faithful to prayer.

After Brunei they flew on to the capital of North Borneo which was then known as Jesselton from the days of the empire, but has since become Kota Kinabalu after the mountain of nearly 14,000 feet which dominates the skyline of North Borneo, and is high enough to be bare at the top because it is above the tree line growth level.

Jesselton was big enough in those days for them to stay in a hotel rather than in a government rest house, and on the Sunday their agent took them to see a bungalow he was having built up in the mountain range which led on and up to Mount Kinabalu itself. In places the road had not been bulldozed very well, and in spite of having a four-wheel-drive vehicle the journey got pretty hairy at some places where the edges were precipitous.

Their next port of call was the lovely town of Sandakan where for some reason they had a Chinese agent called Mr Wong – much to the annoyance of the agents for the rest of the territory, the North Borneo Trading Company. The figures showed that Mr Wong had a fantastic turnover for Colgate which could not be readily explained. Mr Wong could not speak English so he used to always drag out his chief clerk from the office to be with him when he met us at the airport. The poor chief clerk was a rather humble, nervous Chinese, with long unruly raven black hair and a large adam's apple, and for some reason he wore traditional British colonial shorts which came to below his knees. Perhaps he had been a clerk in government service, which would make him a most useful English speaking employee for Mr Wong's organisation – someone well versed in the rules and bookkeeping of the colonial masters!

Abe le Roux had tipped off Tubby to watch Mr Wong as they got to the hotel, and, true to form, he organised things so that the poor little clerk man kept them occupied in the hotel reception while Mr Wong nipped into their bedrooms and removed all the other soap from the bathroom and shower rooms and replaced it with Palmolive tablets, plus a tube of Colgate each!

As they bid farewell to Mr Wong and his clerk and headed off for the DC3 Dakota for the long haul back to Singapore, Tubby vowed that when he came back on his next trip on his own he would try to find out just how Mr Wong had such a large turnover for their products.

It had taken twelve days to work their way up through the Borneo territories and the dear old Dakota was ready for its bus stop flight back to Kuching and then the long haul to Singapore for touch down just before dark.

He and Abe were looking forward to being back and finding

137

out who had arrived from the States, but as Tubby hauled his way up the steep passageway between the seats from the back door of the Dakota he was aware of an above average number of children on the flight. Alas, alas, it had not struck them that this was the end of the summer holidays for the ex-patriate children out in the outposts of the empire with their parents. They were now heading back towards the UK to their boarding schools with labels tied round their necks saying 'to be collected at Singapore by BOAC'. At Jesselton, Brunei, Sibu and Kuching more and more of the little horrors came on board and by Singapore they were glad to see them being herded off to the arms of BOAC lasses who were to see them on their way back to the UK next day.

Two years on when Tubby was heading back to the UK for his first leave, he was extremely glad that he was still in the first class travel category, because it was the same time of the year and he always remembered with a shudder a glimpse through into the tourist part of the BOAC plane and of the frantic chaos beyond. The stewardesses certainly earned their passage handling these precocious horrors.

It seemed to be an ingrained part of ex-patriate life in the outposts of empire to send one's children back to school in the UK – whether they could afford it or not. The ex-pat wives were generally referred to as *mems besar* and many a time Tubby came to hear them voice their longing for the time when their tiny offspring would be old enough to be shipped off to prep school at the age of five or six. No-one ever seemed to take into account such English educational establishments as the Raffles Institution in Singapore which had quite an outstanding academic record, including Oxbridge entrants such as the brilliant lawyer Lee Quan Yew, the founding father of modern Singapore.

23

THE NEW TEAM STARTS TO COME TOGETHER

It had been mentioned earlier that most ex-patriate young fellows lived in company accommodation with servants, called a mess, but Abe le Roux lived in a much more sophisticated mess of Harper's which was actually a very nice flat in a set of apartments called Amber Mansions. Since the number of Harper ex-pats was reducing, Abe had arranged that a Dutch chap would share the accommodation with him. Because of the Dutch Cape background of Afrikaaners and the similarity of Afrikaans to the Dutch language, Abe had many contacts with the Dutch community and, true to the more hard nosed business attitudes of the Dutch, most young ex-pat Dutch trainees had to do tours of five to six years before they could anticipate going home, and were certainly not as well paid, or provided with perks, as were their UK counterparts.

It was agreed with Harper's management that Tubby would move in as and when Abe eventually left for Hong Kong on his way back to the UK, via the States, which pleased the Dutch chap no end since this arrangement meant his carrying on in this pleasant accommodation at Amber Mansions.

Within a day of their return from the Borneo Territories, Jimmy Kevlin arrived from Panama via New York to be the new general manager of Colgate Palmolive (Malaya) Limited. At that point the plan was to set up the new subsidiary in the 'Freeport' island of Singapore, but political developments seemed to indicate that a better place might be in the federation of Malaya. Old-style, colonial civil servants were still an

139

influence in Singapore so just as Jim Kevlin was short in physical stature, it was equally important to keep a low profile as the American general manager of a new American subsidiary.

At that time the federation of Malaya had been independent only two years, headed by the genial Malayan 'Royal'-Tunku Abdul Rahman, while the debate concerning an independent Singapore, or a Singapore as part of the federation, was beginning to hot up. One of the most active voices in Singapore was Lee Quan Yew – then a fiery anti-British orator, though really middle of the road when compared with people like Ong Eng Guan who was a Communist.

While the Malays made up only 50% of the population, with 40% Chinese and 10% Indian, the constitution for Malaya in 1956 gave power to the Malays primarily to get them enthused and interested in putting an end to the emergency caused by the Communists in the jungle. The notorious Ching Peng had been a resistance hero in the war against the Japanese, but when the end of the Japanese occupation did not result in Malaya becoming Communist, he returned to the jungles to continue the struggle for Communism which sadly bred a climate of Chinese versus the rest.

Throughout the Japanese occupation, the Malays had been neutral. The Malays, as devotees of Islam, follow the dictum 'as Allah wills' which fits well with their charming take-it-as-it comes attitude which is summed up in two words in their language *tidak apa*. These two words are pronounced *ti dapa* and were very soon picked up by ex-pats and usually said with a shrug of the shoulders, which conveyed the attitude of 'so what', or 'that's the way it is!'

Although Ted Heath and Herr Willi Brandt of West Germany gained for themselves great kudos and financial rewards as champions of the so called 'Third World', which included Malaya and Indonesia, the truth is that the people in these parts were never hungry, nor need be. Over 60% of the Malay population lived in *Kampongs* (villages) of under 2,000 in population, up and down many of the rivers and back-waters and in the *Ulu* of Malaya, hence their attitude to the

140

Japanese occupiers was more or less 'so what' – life goes on as before.

Sadly, in the world of developing commerce and independent nationhood, the standard mosque education, and the rural background with fish, rice and from the trees abundant food, did not exactly equip them to be competitive. Hence the constitution designated that companies would have at least one Malay on the board of directors and Malay was to be the national language even though it could not cope with needs of commerce and military communication.

Against this background, it was easy to understand why the federation of Malaya was not particularly interested in having 1½ million Singapore Chinese come into the equation, nor for that matter were the Singapore Chinese interested in becoming part of a constitution which was weighted in favour of the Malays.

While Tubby was still operating from the Adelphi Hotel in the middle of town near to the Singapore Cricket Club, Jimmy Kevlin was set up in the lovely Ocean Park Hotel which was on the sea front, six and a half miles out along the east coast road. This location was mainly in anticipation of his wife Rita arriving in a week or so from Panama with their three children. Having grown up in that location they were Spanish-speaking and the two older ones were going to have to face the prospect of suddenly finding themselves in a British military school situation, an extension of the UK education system. Some ex-pat teachers lived in quarters not far from the Ocean Park Hotel, which was situated near the Chinese Swimming Club, so he thought of introducing them for a gentle lead-in to UK-style schooling.

In contrast with the easy going style of UK export whereby Tubby ran things in Iraq and Abe operated here through Harpers, it began to look as though Jim Kevlin was looking over his shoulder very nervously towards New York, and was not going to make any decisions, particularly with the pending arrival of Sears Wilson-Ingraham, from whom he seemed to be running scared already from earlier experiences on the second floor in New York, before Jimmy got his first posting to Panama.

The Harper people, and Desmond Brown in particular, were

getting a bit worked up about the coming visit of Sears Wilson-Ingraham too. Abe le Roux promoted the idea of taking him on a quick swing round the length and breadth of Malaya on a fact-finding visit, since this would give Abe an ideal opportunity for a final swing round the federation of Malaya to say farewell to all the friends he had made amongst the branch managers at the various Harper offices.

The day for Sears' arrival came, but due to air flight delays he did not arrive until late and the welcome party caught up with him as he arrived in a taxi at the Adelphi Hotel. He was a vociferous and most unlikable American, with a short hair-style, and button-down shirt collar and expensive suit one size too small for his overweight figure, as becoming up-market Americans in New York from Connecticut. He announced in a loud voice that someone should settle the taxi which he had negotiated for $20 US. On hearing this ridiculous price for the taxi, all the others present could hardly keep their faces straight and Abe made his escape by saying that he would pay the man off. This he did, to the tune of nine Straits dollars, with words of abuse for conning the poor American, but was of a mind to ask Sears, with a straight face, to refund him in US $20.

Desmond Brown of Harpers was in the reception party too, and as they withdrew to await him in the bar they could not help but notice that part of Sears' equipment was a rather high-powered portable radio with an enormous aerial which he immediately started to extend. Noticing their wide-eyed expression, Sears asked what the time might be back in Rhode Island, USA, because the Americas Cup yachting race was in its preliminaries, and he was determined to keep up with how things were going on.

He was rather an obnoxious, loud-mouthed American, and the type of man who reacts to new, higher management status by trying to demonstrate his position and throw his weight around. This was apparent since messages out of New York indicated he had been given some responsibility for the three new subsidiaries emerging in this corner of the Far East, and it was noticeable that Jim Kevlin, the general manager to be of the Malayan subsidiary, was not at all pleased.

Sears was keen to demonstrate that he was the 'out and about' type of executive, getting into the corners of the boondocks which, since America is so vast, usually means places in the far Mid-west, away from the big cities. In this case it would mean the outposts of the Harpers' branches in Malaya. This was exactly what Abe wanted, and a programme had been worked out with enthusiasm by Desmond Brown, who was to accompany the team of Tubby, Abe, Kevlin and Sears Wilson-Ingraham. This would boost Desmond's standing and aspirations against Harpers' branch managers, and make him Harpers key link with the new boss of things in Thailand, Hong Kong and Malaysia.

The plan was to fly on a Malayan Airways DC3 the next Sunday afternoon right up the east coast to Kota Bharu, where Harpers' had a branch with a local manager. From there they would take the DC3 across the west to Penang via Alor Star, which was the main town of the state of Kedah and the home town of the prime minister of Malaya, the Tunku Abdul Rahman. Penang was a 'freeport' island off the coast of North West Malaya like Singapore, so Harpers had a large branch there with shipping and so on. They would then drive in two cars provided by Harpers to visit their branches throughout the developed parts to the west of the central Malayan highlands, and then go back to Singapore.

As a good Afrikaaner, Abe did not have any particular fondness for Americans, especially this particular brash type, and being bomb-happy about going on leave, he could not resist making fun of Sears from time to time.

Sears had already demonstrated that he was somewhat a strain to be with over meals, and being obviously overweight, he appeared not to have any dietary consciousness. Abe, on the other hand, was perfectly devoid of any excess weight and liked to keep himself trim and presentable. When everyone assembled at Paya Lebar Airport on the Sunday afternoon, Sears caught sight of Abe and Tubby using a set of luggage scales to check their weights before and after the grand tour, since, as far as Abe was concerned, it would be his last indulgence in the lovely food of Malaya.

'Hey fellas!' was a shout they would come to recognise. 'What are you doing there?' Abe replied that it was a necessary precaution in these parts of the world because with heat, humidity and one thing and another, it was the easiest thing in God's earth to add rolls round the middle, so Sears had to get on the scales too.

Following the call to board the plane and the walk out to the tarmac to the DC3, Sears fought his way to the front so that he could grab a seat by the back door, exclaiming that the tail unit was always the safest place to be in if there should be any crash landing. As was usually the case in the late afternoon in September, a localised but quite violent tropical thunderstorm was crossing the back of the island as the Dakota set off down the runway. With the adjustment into a more level position once the tail came up, the plane roared down the big runway to head up and out across the stretch of waterway between the island and state of Johore.

As the Dakota entered the storm with flapping wings on its steady climb, the torrential rain usually outside found its way in via the joins and narrow gaps there seemed to be on Dakotas just aft of the cockpit area. The water began to run down in little rivulets between the canvas seats, and the voice of Sears was heard to exclaim above the roar: 'Do they always take off into monsoons in this place?'

In a short time they had broken out into the glorious sunshine beyond the storm, and headed up the east coast. The take-off and experience of the monsoon squall seemed to have rendered their visitor silent, and Tubby was able to look down on the scenes of impenetrable jungle and then the lovely coastline washed by the China sea, with fishermen's boats visible, beached and no doubt getting ready for the night's fishing. It was down through this great eastern mainland that the Japanese had come swarming on their bicycles and so taken Singapore from the rear without too much problem, since all the fortifications had been ranged for any attack coming from the sea.

144

24

SO THIS IS THE FEDERATION

Kota Bharu was the main town of north-eastern Malaya in the state of Kelantan, which was famous for its local silverwork, and no ex-pat would leave without examples of Kelantan silver, or pots of Kelantan pewter to drink out of. This was a very dominantly Malay area and overall quite idyllic with the whole rhythm of life very much close to nature and the sea and winds.

Because of the mountain range down through the Malayan peninsula, the railway line from Singapore up to Thailand was along the west side. There was a branch which cut up into Kuala Lipis in the central highlands and made its way through the King George V National Park to Kota Bharu. The sales vans and 'Miss FABS' promotion team were on parade for the visitors and the Indian manager of this Harpers outpost branch was most impressed to meet the boss, Mr Desmond Brown from Singapore. The less said about the one night stay the better, and with Sears not able to get an Americas Cup update on his portable he was very unmanageable!

Tubby was to find out that this place was simply not visited from November through to early February, since the area took the full brunt of the monsoons which came down from the Himalayas and Indo-China to cross the China sea. All the idyllic fishing villages hang in there while the gorgeous looking palms are bent back and well-nigh stripped. It was not uncommon for crocodiles to be a hazard in the flood waters which reached to the market places.

The Communist insurgents in the jungles of Malaya knew that Thailand was a place of refuge, and these northern parts of Malaya had great concentrations of armed forces from all the Commonwealth nations.

Away from Thai border areas it was always difficult to tell which Chinese were 'with', or 'not with' those in the jungle, since all Chinese were always under threat of intimidation to supply food, etc. It was the arrival of General Templer, known as 'the rat', which made the system of new villages work, and he was not popular in the process.

Once the Chinese were all concentrated into new villages surrounded by wire, they went out through the gates in the mornings and afternoons to work on the rubber plantations. Those inside the jungle had to come closer to points of civilisation for supplies. This led to the system of patrols out into the *ulu* to ambush them. While the Malays represented 50% of the population at that time, they too were Polynesian immigrants from way back, and the real natives of the Malay peninsular were the Sakai. One would only catch a fleeting glimpse of these people in the dense jungle areas of the central and northern parts. They had become excellent trackers for the military patrols against the Communists, who would set up an ambush once a jungle track was observed.

These patrols into the jungle were the ideal environment for Britain's Gurkha regiments which were in Malaya at that time and had a very good record. The others who were good at these operations were the Royal Marine Commandos and early SAS types. On the flight across through Alor Star, Tubby sat next to one of these hardened bushwackers who had a battered jungle hat, fatigues, and belts of ammo round him with his personalised shot-gun between his knees.

The plane landed on Penang Island at the south end which was a 'black area', with Communists, so it was important to be up in George Town on the north end of the island before dark. Once again they stepped back into the colonial past when they entered the wonderful E and O hotel which sat on the waterfront at George Town with nothing but the sea between there and the beautiful and partly inhabited island of Lankawi, just off the coast by the Thai border and the state of Perlis. This island was one of the places Tubby marked down for a visit once he got settled in on his own.

The E and O hotel was a beautiful old colonial building

which might well have been a fort at one time, overlooking the waters and the safe anchorage between the island and Butterworth. Beyond reception there was a table and seating area with a bar at the other side, but the great delight at the end of a busy and steamy day was to take a gin and tonic, or a *satengah* out to the tables and the chairs on the seafront by the rusty old cannons facing out to imaginary foes long ago.

One could sit here in the cool breeze that came across the water as the colours deepened while the sun went down, and watch a single fisherman working his way along with his single circular throwing net. Beyond, an ocean-going ship would pass, heading out to sea while a Chinese junk in full sail would wend its way slowly in towards the anchorage, round the corner at George Town.

The bedrooms were old colonial style with the old circular fans on the ceilings rather than air-conditioning since there was the cooler air coming in across the sea which made the nights most comfortable, and Tubby really enjoyed being between clean sheets in a nice bed after his experience in Kota Bharu in north-east the night before. Because of the numbers in the party and because it was the non-monsoon time for visitors to come up to that idyllic part of the world, Tubby had ended up in a Chinese shake-down not dissimilar to the one in Kapit, 90 miles up the Rejang River in Sarawak.

Already Tubby had adopted the night attire for ex-patriate *putehs* which was the one-piece round sarong, which you stepped into and pulled tight round the waist and folded over. They were marvellously cool and loose for trying to sleep in the steamy hot tropics, and Tubby had stretched out on the low bed in the Chinese hotel with the ever-present Dutch comfort to curl up against. For insect repellant he had a fan at his feet blowing over him the smoke from a slowly smouldering mosquito coil, which seemed to keep the *nyamoks* (mosquitos) at bay.

The Dutch comfort was the affectionate name for a very long and round, rigidly filled bolster, which was always on beds in Chinese Shake-down hotels. Tubby had never worked out why this enormously long, stiff round bolster was standard sleeping equipment, or how it had come to be standard in Malaya: it is left to the imagination to work it out.

In George Town on Penang Island, Harpers had a very large office and it became obvious that Desmond Brown had ordered that the red carpet hospitality was to be laid on by the directors there, with himself, as the big white chief from Singapore, being the circus master – and enjoying it. They were most royally wined and dined and the only problem was the objectionable company of the visitor from the second floor in New York!

It was here that they picked up the limousines which were to transport the team down through the main west coast centres of Malaya. As they sailed away on the ferry boat across to Butterworth on the mainland from the beautiful island of Penang, Tubby noticed that the beautiful two masted schooner *Xarifa* was anchored off the northern point. It was from this lovely boat that Dr Hans Hass and his fabulous wife Lotte did their underwater filming, since at that time they were the glamorous pioneers of the new form of exploration under the tropical waters with their cameras, flippers and underwater breathing apparatus.

The landing jetty at the mainland end was a hive of activity with the construction of a new terminal and for the first time Tubby noticed the extent to which small and delicate Chinese women formed the workforce which carried and fetched rubble and building materials on shoulder poles. In spite of being engaged in this rough work it was fascinating to notice that they went to great lengths to protect their delicate white skins from the sun of the tropics by having brailings round the rims of their broad, flat, open-pointed hats, and further drapes of cloth at the end of their sleeves which covered their hands. The rest of them was well wrapped up and for some reason the Chinese just don't seem to perspire the same way as ex-pats.

The mainland area across from the Penang Island also reflected the history of Penang area, being one of the original three Straits settlements, for it was known as Province Wellesley. The countryside was fairly flat and well-cultivated, and the area was criss-crossed with roads, so with the road straight and surfaces in good condition the going could be very fast, particularly since the lack of traffic in those days made motoring positively pleasurable. While the fast straight road continued down the coastline through the great agricultural areas, the cavalcade of two cars followed the road to the left and inland before turning south again towards the first major town of Taiping. This was in the huge central state of Perak, which stretched east into the central highland ridge and then encompassed the great tin mining area of Malaya which was centred on Ipoh.

Soon the road was shrouded by dense jungle on either side; this was really bandit territory! As it was lunchtime, where else should they go but the Taiping Club? This was again a lovely beautiful old colonial place with a verandah of timberwork and with all the usual facilities for the young colonial ex-pats to 'do sport' – a lovely green sward of cricket pitch, tennis courts, a bowliing green and the shade of lovely trees round the clubhouse.

Being before the days of air-conditioning in cars, the first thing after the hot drive was to go straight into the bar and shout: 'Boy! – six fresh limes!' This was one of the most marvellously refreshing experiences in the country – the iced fresh lime drink.

The other thing about Taiping which really brought home its role as the front line in the emergency operations against the insurgents in the jungle was the high number of military personnel frequenting the Taiping Club. As Tubby stood after lunch surveying the beautiful scene of the manicured green swards sweeping down from the clubhouse to the *ulu* at the bottom, he thought the knobbly face of an individual in a deck chair not far along was somewhat familiar. On going closer and lifting the hat from the shade of the eyes, he found it was none other than a chap called Willy White, who had been a somewhat roguish and disreputable character in the form below him at school, but had come good studying medicine at Liverpool with Tubby's Penelope. Glory be! He was out here as a military doctor – commissioned too, and posted to the big services hospital facility at Taiping.

149

After the usual exclamations of surprise, they had a quick update of what each had been up to, and in explaining his current medical work in Taiping White did comment casually that the *ulu* just at bottom of the green sward was indeed 'black territory' which one didn't venture into, unless as part of a patrol and heavily armed.

Tubby joined the others in the vehicles to set off on the next run to the great central town of Ipoh – the centre of tin mining. He felt that this was indeed going to be a wonderful country to be in over the next few years, with the tingling excitement of danger around and incredibly changing scenes of vast grandeur and impenetrable jungle.

Travelling east, the road touched the railway from time to time because of the mountains on either side, and they passed by the ancient Malay town of Kuala Kangsar which was really the capital town of this great state. Kuala Kangsar sat on the great Perak River which flowed down and out to sea farther south at Telok Anson from a great lake high inland up on the road to Grik in the northern mountains.

Soon the road swung north for a while and then turned south again, passing great created lakes of water on which floated huge tin dredging machines, which moved the lakes around as they dug out great mountains of the earth at the front to wash out the tin, and then dropped the earth back out at the far end to fill the lake again. At other places they caught glimpses of Chinese tin mines with their incredible, high *palongs* made of latticed bamboo poles. These held a run down of slats for the water blasted out of the tin-bearing hills by pressure water cannons, which was then pumped up for grading out the ore on the way down. In small runaways at the bottom, there would be a gang of Chinese girls up to their knees in the water panning any remaining tin with their huge *dulongs*.

These *dulongs* could be purchased at shops in the villages of this tin-mining area. They were made out of single cuttings from huge logs about four inches thick, and then hollowed out into shallow circular pans. They were favourites for ex-pats to have varnished and polished for use as a decoration piece, or a salad server.

150

The final stretch of road down to Ipoh was through the Kinta valley area which had its own man-made lakes with huge tin dredgers, but also boasted a broad, flat valley with numerous and enormous limestone outcrops called *gunongs*, which is Malay for mountain. They were not exactly mountains, but within this flat valley area they stood up like fingers of French bread, and larger ones were clad with jungle greenery. Some distance from the road, in one particularly large *gunong* with hollowed caves, there had been built a huge Chinese Chin Swee temple, which was a place of pilgrimage.

While the Chinese Hakkas were in numbers in the mining areas, it was obvious by the noise and clatter in the lively streets of Ipoh that voluble Cantonese were the dominant Chinese people in this town and the surrounding area. There was an excitement about Ipoh since the tin mining was going well, and the emergency was being overcome since the arrival of Sir Gerald Templer, in contrast with the dark days when Gurney the Governor was ambushed and shot by the Communist terrorists on his way down the road from Cameron Highlands in his official car.

Tubby was quite overwhelmed when they went into the Ipoh Club, and it became one of his favourite visiting and eating places when back up in these parts of Perak. From his own Caledonian parentage and roots, he could feel the heavy overtones in all the various symbols on the wall that the Scots had been dominant amongst the ex-pats, since many of the emblems would make a proud insignia for any reputable pipe band. No doubt the engineering requirements of the tin industry brought many of the Scots here, but then again, they had gathered in any outpost of the world where there was money to be made, following the example of Andrew Carnegie *et al*. With the historic weighting towards Scottish ex-pats, it was not surprising that one of the four Presbyterian Churches, all named St Andrew's, would be located here in Ipoh, the others being in Penang, Kuala Lumpur and of course Singapore.

They got on the road again the next day, and with the whistle stop nature of this round tour of the Harpers' branches, and

151

the hospitality related thereto, Sears was getting enormously frustrated about the Americas Cup races taking place at home. He could be seen trying to grab opportunities to push up the huge aerial from his unwieldy portable machine and try and tune in for an update on the races on whatever wavelength he might find.

While the railway went almost due south from Ipoh to Batu Gajah, the road was more inland through the same sort of valley countryside, enormous great *gunongs*, tin mining installations of all varieties, which became more numerous as they approached the great tin mining town of Gopeng. These were the mine workings of the dominant company Gopeng Consolidated, whose shares were popular with those who tried to catch a 'top' on the roller coaster of share values, according to the fortunes of tin on the world commodity markets.

Gopeng was also notorious as a very active bandit area, and as they headed south through Lower Perak they were conscious of the fact that their cavalcade of two limos might seem to those in the jungle to be worthy of an ambush, since they might be carrying VIPs. As part of the Sears-bating, an off-the-cuff remark as to this possibility made him wish that he had had a Stars and Stripes to hang out of the car window.

All the time Tubby was scribbling notes on the various places they passed through, with the orbits of the various Harpers' Branches, and places by-passed as they headed on, such as another major town of Lower Perah called Telok Anson where the great Perak River turned to the sea. This would be another minor Harpers branch to visit in promoting the Colgate products.

Earlier, as they had passed through a place called Tapah, Tubby had made note of the road going off to the main large hill station of Cameron Highlands. Being some six thousand feet up in the central range, it would be a haven from the humidity and tropical heat in which they were driving. The road was following the railway again until a place called Slim River where it turned and followed the Sungai Slim (Malay for river), until Slim Village where it turned south again. This stretch of road with very many miles of winding bends following the twists and turns of the river was to become a favourite stretch of road for Tubby, but more of this later.

At this stage, the road touched the second huge state of Malaya called Pahang, which spread right through to the east coast, and at KKB they linked up with the road which came across from the higher part of Pahang state at the second main hill station of Malaya, Fraser's Hill. Another Scottish name! This hill station was not as high in the clouds as Cameron Highlands and therefore not quite as large and popular, but even so it was well over 4000 feet high, and a great place for a break and change of climate.

The town of KKB, as it was known generally, was actually called Kuala Kubu Baru. From there on, the road was into the next state of Selangor and there was more evidence of rubber plantations. Selangor state included Kuala Lumpur, which was the capital of the independent federation of Malaya (Persekutuan Tanah Melayu) established by statute in 1956. Under the democratic constitution, the nine sultans were to take turns every three years as head of state (*Yang di-Pertuan Agong*). As a grand gesture, the sultan of Selangor gave his *Istana* (palace), situated in Kuala Lumpur, to the nation to be the *Istana Negara* – the palace of the nation. The story went that it was so run down and dilapidated that it was a good excuse for the sultan to build himself a new palatial *Istana* with a gold dome down on the road to Klang, twenty miles or so out of Kuala Lumpur towards the coast, and therefore more hospitable as regards climate and weather.

During the following years when Tubby was in these parts and eventually resident in Kuala Lumpur, two of the paramount rulers died, one after having gallstones in spite of being revived by the *bomo* (the Malay for medicine man). The *bomo* got the *Agong* back on his feet again for another year or so with burning leaves, incantations and some secret potions. Some ex-pats tend to write off these incidents as local gobbledegook, but one of the sultans of the huge state of Perak once thought he was under threat from little effigies, or figures made of reeds, being left around, so he locked himself away in one of his four *Istanas* round the state of Perak. Perhaps it was a

153

case of 'the wrath of Allah', since he was a notorious roué with ladies in each of the four *Istanas* round his state, in addition to his 'official' Sultana.

These deaths among the paramount rulers created a certain unwillingness to serve more years than necessary as the *Agong*. There were elaborate funeral processions following the death of each *Agong*, and at this time the Lord Chief Justice of Malaya was Sir James Thomson – a rather humourless Edinburgh Scot who spoke with the deep and rather cultured accent much beloved by advocates from the capital of Scotland. Tubby came to know him subsequently as a fellow elder of the Presbyterian Church of St Andrew's in Kuala Lumpur. Sir James used to sit at the back as a very large and imperious figure. Within the formalities of the Federation of Malaya, he had the grand title of *Dato* and at the ceremonial funeral for the second *Agong* to die since independence, a friend of Tubby's, who was also very high up in the public works department, recalled that as the dignitaries were all waiting around to take their places in the funeral procession, a voice was heard to say: 'Who will be the next *Agong*?' Among muffled mirth another voice was heard to say: '*Dato* Sir James Thomson.' Against the uncertainties prevailing with the next state sultan in line to be the third *Agong*, Sir James could have been a very acceptable compromise solution.

The stay of the visiting party in Kuala Lumpur was again the occasion of excitement as far as the aspiring Desmond was concerned, since this was the main office in the federation, in an imposing building in Mountbatten Road in the middle of town. The dinner for the visiting party with the directors of the Harpers office in Kuala Lumpur was somewhat formal, in that a few reached back to the pre-occupation days. One of these was a very deadpan figure who, with other certain ex-pats, held the position of senator within the legislation process of the new independent Federation, just two years old in 1958. There was a joke around Harper Gilfillan that whenever there was some economic mini-crisis, there would be a piece in the *Straits Times* which would quote Senator Hussey of Harper Gilfillan as saying, 'As long as the price of tin and rubber remains

154

stable, the economic future of the Federation is secure.' Very profound.

They were soon on their way heading south again, but Tubby had noted that one particular Director had been quite knowledgeable about Colgate agency. He was called Sibree, and was about seven feet tall, a stuffed shirt to boot, with a public school voice and mannerisms 'as if to the manner born'. Furthermore, he noted that this Director at KL and Desmond Brown did not exactly hit it off, and wondered if Desmond might see him as a problem for his own foreseeable future in the ranks of Harper Gilfillan, once the likes of Senator Hussey had moved on to retirement.

After a brief stop at the Harper Gilfillan office in Seremban, which was the capital town of the state of Negri Sembilan – the state of the then current Paramount Ruler – they headed on to be in Malacca by nightfall. Turning off the main road south into Johore before Tampin, they were soon into the paddy fields of the historic wonderland which is the state of Malacca.

This was the second major rice growing area of Malaya to the area north of Penang and up to the Thai border, but it had an atmosphere and identity which was totally unique in that it was very dominantly Malay, with mosques among the paddy fields in the *kampongs*, much as one sees towers and spires of churches at English villages across that countryside. Almost as soon as they entered into the paddy field area, they came across the double-wheeled ox carts, with a pointed, matted roof like a Thai temple, pulled by two great oxen. They are seen nowhere else in Malaya and they are part of the uniqueness of Malacca, where the Sultans were very powerful and dominant on land and the sea and in the Straits of Malacca. Because of this dominance, Malacca became one of the three original Straits Settlements by mutual agreement between the sultan and the empire.

The Malays of the Malacca area are very much at one with those on the huge and naturally wealthy island of Sumatra, which is bigger than the Malay Peninsula and part of Indonesia. The narrow straits of Malacca between this part of the federation and the huge island of Sumatra were a natural place for piracy on the boat traffic from Europe which came through headed for Singapore and the seas of the Far East towards China and Japan.

The wonderful and historic buildings of Malacca and the seafront there reflected the arrival of the Portuguese, then the Dutch and finally the British, who came to terms with the sultans of Malacca for their mutual benefit. All the trade and the wonderful products of the spice islands can all be found together in the food of Malacca. The establishments and court procedures of the sultans of Malacca became the norm for the installation of the paramount rulers of the federation of Malaya.

There was at that time a celebrated ex-federation civil servant called Sheppard, who had taken up the cause of Islam, and, through much study, had become the definitive expert on protocol of the courts of the sultans of Malacca. Having been on the *Hadj* to Mecca, he was known as 'Hadji' Mubin Sheppard. Just as the Duke of Norfolk presides over British coronation ceremonies and all that goes with them, 'Hadji' Mubin Sheppard was the presiding overlord at the funerals of the two Paramount Rulers and the subsequent enthronement of their successors. Later, when Tubby was established in Kuala Lumpur, he was to be visited by the very same 'Hadji' Mubin Sheppard at the new Colgate factory.

Harper Gilfillan had a branch in Malacca near the waterfront where one could see the ocean junks tied up and great water buffalos used from the paddy fields lying to cool at the water's edge, tethered to the side with ropes from their noses. Tubby first came across these great beasts in the mud hut colonies along the Tigris River in Baghdad and while one can often come across them being gently led along by a child or with a child sitting on their backs, he had been warned then that they do not like the smell of whites and can react negatively against them. He was warned about this again in Malaya, and indeed it was commented that *Putehs* (whites) are regarded as having an unsavoury smell by Chinese and other local races in the Far East. So, it is not too difficult to understand that these great water buffalo beasts of the paddy fields might not take kindly to ex-pats.

The government rest house where they stayed in Malacca was the ultimate in colonial serenity. A delightful green sward stretched down to palm trees from the grand entrance facing the sea. While staying there, Tubby took the opportunity to buy a genuine Malacca cane to take home for his father on his first leave. Sword-stick versions were common in former times, but none were readily on sale at the rest house.

Under the emergency regulations, the state of Johore between Malacca and the causeway to Singapore was designated a very 'black area'. Ambushes were frequent near 'new villages' in which the Chinese were incarcerated at night, and with curfew after daylight no one was allowed to drive on to Singapore after dark. For this reason they set off in the two cars first thing in the morning and drove down the straight road by the coast to Muar, where Tubby for the first time experienced a local Malay car ferry.

Muar stood at the mouth of the Sungei Muar River and the ferry was a rather ancient pontoon on to which the car was driven, which was then hauled across by ancient chains to the ther side where hopefully one could drive off. It was pleasant to stand with the cars on the pontoon and enjoy the sea breezes and look away inland across the flat areas of Malacca to Mount Ophir, which is over 4000 feet high and the one single piece of high ground in this part of the federation. On subsequent flights in the old Dakotas up and down Malaya it was always the point he looked for when flying towards Malacca from Singapore.

After crossing on the ferry, the road came to yet another ferry at a place called Batu Pahat and by the same Pontoon process, the cars were soon back on to the main road to Singapore at a place called Ayer Hitam, which translated means 'black water'. Since there was no river at this place it didn't seem to fit, but at least they joined the road well south of a place called Yong Peng, which was a very notorious black spot for actions by Communists from the jungle. All along the drive down through Johore, it was obvious to Tubby that this was the main Rubber growing area of Malaya, and there were many great wire-fenced 'new villages' on either side of the road.

They stopped at a small town or *kampong* called Kelapa Sawit in the middle of Johore in order to stretch their legs, have a drink and let the perspiration burn off their clothing. They had plastic or rattan backings to the seats in the cars to form some sort of gap between oneself and the seat, but nevertheless one still got pretty sticky and, whereas in Baghdad and Iraq the heat was so dry you soon frizzled off any damp as soon as you stepped out of the car, the humidity was such here that it did not have the same effect.

Their stopping place was really a row of shop houses on either side of the main road heading to Singapore, and as in most *kampongs*, there was a Chinese medicine shop. Tubby was supping a drink with Desmond and noticed that they were standing across the street from the establishment of the Chinese practitioner of medicine for Kelapa Sawit. He looked in horror at the huge display pictures above the shop front.

This particular Chinese medicine man had cornered the market for dealing with piles, and he had displayed above the shop front huge photo of himself, with a grin of satisfaction across his face, and each hand resting on the raw bottom of two patients he had treated. Tubby gently nudged Desmond and indicated with his face and eyes to look up at the display and watched as his face twisted into utter disbelief.

Sears Wilson-Ingraham was some way up the road trying to get Jimmy Kevlin involved yet again with his radio for news on the Americas Cup when Desmond gestured quietly for him to come across and have a look. Desmond silently indicated with his hand to where Sears should look up and true to form he belted at the top of his voice: 'Hey fellas – come and take a look at this.'

Desmond and Tubby each retreated to the cars and made every effort to get the party on its way before a crowd developed, which would have probably pleased the proprietor of the medicine shop no end. Subsequently, Tubby had many occasions to drive up and down this road from Singapore and always looked out in horror for the great medicine man's shop front at Kelapa Sawit, to see that the dreadful picture of the treated bottoms was still there.

Soon they were entering the lovely town of Johore Bahru, passing the huge *Istana* of the *Sultan* of Johore. Unfortunately the old man was on his death bed by then, but apparently in his heyday before the war he carried a Luger pistol in the glove compartment of his Lagonda, and was known to shoot at the tyres of anyone who dared to overtake him when he was out driving round the roads of his state of Johore.

25

AT LAST – AN END TO SIX MONTHS
OF HOTEL LIVING

Back at Singapore while trying to write up his notes on the trip round the Federation, things were hotting up on the three subsidiaries as Sears Wilson-Ingraham prepared to depart up to Hong Kong to see Frank Hill on progress there.

On the matter of the new subsidiary in Singapore and Malaya, Jim Kevlin and Sears seemed to be set on having the base in Singapore, and they were starting to look for an office in one of the big buildings on the front at Collyers Quay. Before being able to define, or get into, the role of the hander-over of the UK territory of Singapore and Malaya to the new management of the new international subsidiary, Tubby was trying to think about the vast number of territories he had to get round on behalf of the UK subsidiary.

He had fitted in a trip to the Borneo territories with Abe le Roux on his farewell to these lovely parts of old empire. He was beginning now to think about which of his export territories would require his attention first when he picked up remarks by Sears after being in touch with Ken Page in Thailand where the subsidiary was well ahead. It appeared that Ken Page was a none too friendly, abrasive Australian who had his toothpaste factory up and running, but was giving Sears no end of stick since he was not able to sell to his production capacity because of UK Colgate toothpaste coming into Thailand from Burma.

However, the first matter was to see Abe le Roux off on his way to the UK via Hong Kong, Honolulu, and the States, since he was determined to see New Orleans before moving on north to the head office in New York.

The genial Charlie Fell, another director at Harpers who had been through the Jap camps, was also the director responsible for the Messes which housed the young up and comings. He had agreed that Tubby could move in with the Dutch chap at Amber Mansions once Abe left and as to transport, Tubby also agreed that he would buy the green Zephyr Ford car from Abe to help make his departure smoother.

The very next day after paying for it he arrived at Harpers office to find Abe in a stew because the Zephyr had disappeared from outside the Amber Mansions flat in the night. However, they soon heard that it had been found beyond the Padang on the Esplanade, with its bonnet up. Apparently, whoever stole it must have thought the gods or the spirits were against him, because it had a tendency for the thick wired battery lead to spring just loose enough to break contact. Whoever had taken it away had opened the bonnet but had not been able to see anything wrong at all because the lead would look as though it was still in place.

The Zephyr was of the original Ford Consul Zephyr range with relatively small diameter, but very large spongy, tyres and big American style bench seat at the front. The dashboard was a bit like an airplane cockpit, except for the steering column and gear stick. Later Tubby was to find that the fat bulbous wheels at the front very readily got out of balance and as the speed came up towards 60 it used to go through the sound barrier in terms of a great shudder coming up through the steering column.

Having had a final swing round the federation on that rather hilarious trip with Sears, Abe had the final good fortune of bidding farewell to Singapore and the east in the middle of the colourful Chinese Moon Festival. With the circumstances prevailing in China under Chairman Mao, ex-patriate Chinese through Malaya, and particularly in Singapore, had become more traditional than back in China. Perhaps it was a reaction to the fact that they could not readily return, which was something Tubby spotted as having a commercial implication which could be to their advantage.

Singapore at that time was a particularly wild and voluble

place with legions of British Farina Austins as taxis driven by taxi men who looked half-hyped on drugs, with a cigarette in one hand and the other on the motor horn. This they pressed continually as they went round and round the roads, main squares and junctions, often bouncing off one another like dodgem cars. Visitors from up-country in those days, once across the causeway and into Singapore, were quite terrified by the traffic conditions.

Whatever might be going on back in China, the Chinese of Singapore really went to town with their festivals, and the Moon Festival particularly, the fifteenth day of the eighth moon. It was held that it originated with the birth of the Ming Dynasty, to celebrate the overthrow in 1360 of the Mongol Yuan Dynasty set up by Kublai Khan, so the historic and nationalistic overtones made it even more exciting. The rebels against the previous dynasty would pass messages in small round cakes, or by lanterns, so the Moon Festival burst upon Singapore with much light from lanterns and with stalls down the streets selling sweet Moon cakes. Even Abe, the good Afrikaaner, had really taken to the Chinese and other peoples of the east and took Tubby on a walk down Northbridge Road and beyond among the street *wayangs* which seemed to go on all night. *Wayang* is actually a Malay word for 'theatre', but at Moon Festival time the real traditional Chinese theatre was on view in set-up theatres in the streets with all their colour, the smoking joss-sticks, the crashing of the cymbals and the high pitched dialogue. It was a joyous festival time to enjoy, and Tubby had yet to experience the impact of Chinese New Year as celebrated on this island with over a million and a half Chinese.

Abe's departure was almost within a day of the departure of Sears to Hong Kong, but before he left, one of his cohorts from New York International arrived, called José Gomes, and as his name suggests, he was of Latin American background. Poor José was known to Jim Kevlin from his Panama days, and he worked in International Advertising, which took him all around the world on aeroplanes. He was terrified of flying in them. When they went out to the Singapore airport to see

162

Sears and José off, they had to tank him up in the bar until the third and last urgent call, at which he would put his head down and go screaming out across the tarmac and into the plane to a seat which had been organised for him away from any window. He must have been getting paid big money out of New York to counter the stress.

One of the main reasons for José Gomes' visit to Singapore was to check out the relatively new office in Singapore for Grant Advertising, which was an American agency which specialised in overseas locations and hence was used by Colgate with its 44 subsidiaries round the world. The Grant office in Singapore had been set up and was being run by a man called Tom Glaze from UK who had flown Spitfires in the war and was very extrovert.

The media situation in those days in Singapore was quite limited but developing, and certainly not yet into television. The *Straits Times* was the dominant paper throughout Singapore and the Federation, and was in English and run as a British newspaper. Commercial radio was developing and people like Tom Glaze were getting into the action, giving prominence to himself and his own Grant advertising, which would help in buying good media slots for his advertising clients.

There was a Malay paper which was written in Jawi, the Malay script which looked like Arabic. There were Chinese newspapers, though by far the most important media was the cinema, and for the Europeans there was a great variety of films showing to choose from and late shows from 8 p.m. onwards.

The Hong Kong film industry was very dynamic and provided a constant stream of films for the locals, together with the Indian film industry. Legions of locals would flock to midnight shows with frightening story lines and characters – one of the great favourites being the *Orang Minyak*. This was the 'Oily Man' who would cover himself in slippery oil and slither into people's houses, cause mayhem, and could always slip away because no one could grab him and restrain him. The Malay words *Orang* (man) and *Utang* (wild) give the name to

163

the celebrated large ape with the ugly face in the Borneo territory – the orang utang.

Tom Glaze was to prove a very useful advertising agent in the development of ideas for working out substitutes for the lack of a strong single media. He was undoubtedly the original 'Mr Fixer'. Tubby was a great one for local food and having sampled all the dishes in Iraq, he was very keen to sample real Chinese food as compared with the stuff available in UK. Tom Glaze was a great devotee of Chinese food and helped Tubby no end – particularly on the matter of chop sticks, which he soon mastered. His dictum was: 'Eight hundred million Chinese throughout the Far East can't be wrong with regard to chop sticks being the definitive eating tool.' Without doubt, Chinese food tasted better when eaten with these celebrated sticks. After a particularly good eating sensation on the taste buds, Tubby wanted to write down the Chinese characters for the dish so that he could show them in order to obtain the same again. This caused great mirth to Chinese friends who explained that the characters were the chef's own name for his dish, something like 'Dragons' Wings' or 'Mandarins Magic'.

Shortly after Sears' departure with José Gomez, the occasion of Abe's departure from Singapore airport was the occasion for a great thrash out at Paya Lebar and for Tubby to move into the flat at Amber Mansions, which was a great relief after the hotel living he had experienced since arriving in Baghdad in April.

This mess flat of Harpers' on the third floor of Amber Mansions was really quite well appointed and very handily located, being on the fringe of central Singapore, near the start of the big main thoroughfare of Orchard Road which headed out of town towards the Causeway eventually. At this junction where Stamford Road ended and the big Orchard Road thoroughfare started, there was the landmark building of those days, the Cathay hotel, which was really a rather ugly-looking grey concrete high-rise slab, but it did have squash courts in the basement below the parking lots which occupied the lower floors.

From the top of the building there was a magnificent view of

Singapore, particularly of the great new Nicol Highway sweeping across where the old Kalang Airport used to be on the bay. This led on to Geylang and the road east to Changi. Tubby was soon to find out that some of the best Indian curry in Singapore was available at weekends at the back of the Cathay building where an Indian set up his stoves from under a canvas lean-to on the outer car park. On Sundays particularly, the 'curry tiffin' was the favourite lunch with the *putehs* who would be seen driving their cars round into the car park and away with a series of stacked pans with each part of the curry meal, to be brought back later, once the food had been consumed nice and hot.

Amber Mansions were but a stone's throw across from the Cathay in a small road off at the junction with Orchard Road, and as the car turned off Orchard Road the Presbyterian Church of Singapore was directly opposite on spacious ground, where the road did a 90-degree turn. Amber Mansion apartments were on the right, and there were no buildings opposite with rising parkland to Fort Canning Road and the YWCA above. Being a small back road it was possible to leave the cars parked out at the front though there was a lock-up round the back of the apartments for each flat. On the ground floor there was a Jewish couple with their *Mezuzah* on the door post, and a fairly well-off Eurasian couple in the flat above, with the Harper mess flat on the top floor.

Coming in the door of the flat there was a kitchen area to the right with a catwalk across at the back to the servants' quarters, where the in-house Cookie and Amah lived, and the other Chinese couples serving the other apartments.

The coat hanging entrance quickly went into a lounge area and on to the open verandah which also had two ceiling fans. As standard for open verandas such as this, there were the huge heavy chicks (green blinds) made of lacquered bamboo and rattan to roll down against the tropical downpours or half down against the tropical sunshine. On the lovely sunny mornings it was nice to have them partly down with fans on slow turn. A bedroom was off the lounge and Tubby's was to the rear, with that most important item *in situ* bought from

Abe le Roux, the three-quarter horsepower Westinghouse air-conditioner, which he had had fitted into the lower part of the bedroom window, as was standard practice. On the outside you would look up at buildings and see these huge metal vane appendages sticking out with their compressors pounding away at night when one had the air conditioner on. It helped keep one's sanity to have part of the evenings cut off from intense humidity, and it kept camera and films from being overgrown with green mould.

When one is aged 27 everybody getting on towards 50 looks terribly old, and Tubby was rather taken aback when a rather elderly and humble servant, the resident Cookie, appeared down at his car on arrival with his gear from Adelphi Hotel. Cookie was bare footed, with khaki shorts and a short-sleeved T-shirt, and made to stumble up the stairs with one of the bags from the car. The cautious and quizzical expression on his face seemed to be saying: 'I wonder what this one is going to be like?' He broke into a nervous, reactive smile when Tubby made to relieve him of the case but stood his ground on master-servant roles.

Tubby was to find out there was a pecking order, almost a sort of caste system among the Chinese, and the Hainanese, in these Cookie-boy roles, were at the bottom of the heap. After having an Afrikaaner and a Dutchman as masters for the last year or so, Cookie seemed to be excessively humble and servile then as was their normal manner. This had heightened Tubby's anxiety as to how he might get on in the matter of adjusting to life with a Dutchman.

From the great wartime sentiments of Allies being altogether, with the Dutch Queen having been in the UK as a refugee from the occupied Netherlands, he had been somewhat taken aback to hear round the Singapore Cricket Club that the chaps generally referred to the Dutch community in Singapore as 'square heads'. This primarily related to their tough, hard nosed attitudes towards business and he was to find this out for himself. However, Sander van Marken came to be one of the most anglified Dutchmen in Singapore. Being a tremendously enthusiastic rowing man, he was mostly camped out down at

166

the Rowing Club in the Dockland area of Singapore on the Inner Roads.

The hard-nosed Dutch attitude manifested itself in that Sander van Marken did not get paid anything like the British ex-pats, and had a four year duty to do before getting home to his widowed mother and family. It was quite a perk to be in a well-appointed Harpers mess like this, and he came back for lunch readily from the office of Mirandolle-Voûte which was a similar Dutch import-export house to Harper Gilfillan, with its parent company in Plantation House in the City of London. Sander's company also had a parent company office back in Hooft Straat, or one of those prestigious business streets, in that lovely city of Amsterdam alongside the canals with their tall trading house buildings which date back to earliest beginnings of Dutch East Indies. His father had done a seven year tour in Batavia (Jakarta) in the 1920s and his older siblings had been born in the former Dutch East Indies, therefore Sander's four year tour in the 1950s was an improvement.

Since Harper Gilfillan had the agency for the Heinz range of products, Tubby was able to follow the habits started by Abe by having lots of dented tins on the cheap for their pantry, which provided variety for an instant lunch of something on toast, or whatever. Tubby liked to come home from time to time for lunch in order to get away from the pattern which was developing with Jim Kevlin, who in the main wanted to walk round into the various eating houses in Raffles Place, in order to watch the constant toing and froing of the Chinese office girls in their remarkable cheong-sam tunic dresses with the ample slits up the side. It looked all wrong to see a European female trying to carry off these garments, since they simply just did not have the shape for which this particular garment was designed.

After such a prolonged stay in hotels, it took time to get used to the silent presence of dear old Cookie after the first shock on Tubby's arrival in the late afternoon before van Marken had come back. As mentioned, old Cookie insisted on carrying one of the bags up the stairs and, once he had settled stuff in his room, Tubby sat down in one of the armchairs in the lounge area to take in the scene and revel in what was going to be his own place in this marvellous hurly burly noisy place of Singapore. His reveries were sharply invaded by the sudden realisation that silent Cookie was down at his feet starting to remove his shoes as though it were simple routine behaviour towards the new *tuan besar*, having found his beloved Baghdad slippers on unpacking for him in the bedroom.

Tubby had heard about these things amongst the older hands who had been many years in the East, and on the way through Ipoh he had heard comments in the club about a very renowned GP up in Perak whose faithful retainer did just this. In no way could he take on board the thought of a 27-year-old young fellow from the UK having Cookie take off his shoes for him at the end of a tired and weary day. In the nicest way possible he was able to get over to Cookie that the shoe routine would not be essential to their relationship. With the heat and the humidity of Singapore, shoes and socks were certainly the first things to be disposed of for the standard footwear of the flipflop available anywhere in the whole world from the Bata shoe shops, or market stalls.

Cookie seemed almost dumb at times, but once Tubby entered quietly to stand at the kitchen area open to the back, there was a stream of noise with he and Amah chattering away to the other Cookies and Amahs in voluble Chinese and often much hilarity. This contrasted with the rather solemn face he would adopt at breakfast when silently he lay beside Tubby's right hand a little writing pad with a pencil. Cookie had already sussed out who was the prime occupant on behalf of Harper Gilfillan, with Sander van Marken as the guest resident once Abe had gone. Tubby was the one to get the pencil and the writing pad. Sander informed him that this was for the shopping which Cookie was to do during the day, and particularly for the ingredients for their meal at night. Any appearance at lunchtime usually meant something out of the store of Heinz bent or dented tins from the Harpers' godown.

With the humidity of the climate, one had to start each day with a fresh set of clothing throughout and when Tubby went into his bedroom at night he found that, without anything being said at all, all the clothing put off the night before was neatly laundered and ironed and laid on his bed so that the boss man could see that all was done and up to scratch. Not only were the items of clothing duly cleaned on a daily basis but the whole flat was kept absolutely spick and span with shoes cleaned as and when necessary.

It transpired that the eating habits of the Dutchman and the Afrikaaner had been mundane and certainly lacking in variety, and Tubby began to explore with Cookie possibilities of something at breakfast other than set boiled egg, some cereal, and toast and marmalade. Having got favourable reactions from Cookie concerning scrambled egg and poached egg at breakfast, Tubby asked about things like toad-in-the-hole and steak and kidney pie for an evening meal, and perhaps a mixed grill. At the mention of these things, Cookie's solemn face melted into a great beaming countenance as he nodded readily in confirmation of having much experience of these particular dishes being mentioned.

With Sander involved in his rowing club, and Tubby increasingly getting involved in the rugby scene, they tended towards a later meal after 8 p.m., because darkness came suddenly in Singapore on the equator and was complete by 7 p.m. The increasing range of meals in the evening was to delight Cookie who added his bit with vegetables and fresh fruit, for which the Chinese are known to be particularly good and can buy very well. The effect was that Sander began to appear in great anticipation at the evening meals and responded with relish to the introduction of ranges of cheeses to enliven the lunchtime situation beyond the dented tins from Harpers' godown.

To go with the cheeses, Tubby had automatically included cream crackers and water biscuits and celery sticks, and Sander introduced some of the lovely range of Dutch cheeses on to the paper pad for Cookie's daytime buying/shopping list. It was then that Tubby was introduced to the way the Dutch enjoyed their cheeses in that Sander simply took great pieces of the cheese and proceeded to devour them with knife and fork.

After the terrible tight regimen of work with no play during his period of hotel living in Baghdad, with working through the long siesta times from noon 'til four in the afternoon in the dry heat, he was somewhat overwhelmed by the scope for activities available to him in this wonderland of Singapore. He had very much wanted to maintain his flying lessons which he had not long started in the UK, before he went overseas, and had certainly had no opportunity in Iraq. However, the rugger season was getting going at the cricket club, with three games a week, the first team big match being on Saturday afternoon, and then state games according to peformance against other states.

The standard of rugger was very high because of the vast range of services people in Singapore and the Federation because of the Emergency. There was a very competitive interstate competition with Singapore playing Selangor, Perak and other States in the Federation, who had New Zealanders, Fijians, Tongans, Aussies, Scots, Irish and Welsh in their teams. There were many players who had been on the international UK scene or its fringes among the Servicemen who were picked for the state sides.

As mentioned earlier, it became a habit that Tubby's car did not seem to be able to get past the entrance of the cricket club once over the bridge from Collyer Quay, but he was terribly unfit from his prolonged stay in Iraq with no chance of any sporting activities whatsoever.

One of the up-and-coming young executives in the Harper office in Singapore had the same family name of Forbes, but no relationship whatsoever. While Tubby's parents and roots were definitely with the clans in Scotland, with their own named tartan, Hugh Forbes was a rugby product of the great school at Clifton near Bristol. As a very young chap, he played centre for London Counties in 1949 in that celebrated team which has actually beaten the Springbok tourists. Hugh had the ideal powerful build for a centre three quarter for punching holes through for wingers to run-in, or for flattening out any movement developing by the opposition. He took it upon himself to get Tubby fit for involvement in the rugby scene and had him running round the padang for starters.

170

While a public school background was certainly not Tubby's scene it was a fairly dominant factor amongst the chaps who frequented the cricket club, and getting involved in the rugby scene soon brought Tubby an increasingly wide range of friends. Even Sander van Marken, as one of the most anglified Dutchmen in Singapore with his rowing club activities, was heard on occasions to say, 'sports and chaps, this is rather jolly good.' This became quite a catch phrase between the pair of them and they began to develop a good rapport, which helped no end to life in Amber Mansions being very pleasant indeed.

26

BURMA – THE ENIGMA

While things were hotting up on the new subsidiary front, Tubby was desperately trying to work out a trip to Ceylon with his hat on as export rep for the UK subsidiary since Ceylon was to be a high potential part of his territory. However, there was the matter of Burma which did not encourage any visitors of any kind, particularly when nothing had happened there since a rather massive order of toothpaste had gone in almost two years ago. Now that Ken Page with the Thai subsidiary was producing toothpaste for his market there, he was finding trouble because a ready supply of UK Colgate toothpaste kept appearing in Thailand, so it was ordered by Sears from Bangkok that Tubby, as a priority, get himself over to Burma by fair means or foul to find out what exactly was going on.

Fortunately, there was a Consulate for the Union of Burma in Singapore, and he was able to have his passport stamped at a fee of 19.50 Straits Dollars for a three month entry visa, but with the period of his stay to be strictly limited to one week and entry by land route not permitted. Plans had been building up towards a trip to Ceylon before the end of the year and since they were now entering October 1958 it was decided that Tubby should plan to get into Rangoon somewhere about the 17th.

In the meantime, Tubby had progressed in fitness towards having a game of rugby and, duly kitted out in his yellow and black wasp-like Singapore Cricket Club jersey, had his first game with a lower level team on a Monday evening on the *Padang* in the shadow of the government buildings and the great clock tower. By half-time he really understood what mad dogs and Englishmen really meant, when playing rugby in the tropical heat and humidity of Singapore, as near to the equator as one can get at sea level!

His jersey was so saturated in perspiration that it had become twice its normal length, his rugger boots felt as though they were filled with hot water and at one stage in the second half, he thought his time had come to quietly lie down and die. Somehow he kept going, but the presence of the huge clock on the building overlooking the *Padang* only added to the agony since he could see how much longer there was to play before he could retreat into the pavilion.

Once back in the changing rooms – showered in cold water – he sat with the others enveloped in a towel round his waist and with a large flagon of the famous Anchor beer from Singapore Brewery under Dutch supervision. This seemed the obvious thing to do – replace the gallons of liquid lost during the game, but even after an hour there did not seem to be much point in getting dressed yet since the old perspiration pores seemed to be working at full capacity still. Anyway, he had got through his first rugby match on the equator and there were more to come, and besides there were ample opportunities for squash in this marvellous place to help maintain fitness.

Matters were moving ahead at a fair rate on the business front and whether he liked it or not, he was finding that Jim Kevlin's appearance and rather accentuated American accent from Texas were not making it easy for him to establish commercial relationships. Most of those in high positions in the Foreign Exchange Control Departments within the Federation and Singapore were the last of the old British civil service tradition, and his voice alone would visibly cause them to wince. The legal system was also British and the accountancy firms were overseas offices of the majors in the UK. Picking up Tubby's accountancy background, Jim had him involved in recruiting accounting staff for the new subsidiary and was taking him to legal and commercial meetings as a Brit to match the colonial Brits.

However, Tubby's mind was more concentrated now on getting to Burma, and Jim Kevlin could not particularly object to that since the pressure was coming from Sears out of his concern for what was happening to the new subsidiary in Thailand. Tubby had booked his flight out on BOAC for the morning of 16th October on a Britannia prop-jet plane they were now using on the Far East routes. They were called Whispering Giants because of their quieter engine sounds against the old piston engines with their flaming exhausts. They were indeed lovely planes and quite elegant in appearance, but jokes were beginning to fly around about their performance and poor time-keeping so that it was becoming difficult to stand up in the British camp and say three cheers for BOAC.

Tubby's flight on the Britannia out of Singapore was due to leave at 6 a.m. or thereabouts for its return to the UK and on checking on the 15th, there were messages that the Britannia had got delayed somewhere along the route at Dubai. When it came to the morning of the 16th he went into the Singapore office in anticipation of a call from BOAC as to when the Britannia had arrived and been turned round, and would be ready to set off again back towards the UK. Tubby left his bags packed at home ready and the call came in the late afternoon saying to be at Paya Lebar for take-off at 6 p.m.

A taxi was ordered to come to Amber Mansions to take him out to the airport, and he dashed back in a tropical downpour and darted into the flat where Cookie was ready to help him stumble down the stairs with his case and small portable typewriter. He waited in the small downstairs entrance for the taxi to appear and Cookie – ready for all eventualities – had brought down his good and faithful Singapore umbrella, which was standard equipment for all people in Singapore. These were of paper, bamboo and sticks, all heavily lacquered and sewn together so that they would open out with a crackly noise as the sticky paper unfolded. They were painted green down their bars so when they were closed up they looked like green rolling pins and once open they had a beautiful network of handmade spokes. They were most effective since the tropical rain came straight down and if you could keep yourself firmly underneath them, they diverted most of the floods to one side

174

or the other. As Cookie opened the umbrella, two enormous cockroaches with waving antennae fell out. These nasty, enormous things, the size of a finger, were an ever-present feature of life in the tropics, but without batting an eyelid Cookie gave both kicks with his bare feet before they could think of opening up and taking off or scuttling into a corner. Tubby literally fled from the spectacle into the taxi, his *barang* (baggage) thrown in after him. The taxi made good time to the airport through the tropical downpour with the driver's hand incessantly hitting the hooter button as he bounced in and out of the traffic and flood water.

In those elevated days Tubby was still travelling first class and once they were boarded and moving off away down to the end of the huge runway for take-off, it appeared that the only passengers were himself and one other chap, both seated in the first class compartment which was then located beyond a curtained bulkhead at the rear where the huge graceful tail unit of the Britannia was attached. Tubby was seated at the very rear and with the curtain undrawn between the first and the rest of the plane, he could see right down to the galley and then the cockpit at the far end where the front of the Britannia came to a narrow point and the whole plane looked like a folded paper dart.

They taxied down for the take-off as the rapid turn to darkness in the tropics began to happen and the captain came on the intercom to explain what they already knew – that the Britannia was twelve hours late, but because of this they were going to have to touch down at Kuala Lumpur for a large number of ex pats heading home who, because of the on-off circumstances through the day, had not in the end come down to Singapore to pick up the flight there.

At this announcement, Tubby began to run through in his mind the various factors concerning the Kuala Lumpur airport. Firstly, it was an old fighter strip at the back of the town with a small airport building, with a six foot wire fence outside a peri-track which only went down one side anyway. Secondly, the runway was not very long, and thirdly, a novel feature was the fact that a railway line ran along the main approach landing

175

end from the south, and for some historic reason the railway line was up on an embankment!

The other novel feature about this ex-wartime strip which acted as Kuala Lumpur airport was the fact that it had no lighting and when occasions like this occurred, large crude metal oil lamps with big oily wicks sticking out of the spouts were placed down each side of the runway and lit by runners with flaming torches. It was not long before the Britannia was up from Singapore to Kuala Lumpur in the darkness of the night and as they started their approach it was obvious that the captain had been putting all these factors about the airport into his mind as well.

First there was the slow down as the long, thin nose wheel and the rather unique main undercarriages of the Britannia, with four small wheels on end of long telescopic forks, came down from the near-engine nacelles. Then Tubby could feel the braking effect of all the flaps coming down as the plane was set in a steep descent altitude similar to when a plane is coming in for an aircraft carrier landing. The Britannia did not have an arrester hook and there were no wires across the landing zone at Kuala Lumpur. By the rate of descent it was like being in a lift rather than flying on to a runway and he could imagine the big blip over the Captain's head which read: 'Thinks – there is a railway line on an embankment before we touch the end of the runway!'

As they hit the tarmac the whole plane jarred as the telescopic wheel gear went up to its maximum and then the nose wheel must have been bent nearly to breaking point as it took the full pressure of the reverse thrust of the four great prop-jet engines, and even the Whispering Giant began to roar.

What added to the hair-raising experience was the fact that Tubby's metal encased lightweight portable typewriter which had been on the floor by his feet took off and went down the full length of the walkway and ended up in the galley area with a clump. When they eventually came to a halt it was obvious that they had not become impaled by the six foot wire peri-fence. The Britannia began to taxi round towards the airport building and he looked out to see the oil lamps still flickering on each side of runway – in spite of reverse thrust.

They were soon about half filled with families and other passengers, and one could feel the relief in the chatter that they were glad at last to be on a BOAC plane heading home. Soon the great giant began to taxi out to the end of the runway for takc-off. As it straightened up, the pilot obviously began to go through the take-off routine before the propeller noises then died down to a regular vacuum cleaner noise. Instead of the roar for take-off, the intercom came on to announce that lights showing in the cockpit indicated that all was not well with the landing gear and the braking systems in one of the four wheels on either side, so they would have to taxi back to the airport building and have an engineer see what he could do.

After two hours they were informed that a hydraulic braking system had gone on one of the eight wheels across the two main undercarriages, and so that they could get on their way the engineers had isolated off hydraulics from the faulty wheel. Soon the great four engines were revved up and the blades put to full pitch and there was no problem taking off since this plane could certainly get off the ground readily with its tricycle carriage attitude without having to run a third of a way down the runway to get the tail up. Tubby wondered if the oil lamps had been blown out one by one as the plane roared off into the darkness.

As he flew on through the night towards an estimated arrival at Rangoon Airport now at about 2.00 to 2.30 a.m. his mind turned to comments on the shambles which had become the Burma of that time. Following idependence, the left of centre stance taken by the Burmese meant the British were told to clear off quickly as soon as the hostilities with the Japanese came to an end. Tubby was told that the only vehicles he would see were those left over by British armed forces and that the country was divided now into unofficial states, or bandit territories, run by particular interests such as the Karens who controlled that part of the country in the upper reaches of the Salween River along the north western borders of Thailand,

177

the fierce Shans in the border regions to the north and east of China, and of course the drug barons who ran the golden triangle which made up the upper reaches of the Mekong River touching Burma, Thailand and Laos, and the Yunnan Province of China.

As Chiang Kai-shek and his Kuomintang, who once ran China before Chairman Mao and the long march, retreated off to Taiwan, a large remnant of Kuomintang, when cut off by Chairman Mao from the others, moved across into this lucrative golden triangle for opium growing on a large commercial scale. They ruthlessly organised the trade and geared-up the distribution channels for after the December/January harvest when even fast light aircraft are used to transport the raw opium which converts to morphine and further refines into heroin.

In contrast with all these negative aspects to anticipate and cope with on his arrival, he went on to think more of the mysterious Burma which he heard about as a child and at school. This incredible country was part of empire, and known as the 'Rice Bowl of the Far East' for by climate and fertility it is ideally suited to the growing of rice. Having grown up as a child in a place like Birkenhead, he could not help but be aware of all the great ships which came and went to particular parts of the world, and the individual flags and colour schemes of the various shipping lines. His mother had a cousin from Scotland who had attained the rank of First Mate with the Paddy Henderson Shipping Line, which operated two well appointed passenger-cargo ships called the *Moulmein*, after one of the main port cities of Burma after Rangoon which is at the mouth of the other great river, the *Salween*, which was the name of the other ship.

These boats were beautifully appointed with black hull and black funnels and white superstructure, and from visits of Cousin Jimmy to his mother, and childhood visits on to the big ships themselves at their birth in Birkenhead docks' West Float, he knew of Rangoon as being the fairest city in the Far East, with great gardens and lakes; of the Road to Mandalay; of Burmese teak and the wooden boxes of Burmese cheroots –

178

cigars – which were brought for his father. From this contact with these lovely big ships, even in wartime when they all became painted uniformly grey with guns on the bow, he had grown up with a great wonder of these places in the East. Here he was about to fly into Burma and see what it was like now, Rangoon, the beautiful, on the side waters by the Irrawaddy River.

Rangoon airport was some 20 miles out of Rangoon and since it was built as the staging post for the flying of resources into China and, in later war years, all the equipment necessary for the Burma campaign against the Japanese, it had then the longest runway in South East Asia. There was more to come than Tubby had anticipated as he disembarked from the plane at Rangoon Airport and saw a rather shambolic medium-sized bus was to be their transport over the 20 miles into Rangoon. The checking process was laborious and Tubby took this to be just part of general attitudes to life in Burma at that time, but eventually his entry visa was again stamped for his stay of one week's duration. By the time they got on to their bone shaker bus and started off into the dark, he was not aware at that time how long the journey would take and what it might be like, but the monsoon rain had started to come down in earnest. They got on their way.

It had been a very long day, and Tubby had actually begun to doze as the bus lurched along the uneven roads at a reasonably steady pace, but he came to his senses in a flash as the bus came to a jolty halt and heard the tense chatter of the driver as the bus door was pulled open by armed troops in tin hats and capes, since the tropical rain really was pouring down. Being less than six months away from his hair raising experiences with mobs during the revolutionary period in Iraq and thereafter, Tubby had developed a high degree of sensitivity to voice exchanges even when not familiar with the language. Other experienced overseas hands can recount how sounds of running feet, or just seeing people running, can act as alarm signal since in these places people don't readily run around unless there is a good reason for making haste.

It was a most weird sensation to hear voices increasing in

tension while trying to peer out through the rain-splashed windows into the limited light thrown back from the headlamps of the bus against the jungle on either side. Tubby was not sure if the driver had conveyed the fact that he was a routine bus taking passengers from the airport to Rangoon, but the rain-soaked troops with their guns did back off and the bus began to trundle again through the night along the uneven jungle-clad road.

The journey seemed to go on and on and the rain seemed to go on and on, when suddenly the bus was stopped again and once more they could see tin-helmeted rain-swept troops who were not likely to be in a very good humour. Again the exchange started with the driver and Tubby began having vivid recall of the film of Graham Greene's *The Quiet American* with Michael Redgrave, and Audie Murphy as the CIA man in Vietnam. This old, high-tension film covered the early 1950s years of the Vietnam situation, with Michael Redgrave as a two-timing pressman returning to Saigon from the major annual upcountry Cao Dai festival at Tay Ninh. They were having similar threatening ambush experiences as they headed back to Saigon and the film climaxed with carnage from a car bomb in the square in Saigon where the celebrated Continental Palace bar was located. At this stage, Tubby was not aware that within 18 months, he would be standing in that very same square in Saigon.

Listening hard in the semi-dark of the vehicle against rain bouncing off the top, he could only gauge once again what was going on up front by the tone of the voices. All of a sudden he wondered if they were to be taken out and lined up to be shot by these rebels, or whoever they were. Just as suddenly they backed off for the bus to get on its grinding way again. Through someone on the bus who had some knowledge of Burmese, a picture began to emerge of a revolution, military coup, or whatever, and Tubby thought to himself, Baghdad, here we go again.

After what seemed an eternity, they could feel that the bus seemed to be on some sort of more formed road and, through the rain swept windows, it would appear that they were beginning to enter Rangoon itself. Before long they were being unloaded at that monumental edifice of colonialism which was called the Strand hotel. It was so late and Tubby was so worn out by then from his long flight since leaving Singapore that he did not take in too much other than there were rats scurrying around an enormous hall-like lounge area which had great murals on the wall, visible in the semi-light from ornate chandeliers from a past era of splendour.

Before leaving twelve hours late, he had been able to fire off cables to Ben Henry, his agent, who ran the local office in Rangoon for Muller and Phipps, and had arranged for Ben to meet with him at the Strand hotel on the next morning which would be a Saturday. The habits of the Raj were apparently deeply ingrained in that the working week seemed to still involve a Saturday morning with a Sunday close down. He wondered what manifestations there would be in Rangoon of the apparent coup which had the troops out in the countryside stopping their bus in the early hours.

The next morning, the Strand hotel appeared to be an oasis of non-activity as compared with the revolution Tubby had recently experienced, or perhaps things were going on outside on the streets.

He went into the huge lounge area and sat at one of the numerous tables to take in the incredible scene of this place, now in decay. The Strand hotel was certainly the meeting point for any who were in Burma for business or cultural reasons. He became aware of German voices from a group of people at a table across the room in very up-market European suits sitting round one large gentleman smoking a big cigar. He was obviously the leader in the group and Tubby suddenly realised he was none other than Erhardt – the renowned economic miracle worker of the West German *Wirtschaftswunder* started under the guiding hand of that unsmiling elder statesman Dr Konrad Adenauer who had become chancellor of West Germany after the Berlin airlift had galvanised the post-war European scene this side of the Iron Curtain. Erhardt and his cohorts appeared to be in animated conference about what to do next after what had been happening in the night before.

181

Tubby did not know anything about Burmese history other than it had been pink on the map as part of the empire and had been the scene of tortuous fighting against the Japanese with the purpose of keeping them from getting to India and trying to keep Chiang Kai-Shek in the war via the Burma Road before it was cut. General Slim had been a main figure and that strange Lawrence-like character Orde Wingate with his Chindits had been part of the post-war legend.

It was certain that his knowledge or wartime memories did not include any awarenes of a patriotic war-like Burmese race. Therefore, he was most intrigued by the huge wall paintings round the lounge of heroic scenes which had as the centre figure a Burmese patriate in military uniform which featured a large military cap rather of the type preferred by Russian generals.

When Ben Henry appeared on schedule the poor man was immediately bombarded with questions about these patriotic paintings, and apparently this was none other than General Aung San who led Burma on the road to independence from Britain, and who was obviously regarded as a great heroic figure who would have led Burma on to great things if he had not been assassinated, resulting in Burma's descent into the utter economic chaos which was all there was to see in October 1958.

Because of the chaotic situation in Burma with regards to trade, the Muller and Phipps office in Rangoon could certainly not support an ex-patriate presence, nor would this be worthwhile, so dear old Ben Henry was the manager of their office in Rangoon. Ben was anglo-Indian with a bald head and a fringe of grey hair round the edge. With his glasses up front and without the remaining hair round the edges he would be not unlike the Mahatma Gandhi of India.

The interest in the murals and all the questions about Burma helped to break the ice and establish some sort of relationship and Tubby was interested to hear what Ben Henry could relate about the times when General Aung San had been assassinated to the present moment. Ben tried to explain that, to the best of his knowledge, it appeared that the army and a General Ne

Win had taken over the country with the object of restoring a kind of socialist form of normality out of the chaos of corruption which prevailed. The General's proclamations talked of a start to unify the country once again instead of the states-within-states situation prevailing, with some organised by Karens, or Shans, or exiled Kuomintang Chinese, and other local bandits in particular parts.

Even with the very limited time available by his entry permit, Tubby had fondly hoped he might make the train journey up-country to Mandalay to see all the mysterious shrines and temples on the way, but he was gently informed that even without the intervention of General Ne Win and his army, signs at the railway station usually intimated that trains would leave for Mandalay as and when there might be a clear track all the way and no troubles from local war-lords.

No one need be hungry in a place like Burma since rice grew anywhere and everywhere but it certainly wasn't exported any more as in the pre-war days when it was renowned as the 'Rice Bowl of the East'. Indeed, the famous Burmese teak was priced out of world markets too, in that taxes were levied by the various bandits as it passed downstream through their areas (as on the Rhine in long ago days) so that by the time it reached Rangoon to be shipped abroad, it was beyond the economic price ranges on the world market.

As mentioned previously, it was always good to establish early good relationships with people like Ben Henry by showing lively interest in Rangoon and Burma and all that it had been before in its past glory. It was resolved that they would go to his office and have a look at the facts and figures so that Tubby could find out about past huge orders for toothpaste which had come in from the UK for the Burmese to clean their teeth with. On Sunday shut-down day, it was agreed Ben would take him on a grand tour of the sights of Rangoon and the surrounding areas since he confirmed that the streets seemed to be normal by Rangoon standards. In contrast with the troops they met out in country the night before, taxis were waiting ready outside the Strand and Tubby saw with his own eyes what he'd been told – all the vehicles were predominantly leftovers from the British at the end of the war, and somehow they were being kept going by fair means or foul.

The level of dilapidation had to be seen to be believed, with scaffolding hanging half off many buildings since their repair work had been given up long ago. Most appalling was to notice that the huge monsoon drains on the scale of those seen in Singapore were all filled with rubble and debris and thrown away bits of vehicles.

While in the business area they were able to get to Ben's office, and it was noticeable that most other streets were greatly choked by the fact that there were traders' stalls on the pavements and beyond, down both sides of the streets. Indeed, Ben confirmed that more trade was now done on the streets outside than inside any shops which still managed to keep their doors open.

Ben had been most intrigued to hear of Tubby's family having had past shipping connections with Burma and indeed he well remembered the days when the port of Rangoon was one of the major ports of the Far East with the great liners and boats coming in and out. From the exterior, the office building had been very similar to those from the colonial days in Singapore, but for the decay and lifts which had ceased to work a long time ago, so they made their way to the third floor up the stairs. Inside was like entering a time capsule since furnishings and decor resembled old offices in Liverpool which Tubby visited in the Albany buildings near to the old Cotton Exchange.

As they left the office at the end of the morning and Ben was to see him off in a taxi back to the hotel, Tubby commented that all the taxi men, with one elbow out of the car window, were smoking Burmese cheroots, which he thought must indicate that they are about ten a penny, or certainly abundant enough for everyone to smoke. Ben laughed at this and asked if he would like to see what was in them. Before he could say anything, Ben had got hold of one from the taxi man and took the lovely Burmese cheroot in his hands and snapped it in half to reveal that inside was nothing but chopped stalks from tobacco leaves. These stalks were then rolled in thick outer leaf so that they looked like a good cheroot as far as Tubby could see, but they must have been a powerful smoke. Tubby then made sure that he took Ben with him when he went to buy some good quality Burmese cheroots for himself.

Back at the Strand hotel there was an air of tension about but certainly nothing resembling Baghdad in the first few days of the Revolution, and indeed the week that followed. However, he did find out from reception that Erhardt and his West German cohorts had gone off to the airport for their Lufthansa plane to clear out, obviously aware that Burma should be left alone for a while.

While at lunch, Tubby was aware that there was a table of Brits over in a corner who didn't seem the usual commercial types, so he went over to say hello. It turned out that they were engineers and maintenance staff of BOAC who were there as part of the ongoing folklore surrounding the Britannia aircraft. In spite of the Rangoon airport runway being the longest in South East Asia, there was a Britannia in the paddy field at the end of the runway, having made initial touchdown but half way along the runway. The boys from BOAC had been there a few days now and reckoned it would take them at least a fortnight before they got the plane back out and on its legs again and then some more before it would be ready to fly off. They too were concerned as to what the new change in regime would eventually mean in terms of their being able to carry on and get the Britannia off and in service again.

It was generally agreed that the state of affairs on the streets of Rangoon at that time seemed to be safe for a walk about with the cine-camera, so he set off on foot making for the docks where he had heard that there was a concrete pyramid which was the result of a shipload of cement as aid from Russia. The cement had been unloaded on to the dockside to get the ship turned round and off again, and then the rains had come and so the pyramid of cement bags had become a permanent emblem of how not to run a country.

The dilapidated buildings, the state of the road surfaces and the drains, the vehicles which bounced along these roads and the vultures circling overhead, all confirmed the suspicion that the whole place had somehow muddled along from the day when wartime armed forces moved down for the fall of Rangoon on 3rd May 1945, and were then precipitously asked to go off home.

When he reached that part of delta which was the dock area, the water was black and the place seemed to be mainly silted up. He actually saw two fellows up to their armpits in this water pulling a net between them for fish which he could hardly think would be edible. He did see one or two uniquely shaped and carved wooden river boats which were probably being pressed into service again because of the general deterioration of anything mechanical and non-availability of spare parts. Tubby came to the conclusion that the people managed to keep going because nature had given Burma luxuriant crops and valuable raw materials and as long as people are reasonably clothed and fed, there is less inclination for mass uprisings, and besides there was practically nothing to be looted anyway if a mob should get going as he had seen in Baghdad.

Ben Henry appeared in the great hall of the Strand hotel on the Sunday morning looking extremely relaxed in a lovely loose long sarong. The ones in Burma appeared to be a bit more upmarket than the generally used sarong, the likes of which Tubby had adopted for bed-wear, and Burmese called them something which sounded like *lonjeen*. He was pleased that Tubby's complimentary remarks endorsed his relaxed attire.

Ben appeared to have given some thought to the grand tour they were to embark upon on this day off when all seemed still to be relatively normal round about Rangoon. Like most countries in these parts, there was a shift towards the left and the influence of Communism, but no armed insurgency like the situation in Malaya and in Indo-China which was probably due to the diverse warring factions which already existed in the country, who had plenty of opportunity for aggravation amongst themselves. Burma is the fabled country of the Buddha and his followers, and as if they didn't have enough temples and pagodas already the first viewing was the most recent pagoda on the outskirts of Rangoon called the New World Peace Pagoda. As the name belies, it was financed by Eastern Bloc money in order to show the friendly respect of Communism. It was a simple large round *wat* with the gold circular pointed top reaching up to the sky. The outer walls were still covered in scaffolding, but inside was an enormous cross-legged Buddha with all the usual trappings and decorations.

From there they went on to a great cleared area of vegetation in the centre of which was a huge hillock of uneven tufted grass which could easily have covered a rugby field. As they approached they came to a large ceremonial bell, the type usually seen outside Japanese temples, with a huge log hung horizontally with ropes attached for the swinging thereof to bang the end against this enormous ornate bell. Strangely enough, there was also a piece in English engraved on to this enormous bell telling that it was donated by Buddhists of Japan and had been brought by their delegates in 1956 for the great gathering, or synod, of world Buddhism.

Tubby confessed not to know much about Buddhism in great detail, but they appeared to have as many and varied denominations as does the Christian church, with the Chinese variety being particularly centred on ancestral worship. It would appear that when they have a world convention or synod of this type there must be a preference for meeting in a cave, because Ben then led him to the gates of one of the entrances into the mound and he could not believe his eyes at the extent of the interior. The whole thing was fitted out with rows and rows of seats all round the edge like a huge stadium with the large central oval area clear of seating, which gave prominence to the pairs of enormous gold covered pillars which supported the roof. The mind simply boggled at what it must have cost in this peculiar run-down country to have the meeting place ready for 1956. However, Burma was not only abundant in vegetation and the growing of crops, but was also well endowed with precious metals which were much in evidence in all the shrines they passed or looked upon dotted all over the place. They were all of the high-walled, circular type with central gold clad spires rising up into the sky.

As they drove on from the great artificial cave round the outer environs of Rangoon, Tubby noticed the dilapidated houses and peculiar great wooden framed hand carts which had wheels as big as those on ancient siege guns being man-handled by four at least. Additionally, there seemed to be a festival forthcoming because there were many pairs of people carrying rows of red lanterns on a great pole stretched from one shoulder to the next. Everywhere there were men doing their stint as Buddhist monks with heads shaven, saffron robes and their black alms bowls, and it did seem to be true that in this land everyone seemed to wear a smile.

Buddhism claims to be not so much a religion but a complete way of life, the followers observing the first precept of the Buddha which is to act for the welfare and happiness of all beings. It therefore followed that Buddhist monks are reluctant to become involved in such worldly things as politics, but now and again they do and they can assassinate such national heroes as the great General Aung San – possibly because his form of independence was going to be authoritative.

After the forebodings on the journey in from the airport in the rains of the night, the general state of affairs round Rangoon that day did little to indicate the convulsions that this country would go through subsequently. Aung San Sau Kyi, the daughter of General Aung San, ended up under house arrest in Rangoon some 30 years later (in spite of winning the Nobel Peace Prize) under the same General Ne Win, who was in the process of taking over at that very moment in 1958, and still running the country in one form or another, or certain segments of it.

Tubby and Ben Henry were getting on extremely well and his ongoing patter probably distracted Tubby as they drove along in the car from noticing exactly where they were going because Ben had cleverly kept the great Shwedagon Pagoda of Rangoon until the very last. As far as Tubby was concerned the car stopped close up at the front of what was a very massive entrance to something. The common guardians of many of the holy places were carved dragon-like dogs, unique to Burma, sitting on their haunches looking out at all who should come

188

near with their big teeth and dragon-like heads. They were called *chin the* (pronounced 'chin tey') and the two confronting them at this particular entrance were positively enormous, with a covered staircase leading upwards between them.

They mounted the stairway and emerged at the top on a huge platform area of shrines with beautifully inlaid stones. Tubby simply stared round taking in the sight of all the shrines which seemed to be without number, all round the edge. He could well believe the legend that the eight hairs of the Buddha were lodged in the base of the great pagoda showered with jewels, because all these mini-shrines just seemed to glitter and glint in the sunlight. But his eyes were soon taken – nay drawn – to the magnificence of the great gold Pagoda which rose from another circular base at a higher level above the platform to 300 feet into the azure sky.

It was like a great ornate bell which had been placed upside down on the great circular base with its handle tapering off gracefully and symmetrically to the ornate pinnacle on top. Its sheer size and presence and total encasement in gold leaf had one transfixed. The Great Wall of China is the one manmade object which can be seen from satellites far out in space, but Tubby proved to himself on a later high trans-flight over Rangoon in good conditions that this enormous and beautiful pagoda can also be seen from high up in the sky when one knows what one is looking for.

Soon Tubby came out of his trance and got his cine-camera working with the telephoto lens on the top and in no time he had to replace the film. Ben Henry soon joined in the act and held the camera so that Tubby could get some footage of himself at this great and magnificent centrepiece of life in Rangoon. It was indeed a centre of life in Rangoon with pilgrims and worshippers coming constantly all the time, with parents and children laying down their prayer mats and kneeling before whatever shrine was of particular appeal and interest to them. But like all holy places round the world, there are those who cash in on the pilgrims and there were numerous stalls selling flowers and other decorative items and even gold leaf which pilgrims could pay for and then carry up to craftsmen who were fixing the gold leaf to those parts where the gold cover was thinning.

Ben was insistent that they went on to the huge round next layer of the base, and Tubby was most amused to find that a gate one had to pass through into this higher area had in English, no less, a sign – 'Men Only'. Indeed, the sign was not unlike something at home at the entrance to a toilet facility. The whole area surrounding the site of the pagoda was high ground with magnificent trees and vegetation all round, and it was with some reluctance that he followed Ben down a similar laid staircase at the opposite side lined with ornate gold pillars. They emerged from between two more *chin the* into a garden area with two large oblong ponds on either side of the pathway leading away from the exit.

They partook of some refreshment looking back up at the magnificent pagoda and the placid green water of the two ornate ponds was occasionally rippled by the heads of the turtles which swam around in these ponds. The stall from which they had bought their refreshments also had round rice balls and Ben bought several of these, suggesting that Tubby stood with his cine-camera ready for when he tossed one of these rice balls into the placid water of the ponds.

Tubby was horrified to note that as soon as the rice ball landed on the green stretch of water it exploded into a frenzied activity as piranha-like fish literally demolished the ball as one looked at it. This was done several times for good film footage but it was obvious why these were not paddling pools, because if one's foot went into this water you would lift out a skeleton foot devoid of flesh. The turtles with their horny skin were able to swim around and enjoy the water unharmed.

The drive away from the pagoda was through magnificent parkland which even in its then state of neglect could be seen to have been very much part of the legend that Rangoon had been the fairest city of the East. At the far end of the park Ben stopped the taxi and suggested that Tubby got out and took one last look at the Shwedagon Pagoda, and indeed it was a magnificent sight across this great area majestically rising up into the sky, beautiful in its symmetry and flashing gold.

On his walk-about on the Saturday afternoon, Tubby had noted the fact that the stalls which littered the streets had fair quantities of his UK Colgate toothpaste and some Palmolive soap to boot. Arriving at Ben's office on the Monday morning with the realisation that he had three days in which to get to the bottom of what was going on, they worked out a strategy, and they would start by Ben introducing him to the sources from which those market traders obtained their toothpaste.

Tubby had found that in Singapore and Malaya the traders were predominantly Chinese, as were wholesalers and bigger level businessmen, so here in Rangoon and in Burma the Chinese *towkays* were a dominant factor in the handling of goods for the retail trade. Ben drew up a shortlist of those whom he, as Muller and Phipps, had dealt with when the last big load of toothpaste and some soap had come in 18 months to two years ago. The best way to get on terms with these Chinese was to eat with them and show an enthusiasm for their food, their customs and business acumen.

This was not difficult to Tubby since he really did like Chinese food and it was all such a new and a wonderful situation to be in, but he had not bargained for the bathhouses, massage parlours and 'other' places he would end up in over the next three hectic days as he integrated himself with the particular group of Teochew Chinese. They did indeed have the most widespread network of business connections through-out the Far East from their native area of China round Swatow which is up the coast from Hong Kong. Piece by piece he began to put together a picture which was centred on currency. He began to suss out that much of their jolly friendliness centred on the idea that he was Mr Colgate through whom they might get their hands on other big landings of toothpaste via Muller & Phipps. Though there was not the slightest hope of this, Tubby realised that it could be abundantly helpful if he let them believe that he might well be 'Mr Big' who could open the flood gates again!

The currency of Burma was Kyats (pronounced 'chats') and with the chaotic state of Burma, Kyats were valueless on world markets. Nevertheless, the country was so rich that there was money to be made and the trick was then to turn the Kyats to Thai Bahts, since the Thai currency was the means into Yankee dollars and thereby real money.

In the framework and terms within which these *towkays* organised things in Burma they had spotted that these UK Colgate goods could be the means of converting their currency, as Tubby had found with Moshe in Baghdad. These Chinese *towkays* had garnered all the large supply of Colgate and Palmolive soap which had come in to Burma some 18 months to two years previously, paying for it in Burmese Kyats.

They trickled enough out into the market to supply the stalls and the needs of those main centres where there was a market, but the vast bulk of the supplies bought from Muller and Phipps had been taken across to Moulmein and then up the Salween Valley to the area controlled by the Karens. For their take on the goods they arranged shipments over into Chiang Mai, duly bribing the Thai customs officials as necessary.

It was absolutely fascinating to find out how they could manage things to their financial benefit and later Tubby was to find out how the network of Chinese traders across the East could spot a price differential in a flash and then turn it to their advantage by shipping stuff around in san pans and junks throwing the most carefully worked out marketing plans into chaos. This was exactly what Colgate was up against. They had established a factory with pioneer industry tax advantages in Thailand but couldn't sell production capacity because UK Colgate products had been hijacked and were being readily supplied over the border and into Chiang Mai as currency.

Feeling sure that he had now got to the bottom of what was actually going on he sat down with Ben Henry and tried to do some sort of sums on the quantities that had actually come in and gone through Muller and Phipps' books and tried to calculate the dates of shipments and how much stock might be left for conversion of their currency into Thai Bahts. His permit ended on the 23rd so he used his plastic IATA ticket to arrange a flight across from Rangoon to Bangkok to meet up with Ken Page, the general manager of the new subsidiary there.

Because of the distance to the Rangoon airport, Ben Henry

192

did not come to see him off and besides, it was felt to be prudent that Ben should stay in Rangoon since there was an air of tension developing though there were no sights of troops around the streets or signs of Buddhist monks getting involved in riots and politics yet.

When Tubby reached the airport, he was able to go down some way to see the far end of the runway, and sure enough there was the big tail fin of the Britannia visible, stuck up at an angle into the sky. It was the final touch to the charming chaos which was Burma.

27

BANGKOK – THE VENICE OF THE EAST

The only flight that Tubby could manage was by the so-called Rangoon or Burma Airways which had been set up by commandeering planes of other airlines, and he looked across the tarmac with some trepidation at a rather dilapidated DC4 in the livery of their airline. However, before they got the call there was a commotion as a posse of military vehicles appeared surrounding one particular car, out of which emerged two Eastern European-looking gentlemen. Tubby had had the experience in Baghdad of seeing many Eastern Europeans appearing through the authority of the United Arab Republic once all other nationals had cleared off, except for the British, and it transpired that this was a Russian Embassy official of some significance being expelled by the new regime of General Ne Win.

Russian Boris, and what looked like a sinister unsmiling KGB man in attendance, were kept very separate and indeed put on the plane first. By the time Tubby got on board the DC4, Boris was seated up front with his KGB friend in the outside seat so that nobody, but nobody, was to get near them to have a word with Boris as to why he had been asked to leave Burma.

Tubby had not been very impressed with the state of the RAF DC4 which had flown them from Cyprus back to the UK after he had got out of Baghdad, but this DC4 was a real boneshaker with bits of green mould round the windows due to the tropical damp, which made him wonder about the state of the flight deck. He was very glad when he could look down and see the broad Chao Phraya River and the numerous *khlong* waterways which dominate Bangkok, and noted the limited number of bridges across the broad river. The other thing was the number of Buddhist temples which Tubby immediately noted were entirely different architecturally from the circular style favoured in Rangoon and Burma. Here they were almost church-like but with beautiful red and saffron roofs, except for the five towers of great Wat Arun or Temple of Dawn which sits by the river with a square-type form and ornately carved piers narrowing to the pointed top.

Tubby was met at the airport by Ken Page, the general manager of the new Thai subsidiary, and while he was Australian he did not look or converse like the usual macho Aussie, Tubby suspected he was probably first generation. He wasn't sure whether he had a personality problem, or whether it was due to the effects of the trip upcountry to Chiang Mai he had just completed which in those days was very rough going indeed, but he was not exactly friendly. Perhaps it was all the UK toothpaste he had seen in the market at Chiang Mai instead of his own Thai factory toothpaste.

In order to cope with up-country trips, his vehicle was a long wheelbase landrover, but even so the hazards encountered on his journey had removed the silencers from underneath which made the rather big, angular vehicle sound like a huge tank. Ken recounted that at one place up-country he had come across an overturned bus with half-bodies visible from underneath where the roof had landed after the vehicle had turned over.

Tubby had thought Singapore was chaotic, but the traffic in Bangkok simply had to be seen to be believed. He understood that there were 44,000 tri-shaws licensed, some of which were motorised. Throw in this lot with innumerable taxis and all sorts of other vehicles with only two bridges across the river, and you had stock-car racing on a grand scale. Being high up on the big landrover he felt relatively safe and the removal of the silencer caused it to emit a sound which helped to make other vehicles scatter, or drivers look over their shoulders to see what was coming.

As they passed one of the great stoneworks at one of the river bridges adorned with a statue of an earlier king than the current King Bhumibol, Tubby almost jumped at the sight of troops in place at the bridge entrance with guns set up with a range of fire to take in anything untoward that might happen from the streets in that area. Ken Page explained that while King Bhumibol and his beautiful Queen Sirikit enjoyed almost godlike adulation, as a supreme symbol of unity over all their subjects, it was a pretty violent society underneath and required a pretty heavy hand while keeping a facade of constitutional democracy. That heavy hand was a General Sarit – a large, uncompromising godfather character.

The reality behind anti-drug stance by Thailand on the United Nations scene was that drugs were controlled by General Sarit, and the explanation for the troops out on streets was that he had staged one of his coups against some threat or other. This usually meant that some Chinese *towkays* were 'docked' for encroaching on his commercial interests, and the odd godown would be burned down. Later in his short stay, Tubby was given a glimpse into an 'official' opium den which was some vision of hell on earth, with customers using opium pipes looking like the emaciated terrible immortals called the strulbrugs in Jonathan Swift's *Gullivers Travels*.

Tubby took note that this was yet another place where he had to be very alert and keep his wits about him with regard to outbreaks of public disorder and street violence. He felt somewhat secure as they arrived within the confines of the Erawan hotel which had a swimming pool and every kind of mod con demanded by American tourists, who were in this place in abundance spending their Yankee dollars. Additionally it was a relief place for Americans to come from the traumas of Vietnam for a spell.

That night they went to the wild frenzy of Thai boxing for which the place is famous, so they did not dine at the many floating diners on the famous *khlongs* which are a feature of the city, similar to the canals in Amsterdam. Ken Page was not a gourmet and he commented that the dishes were usually washed by putting them over the side of the boat in spite of whatever may be in the *khlong* waters.

As they walked back through the streets of this wild and

exciting place, Tubby noticed great waves of noise and excitement coming from lit cellars or arcades off the side-walks which were lit with neon signs. Under these emblems of Western culture there were still the pavement sellers of coffee, tea, and drinks who carried everything on shoulder poles – including the tea urn. Tubby noticed that at the entrance to these noisy arcades there were tables with rows of jars of water containing very ornate fish with a piece of cardboard or paper between each of the jars. These were the famous Thai fighting fish and they provided the action for what were in fact gambling dens.

The fish had similar temperaments to the fighting cocks of Sarawak, and their potential fighting reactions were usually gauged by placing prospective opponents in their jars alongside one another and then removing the paper from between to see their reactions once they spotted one another through the glass. They were then taken to the centre of a table where the punters all gathered around and then the two fish were popped into a jar together to fight to the death while fistfuls of Thai Bahts changed hands rapidly.

On the next morning, Ken was going to be delayed by getting his landrover seen to, and being an early riser Tubby went down through the streets to the river at a point where one of the *khlongs* joined, and he could see how much this incredible city lived to the rhythm of the river. Because of the restricted number of bridges over the river, school children and workers were coming down in a steady stream to the water's edge and stepping on to all manner of boats as ferries to the other side. Some he would never have set foot on since they had hardly any clearance of the waterline once they were filled with people.

In addition, there was quite a flow on the river which meant that as soon as the boats untied and set off they began to go on an angled journey across the river against the powerful flow. At the other side they resembled aeroplanes coming in to land when there is a cross wind and they straighten up from their angle of drift just before the wheels hit the decks.

In addition to the hazards of crossing against the current,

Tubby began to see that there were enormous rafts of teak logs on their long journey from the forests away up-river. Their journey to the sea must take a long time because each of the rafts had a hut built on in the middle as crew's quarters for the journey. The huge log rafts had at the front a tug boat but it seemed to Tubby that it should be better at the back as the whole huge log raft seemed to be pushing the boat along rather than being pulled. The whole river was a fascinating mixture of east and west. While the Japanese had been here during the war without any resistance it was notable that there was still wartime camouflage on oil installations across the river against possible bombing once the tide of war began to turn and the Japanese forces retreated back towards the land of Nippon. There was an abundance of temple tops and roofs visible and pointed Wats and among these there would be a big yellow Shell petrol sign visible at various places along the waterfront.

At the office they completed their council of war on the situation of the toothpaste from Burma coming into Ken's northern territories, particularly where he had been on his recent trip. With Tubby's indication that the supplies must be beginning to run out and the dealers in Burma would have to turn to other means for converting the currency over into the Thai Bahts, it was going to be a case of waiting for signs of this and then going heavy with promotion of the locally-made Thai toothpaste.

Tubby made plans to get back the next day and used his plastic IATA card to get a Qantas flight for the hop to Singapore. With this done he took the opportunity to buy some of the renowned memorabilia of Bangkok. When you do not know about gems you simply do not go out and buy them in a place like that and through a contact of Ken Page he was able to acquire a nice black sapphire which he would get set in a ring in Singapore where the Chinese had goldsmiths galore and would not use anything less than 22 carat gold. For his beloved Penelope back at home in the UK, what better than a good length of the beautiful and famous Thai silk. What he had never heard about, or ever seen before, were the sets of cutlery made in beautiful Thai bronze with black ebony handles, and he was delighted to find a particularly beautiful set of half a dozen pieces in a custom-made wooden case lined with velvet.

On the way to the airport on the morning of departure, Ken Page insisted that he pay a visit to the world famous Pasteur Institute in Bangkok which was renowned for its work on anti-venom snake serums. There were numerous snake pits set in the grounds which one could lean over and look down on to watch huge cobras emerge from stone shelters resembling large beehives, to swim through the small water moats when over-heated. They certainly looked particularly sinister and menac-ing when they rose up and expanded their huge necks and show the enlarged coloured patches called eyes on the front and rear of their extended hood.

The Qantas plane was on schedule which was a blessing after his recent experiences and it was the much larger Super Constellation in white and red livery with the huge streamlined extra fuel tanks on the wing tips. In terms of space inside and smoothness of flight it was a great improvement on the old wartime Constellation which had carried him on his first flight from the UK to his eventful stay in Baghdad. It felt like coming home when they swung over Singapore and he could look down on the beautiful greenery and recognize the outlines of the island and see the beautiful white Sunderland flying boats moored at the RAF Seletar at the back of the island facing Jahore.

As he emerged into the airport building at Singapore it was as hot and sticky and humid as ever, which was heightened by the large numbers of passengers passing through at that moment. Standing out like a beacon amongst the crowd was a British type of the old school in a white pith helmet (topee), white jacket with raised colonial collar, and frayed old school tie. He raised his hand and flicked with his finger and thumb and Tubby watched in amazement as an Indian bearer standing some ten paces behind in the crowd came forward with a brolly in one hand and a Qantas bag over his shoulder. He laid the brolly down parallel with his feet and opened the Qantas bag, got out a packet of ten cigarettes, gave one to the gentleman in the white topee and jacket, lit a match and held it up for his master to take his first puff. The deed having been done, the bearer replaced the cigarette packet and the matches in his Qantas bag, zipped it up, picked up his brolly and retreated again through the throng to stand waiting at attention at the regulation ten paces behind.

Tubby just could not believe his eyes and at that moment caught sight of the chap from Qantas whom he had met at rugby and said: 'In the name of God, who on earth is that in the white helmet and jacket with the faded college tie?' The Aussie burst out laughing and related getting amazing cables for special treatment for this chap because he was none other than the archaeological correspondent for the *Illustrated London News*. He was on his way to visit the Niah and mount Mulu caves and excavations in fourth division of Sarawak. Ah, for the days of the Raj, thought Tubby, as he headed out for a taxi back into Amber Mansions for the comforts and food of dear old Cookie once again.

After such an eventful and hectic trip to yet another part of his far-flung territories, it was good to be back in his care and van Marken was continuing to be delighted in his extended stay in this Harpers' mess. As Tubby unpacked his bag he knew that by the end of the next day all his clothes would have been laundered and laid out on his bed.

28

THE PRESSURES BUILD UP

The green Zephyr hadn't been stolen any more and on his way in to Collyer Quay and the office in the morning he always surveyed lovingly the legions of Chinese children heading for school, immaculate in their brilliantly white cleaned tops with their abacus and their school bags over their shoulder, thinking how much of his wonderfully bubbly FAB detergent had been used to get all this clothing clean.

At that time there were a million and a half Chinese on the island of Singapore and breeding at the rate only Chinese can. It was amazing to Tubby just how they lived in one or two rooms in the traditional houses with red roofs or in some blocks of flats which were then appearing. As the family grew in numbers, the bed would be put up on higher legs so that some could sleep underneath as well as those on the bed. Again he was greatly heartened to go up and down streets where these new blocks of six storey flats were located, to see that all along each verandah were huge poles sticking out with the morning's washing hanging along drying in the morning sun before the rains came towards the end of the day or in the afternoon.

As Tubby drove into the car park at Collyer Quay on the sea front by the Inner Roads, the little Indian lad he had taken over from Abe le Roux greeted him with big smiles and ran alongside with his bucket and washing gear to direct him into a parking slot and collect his dues for the week, which included giving the car a wash.

His first priority was to button down his report on what he had found going on in Burma and confirm estimates to Ken Page in Bangkok as to the likely run out time of the UK toothpaste being used for converting currency. However, there were also messages from London reminding him that Ceylon was a top priority as a high potential market for UK export, with Singapore and Malaya going over to a new international subsidiary. John Steele, as new boy in the export manager's post, was wanting a report back in London for future planning for Ceylon. On top of this, Tom Glaze of Grant Advertising in Singapore was on at him about a new office of Grant Advertising in Colombo with a letter of introduction to Reggie Candappa, who was the Sinhalese manager of their Ceylon operation.

As a counter to this pressure on him to see the Grant Advertising operation in Ceylon as the guy from Colgate who was going to do big things there, Tubby had letters and details and files from London about their agents, Messrs Rajandrams Limited and UK export's current advertising agents who were a local go-ahead company called International Advertising Services Limited. One of the joint managing directors with the name of Tim Horshington had a letter waiting for Tubby, with a copy of the most recent IAS Limited house magazine which was very much a PR document telling all interested parties in no uncertain terms how good they were.

Matters had moved along at such a pace that he just simply had to book a flight for 30th October which gave him less than a week to get organised. After his problems with BOAC and the Britannias, he was determined to try another airline and booked on the Dutch KLM flight from Singapore to Ratmalana Airport north of Colombo. It was an early morning flight which would get him there mid to early morning, which is a good time to hit new faces and new places when one is relatively fresh.

Whether he liked it or not, he was getting drawn into the new subsidiary activities and he was regaled by Jim Kevlin about these British stuffed shirts who were still the civil servants running the foreign exchange control department in Singapore. "Why was it that Americans were so disliked?" Kevlin wanted to know. He was beginning to form the opinion that in appearance and voice he was not exactly the ideal

American to head up an American multi-national subsidiary in what was still a very British Colony, with the other part across the Causeway still very much run the same way as when it was part of Empire until 1956. Jim was certainly beginning to show some paranoid attitudes towards Bill Bailey and Desmond, and some of the other directors at Harpers who were very very British, since to him they must have seemed on great chummy terms with those other *puteh* ex-patriates of UK origin still in high office.

On the other hand, from attitudes emerging in odd conversations, he was perhaps missing his wife, and Rita and the three kids were due any day from Panama, after making their way across the Pacific in the old Pan Am Stratocruisers which still operated en route from west coast USA, and took well nigh a week via Honolulu, Guam, Manila and Saigon.

One Chinese clerk of middle age called Yim Ah Hoi had been recruited, and it had not been yet resolved whether we would just carry on using Harpers as a book-keeping system and then produce a set of consolidated accounts for the subsidiary to offset management cost overheads. For banking facilities, they were under pressure to place business with newly opening American banks in Singapore, but the hugely important and influential Hong Kong Shanghai Bank was advised because of its establishment influence throughout the whole of South East Asia. After all, the top men of this bank and Jardines had their dwellings up above the governor's residence on Hong Kong peak!

From his start in life in professional accountancy after school, Tubby had demonstrated that he had a good idea of what was going on and what needed to be done, so he was handed by Jim Kevlin a huge loose-leaf volume which had on it in big letters 'ADI'. This had come in from the international accounts division in New York and was affectionately known round the world throughout the 44 Subsidiaries as 'the ADI' which stood for Accounts Department Instructions.

The accountants retained were Price Waterhouse – again terribly British and difficult to communicate with for Jim Kevlin. His words to Tubby were: 'You've been in accountancy, go over and see these Limies, and show them what needs to be done from the ADI.'

Once Tubby had given the volume a thorough going over and checked out some questions, he went over to see Price Waterhouse, and the partner almost backed off in amazement at the sight of this great black book. But, like Tubby, once they got into it together, he was mightily impressed because in very clear laid-out form it was indeed the bible as far as concerned any activity which any overseas subsidiary might get involved in – accumulated from experiences in 44 very diverse locations around the world.

Together, they were soon able to work out the suggested simple bookkeeping framework which would allow them to fulfil the requirements of New York for all overseas subsidiaries which were the cabling of P&L account within 24 hours of the end of a month, and a balance sheet format by the 28th day after the end of the calendar month. Later when they were to get involved with setting up more subsidiaries with manufacturing, again the ADI had sections appropriate to whatever circumstance or situation was to arise.

All this work pressure was leaving little time for Tubby to get integrated into the gang at the cricket club, and the rugby crowd particularly. After the trauma of his first game on the *Padang* he found that the heat and humidity of Singapore seemed to keep muscles loose to prevent stiffening up, as in UK when not playing regularly. So he managed a Wednesday night game to keep his hand in. After the game, sitting as required wrapped in a towel waiting for the perspiration to stop pouring out while replacing it with jugs of ale, Tubby got talking with one of the great characters of the rugger scene in Singapore at that time – the one and only Derek 'Scoops' Urquhart.

Scoops was a product of the public school system, being the son of an ex-pat who was in business with other ex-pats with an Import House in Colombo, Ceylon. From the household servants, Scoops had actually grown up speaking Tamil fluently. This really got them talking because Tubby had mentioned his pending trip to Ceylon, and Scoops was able to give him some

204

background to the former colonial scene which still prevailed there, though Ceylon had gone into independence within the Commonwealth with India and Pakistan.

Scoops had recently been on leave to the UK from his job in Singapore with Straits Steam Ship Company, which was the local shipping company of the great Blue Funnel Line, which was the name throughout the shipping world for the privately run family company of Alfred Holt and Son in Liverpool. Headquarters was a huge office building called the India Building which had been gutted by fire bombs in the war and Tubby had actually started work in a chartered accountancy firm which was across the street under the shadow of the big Holt building. The Holt family had their own ship's architects, and their fleet of Blue Funnel ships were always immaculate with a straight up and down funnel and mast appearance unique to themselves. The skippers followed laid-down shipping routes round the world and to the Far East as their speciality, which were not the same as the shipping lanes generally followed by other carriers.

Anyway, Scoops related an evening returning to a flat in the area round Earl's Court in London in an inebriated state which caused him to express his feelings in loud Tamil after being unable to find his key. This prompted a window to be flung open high on another building by an irate sleeper who had been woken up and who began to regale Scoops back in Tamil about having been woken up at an unearthly hour.

Scoops was very much of the old world, favouring a high hair parting and combed back hair, with nose and face which bore evidence of being caught at the bottom of the scrum a few times. Scoops related that his parents had sold out in Colombo and Ceylon some years previously, since the old days had gone. Before settling in Australia of all places, they had gone on a tour of similar places that had once been outposts of empire and had come across this incredible club in South West Africa outside Windhoek. A variety of ex-pats from military and far flung colonial services had gravitated there to see out their days in the manner to which they had come to expect as norm.

The club had bearers and was akin to descriptions Tubby had heard of the Light Horse in Calcutta. The system at this unique club had been carried to extreme in that they had the floor demarcated by regiment, or particular branch of the services, or particular foreign service location such as the Sudan civil service types, who were fairly renowned among old colonial overseas types to be the most arrogant, idle and lacking in grey matter. Anyway, the incumbents of this club, in this outpost of former empire, closed the ranks once a week on a Friday night when they crossed their lines and all had Sundowners together as the flag was lowered to the appropriate bugle call.

Returning to the work front, before the week was out, everyone went to the airport for arrival of the big old Boeing Strato-Cruiser which flew in on its next to last stop before going across to end its long trip across the Pacific Ocean at Djakarta in Indonesia. Poor Rita emerged looking somewhat bruised and battered from the long journey and carrying a little toddler called Gita who could only speak Spanish, and the two older ones, Jamie and Kate, who managed some American school English but again primarily conversed in Spanish. It was going to be quite a change for them to go to the British school in Alexandra Army Barracks run on British lines with British teachers.

In those days, the Singapore Raffles had got a pretty run down reputation from the point of view of cuisine and from not exactly pristine bed linen in the rooms, and having the large British services NCO's club almost opposite the evening hours were usually filled with raucous sounds from those coming and going there. After a look round, Jim had made the very good choice of placing the family in the lovely Ocean Park hotel by the seaside out at Galang near the Chinese Swimming Club as their abode until they fixed up accommodation. Tubby hoped this would keep Jim occupied while he was away on his next trip.

The 30th came for his flight day to Ceylon and he was jolly glad to be getting away from all the new subsidiary build-up and pressures. He snuggled himself into the seat in the first class compartment of the KLM DC4 with the prospect of enjoying the comforts of the Royal Dutch airline, knowing that he could take it out on Sander back in the flat if all didn't go well.

The DC4 taxied out to the end of the long runway at Paya Lebar and went through the revving and checking of each engine in turn, then it began to sink in to Tubby that the checking was taking a bit longer than usual and surge of engines wasn't forthcoming which would put him back in to the seat as the plane surged off. Instead, the Dutch Captain came on the intercom and announced that unfortunately they had a problem in one of the engines and would have to taxi back to have their engineers look at it.

Tubby began to feel like Jonah on the boat in the storm, hoping that other passengers would not find out about his experiences with Britannias and mark him out as being the reason for having to go back. After an hour and a half they were deemed to be fit to go again and this time they did go through the checks on schedule and then surged off down the runway, heading for Ceylon. Alas, as far as Tubby was concerned, it had thrown out his careful plans for a mid morning arrival into the Ceylon situation as the first UK rep to hit town for a long, long time.

29

CEYLON – THE BEAUTIFUL

From its outline on the maps, the island does indeed hang from the tip of India like the pearl of the Indian Ocean and in the Hindu classics it is known as Lanka, the resplendent isle. As they flew in, Tubby could see something of the magnificent mountains and valleys and the incredible terraced paddy fields for rice growing before they swung round Colombo on the coast and turned down into the landing at Ratmalana.

During the flight, Tubby had started to perspire profusely as though he were developing a fever for no apparent reason, but other than feeling a bit sticky and uncomfortable, he had almost forgotten about it until they were making their approach and he felt it coming on again. While Tim Horshington of International Advertising Services Limited had mentioned that Tubby would be met at the airport he was conscious of the fact that the plane had been delayed by the gremlins almost two hours and it was now gone lunchtime.

As he came out of the Customs and Immigration gateways into the welcome lounge, he was greeted by the very competent and extremely well-modulated voice of a very black but western-featured gentleman of similar height to himself. This was Tim Horshington, who immediately introduced Tubby to the diminutive gentleman on his right as none other than Mr Rajandram, founder and guiding light of his Colgate agents – Messrs Rajandrams Limited. He was old enough to be Tubby's father and carried his years well with his Hindu spot on his forehead. Dressed in shirt and slacks and tie, as was Tim Horshington, he was quite Indian looking but for the way his diminishing hair was parted and greased down.

For all his Western features and hair style and voice and

stature, Tim was very much a black Tamil since they can be very black indeed against the more brown Sinhalese. While the greetings were being exchanged plus the general exchanges between other passengers emerging and the various reception parties, he had been aware that there had been two superior looking Indian gentlemen in their white dhotis garments disembarking, therefore did not take much notice of photographers and flash bulbs going off.

They went to the lounge area and had soft drinks together, after Tubby had thanked them profusely for waiting for him, and explained what had happened to the KLM plane in spite of trying to avoid BOAC delays. Before they could embark on any plans for the remainder of the afternoon, Tubby had to say that he was feeling ill and that it might be better for him to get signed in at the Galle Face hotel in Colombo and see if he could sleep it off. Mr Rajandram went off in his chauffeur-driven car and Tubby had noticed already that he was very status conscious as a leading Colombo businessman. Tubby went off with Tim Horshington who summoned up his transport with an authoritative click of the finger.

Listening to spoken Tamil always fascinated Tubby since it came out in bursts like machine gun fire, usually with hand actions to go with it, so with quick-fire instructions in Tamil, the driver was soon on his way to the Galle Face hotel which was in central Colombo towards the seafront and again a very imposing colonial edifice with its own swimming pool.

Tubby had noticed and commented on the large number of ships which seemed to be anchored in the outer bay waiting to come in and was informed that labour troubles were becoming a problem and some of the ships had been waiting for nearly two months to get a berth to unload. He had also noticed that the streets were fairly congested and the vehicle had problems moving in and out and round rather enormous slow moving bullock carts which still seemed to be a normal mode of transport for goods coming through the port.

Tim Horshington was obviously bursting to smother Tubby in a hectic programme of engagements with the aim of keeping Grant Advertising and Reggie Candappa at a minimum level of contact. He had a paper prepared which was accepted for review on the morrow and not before. Once in his room at the Galle Face with the door shut, Tubby was able to drop his mask of bonhomie and energetic Colgate businessman, and collapse into bed to fall asleep very rapidly under the ceiling fan turned up to maximum, since air-conditioning was not part of the amenities of the Galle Face hotel.

He woke with a start to find that it had gone dark and was now early evening, and he found that while he thought he was lying in a bathtub full of water he was actually still in the bed and soaked in perspiration. He definitely felt better, so whatever bug had attacked him, it had worked through in some miraculous way or other. After taking a shower he set off for a swim in the hotel pool adorned in his towelling jacket and felt even more better to the extent that he even felt hungry enough to dress up in suit as was befitting the Galle Face hotel and the magnificent colonial dining room, where he was descended upon by the Maitre and attendants of various kinds.

After the hectic week he had had in Singapore after returning from Bangkok, he was quite glad of an evening on his own to be able to put down on a paper for himself the sort of programme he had in mind. He was determined to get to grips with the whole retailing/wholesaling situation and consumer potential of the Ceylon market using prize export territory of Singapore and Malaya as a measuring stick. However, Tubby did make a mental note that not all the peoples of South East Asia were so industrious and fastidious about their laundry and personal care for rapid consumption of lots and lots of Palmolive soap, toothpaste and of course the bubbly FAB.

Before taking his leave after the brief meeting together at the airport, he had established that his first port of call would be to pay homage and respect to Mr Rajandram, and it was the ebullient Tim Horshington with the obligatory '50' tin of cigarettes in hand who bounced into the Galle Face to conduct him on his way once breakfast was attended to.

The office of Messrs Rajandrams Limited was a reasonable office in a busy commercial section of downtown Colombo, not

210

far from the great clock tower up from the harbour front. They had to walk through the hustle and bustle of the street scene before getting to the entrance and the staircase up to the offices, and Tubby noticed that there were quite a number of distinctly dressed Afghans and Nepalese. They brought their precious stones and other additional objects unique to the northern mountains for sale and they would lay on the pavement the load from their backs. Some of them played on what looked like strange wind instruments, but he was informed that uniquely to Ceylon, and Colombo particularly, their real trade was lending money. Tubby was quite intrigued at these Afghans from the high mountainous areas of the north because the prime money lenders to people generally across the Far East were the big turbaned gentlemen from the Punjab in India.

As Tubby and Tim Horshington reached the top of the stairs to the busy offices of Rajandrams, the scene was once again of a very typical British-style colonial office, with desks according to status; against downdraught from ceiling fans each tray had a weight, and there were blocks with spikes to hold papers from being blown around off desks. It was not quite as bad as in Japan where Tubby understood that such an entry as theirs would result in all employees standing at their desks and bowing in their direction. There was a general air of servility as they advanced to the entrance of the office of their revered and respected proprietor.

Tubby was always an early starter and this had gone down well with Mr Rajandram, who also liked to lead his staff by example, being at his desk early. He was sitting resplendent with two others on his right and left as they were ushered into the room.

After further apologies by Tubby for the events of the previous day and assurances that he was feeling very fit and well again, he was introduced with great pride to the young Indian gentleman on his right who was none other than the son and heir of the business, called Maharajah. Apparently Hindus do not have a family name which carries on as with Europeans, therefore that was his name in his own right though

211

the old man's name – as founder – would continue as the business name for goodwill.

The other Indian gentleman present had a most pleasant presence and while 'Indian' in appearance, he was neither Tamil nor Sinhalese, but when he was introduced as the manager, one John Fernando, Tubby realised that there might have been a Portuguese bloodstrain from back over the centuries. Before Maharajah and John Fernando left the room, it was commented to Tubby that John would accompany him on his travels, which rather took Tubby aback. As far as he was concerned, he had yet to work out what his travels would be to assess exposure to the market, study means by which their consumer goods reached the buying public, and how they might be marketed into a significant level of turnover to support local manufacture.

Tubby always believed in finding out just what motivated his agents and this was usually done by prompting them to talk about how they had become Colgate agents. Little Rajandram responded to this and was soon telling Tubby how hard he had worked to build up his business in Colombo and beyond. He began to get particularly animated when he had reached the point in the story where he was beginning to be recognised as a sound businessman in Colombo from his ability, business standards and owing nothing to any man. At this crucial stage in the history of his company, when he was on the brink of acceptance by the business establishment, an Afghan had appeared in his office and had made some remarks about his possibly needing some money.

By this time he was standing to his full five foot two behind his desk and had become almost white at the memory of his rage at that time. The very thought that it might get round the Colombo market that an Afghan had been seen entering his office! With eyes piercing into Tubby, he shouted in a high pitched voice, shaking his head, 'I threw him down the stairs – I threw him down the stairs and bundled him out on to the street for all to see.' Tubby just did not dare look at Tim Horshington who was biting his lower lip almost to the point of agony to prevent the semblance of a smile crossing his face.

Somehow he managed to make a studious remark to the effect that it was good to know that the agency for Colgate Palmolive was in the hands of a businessman of such stature in Ceylon.

Tubby's strategy was working and he was establishing a good relationship with dear old Rajandram, who then insisted that Tubby accompany him as his guest at the Rotary lunch in Colombo the next day. This would be the nearest that Tubby had ever got to Rotary since in those days it was certainly a very exclusive gathering limited to one from each profession. He remembered that growing up in one of the wealthiest Presbyterian churches in the whole of England back in Birkenhead, their incumbent Reverend of some 20 years, or more, was the Clergy member of Rotary in Birkenhead and even made President for a year, by rotation.

He made an appointment to meet with Mr Rajandram at the end of his travelling round Ceylon seeing all facets of the whole process by which their goods were marketed and sold. He would then reason to Mr Rajandram the outline of the suggestions and propositions he would wish to put to the export manager in London. He was once again assured that John Fernando, as manager of that part of his business that included Tubby's products, would be in attendance and would be glad to learn from his experience in going round Ceylon together.

Tubby then left for the offices of IAS – the hotshot advertising agency run by Tim Horshington and a Sinhalese lady by the name of Estelle Goodchild (via marriage) who had top London West End advertising agency experience. Tim had gained his top level advertising experience in Australia with no less than the prestigious J. Walter Thompson Agency. With this calibre of leadership it was run at top international standards and besides, they were determined to make sure that Grant Advertising and Reggie Candappa were not going to have a look-in on the Colgate account.

As an opening shot Tubby was presented with a large white folder with his name and 'Press coverage on visit to Ceylon' on the front, all with the compliments of International Advertising Services Limited. Tubby opened the large white double spread folder to find six mounted press cuttings with photos covering his arrival by KLM Royal Dutch Airlines. Tubby was quite taken aback to see it written up not only in English, but also in Sinhalese and Tamil script. He was absolutely amazed considering how awful he had felt that the photographs had turned out so well from the popping flash bulbs at his arrival meeting with Tim Horshington and Mr Rajandram. One photo actually showed his resplendent leather briefcase provided at the start of his career in export. By then it was adorned with a large BOAC sticker and a Middle East Airways roundel which had particular significance since the airline had flown him out of the bloody Baghdad situation.

Tubby was also given a copy of the quarterly IAS house PR magazine before being taken on a detailed tour of all aspects of the agency which were very much on West End lines with the addition of the great feeling that all and sundry in IAS were one team. Almost as a throwaway line, Tim Horshington mentioned something about having to go round to Radio Ceylon about his programme and in the car going over he explained that through opportunities in Australia he had got into broadcasting and now hosted a music/chat show type programme regularly on Radio Ceylon. As part of the treatment Tubby was being subjected to he got a great welcome at Radio Ceylon and lunch too.

Since Ceylon had been the headquarters of the whole of the South East Asia Command in the Pacific war against the Japanese, Radio Ceylon was noted as having one of the most powerful sets of transmitters in South East Asia, and a young British type called Clive Bates joined them for lunch. He was very much of the old British school in appearance and manner, being the son of wealthy ex-pats, and he now considered himself very much part of the independent scene of Ceylon, however chaotic.

It became very clear over lunch that the 'buzz' thing in these media circles of Colombo at that time was to do with the recently much acclaimed film *Bridge on the River Kwai* which was actually in Ceylon since it was not politic that it be made at the real place in Thailand, because of the now important

214

pro-American role of Thailand on the South East Asian scene with Communism rampant in China.

It transpired that young Clive was very much into the local amateur dramatic scene and, resulting from this, he had a minor part at the beginning of the film as one of the group of four officers in the notorious prison camp with William Holden discussing escape which Alec Guinness as leader of the British prisoners would not tolerate. Young Clive in his part got shot by the guards trying to make a run for it.

The inside stories on the making of the film were most interesting and Alec Guinness was universally regarded in high esteem by all the locals in that he did not behave in the prima donna fashion of the other leading stars and was most ready and willing to talk to people like young Clive about acting, giving advice.

The other most interesting factor concerned the extras who made up the prisoners under Alec Guinness who worked on the railway bridge, other than those like Harry Fowler who had the speaking parts in the front ranks as and when those shots required it.

The history of Ceylon is the same as Malacca in Malaya in that the first Europeans to arrive were the Portuguese whose architecture and customs and names remain though they were replaced by the Dutch who actually gave the island the name of Ceylon, and they too left their mark in terms of names and buildings. Then the British arrived and really did colonise the island into the interior to make it part of the empire, as throughout the Far East. The three waves of European influx had left a mixed segment of population who were neither local nor European, but had names like DeSouza, or DeSilva, Van Belts, or some other Dutch and British names. In the case of Tim Horshington, the name had come from his father who, on becoming Christian then a Church of England clergyman, changed from his Tamil name to the name of Horshington, the name of the missionary who led to his conversion and entry into the Church of England ministry.

Anyway, the males from these mixed blood origins were generally known in Ceylon as 'Burgher Boys'. Since they were not really recognised by white races, or the local races, they were generally by no means well off. The money they were able to earn as extras during the making of this renowned film gave them a once in a lifetime opportunity to escape from the confines of the 'Eurasian' handicap, and many of them used the money to buy their passage out to Australia or America for a new life.

It was a sad reflection on the politics since independence that Tubby picked up signs and comments which indicated that racial and religious tensions from many years ago before colonisation had been used for political ends. Sadly Trincomalee and Jaffna in the predominantly Tamil areas of the north and east were not on the itinerary suggested, only the major towns to the north of central area and down through to Kandy.

In the few days remaining before they would be setting off, Tubby had to fit in his visit to Grant Advertising which turned out to be a quite typical set up for a branch of an American Agency. It did not have the same local feel as IAS and probably might not have this necessary ingredient in its ideas for advertising and marketing the Colgate products to the locals. However, Reggie Candappa did introduce Tubby to the wonderful Mount Lavinia hotel south of Colombo over lunch and he vowed that on a subsequent visit he would stay here rather than the Galle Face. This marvellous hotel, perched above and amongst bending palms, had a view of a bay with sweeping beaches which were the home territory for the local fishing catamarans, which were crude dug-out logs with an outrigger but which could skim along the waves propelled by their square sails which were often made from flour or sugar bags, as is fairly standard in the East. It certainly was a most relaxing and idyllic place and Tubby could well imagine that it was the ideal location for watching the fabled sunsets which were part of the magic of the west coast of Ceylon.

The rest of the time before going inland was spent busily with John Fernando visiting the market scenes in Negumbo to the north of Colombo, then going down the coast road to Galle on the southern tip of this glorious island. The drive down the road to Galle was an experience of utter wonder and delight in itself. With hardly any traffic on the road, Tubby was able to take in the views of great stretches of empty tropical beaches with bending palms. At one point where they had stopped to take in one of these scenes with the cine-camera, he was confronted with the sight of an enormous reptile of almost crocodile proportions and called a telaguyah locally, as it plodded along headed for undergrowth and some water beyond.

As they headed on down towards Galle, Tubby had his first sight of a marvellous mermaid. There across a lagoon with a backing of palm trees, she lay resplendent at the head of a beach, her long hair, pink bosoms, and long fishy tail declaring on the advertising hoarding above that whilst she had no need of shoes she would recommend the ever-present Bata shoe shops for footwear.

The first thing they came to at Galle was the massive wall fortifications guarding Ceylon's most important point of landfall for those intrepid mariners and navigators who opened up the trade routes to the Far East, and China beyond, centuries ago. The views from the top of these fortifications were simply breathtaking in the dazzling sunlight, as catamarans with their outrider floats and their single big sails filled with a strong wind made good runs across the white-topped surf. It must have been a most welcome sight for captains of those ships, the Portuguese, then the Dutch, and then the British, as they would refurbish before the long sail of open sea to the Straits of Malacca. It would be the same for those coming west, once they had left the shelter of Sumatra to head out across the wide ocean, to make welcome land fall and safe harbourage at Galle.

It was the replica of Malacca in Malaya with the distinctive buildings reflecting architecture of the three maritime nations which had made claim to the place in their turn and left some of their people whose names appeared on buildings and shops. It was marvellous to be able to visit these places before the pollution of tourism began to exploit them and unsettle a process which had been going on for centuries. Like Malacca, Galle had same dreamy sleepiness, since both had been bypassed and superceded as mariners ceased to be reliant on wind power, and the increasing trade of the powered ships preferred the likes of Colombo and Singapore where much bigger and better docking facilities were developed. Both Galle and Malacca had evolved a uniqueness in terms of ethnic mix, while families seemed to maintain some sort of distinctness from their origins, yet they had blended with the others in a wonderful mix which manifested itself particularly in the food and the market places and the products available therein.

It was with some reluctance that Tubby bid farewell to Galle and headed back with John Fernando, and having brought swimming things they stopped by an isolated fishing village. Tubby was able to have his photo taken in true tropical paradise poster pose against a beautiful palm tree reaching out across golden sand and surf in glorious sunshine. As they dried after their swim he was able to examine fishermen's catamarans on the beach being prepared for the next outing to fish for their livelihood. The big dug-out log which was the boat had a mast with an enormous crude sail, and heavy great logs lashed on fore and aft held the other smaller outrigger or float, which helped the whole contraption to remain steady and level on the water while crossing racing surf. It was fascinating to watch what was really a big, heavy and clumsy-looking sailing device being brought in with such dexterity by these seamen, riding on the top of the waves for the rush up the beach with great momentum, while their family and friends were ready to grab the outriggers and posts and carry on running them up the beach as far as they could go.

There was one more night on his own in the Galle Face hotel before Tubby was to set off on the tour of inland cities and towns, and he was glad of the night on his own to write up his notes on what he had seen of Colombo and the south-west corner of this island so far, and the first impressions of their agents and the two ad agencies. Next day was the 5th November, and he was packed and ready in shorts for the journey, since he had been warned that it could be hot and sticky which was in great contrast with Bonfire Night at home in the UK – long dark nights, the winter coming on and the build-up of excitement for Guy Fawkes.

The road gradually left the coast and after some time they headed inland for Kurumegala, which was not in the mountainous areas although rivers did run down through to the sea and it was difficult to make out the gradual up and down of the underlying countryside since they were driving steadily through jungle areas. The car had a driver, and John Fernando was sitting up front while Tubby and Tim Horshington occupied the back seat. Coming up to lunchtime there was an exchange with the driver, and the car turned off the surfaced road into a jungle pathway which twisted and turned for a while and then rounded to what was the upper reaches of a river valley, but all deeply clad in jungle.

Tubby was delighted to see that they had drawn up at one of the old colonial government Rest Houses, like those in Sarawak, which once again dotted this island as an ex-outpost of the Empire, for the civil servants of old to go about their governing of the island. There was a minimal clearing of trees for the Kuranegala Rest House, and because of the lack of a level space the front verandah area was on timbered legs and it was a lovely day for dining out at the tables laid with white cloths on this verandah, looking across the tops of the jungle trees with the noise of water somewhere way down in the green mass.

After a rapid exchange with the staff of the Rest House, Tubby was informed that there were working elephants nearby and that he might like to take his cine-camera and go down into the jungle to see if they could catch up with them at their work. After about a quarter of a mile of manageable undergrowth, they came across tracks which had been formed by great logs being pulled along. After hearing voices, which gradually got louder, they were aware of crashing sounds and then came upon two huge working elephants with the ever-present *mahoots* who handled these huge masses of living machinery for the pulling of great felled trees down towards the river. The *mahoot* sat, as usual, astride the head and higher neck with long sticks with a point and hook at the top. The elephants had a huge leather halter round their necks, to which chains were attached down either side to be latched on to the huge logs, which they then dragged along through the undergrowth.

One already hitched to a huge log went on its way down the slope weaving a passageway as straight as it could between the trees, while the other was about to be attached up. The sight of a white colonial boss man with a camera brought an immediate response from the *mahoot* to demonstrate his prowess with his great elephant. In rapid-gunfire Tamil he instructed the great beast to raise its foot up at the front for him to slide down on to it and then step lightly onto the ground, and Tubby immediately burst out laughing as the ridiculous thought went through his mind – of how strange it was that an elephant understood Tamil. With his previous experience of elephants being only in zoos, he had a particularly memorable childhood experience of being extremely high up on a swaying seat on an elephant in Edinburgh Zoo, which responded to instructions from a Scottish tongue.

It really was a wonderful experience to come across these great beasts at work in the dappled sunlight which came through from the high treetops. For his final trick the *mahoot* again spoke to his beloved elephant in Tamil for the foot and leg to be raised like a lorry tailgate to take him up within reach of the end of the great flapping ear which he got hold of, and then he hauled himself back up with great alacrity on to his commanding seat overlooking the great noble head and the protruding trunk hanging down in front.

Back they went up to the Rest House, and Tubby was really ready for lunch, so it was utterly wonderful and simple to sit down at a table with a beautifully laundered white cloth and have curry and rice laid before them, as served and eaten by the locals – a change to it's being served up for western eating habits and palates in a restaurant playing piped Indian music. It simply had to be a long, leisurely lunch since it was good, fiery south Indian curry and tasted utterly marvellous. Tubby was fortunate to have grown up with the taste of curry, since his maternal grandfather in Scotland had been born in India and curries were part of his normal diet.

His mother used to relate an incident from her childhood in

the then remote fishing village of Tarbert in Argyll in the Western Highlands in those peaceful days before the World War One, when it was common for children to beg their parents to let them go bare-footed for the summer. As she was playing across from the house where the fishermen's nets were hung up to dry each morning, a retired major from the Indian Army service, coming up the road from the shops down beyond the harbour wall, encountered the smell of curry coming from the house where Tubby's grandmother was preparing a meal for the evening. The poor major could not restrain himself and proceeded to the door of their house followed by audience of inquisitive children who stood around completely fascinated as the major begged for a taste of the curried dish, which was well on in preparation since the curry process starts the night before.

Tubby's mother inherited from his grandmother the skills in preparing curry dishes brought back from India by the family. This held them in good stead because with the wartime shortages they regularly received bloody parcels of fresh rabbits which had been shot by a gamekeeper uncle in the Scottish Highlands, and his mother would often curry the rabbit meat. As Tubby sat there on the verandah of the Rest House in the middle of the jungles of Ceylon, he felt he had come the full circle as he sat back and savoured the glorious curried meal, but his reverie was broken by the call that they had to go.

Tim Horshington and John Fernando started off down the track again, suggesting that before they set off on their journey they should take Tubby down to the river, and when they eventually broke through the cover to the water's edge Tubby was confronted with an idyllic scene which was to remain etched on his memory for ever. The river straightened out after a bend which was not fully visible, and the sun streaming down on to the waters marbled the surface where there were small eddies; directly across there was a small tributary where beams of sunlight broke through the trees.

Right there before them were the two elephants he had seen working earlier with their *mahoots*, enjoying their treat at the end of a strenuous day. Both lay on their sides, half a head and half an ear and up to the hump of their big bodies above the

221

level of the water, and every now and again their trunks would sweep up in a lazy arc and spray the exposed parts with jets of river water. Eventually they got up, and the *mahoots* were lifted up again by one leg and one ear on to the tops of their heads, and one set off homeward bound down the river, while the other went slowly across the shallow waters. Tubby's last sight of this lovely big gentle beast was it strolling away down the tributary river across into the dappled light coming down through the canopy of the trees.

Tubby then caught up with the others who had strolled upstream and rounded the bend, which revealed a sweep of the river up to where it had come round from a gorge, and there was a mud bank stretching out from the inner side of the bend before them. He suddenly realised he was at the very spot from which Alec Guinness had strolled out across the mud bank at the end of *Bridge on the River Kwai* to where the lowered water level in the morning had revealed the cable to the high explosives designed to bring down his beloved bridge. As Tubby shaded his eyes and looked up beyond this scene from the film, he could see the remains of the main support timbers for the twin towers on the stone outcrops on either side of where the river came through the gorge.

The others had not mentioned why they had come to this particular spot for lunch on the journey to the northern parts and they were quite amused and fascinated by Tubby's reactions. They then climbed up through the jungle to the spot away up above the bridge where the actual rail track had been laid for the engine and the train to come down and then crash through the bridge as it was blown up by the charges set in the night. It was quite a strange experience to walk down where the track had been with bits of the timber still about, and he could almost hear the singing of the troops in the film as they marched through having completed the bridge. It was a most delightful spot and must have made for some very pleasant film-making.

It was then back to the car, and the driver set off in what was then the late afternoon heading for Anuradhapura, a major capital of the Sinhalese. It went dark while they were driving

222

along and at one place Tubby became aware from the car windows that there were a lot of people running about, and he began to wonder if they were going to run into some riots. This fear was heightened as he was aware of a glowing colour in the sky reflecting what must have been a large-scale burning area, and as they rounded the next bend he saw that it was a huge bonfire with a guy on the top, and the whole spectacle was surrounded by an enormous mob of people lit by the orange flames. Tubby remembered that it was the 5th November and he exclaimed in amazement that the British colonial influences were such that people had taken up the ritual of Guy Fawkes' Day, and he asked that they might stop to watch. This was immediately countered by a stream of words from Tim and John Fernando to the driver and he felt the acceleration of the car as it was explained to him that it was a ritual cremation taking place, and it certainly had nothing to do with it being the 5th November.

The next morning was spent on intense research and fact-finding on the wholesalers and general trade situations and channels of retail distribution in this important central and northern city of Anuradhapura. After an early lunch, Tim and John insisted that they took a run round what must be one of the largest number of relics of Sinhalese architecture round and about this great city, where Buddhism was introduced to Ceylon.

As expected, there were numerous wats or pagodas, which in Ceylon they call *dagobas*, and once again they were distinctive in their architecture and design from the Buddhist shrines and temples which Tubby had seen throughout Rangoon and Thailand. The ruins round and about in jungle areas must have covered quite an enormous area and it took some time before they left them behind and were on their way to the incredible Lion Rock Fortress of Sigiriya.

They stayed the night in the government Rest House after taking in the market and other distributors in the nearby town. It was a beautiful morning when Tubby emerged from the Rest House, with beautiful white egrets foraging in a large shallow lake on which they were beautifully mirrored. In time past this area had settled into jungle-covered plain, since the geological phenomenon of Sigiriya just stood there totally on its own, 600 feet in the air. After inspecting the foundation ruins of what was once the king's palace and outbuildings, in around A.D. 500, they started on the climb to the top of this great rock fortress where King Kasyapa took refuge after an episode of patricide, to be on look-out for his brothers coming to get him in revenge.

The start of the main steps up from the bottom were between huge claw like feet carved from the foot of the Lion Rock. Half way up, a precarious metal fire escape ladder led to a metal walkway under an overhang area, which was decorated with incredible frescos of palace beauties of the day which had somehow been preserved from erosion due to the overhang conditions. Once on the top, the spectacle was breathtaking and the facilities and buildings on the top must have been up to palace standards, since Tubby had himself filmed reclining on what must have been a stone couch above a small mini-bathing pool. He could just imagine how the king could lie at ease while keeping a look-out for who was coming from hundreds of miles around. Away to the south could be seen the ranges of the mountains of the tea country above Kandy, which ended up in Adams Peak – the other great Buddhist holy place on this fabulous island. From this incredible palace area 600 feet above, it was possible to look down and see the extent of the palace buildings which had existed from 1,400 years earlier.

From there they reached the Rest House at Polonnaruwa, which housed the Queen and Duke of Edinburgh on a previous visit to the island, when returning from Australia. It overlooked a fabulous tank, the word used in Ceylon for the incredible reservoirs, which were built as a highly efficient storage and irrigation system by King Porakrama the Great in around the twelfth century. The whole place was littered with the ruins of incredible buildings built by this king, in what was believed originally to be a seven storey palace in a fortress, and administration buildings reflecting a Hindu influence on the architecture. However, what amazed Tubby more than anything was the almost Greek or Roman appearance of some of the buildings, until a glimpse through to a centre point revealed a statue of the Buddha. Indeed, at that time it was a privileged experience to visit this tremendous area of fabulous buildings and film the famous huge reclining Buddha statue in stone, because tourism was discouraged and in the grass at these fabulous places there were signs saying: 'Do not take photographs.'

Shortly before they left, aiming to get to Kandy before the night, Tubby was walking through the commercial area with his cohorts when he saw another European rep coming towards them with his Sinhalese/Tamil cohorts. He turned out to be an American with Union Carbide, whose Ever-ready batteries were similar high turnover goods to his own Colgates, and he too believed in getting out and about with people on the spot to have a good look at how the whole trade processes functioned, to get the goods through to the consumers. He was responsible for overlapping areas to Tubby and they parted wondering if they might bump into one another again.

Being late in the day, Tubby was not able to take in the wonders of the hill country, now famous for tea, as they rapidly descended into Kandy for the night. The whole wonder and beauty of Kandy was to bowl him over on the beautiful sunny day to which he awoke. Flowers and the wonderful colours of bougainvillea in abundance adorned this fabulous town which rests in a hollow amongst the high tea mountains. The streets run down to the beautiful lake which is the focal point of the town, and he was taken on a drive round to the far side and looked back across the lake at the town shimmering in the sun with the famous Temple of Tooth built into a hillside. Unfortunately, with his visit being in November, he was not able to witness the great historical pageant of Perahera which is held in August, when the sacred Tooth relic of the Buddha is paraded on an enormous Maligawa elephant decked in velvet and gold, followed by a long procession including the famous Kandyan dancers. There is a great array of incredible masks of mythological figures used in Kandyan dancing and Tubby was able to buy some miniatures to take away for wall decorations.

While the elephants are chosen particularly for their size for

225

the Temple of Tooth, they are a great work beast in this part of Ceylon, up in the tea plantations. It was here that he heard of an incredible episode whereby four planters, somewhat the worse for drink, were driving at speed in the darkness of the night when they were aware that the road was impassable ahead due to the presence of an enormous elephant. Having stopped the car they began to sober up rapidly as the great beast began slowly to proceed towards them with measured step until it filled the vision through windscreen to tower over them. Before it could step on to the bonnet, its sensitive trunk touched the radiator, which was overheated from speeding, and the great beast reared up and trumpeted enough to rattle the windows and shake debris from trees round about. This completed the process to being stone cold sober, but the beast fortunately did not come back down with two legs on top of the car and instead shot off into the bush.

Before they left wonderful Kandy, Tubby was fortunate in that his companions insisted that they visit the celebrated Peradeniya Botanical Gardens which had been the headquarters of South East Asia Command in World War Two. A drive round these extensive and fabulous gardens confirmed why it had been chosen, and to have been stationed there must have been great way to spend the war. They drove through two sections of the winding way through the gardens, which were lined by enormous cabbage palms and great palms which reached hundreds of feet into the air, before they arrived at the absolutely fabulous orchid houses. It was a wonderland of colour and variety and an exciting introduction to these exotic plants which Tubby would never forget for the rest of his life.

Once out of Kandy it was not long before they began to soar up the twists and turns into the high tea country with scenes from the famous Brooke Bond tea advertisements everywhere, and whole hillsides covered with tea bushes and Tamil ladies nipping away with their nimble fingertips and casting the leaves over their shoulders into the wicker baskets. Tea factories were perched on the hills up each valley, and now and again they would see by the factories an odd tree which was in fact a tea bush allowed to grow and seed which made it even more fascinating to see how the acres and valleys of the tea bushes were kept at the hand height by the picking of the leaves when they were just right for the blending of a British cup of tea!

On and on they went for over 6,000 feet, passing the highest point in the road before the descent into the lovely centre-point of the high tea country, Nuwara Eliya, which in some ways seemed more British than Britain, with a famous club of the same name as the meeting point for the tea planters for miles around. There were hills and mountains all around, a climate to surpass anything back at home, an English summertime during the day, log fires and a tweed sports jacket for the cool evenings, and a Sundowner of malt whisky in the club. Tubby just simply stood and took it all in and found himself thinking of the lot of the rubber planter in the Malayan jungle – not only the steaming humidity to cope with, but also the threatening high tension of the Emergency. He thought to himself that he shouldn't ever listen to any tea planter who might bemoan his lot. This was indeed heaven on earth, and Tubby made a note that the Nuwara Eliya Club had a reciprocal membership with the Lake Club in Kuala Lumpur, so that if he ever came to be based there one day he could join. He would then come back to this beautiful island and the high tea country to walk into the Nuwara Eliya Club with full member's rights.

From Nuwara Eliya they headed south in glorious sunshine, seeing from time to time the sight of delightful waterfalls or gurgling streams which danced their way down through the valleys and under rocks to emerge again 20 yards further along and go on their bubbling way. They finally broke out of the wonderful high tea country at Haputale Gap where they all got out of the car and stood in silence at the vista of the whole of the southern part of Ceylon stretched out before them. One set of lower hills, then the terraced paddy fields, reached down to the plains and on to Galle on the coast by the dazzling sea. It was easy to feel like a king looking out over his whole realm from this spot, or Christ at his temptations being shown all the kingdoms of the earth by the devil.

From Haputale Gap the road descended quite rapidly and

swung around to the north below Adam's Peak. It was dark when they returned to Colombo and the Galle Face hotel. All the way back on the way to Colombo, Tubby had just sat quietly locking into his mind and memory the sheer beauty and variety of sights they had experienced in the beautiful high tea country of this jewel of an island. Before his return to Singapore on the 14th November he had to work up to the hardest part of his visit.

It was most opportune to have this incredible experience at his age, and all on an expense account, but it had to be paid for by the resulting business his trip would generate. Therefore he had set aside the next day to be on his own in the Galle Face doing his sums, in order to turn all his notes and conversations with all the people in the trade, advertising and marketing division into potential turnover figures for the export department. Not only would he have to justify his projections for the three major products of soap, toothpaste and detergent in the short term, but also in the long term for toothpaste and detergent, as the basis for investment in local manufacture.

While Tubby had only the experience of going into Iraq for a two to three year period which had been cut short, in four months he had experienced what a new van selling operation alone could do to boost turnover. In that short initial period he had cleared all the Hasso Brothers' stocks in Baghdad for a desperate replacement shipment from the UK, which had then been held up coming from Basra to Baghdad. The trick would be to widen the horizons of Mr Rajandram to a vision of the sort of volume he must anticipate going through his warehouses compared with what must be regarded as a trickle currently. Tubby had made the assessment, that long term, his organisation under his son, Maharajah, could take things up to a point where volume would be meeting the required turnover to support a local manufacturing facility, as had happened in Singapore/Malaya, Thailand and Hong Kong. By the end of the day Tubby was pretty knocked out from the figure work, but was soon revived by the prospect of going to sample a wonderful range of local curries and extras in the home of the Horshington family.

It was a beautiful and fascinating experience to hear of the lovely marriage which had developed from an arranged marriage even though the Horshingtons both came from Christian/Tamil families. The sad aspect was hearing how they had had to adapt to help the children cope with changes and pressures on the political front as the people of the island evolved to independence, against the ethnic pressures exerted by two main blocs of different basic languages and religions.

Since Tim Horshington had very real experience of up-to-date marketing, promotional and advertising techniques, Tubby was able to check out with him his ideas for increasing through-put into the trade and points of sale, while inducing the consumers to buy with advertising and promotion. Tim Hor-shington was very enthusiastic, though Tubby was never quite sure if the prime reason for his excitement was the thought of billings from advertising and promotional work which might come to IAS. As an inducement, Tubby had conveyed to him that he had not seen anything in Grant Advertising to recom-mend the switch from IAS, however great the pressures might be from New York for a US branch agency.

The next day he ate his breakfast with some apprehension about the meeting to come with Mr Rajandram, and once there he found with him young Maharajah for the next generation, and of course John Fernando, who had been with them on the trip and had obviously reported back to the old man.

Tubby was well aware that when he came to the actual figures they may be hard for the old man to take on board, so he led in with a resumé of the places they had visited and his opinion of how the trade and market worked at the various levels of distribution out to the main centres, since Colombo would be the landing point for the imported products initially. During the build-up process, he did notice that John Fernando was beginning to nod in approval and confirm his agreement and young Maharajah seemed to be enthusing at the future prospects. When it came to the figures for the three main products, the level of ordering, and the time schedule Tubby would like to put through to London export, the old man went somewhat pale again and Tubby deemed it was now his turn to shut up and allow them to resort to their own language. It was absolutely fascinating to listen to the rapid-fire Tamil while watching the body language which went with it.

From this Tubby was able to get a feel of how things were moving under the to-and-fro of the arguments and discussions, and by the time the dust settled a bit he was brought into the proceedings again. It did appear that in spite of the tale of the Afghan money lender years ago, the financing of such quantities of toothpaste, soap and detergent would need to be worked upon.

Fortunately he had gained enough of a rapport with all the parties involved to be able to have a frank discussion and establish certain ground rules which were the basis of his communications to the export manager in London. It certainly helped that Tubby was able to confirm that IAS Limited would be the advertising agents, since Mr Rajandran held Tim Horshington and Estelle Goodchilde in high regard. Dear old Rajandram was still trying to come to terms with the scope of business volume which he might eventually attain, but nevertheless there was an underlying air of excitement as they all went out for lunch together.

Tubby had asked that he might be dropped back at the Galle Face and left for the rest of the day, with a promise that a car would collect him and take him to the airport in the morning. Tubby was on a bit of a high after getting through the meeting more or less with his volume figures intact, and was keen to get his report and projections off to London to initiate the export process. He thought he might type on the flight back across to Singapore but he fortunately compelled himself to sit down and get as much done as possible in the remainder of the day, followed by a swim in the pool at the Galle Face and a good evening meal.

He felt in good form in the morning over breakfast. It was good to have nailed down the visit to Ceylon since he was well aware that once he hit the ground in Singapore he was likely to get enveloped in the increasing pace of the moves towards the new subsidiary. John Fernando arrived with transport to take him to another airport serving Colombo called Katunayaka, since after the entry episode with KLM he thought he would go back by Britannia and dear old BOAC after all. The airport buildings in those days were somewhat primitive and one sat or stood around with the other passengers waiting and even mingled with those who came off the plane when it eventually arrived – about an hour late, which was not too bad for the Britannia.

Tubby was quite fascinated to notice that among the rag tag mixture which came off the plane there was Jack Kramer, Kenny Rosewall, Frank Schroder, the two incredible Panchos (Gonzales and Segura) and some other exponents of the power tennis group who had broken off to form a professional circus and had therefore been debarred from Wimbledon. Here they were out of the glamorous spotlights in some backwater airport in Ceylon for a scheduled day of exhibition matches to a fee-paying crowd. It was always fascinating to Tubby to see people like this in their ordinary working day situation, away from the spotlight of the hyped-up glamour. Tubby remembered during his stay in London seeing famous stage actors flitting away from the back doors of theatres in the West End in the shadows after the show. They would pull up their collar round their ears against the wind and the rain, and slip away into the night, unseen and unnoticed by the fans who had been clapping with a standing ovation just fifteen minutes previously. In reality these men were transitory nomads plying their trade and tennis expertise to the highest bidder.

Tubby was soon settling himself into his first class seat at the rear of the Britannia for the relatively short journey across the sea to Singapore. He was about to set up his typewriter on the feeding table when he discovered he was sitting next to a New Zealand tea merchant returning from a buying visit to Ceylon and who turned out to be an elder statesman in All Black rugby circles in New Zealand.

Some years earlier Tubby had received from his uncle in South Africa a pictorial booklet on the mid-fifties epic tour by the All Blacks to South Africa and the test matches against the Springboks. He had vivid recall of the photographs of the legendary Kevin Skinner holding back those three neanderthal

Africaaner Springbok forwards answering to the names of Yap Bekker, De Toit and Koch, with the support of a ghoul-like All Black forward called S F Hill.

He began to listen enthralled as his tea merchant friend from New Zealand began to relate some inside stories about the return tour of the Springboks to New Zealand. They won the first test against the All Blacks with all sorts of things going on in the front row in order to stop the New Zealand hooker Hemi from seeing the ball properly when the scrums were down.

The reputations and power in rugby at this level were such that the legendary Kevin Skinner had apparently retired. He was sent up to the hill country to fell trees and hump sheep around to get himself totally fit for a come-back in the second test against the Springboks. The legend had it that Kevin Skinner sorted out Koch, De Toit and Bekker by propping first on one side and then on the other in the second half, to make the series one-all. The rugby stories and folklore Tubby picked up on this trip gave him ample to regale the faithful in post-game bar situations for many years to come.

In BOAC Britannia terms, the trip was proving to be uneventful until they had had their good meal, and the captain announced that his antenna at the front had picked up the outline of an anvil-shaped thunder-head some distance ahead, which he would attempt to avoid by going round it. However, the waiter had just arrived near their seats with his tray full of liqueur bottles as the turbulence of the thunder-head caught up with them. It was simply magnificent the way he placed himself by the shoulder against the bulkhead and delicately cast his free arm round this selection of expensive and delightful liquids in a loving caress to hold them safe until the shudders began to subside. From Tubby's long viewpoint seated at the back, the tail unit seemed to return once more to be in a straight line with the rest of the plane's fuselage.

30

LIFE IN SINGAPORE EVOLVES

It was dark when they reached Singapore, and Tubby began to think that his ongoing, non-existent tax status might be at an end since the immigration officer on duty turned a bit awkward. His passport was stamped on the 15th November 1958 with a special pass only valid for two weeks, within which time he was to report to the immigration department. Once back in the solace of Amber Mansions and the tender administrations of Cookie, he made a note in his diary writ large: 'See the immigration department within the prescribed time' so as not to jeopardise this wonderful set-up he was enjoying in Singapore as non-taxable and not really resident.

Van Marken had given the old Zephyr a run from time to time since Tubby had been away for two weeks. Back at the office he somehow had to fend off Jim Kevlin on matters concerning the new subsidiary and the Singapore/Malaya activities which he was supposed to be handing over, with his second job hat on. Tubby managed to do this long enough to get his report done and sent off to London export. It caused quite a stir with the figures in his report endorsing a longer term potential for local manufacture in Ceylon.

Jim Kevlin was particularly jumpy with a certain buzz around Harpers and the Singapore scene, since the legendary and dynamic Bill Miller was arriving the next day on a brief stopover before he finished as president of Colgate International. This was the big boss Yank with a moustache that Tubby had heard so much about when he first joined the UK subsidiary. Bill Miller was the UK general manager who had a moustache which had moved Tubby to keep his after the friendly words from John Steel about some Americans' aversion to them.

He duly arrived and was very thrilled with the way Singapore/ Malaya export territory of the UK subsidiary had blossomed into becoming a new 45th or 46th subsidiary to his Colgate International chain of overseas ventures, which were producing billings and profits approaching the level of the huge domestic Colgate Palmolive Company of New York.

The big news Bill Miller had was that his successor was going to be someone called George Lesch, who was a second generation German American from the Milwaukee area on Lake Michigan which a wave of German immigrants had settled and made their own. He was an accountant and very dynamic, and at the time Jim Kevlin and Sears Wilson-Ingraham were up-and-comings on the second floor in New York, the Lesch legend had been developing through his exploits in the Mexican subsidiary. Apparently stories which circulated round the international company were that he had gone into an ailing subsidiary in this hugely high-potential country south of the border, and had put into operation dynamic marketing plans which started to boost volume and local manufacture considerably although not so profits initially. Apparently he had the strength of character to ignore New York's cables until he saw when it was the correct time to cut back on the higher level advertising, promotional and marketing budgets, and New York began to stand in awe as the profits rolled in.

Jim Kevlin stood in awe of the dynamic Bill Miller, who was a large physical presence anyway while Jim Kevlin's small stature didn't help, but the news of George Lesch being the potential big boss of Colgate International caused Jimmy to break out in a sweat. It had been a puzzle that they hadn't heard much from Sears since his bombastic performance on the initial trip round Malaya with Desmond Brown and the other Harper entourage. Perhaps the move of leadership to George Lesch was the reasons for his demise; they would have to wait and see.

Tubby found all this closeness to the pace-makers of a multi-national American organisation of this scale too sudden and enormous to take on board. He could see it was the same pyramid mentality which operated with the American presidency. All sorts of things can go on during the elections, but once the man has the mantle of president everyone seemed to fall in line and look to the leader. The majority never seemed quite to grasp the point that people like Bill Miller and George Lesch stood out because they acted on their own initiative and thereby moved up the executive ladder. Tubby listened in complete fascination one morning when a call came through to his office from the general manager of the Venezuelan subsidiary for Bill Miller, who happened to be standing there talking to Tubby about his happy days as boss of the UK subsidiary. Bill Miller took the call and there was an exchange in a mixture of Spanish and English which made it clear that the call from the general manager of the Venezuelan subsidiary was to check with Bill Miller that he could fire the factory manager. By the answer given and the way it was given, Bill seemed to be wondering why the man was a general manager if he had to call from other side of the globe to get Bill's approval.

Once Bill Miller had gone on his way, Tubby took the opportunity to get among the selling operations of their products on Singapore island, since he believed wholeheartedly from his own selling experience in the UK that one must get integrated into the front-line scene.

There was no direct selling organisation as such, and Harper Gilfillan's big godown was the centre point from which the products moved to what he would call in the UK the wholesale trade.

The clever and very profitable marketing strategy on low export budgets had been to develop promotional teams of ladies going direct to the consumers with vans, and there were two such in Singapore. The teams were known as Miss FABs and they were made up of six girls with a supervisor, all dressed in smart white uniforms and operating from mini-bus vans which had sound equipment for broadcasting advertising jingles, in Chinese for Singapore, to create attention when they were in an area doing their door-to-door selling. Their visitations had become quite exciting events in the densely populated dwelling areas of Singapore, because of an annual promotion whereby gold rings were given away to consumers who could produce a packet of the wonderful FAB detergent when a Miss FAB knocked on the door.

It had reached the point where sometimes folks appeared with about ten packets, and others got the message wrong and were found to have tipped all the packets out on a big sheet so they could sift through the powder and find the ring, which was 22 carat gold. The Chinese acquisitiveness for gold was well known, provided the article was genuine, and to ensure this the rings came from a reputable goldsmith, with a certificate for each ring confirmed with his 'chop'. This was the word used for the ivory-headed stamp with Chinese characters for the goldsmith on each of the certificates, stating the weight of gold in each ring and its value.

Tubby went round to the Harpers godown in Havelock Road to meet with the Miss FAB teams as they arrived back after their day's operation. As usual, the Chinese seller of seaweed juice arrived with his shoulder pole supporting his big flagon of seaweed juice, and on the other arm the glasses, and water for cleaning them. The liquid seaweed juice was renowned as a great restorer of the blood from the fatigue of their day out and about in the tropical heat, and Tubby talked to them as they relaxed at the end of a busy day.

One of the team leaders was a very striking, tall Chinese lady called Miss Lym, who ran her team as a strictly controlled unit, whereas the other team was a bit more relaxed under the motherly care of a rather large and round Chinese-Eurasian lady called Dolly Quintell.

Their vehicles were Bedford mini buses in dazzling white, emblazoned with logos of Ajax, Palmolive soap and Colgate toothpaste. Once Tubby had finished with the Harpers chap, who was then Dirk Deganhart, he was interested in having a look round the godown and was shown round by the huge Chinese in charge, whose name was Bah Seng. Behind his desk near the entrance Bah Seng resembled the ever-present Buddhas Tubby had seen in the temples in Ceylon, Burma and Thailand, or the character – Odd Job in the film – *Goldfinger*.

On the celebrated trip round the federation with Sears Wilson-Ingraham and the entourage they had really just passed

236

through Johore from the causeway and back, so Tubby was quite keen to drive out and across the famous Causeway, and see how the trade set up compared with the Federation mainland. The Federation had been independent since 1956 with the constitution weighted towards the Malays at half of the population, whereas Singapore Island was 90% Chinese and a free port. This meant there was a price advantage which brought many folk from the Federation across the Causeway to the rows of stalls on the Singapore side, run by Chinese entrepreneurs. This trade was much resented by the Malay Police and customs officials on the federation side and every now and again they would seek to make an example of someone coming back across the Causeway laden with goods bought on the island.

Because Singapore was still 'British' and had the same time lag for replacing motor tax discs on the windscreen of the car beyond the end of the month, Tubby had yet to renew his. He had not realised that in the Federation, Motor Tax renewal was strictly kept to the first day of the month. This was often used as a means of making a point against people who came across the Causeway from the Island if it was spotted that their Motor Tax disc was out of date according to Federation rules. Tubby was caught up on this and taken to a Police Station where he had to wait for some time until a very large and imposing Sikh Police Inspector with large khaki turban around his head came back from his lunch.

Noting the inspector was a Sikh, Tubby did remember that, with the balance towards the Malays, the federation was in reality an Islamic state, so besides producing his international driving licence, he fortunately had with him his Iraq driving licence too, all made out in Arabic script to which the Malay script, called Jawi, is very similar. Whether this carried some weight or not he was not quite sure, but it was certainly studied in some detail and he was eventually allowed to go on his way with a severe ticking off.

Once again he thought he was going to be rumbled as to his non-resident tax status by being caught with his out of date road tax, so he made haste to get back across the Causeway into the safety of Singapore. The very next day he made sure he got his car tax paid and the proper disc in his windscreen, and on the 22nd November went to the immigration department seven days earlier than his special pass allowed from the airport on his return from Ceylon. Fortunately there was no problem, and his passport got a stamp extending his status to the 20th January 1959, with a note that he was to obtain an identity card. He could only think that the official on duty on the 15th November when he flew in from Ceylon was reacting to anti-British rhetoric building up to forthcoming elections. Thus he made a note in his diary that he must aim to start 1959 with a proper visit again to Sarawak, Brunei and North Borneo in order to get him out of Singapore again for re-entry on yet another two month visitor's pass.

While Tubby was doing his best to maintain his non-tax status, as per the example of his friend in Baghdad – the Horlicks rep, alias The Card, he was horrified to find out that Jim Kevlin was getting more and more bogged down with the British civil servant types and had gone and registered himself in Singapore for residency. How long before they asked for names of the other ex-pats on the payroll? Then he relaxed as he realised he was not on the payroll of the new subsidiary – he was London export troubleshooter for the vast areas of the Far East.

The food and the variety thereof back at the flat at Amber Mansions was getting more and more wonderful as Cookie's hidden talents were brought out into the open. Sander van Marken was making efforts to get back to the flat for evening meals more regularly in spite of his fanaticism over rowing, which took him from work down to the Rowing Club at the docks on the Inner Roads each day.

Tubby's social life grew and expanded from his involvements with the rugby season at the cricket club, though his schedule of away trips had been restricting his rugby involvement to the minor games on the Monday and Wednesday evening. However, he was telling Scoops Urquhart about his adventures in Ceylon and how things compared to his childhood experiences when his father was there, when Scoops asked if he would play for the Tankards this coming Saturday for a fixture arranged at the Naval Base against the Senior Service personnel. Apparently, the Tankards was a rugby club on Barbarians lines in that it had no club house, always played away fixtures and raised teams by invitation. Founders and leading lights were Scoops and a Dr Paddy Bye, who was in a GP practice in Singapore and quite fanatical about his rugby.

The Tankards' club colours were all white like England but with a black tankard over the left breast and black socks with white tops. The club had been formed to help people like Tubby and other business types passing through to have a game, and also the vast range of service people on the island at the various bases for air force, navy and army. They, too, were en route with the Emergency, and starved of competitive games, so the Tankards provided a great opportunity to meet up with a lot of others who were keen on the game. Because of the pool of talent available on Singapore at that time, the Tankards had built up a good reputation and even progressed to a silver summer tie with black tankards on it and a black winter tie with silver tankards on it, ordered from a tailor's shop in Cambridge.

Anyway, Scoops asked Tubby if he would play loose forward for the Tankards against a Navy team at the Naval Base the next Saturday, and thus it was they gathered at this great historic establishment on the north side of the island, looking across the narrows to the mainland and some miles down from the Causeway towards the Seletar RAF base – home for the Sunderland flying boats.

The accepted, but never mentioned, motivation for Scoops to organise the Tankards was that it allowed him to pick himself at full back and play the captain's role from there. Anyway, he did have a fairly hefty boot on either foot for clearing the line. Tubby knew quite a few of the others from the rugger circles and the cricket club, but even so he was impressed by the size of his fellow forwards. One huge bloke was a regular with Blackheath and was out from London from Butterworths, the printers of the paper currency of the North Borneo company.

239

What they had not been aware of was that after Scoops had arranged the fixture, HMS Ark Royal had come into the Naval Base on the Thursday night. Besides having a huge complement of crew, there was a peacetime tradition in the navy that capital ships of this size showed the flag. For this the crews often contained top flight athletes across various sporting disciplines so that the British Navy could always be seen to give a 'good show' whenever they touched the port on official visits. Anyway, as the game progressed it was soon apparent that the naval side was brim-full of fairly talented blokes such as Tremayne Rodd of Scotland and London Scottish, besides those from Ark Royal which had a big enough flight deck for them to keep fit. They were really relishing being back on lovely turf and having the great sporting facilities of this historic Naval Base. The Tankards got a fair old drubbing for Tubby's first occasion, but the disappointing defeat was more than recompensed by the vast social facilities available at the Naval Base, and at one stage later the Tankards' scrum half was seen going headfirst down a bowling alley having failed to release his fingers from the holes of the big heavy ball at the right moment.

Scoops lived in a fairly palatial Straits Steam Ship mess and part of his aura and mystique was the fabulous old American car he had which had the push-button electronics to move back the canvas top and stow it into a space before the boot and close the lid. Once stowed down in this way the big black car resembled a large long bath behind a large bonnet and windscreen. When they came to leave at goodness knows what time, the car would not start and had to be abandoned for collection the next day.

On the Sunday morning Tubby took Scoops out in the Zephyr to the Naval Base where they looked up some chums from the night before. A particular surgeon, Captain Sam Ross Wallace, insisted that they repair to the mess once he heard the story that the old American car had packed in, and they were going to proceed with the hair-raising experience of pulling it back behind the Zephyr. Sam Ross Wallace was a bit of a social climber really since they found out he was a dental surgeon really, and tried to hide the fact. His main reason for hanging around the Tankards appeared to be that one of the gang, called Mark Chilton, who was with William Jacks (M) Ltd, had a father who was a celebrated air Vice-Marshall, or something of that level, and was therefore worth getting acquainted with by someone with aspirations to climb the ranks in the armed forces.

Eventually they got Scoops' big old American tub safely towed back to Singapore at his mess to await repair and thus ended another most eventful and interesting weekend. Tubby was certainly beginning to revel in this fortunate state of affairs which he had dropped into, he even began to come to terms with the incredible humidity and without doubt the haven of his air-conditioned bedroom was a major factor.

After the episode across the causeway in Johore and the Sikh Police Officer and his eventual extension of his pass to the 20th January 1959, Tubby started to make plans for a second visit to Sarawak and the Borneo territories. He was first and foremost the export rep for the UK subsidiary despite the pressures and demands that were coming upon him from Jim Kevlin to help with recruitment of staff for the new subsidiary, which was going to be known as Colgate Palmolive (Malaya) Limited.

Tubby found that the Harper Gilfillan chap now in Kuching office was a man named Graham Wood who had come back from leave to this new posting. It was considered a bit of an outpost like Sibu, where the big red-headed Frank Burke-Gaffney was based, and Tubby thought to himself that this posting had probably been chosen because Graham Wood was considered to be a bit of a loner. Tubby had met him briefly on the trip through before he had gone on leave from Taiping, and had been impressed by the fact that he was the only Harper Gilfillan executive who could speak Chinese since he had become fluent in the Hokkien dialect. Everyone learned to speak Malay as the easiest and most popular means of verbal communication, which in reality was an equivalent to the pidgen English used in West Africa, and throughout Singapore and Malaya it was known as Bazaar Malay.

There was certainly pressure developing in the Federation across the causeway for Malay to be the national language, though it could not really cope. Jim Kevlin and Tubby had started to take lessons in Malay, but alas, the teacher was a very self-opinionated Malay of the Singapore minority, and they soon found out that they were not picking up the sort of Malay to communicate with in the market and with people in general. The realisation of this came to Tubby when he came back into the office in Collyer Quay one day and said to Yim Ah Hoi, 'Mana Tuan pergi?' (Where has the boss gone?). Yim hardly looked up from his desk but just shouted after Tubby as he went to his room, 'Disipi – Harpers.' Tubby came back out of his room and repeated, 'Disipi – Harpers?' to which Yim replied, 'He's gone to Harper Gilfillan.' Between them, they worked out that 'Disipi – Harpers' was Bazaar Malay for 'Dia suda pergi ka Harper Gilfillan.' which was the Malay Tubby was being taught.

It was understandable that Tubby, with all his tripping around, was quite glad to have the lessons lapse and he found he could do far better out in the market place, or by going out and dining with Yim and the Chinese salesmen to lovely eating places like the People's Park at the far end of North Bridge Road, where the local people would go and eat after work, particularly on a Friday evening. The People's Park was a great shopping and eating area where one sat on stools at bench tables where all manner of marvellous Chinese food was served up. Also, it was a great way to pick up the local feel of the real Singapore and get to know local staff and establish a rapport with them, and learn the language and their customs.

Singapore really was a wild place at that time with the electioneering scene warming up towards the prospect of independence, with Lee Quan Yew, a brilliant lawyer and orator, giving anti-British speeches, while a little Chinese with a black head of hair and big glasses, Ong En Guan, peddled the Communist line as per Chairman Mao. The other contender of note who was active in the political field was a rather smooth Eurasian gentleman called David Marshall who had a sort of socialist middle of the road party called the People's Party.

After Tubby had seen the inside of an opium den in Bangkok he felt that many of the trishaw men who peddled their three wheel taxi cabs round the streets resembled the inmates. There were tales of children being sold into *wayangs* – Chinese theatres – to help pay for drug habits. The Triads, or Chinese Mafia Tongs, were also active, and once there were two or three slashings in the streets a day, there would appear in the *Straits Times* a report that Gurkha troops had been brought in to patrol certain areas of the city. The street murders would subside since the sight of the immaculately turned-out Gurkha troops, two by two, walking round the streets with their famous *kukri* knives at the back of their belts was enough to make any Triad killer have second thoughts. Triad activities were strictly among the Chinese and never involved the other races in the Singapore mix.

With no changes of seasons, the regular arrival of darkness at about 7 p.m. and the usually glorious sunny morning for going to work, one soon became detached from UK living, and it was interesting that the UK became no more special than any other country round the world in terms of prominence and reportage in the media of any events and politics going on back home.

While humidity became just part of normal living, Tubby could not quite get used to the tremendous tropical downpours which could happen often at knocking-off time when people were all about to go home from work. Most people had their lacquered parchment umbrellas, but it was always highly amusing to see the number of office workers make a run for it across the street by holding just a flattened folded newspaper over their heads which turned into sodden papier-maché almost as you watched it. The trishaw men simply carried on as before knowing that the heat was such that they would dry out once the downpour stopped, but it was the driving conditions which Tubby found most alarming.

The traffic was chaotic enough around Singapore with taxi men pressing on the hooters and bouncing off one another at corners, but when the tropical downpours came and the car windows had to be shut they would immediately steam up. One time he was coming back via the Bukit Tima Road when a tropical downpour came on and he reached Newton roundabout to find that the monsoon drains had ceased to cope and the roundabout area had become within minutes a mini lake with five roadways emerging from it.

Having five weeks or more before setting off for Sarawak on New Year's Day, he had been able to develop some sort of pattern to life in Singapore, which was centred round the cricket club and the Tankards rugger team. Scoops Urquhart had a yen for the secretary to the High Commissioner, a lively character called Liz Graham who used to breeze round Singapore on a scooter, and it was always quite a hoot to see the High Commissioner's Rolls Royce stop in the street near Raffles Square, or somewhere, and the *sais* would open the door for Liz to get out of the back, then open the boot and lift out her scooter for her to drive off round the shops or wherever. Liz lived in a mess for civil service girls with Jean Tierney and others who were all part of the social circle.

In the lift one morning going up into the office building in Collyer Quay, Tubby bumped into an elder statesman in Singapore called Andrew Gilmour. They had met in the cricket club and found that he had an office on a higher floor, where he was secretary and sort of founder of the British European Association. Andrew had twelve years of colonial service and latterly the experience of being a Japanese prisoner-of-war after the collapse of the island, and with many Dutch from the former East Indies and other Europeans now in Singapore in some numbers, he had formed this new association. This had happened some two years earlier, so Tubby became an early member and thereby a recipient of the monthly magazine called *The Beam*.

By now Tubby played possibly two games of rugby a week and squash fairly regularly, once he began to find others who lacked finesse like himself and simply wanted a good bash around the court. Very early on he had had a game with one of the regulars in the club called Alf Willings who was quite a good wing three-quarter and a good fast bowler in the cricket season. It was a farce for Tubby to play with him since he was

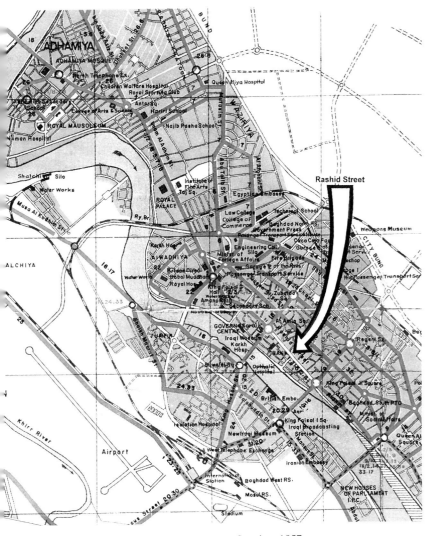

Rashid Street

Street map by Baghdad Passenger & Transport Service, 1957

WANTED –
Have you seen this man?

The leader, Abdul Kerim Kassim, saluting the people

Tankards XV at naval base, November 1959

:d MGA, Ipoh Station

:cottish Aviation Twin Pioneer.

Photo by AIR-BRITAIN

Tubby greeting Mr Rajandram at Columbo with Tim in background
Photo: The Associated Newspaper of Ceylon Ltd, Columbo

Tubby with Tong deputies

FAH Studio, K.L

the market with Miss FABs and Towkays

van Marken

Cookie and Amah at
Amber Mansions

so good he could just stand in the middle and dictate the ball all round the place with the minimum of effort. Tubby began playing prop forward since he was now a very fit 200 pounds and with a spell of more regular play he made the Saturday Club side for the odd game before going off on his travels again.

There was a particular amusing Irishman in the club called Eddie Flannigan who graduated from Trinity Dublin and made his living as a laid-back rubber broker on the exchange in Singapore. The two Celts struck up quite a friendship and Flannigan began to refer to him as Brian Boru because Tubby would recite on rugby occasions verses about the revered Irish Celtic chief of that name, and his celebrated and very original contraceptive in those far off days before Rome and the Holy See became the power in the land.

Tubby tried to establish a discipline whereby he wrote to the folks at home on a Sunday morning sitting out on the verandah at Amber Mansions, but it came to pass that he had to be finished by 11 a.m. or so, because before noon the phone would invariably ring and the Dublin voice of Flannigan would be there, him having just surfaced and still somewhat slurred. Tubby would catch enough just to hear the words: 'Brian Boru – I'll see you down at the club shortly.'

There was a tradition among the ex-pats in the Far East locations to resort to eating a curry tiffin at Sunday lunchtimes when a crowd would gradually come together at the cricket club drinking their Anchor beers before moving off somewhere. One certainly did not eat a curry tiffin where the catering staff were Chinese, since it was usually hotted up by cutting in large lumps of hot chillies which are stronger than curry powder. More often time would run on towards 4 p.m. when the spirit moved them to go round to the lovely English-style pub run by two old dears called the Tangle Inn, where they served the most marvellous Nasi Goreng. By strict translation this is fried rice, which is what the dish primarily is, but done in a marvellous round wok with all sorts of things chopped up in it and topped with two marvellous fried eggs to which would be added soy sauce for a really rounded, wonderful eating experience.

245

Before the evening meal on Sundays, Tubby would seek to maintain his kirk heritage by ending the day with a walk round the corner from the flat to the Singapore Presbyterian Church which was presided over by 'Bishop' Greer. Although part of the Presbyterian Church of England, as were the other three ex-patriate Presbyterian churches with the name of St Andrews' in Kuala Lumpur, Ipoh and Penang, they were actually run far more on the kirk lines of the Church of Scotland – which in Scotland are known as the parish churches to which most ex-pats attending could relate.

'Bishop' Greer in Singapore was very much of the polished Edinburgh Kirk style, a long-term incumbent, and of the generation of ex-pats who had been through the Japanese occupation and prison camp experiences following the surrender of the Island and the march out to Changi. In addition to being the minister in charge of the Singapore church, he had responsibilities for the scattered ex-pats across Sarawak and the Borneo territories and made visits to administer the sacraments at least four times per year to fulfil Church of Scotland requirements. None of this once or twice a week Eucharist which the Anglicans and Episcopalians have. Alas, as per Tubby's choirboy memories, the sermons of 'Bishop' Greer were too long and too dull.

After Tubby's enlightening experience of Christian fellowship with the Hasso Brothers in Baghdad, and his ongoing experiences now in the Far East, there was a deepening awareness as to just how far mankind can lose sight of the true understanding and vision of Christ's Church as a spiritual bond of believers. Throughout the world man-made denominations with rituals, orders and vestments socially suited to an earth-bound dimension had been substituted for the truth – eternal and spiritual. Little wonder that these temporal substitutes had become the contention for so many wars and cataclysms – particularly in Europe where the initial impetus from the dynamism of Christianity had been so vital an ingredient.

In complete contrast he had met up with a dear lady in Singapore called Celia Downwood whom he remembered going off with great affection from his home church in 1938 to be a missionary in China. Her experiences were not unlike those of Gladys Aylward's life story in that she became fluent in the Teochew dialect in the Swatow area of the mainland away up north from Hong Kong and had ended up totally on her own in a small place called Swabue and had had to flee from there further inland to Wukingfu from the advancing Japanese army. It wasn't until 1944 that she got out via an American plane from Kunming over the Himalayas to Calcutta after a horrendous journey of hundreds of miles by land in a charcoal-powered lorry.

After a year's leave she was back in Swabue doing what seemed to be 'real' missionary work by just simply living and witnessing her Christian way of life and being part of the community, and she was still there in 1949 when they were overrun by the Communists' advance. She was obviously held in such high esteem and was so much integrated into the community that it wasn't until the conflict in Korea in 1951 that the People's Republic decided to get rid of her as a foreign imperialist. However, it was some seven months before an exit visa was produced and she was dumped in Hong Kong without any of her worldly possessions accumulated over the years.

Alas, by the time Tubby met up with her she was sadly 'piggy in the middle' between the Chinese Christian Church in Singapore, many of whose leaders had come out of China, and the four churches of St Andrew's for ex-pats, whom they considered to be Heretics by their standards, even though their origin church in Swatow had been founded by the Presbyterian Church which had financed Celia and others before her to go out to China in the first place.

Many months later Tubby was to bring her back from the hill station of Frazer's Hill, north of Kuala Lumpur, where she had been recuperating after an illness. On the way south through the black areas of Johore his car broke down and they had to stop at a garage near Yong Peng, a terrorist black spot. Because of the chaos in China in 1938–1939, when she first went there, she had not been able to go on a course to learn Mandarin and had therefore learnt to read and write the characters, but spoke the local dialect of Teochew which gave her freedom of speech with the Hokkiens as well. She commented once they were on their way again that the Chinese in the garage at Yong Peng were talking Mandarin amongst themselves, which was the standard dialect established for the Communist insurgents in the jungle.

There were two other missionary ladies who worked and witnessed like Celia Downwood as part of the Chinese community in a fenced new village in the Johore black spot area round Kulai.

Agnes Richards and Joyce Lovell simply lived out their Christian faith in this new village and were much loved by the locals, having had initial experience in the North of China so that they did speak Mandarin. Joyce was a midwife and her 'put-put' Morris Minor car was known throughout the whole area as she went on her missions of mercy at all hours outside the new village, and it was said that the distinctive sound of her car meant that she never got ambushed which was a common hazard for most others, and particularly the rubber planters.

Being aware of the celebrated Somerset Maugham stories about Raffles Hotel, the planters and their wives and their goings-on, Tubby began to hear incidents of what it was really like trying to keep a rubber estate going at full output with Communist insurgents moving about from the jungle. He was soon to experience it for himself because a weekend Tankards fixture had been arranged at the huge 19,000 acre Dunlop rubber estate at Ladang Geddes which was on the eastern edge of the state of Negri Sembilan, north of Johore and Malacca.

It was now into December and they were to be there by lunchtime, so they had to set off in their cars early on the Saturday morning, and with Mark Chilton Tubby drove into the Naval Base to pick up two officers from a destroyer flotilla recently docked. Scoops had got their names for invitation from Ronny Loughton who had arranged the Naval Base XV a week or so earlier.

Soon they were across the Causeway and out of Johore

248

heading north, crossing the only east/west road at a place called Ayer Hitam. This was really black bandit territory and could not be motored through after dark because of curfew, and from there on, the road passed another huge rubber estate establishment before Labis where they crossed the railway heading north. The road up through Johore followed the railway line as both ran along the western edge of this enormous empty *ulu* area of Malaya which was being designated wildlife sanctuaries and reserves. This huge empty area stretched across to the east coast along the China sea where there was then no road going north/south, and the Dunlop rubber estate to which they were heading was at the western side of this huge empty area of jungle and swampland.

The town of Gemas was where the great northern railway line split off because of the central highlands to the north and one railway line went left then to go round up to Kuala Lumpur and on up the populated west coast, while the other line went right up through the middle and ended up at Kota Baru in the north-east monsoon-ridden areas. The extra mileage by the normal road system to get to Rompin and the estates just north at Bahau was pretty tremendous. Fortunately they had heard from some chaps in the Gurkhas that for easy access by the Emergency troops against insurgents, the sappers had cut a laterite road through from Gemas to Rompin. At Gemas they had met up with another car which had picked up two South Africans with a Gurkha regiment based in the area at Muar, further west, and were soon bashing it along this huge red laterite road carved out through the jungle. Tubby was amazed to see just how utterly thin was the layer of soil from which grows the whole tropical jungle, because of so much leaf mould and rotting vegetation continually providing nourishment and the abundant supply of rainwater. Once the jungle trees are removed, nothing but this arid-looking, very red laterite remains which is soon eroded by the rain.

The day they were travelling was very dry and Tubby soon realised that by going in convoy line-astern he was driving in a continuing barrage of red laterite from the car in front, so he stepped on the accelerator so that he could get alongside Tom

249

Loughead's car and continue the journey line-abreast with both clear of any laterite slipstream. When Tom Loughead looked in his mirror and saw the manoeuvre, he thought that he was going to be overtaken and end up in the laterite stream. It wasn't long before both cars were screaming along this laterite road at nearly 90, waving at one another until somebody yelled from the back seat that there was a point ahead where the road was going to enter a gate and one or other of them would have to throw out the drag chains because they simply couldn't get through together. Fortunately this was done in time for both to pass through line-astern and at manageable speed.

When they turned into the estate area, it was absolutely fascinating to see what that great economic machine called the British Empire had done to create a huge, profitable and tightly managed rubber industry in this equatorial Malay peninsula from rubber plants spirited from Manaus on the Amazon and nurtured in Kew Gardens while estates like this were being prepared for the full-grown rubber trees with organised daily tapping of the white sap.

To grow rubber trees to provide a steady stream of the product on this commercial scale, the estate was divided into three parts, one of which had trees being tapped daily for the latex, while another third was growing, which by 1958 had reached a short four year period or so to be ready for tapping, while the third part was being cleared of old trees ready for replanting.

The actual rugger field or *padang* was just off the estate, overlooked by the usual well appointed ex-pats club with bar facilities and the odd rooms for overnight stays. There was a great cheer when they arrived since the visit of an invitation rugger team from Singapore was a gala occasion for the isolated rubber planters for miles around, many of whom had offered accommodation to the visiting Tankard players. The weather was good, the pitch was good, the match was not too strenuous and they had a fairly comfortable win. It was obvious that the evening gathering was to be the main event.

Looking at the map it could be seen that the estate was established on higher ground and at the headwaters of several tributaries of rivers, which eventually wended their way all the way down to the east coast. This was simply not the gorgeous hill country of the tea planter recently visited by Tubby. This was the steaming hot tropical Malayan jungle, with the added tension of the Emergency, and Tubby noticed that most of the vehicles parked outside were armour plated Landrovers.

The plates on the windows at the sides and the windscreen would be screwed down for when they set off back to their estates and they would peer through slits in these overlay plates. There were high powered carbines and heavy-duty revolvers and related ammunition bands, and it took a special breed of character to live and work in these conditions. They were indeed, and among them was one particular old character in a pith helmet with a light suit and waistcoat of older colonial times, who could tell of still keeping the estate going in the confusion when the Japanese appeared out of the jungle on their bicycles and went on to Singapore before they returned later to take over whole peninsula.

It was easy to understand the underlying tension which prevailed even though the evening was developing into quite a thrash. The system of new villages in which the Chinese tappers lived enclosed overnight, had brought about the desired effect of bringing those Communists from the jungle nearer to the points of civilisation in order to get food and other resources. This meant they were round the rubber estates more, with very nasty episodes for planters and the tappers, since any considered to be informers were often impaled on trees as an example.

While there were armed forces from all the Commonwealth countries, including Fijians for a short while, fighting in the jungle trying to winkle out the Communist insurgents, it was the Gurkhas and South Koreans who were most feared because of their totally uncompromising attitude of taking no prisoners.

The ambush tactics particularly suited the Gurkha troops from Nepal, and one planter related how he had had a near miss one evening when he had avoided an ambush and had radioed up the position to the local Gurkhas. They moved quietly into his area and the next night he remembered some-

251

thing in the latex rooms which he hadn't done and nipped out from his bungalow on foot when the pathway had opened up before him and a Gurkha's head and shoulders appeared and told him in simple terms to: '. . . . . . off.' This he duly did and it was two nights later that he awoke to intense gunfire some distance away in his plantation and next morning quite a number of Communist dead were stacked up waiting to be taken away.

After hearing other incidents being related of tensions boiling over with shotguns being fired in each other's armour-plated vehicles, and card games ending abruptly with a grenade being put on the table, Tubby began to hope he would get to his lodgings safely that evening. He and Scoops were to be billeted with a Tony Pitt, who was a very jovial roly-poly mustachioed planter based some miles away on a smaller estate.

Some estates looked pristine clean with the bottom parts of the trees painted white, while others just carried the scars of the daily tapping on an angle to a 'v' point on the bark where a little peg allows the latex to come off the wound and drip down into a little cup which is attached round the trunk.

Tubby's senses soon sobered into a heightened state of alertness as he sat alongside Tony Pitt riding shotgun in a Landrover with all the plates down and just the slits to see out into the road ahead in the headlights. When they passed through areas where they did have whitened trees it was like travelling through a blackened war cemetery. When they passed through other areas where the trees were just cut for tapping there wasn't the throwback from the white of the tree trunks, there were just the eerie lights and shadows and the straggly branches disappearing into the darkness above the level of the headlight beam. He began to wonder what he really would do if a slant-eyed figure in cap with a red star on the front appeared from among these rows of blackened trees for a grenade to be lobbed at them followed by bursts of machine gun fire. It was indeed a very sobering experience and he was quite glad to reach Tony Pitt's bungalow to get bedded down for the night.

Beyond the mature trees on the areas being tapped, the rubber plantations can be very messy places, particularly where the muster takes place. The muster is the start of the planter's day when the tappers all gather with their specially-headed knives sharpened, since their real skill is just to re-open the angled wound on the bark sufficient for a good run of latex, because too deep cutting shortens the life of the tree for tapping purposes.

Once the tapper has done all his allocated trees and set the little cups up he comes back again for a break before he goes back on a second round to collect the latex and gather it all in before it begins to get tacky. It is all rather smelly and messy as the latex is prepared in big vats for turning into latex sheets which are then dusted in powder to minimize their stickiness, and then all laid on top of one another until they make up a transportable bale wrapped in other big latex sheets which seal the bale into a big, very heavy block of latex. These are then seen precariously balancing on the back of Chinese lorries which are stacked so high that it is prudent to make sure that overtaking them is done as quickly as possible before any fall off on to the car.

Once the tappers are back for the break while the latex is dripping, the planter usually gets back to his bungalow for the celebrated planter's breakfast. They are usually raving hungry by then and the planter's breakfast consists of a huge plate of fried everything accompanied by two large pieces of fried bread, washed down by big mugs of tea.

On this Sunday morning Tubby woke up to find Scoops sitting on the other side of the bed making increasingly aggravated mumblings while stirring a tumbler of water. He found that the state Scoops was in he didn't realise that he had put one alka seltzer into the water and the polythene insert from the container top, which was failing to dissolve in spite of all his attentions with the spoon.

When they eventually began to move about, they heard Tony shout something about a crocodile being down in the bath. When Tubby got there he found that there was indeed a small baby crocodile in the bath which Tony had found by one of the small rivers. Tubby reached down to it with his toothbrush and was absolutely horrified by the aggressive response in spite of its small size. At any approach it was up high on its front legs and snapping away with its big mouth and teeth. When they did eventually emerge they found that the bungalow had a beautiful verandah from which the ground dipped away and there was the smell of fried bacon and eggs, bread and lord knows what. The radio was in those days still broadcasting the C of E morning service for ex-pats and Tony Pitt was holding a prayer book in his hand while parading up and down his verandah, clad only in a wrapped round towel which didn't exactly enhance his roly-poly figure.

Strangely enough, Tubby did actually feel like his planter's breakfast and thoroughly enjoyed the experience of this unique meal on a real planter's bungalow verandah in the company of a real planter as host! They eventually joined the others who had drifted to the club by the rugger ground for a 'hair of the dog' and it was post-lunchtime before they got on their way. As the sun was going down and yielding to the tropical darkness, Tubby was back at the naval base enjoying a Sundowner of traditional naval pink gin on HMS *Cossack*, tied up abreast the other destroyers in the flotilla.

This was the third naval vessel to carry this famous name of *Cossack* from the one Tubby remembered in the war which had sped into the enemy-occupied fjords of Norway and rescued merchant seamen from a German tanker *Altmark* which was returning from fuelling U-boats in the Atlantic, and was carrying these merchant seamen who had been picked up from torpedoed craft.

The daring exploit of HMS *Cossack* in those dark days of the war had been mightily welcomed as something to shout about to boost the morale of the nation. Tubby was fascinated to walk round the wheel house on the destroyer and read the plaques commemorating this and other exploits in the history of this famous ship's name.

On his return to Amber Mansions from this fascinating weekend Tubby made a note that Tony Pitt would be sailing

254

home on leave from Singapore docks in February after Chinese New Year and all were invited down to the boat to see him off which was a great thrash to look forward to.

The build-up to Christmas was just not as heightened or noticeable in these parts of the world, nevertheless Harper Gilfillan had the agencies for Courvoisier brandy and VAT 69 whisky, and the stocks had been built up for the festive season and for the Chinese New Year, which came towards the end of January 1959. One evening at the cricket club, Tubby found the chaps from Sime Darby working out what they called a Hennessey Rota. It was a proven commercial fact that you were home and dry with your product if you could somehow get over to the Chinese in particular, that it gave them plenty of instant energy and in crude terms – lead in the pencil.

This had been achieved for Brand's chicken essence of all things which came in delicate small jars, and Tubby had had great difficulty trying to keep a straight face when in general talk with a salesman one day about a recent inter-office football match, the Chinese related how part of his preparation had been to take ten jars of Brand's chicken essence the night before.

The most celebrated product which had got over this message was Hennessey brandy and indeed there were hard research facts to show that the per capita consumption of brandy in Singapore and Malaya at that time was second only to France. Apparently, one of the senior directors bearing the Hennessey name had become a living legend since he came out regularly through these parts at this time of the year for the Christmas and Chinese drinking periods, and he was due shortly.

It was a fairly accepted fact that people like him in major drink companies had an alcohol tolerance level away above other normal mortals, and Mr Hennessey could go from one event to another apparently unchanged while those young chaps dedicated to accompany him from Sime Darby, the agents, fell by the wayside and had to go for a period of washing out afterwards to prevent the DTs setting in. Hence their sitting down together to establish a rota whereby they could bail out before things had gone too far, and the next one would slot in to take over while the others tried to recuperate for the next episode.

Makan was the Malay word for food and the Chinese *makan* was the term used for great gatherings of Chinese *towkays* (wholesalers) to celebrate the visit of Mr Hennessey and to impress upon them that his brandy was indeed the greatest stuff. Big sit-down Chinese *makans* were usually all at round tables and there were courses of about thirteen dishes – always an odd number. The great sport was to go round these events from table to table shouting, '*Yam Sing*' which meant that everybody had to bottoms up and empty their glasses of brandy.

Old Hennessey had become legendary amongst the Chinese in that he seemed to be able to '*Yam Sing*' all round the place and, not only that, he could go on and do two of these monster Chinese *makans* in one night. Whether old Hennessey was actually old or whether it was the drink over the years, but his appearance of older age certainly gave him status with the Chinese due to their attitude of reverence to the elderly, and ancestors in death. Anyway, he would walk away from these Chinese *makans* waving benignly to them while they all cheered and clapped and almost worshipped the ground he walked upon.

With the build-up to Chinese New Year some six weeks ahead, Tubby thought that it might be a good idea to produce a calendar for the trade for 1959 with the names of Colgate Palmolive (Malaya) Ltd and Harper Gilfillan & Co Ltd. This would be made gaudy and full of the Chinese characters for the greetings for the Chinese New Year and with all the symbols and pictures of the twelve animals which made up the cycle of the Chinese year. Without doubt the Dragon was the best of the lot and any Chinese worth his salt would try and have a male child born in that year. Failing that the Tiger was next, then there were Rats, Rabbits, Snakes, Monkeys, Cockerels, and, alas alas, the next year was going to be the year of the Pig, which didn't exactly appeal to Tubby. Nevertheless, he thought it would be helpful all round to have a good personal session with three of the long term Harper Chinese salesmen involved with their products in his office with Yim Ah Hoi, their clerk, who was becoming involved in the office scene for the new subsidiary.

It turned out to be one of the most hilarious and useful experiences, because they first listed each year from the next one to come, with the character and picture of each animal. Then Tubby asked each in turn to give him their opinion as to expected attributes for those born in each of the twelve. It emerged that the animal names also had a related property such as metal, water, wood, fire, earth, so starting with the Pig and wood, Tubby sat back absolutely fascinated as they put their ideas down on paper and then tested them on each other, first using their own Chinese dialects and then cross-referencing with other dialects. Tubby always felt inferior in that while he was trying to get to grips with some Bazaar Malay, these individuals could speak the Bazaar Malay, English and at least four dialects of Chinese, which were in effect entirely different languages although there was uniformity of the characters when it came to the written word.

At times the gathering in his office began to sound like Chinese theatre without the crashing gongs and cymbals because they became very vociferous and animated as their ideas were exchanged, before eventually coming to consensus that the Pig could bring either prosperity, or poverty, depending on which way you wanted to look at it. It was quoted that it was quite familiar for wealthy Chinese to have a wife born in the year of the Pig for breeding, while having an alternate, a dolly-bird, wife with the figure for a Cheong Sam dress, for taking out to official functions when a decorative and attractive wife was required. Even the Snake, which came out with evil-deceit could have cunning as quite a useful attribute to a child born in that year. Attributes such as benevolence, courage and fidelity were kicked around for the Cock and water and the productive reputation of the Cock was referred to as possibly no bad thing for the male Chinese psyche. At the end of the session they did come away with an agreed format to take to Tom Glaze at Grant Advertising Inc. for a mock-up and, for Tubby, it proved to be a superb exercise in terms of building up relationships with Yim and the salesmen, and gauging how they might behave and respond to higher responsibilities in the future.

After the whistle stop tour through Sarawak to North Borneo with Abe le Roux when he had hardly arrived out in the Far East, Tubby was looking forward to his first visit on his own in order to go into much more detail, since this would be an important remaining part of his London export territories with Singapore and Malaya going over to the new subsidiary of Colgate-Palmolive International. Additionally, he had been particularly fascinated to find that life there was exactly as some of the older hands in Malaya described things in Singapore and Malaya prior to the war.

He had managed to obtain a copy of *SARAWAK 1957*, the official year book for this very particular and very special domain of the Rajah Brooke family whose influence was still running this outpost of the empire. It was a hard bound book, priced at Straits $3, US $1, 7/6d Sterling, and Printed and Published in Kuching at Sarawak Government printing office by E W Goodwin OBE, government printer. It reflected the pace at which government and commerce were conducted and was quaint and old fashioned in its presentation, with the authority of the empire. On the hardback it had a dust cover with beautiful colour photograph of Astana – the Palace of the Rajah Brookes – across the river at Kuching with its manicured lawns and his official white barge (*sampan*) being rowed across by Malay oarsmen fore and aft in black *sonkos* (black turban-like hats) with the British flag hoisted at the stern.

Additionally he had been able to purchase a wonderful pictorial book on Sarawak by Hedda Morrison, whose black and white photos were simply incredible. The book had only been published in 1957 by this German lady who was married to a district officer and had put together this superb record of the races and districts and rhythm of Sarawak from accompanying her husband on his trips as administrative officer in this tried and tested system of colonialism which had worked extremely well throughout the British empire. These two books had heightened his appetite for the revisit and after being in touch with the new Harper executive over in Kuching he was even more thrilled at the prospect of the trip. Graham Wood had been back from leave in Kuching long enough to get his feet under the desk and confirmed that other than the Malayan Airways flight out to Kuching and his non-stop return from Sandakan at the far point of North Borneo, Tubby could fix up the rest of his hopping around on Borneo Airways as needed.

The other thing that Graham Wood had found out and passed on to Tubby was that there was to be a New Year's Day party for the ex-pat fraternity in Kuching to be hosted by a White Russian couple who had become major players in the social scene at Kuching since they had settled there, having had to move on from Shanghai where many of the White Russians had ended up after managing to get out alive from the post-revolutionary scene in Russia.

From the experience of the run through in early September, Tubby was able to plan out a fairly detailed schedule and communicated the outline of this to the other agents along the line since Harper Gilfillan were his agents only for Sarawak. Once into Brunei and North Borneo he was in the hands of the North Borneo Trading Company, which like Harpers was an outpost of a parent organisation in the UK in Plantation House. Finally at the last outpost, Sandakan, round the top north corner of North Borneo and south of the great Mount Kinabalu, he would have the anomaly of Mr Wong, the Chinese agent who seemed to get rid of more of his Colgate products than the North Borneo Trading Company covering the rest of North Borneo, Brunei and the island of Labuan.

With these plans well in hand, Tubby warmed to prospect of being away again since on the new subsidiary front he was becoming the diplomat or herald between the very American Jim Kevlin, raw from his first overseas subsidiary post in the Yankee satellite country of Panama, and the very British chaps of Harpers, and the Winchester types in the colonial service, still with their fingers on the Foreign Exchange situations in both Singapore and the federation.

Christmas was rapidly upon them, though the build-up and hype was not as it would be at home, and he and Sander van Marken were able to indicate to Cookie that he would be almost stood down for the festive season since Sander had so much happening on the rowing front over the Christmas holidays and he had Christmas fixed up with other Dutch expatriates in Singapore.

Tubby had an invitation to go round to the Kevlins in the evening of Christmas Day and a Tankards fixture had been arranged out at the New Zealand Canberra Squadron Base at Tengah which was some 14 miles off the Bukit Timah Causeway Road into the extreme *ulu* of the north-west corner of this tropical island. Since it was Christmas Day it had been agreed that this would be a morning fixture and as they gathered at the cricket club they did start to enter into the spirit of Christmas Day.

They got on their way in good time, and on their way towards the swamp parts of the island it became obvious that Singapore was getting a touch of the monsoon season on that morning. Sitting virtually on the equator, the island is steamy, hot and humid with good tropical downpours once the convection can get going with the heat of the day, but as they drove due west into this isolated part of the island where Tengah Base was situated it was a thoroughly miserable wet monsoon morning.

While this was a New Zealand squadron base, there were no white faces on sentry duty and indeed there seemed to have been a squad of Malay soldiers brought in for the day; once inside the base it was obvious why. Everybody seemed to be well on their way into the festivities of Christmas Day already and while the first half of the match was reasonably normal, by the second half it seemed at times as though it was 30 a side instead of 15. The game finally petered out in hilarity and after showers all retreated to the mess bar. Eventually they reached Scoops Urquhart's place some time in the afternoon where his good old Cookie had prepared a turkey for a traditional Christmas meal and somehow he did get tidied up and made the Kevlins' for the evening.

Not surprisingly, Boxing Day was spent quietly at the flat getting back to normal and getting some thank you letters off to the folks since his swing through the Borneo territories was scheduled to take nearly three weeks and he could not leave these essentials until his return. In the intervening days he finalised his schedule plans and made urgent calls concerning disturbing reports which had come through about unauthorised shipments of Palmolive soap landing in large quantities on Labuan Island, spreading into Brunei.

Being on his way on New Year's Day he kept out of mischief on New Year's Eve, though he did meet up with the Scottish chaps from the Ben Line for a few scoops before retiring. The Ben Line, based in Edinburgh and Leith, had a large mess in Singapore with Big Gibson and George Allen, leading lights on the rugger scene, having been on the fringe of Scottish international rugby. The Ben gang usually left the club in convoy for the mess and any motorised confrontation with the wild Chinese taxi men of Singapore would usually mean that there was a whole pack of fierce Caledonians to deal with.

31

SARAWAK REVISITED

There is always a first time for everything, thought Tubby. Who would have thought that he would spend New Year's Day 1959 sitting in a wartime Dakota plane belonging to Malayan Airways, heading due east across the South China Sea on the 400-mile hop from Singapore, having left at 6 a.m. He was quite excited about his re-visit to this outpost of the empire and having studied carefully the *SARAWAK 1957* year book, he was even more enthralled at the picture of benign colonialism and a place and peoples who seemed to tick over to a pace mostly attuned to the rhythms of nature across this territory spread west to east just north of the equator.

He was determined to see as much as possible of this remarkable area since he enjoyed flying and particularly at the primitive level he had found on his first trip. When he had found that the Sarawak Steamship Company still had a coastal vessel called the *MV Rejang* by which they operated a service between Kuching and the Rejang River and took passengers, he had Graham Wood of Harpers book a passage for the late afternoon of the next Monday, the 5th January. This would give him what remained of New Year's Day and three more days to do the important Kuching area from which five divisions of the colony were governed by the current member of the Rajah Brooke family and his squad of district officers.

After his hectic existence in Singapore from his return and over Christmas, this long flight was a good opportunity to do his homework and go over the details of his three week schedule which would bring him to the far end of this Malayan Airways two-way airbus system at Sandakan in North Borneo. However, he was to find out that he was not yet in touch with

262

the monsoon seasons, since he had not yet experienced the federation of Malaya in the north-east parts, only experiencing Singapore and its equatorial climates so far. The plane was within an hour of Kuching on its long haul across the South China Sea when Tubby was aware that the plane was going somewhat up and down instead of just steadily forward, and the noisy rhythm of the twin engines did not seem to be quite so constant. Looking out of the window by his seat he realised that it was now all level grey with evidence of torrential rain from time to time, nothing else visible at all.

As they got nearer to the four hour duration of this long, one-stop flight he was pleased that he really did enjoy flying, because with the constant grey scene through the window the only way in which you knew quite what was going on was the fact that your body weight would be totally pushed down into the seat one minute as though one had tripled in weight. Next minute your body was weightless and held by the safety belt with a space between one's bottom and the seat. It was fortunate that the captain had given due warning that everyone should belt-up again before these physical manifestations took place. From the previous trip which had been in benign weather, Tubby remembered the Dakota had to fly past Kuching and then swing sharp right and come in from the sea between two promontories at about 1000 feet, since some ten to fifteen miles to the west of Kuching was Mount Serapi at nearly 3000 feet.

The DC3 Dakota was of very advanced design when first introduced in the late 1930s for commercial flying, with good stout low wings and the cockpit stuck out at the head of the two engines, which were fine for the pilot and co-pilot seeing out in a normal landing and taking off situation. This was far from normal and it was obvious by the motions of the plane that the pilot had decided to try and do a dive through the grey of the monsoon storm clouds which sweep down the South China Sea to try for a land sighting to home in on the Kuching airstrip: after all, at that time it was designated as an international alternate: ICAO Class S3. 4,500 feet metal runway.

After the pilot had attempted three such diving attempts

through the grey realms of the monsoon, with passengers alternating rapidly up and down, he announced on the intercom that his fuel situation was such that they must make straight for Sibu, which was the next airbus stop on their course east situated on the Great Rejang River. Sibu airstrip was rated ICAO Class E5 with a 3,600 foot metal runway, and fortunately the visibility was fine, Sibu being much further inland from the South China Sea.

After the fun and games of trying to get into Kuching, Tubby was relieved to find that Frank Burke-Gaffney at Harpers had had a phone call from Kuching about the flight problem and had come to the airport building at Sibu. Frank was able to assure him at once that he had not missed the other Dakota 'bus' returning to Singapore from Sandakan, since they crossed at about Sibu, and that meant Tubby was able to fly back to Kuching without delay.

The airport buildings in these places were small and single-storey with a glass-windowed control tower on the top. They sat down together in the lounge on a wall chair backed to the window, open on to the tarmac. He was telling Frank about his booking on the *MV Rejang* for the following Monday, which would mean coming in from the South China Sea up the Rejang River early Tuesday to the lesser towns of Sarikei first, then Binatang, when his words stopped in his mouth at the arrival of a flying insect on the back of the chair between them which resembled an enlarged mutation of a bluebottle.

Having grown up before the days of universal refrigeration in homes, Tubby held a distinct dislike for bluebottles because of what they could do in terms of carrying germs and laying of maggots' eggs, and to see one sitting there which was bigger than his fingers was almost too much to contemplate. While Tubby's voice had petered out, attention riveted on what this enormous bluebottle mutation might do, big Frank maintained his concentration on the conversation while nonchalantly reaching out with a hand and picking the beast up and lobbing it out the window, all in one casual movement.

They both burst out laughing at what had happened and Frank explained that they were sometimes known as screeching beasts because of a somewhat awful noise they could make. He told Tubby it was common practice for the youngsters there to play with these things by catching them and then tying a string round them and making them fly round, at times emitting their noises.

They returned to the conversation which concerned the arrival next Monday on the *MV Rejang* and Frank mentioned that Harper Gilfillan's latest plaything had arrived in the form of a jet boat for him to use when doing his shipping duties. This latest device apparently had some sort of jet motor instead of the traditional outboard with propeller in that it took the water in and jetted it out the back and steered by shifting the direction of the jet. It was going to be Tubby's pleasure to be met at Binatang since Frank would be there that Tuesday morning doing a shipping agency job on a newly arrived freighter and Tubby would be able to transfer to Frank on the launch rather than waiting for the *MV Rejang* to finish its journey up to Sibu.

They had just finished their conversation when the call came for Tubby to go out to the Dakota which had come the other way and soon he was on his way back to Kuching, to be met by Graham Wood at the airport building. Graham Wood had a Morris 1000 saloon which he had acquired for his new posting to Kuching on return from leave and as they drove in to the office from the airstrip Graham told Tubby how he had actually seen the Dakota on two of its dives through the grey overcast, but with the low wing roots the pilot had obviously missed a glimpse of the airstrip and they had watched the plane disappear back up into the gloom.

Graham Wood was quite delighted with his posting over to Kuching in Sarawak since he was considered to be a bit of a non-conformer for the more sophisticated postings in Singapore and Malaya because of his mixing too readily with the locals. However, through this non-conformism he had become fluent in the Hokkien dialect of Chinese. With his aptitude for getting on with the locals, he was very fluent in Malay, which in Sarawak was the link communication with the main local tribes of Land Dyaks and Sea Dyaks, known as Ibans, and indeed with the lesser and more strange native tribes from which some males became policemen and talked Malay first before English. Round the Kuching area, Ibans dominated except for the coastal and fishing village areas where the tribes people were Melanaus.

As they started to go over the programme for Tubby's visit it was obvious that Graham had done a lot of homework on this colonial posting since he came back from leave and he mentioned hearing of some old letters that had been found, written by a young fellow who had come out to the Borneo company in the 1800s and had experienced the massive volcanic explosion of Krakatoa situated at the tip of the island of Sumatra across from the island of Java. This young chap had written home to his mother about the noise of the explosion having been heard in Bangkok 3,000 miles away, and how the river at Kuching had started to flow in the opposite direction from going out to the sea and that the level had become so high that they were contemplating having to move their office further inland to higher ground.

Driving round the ordered centre of Kuching, with many established government buildings, a recreation ground for athletics and sports, a teacher training college and a hospital, it was hard to believe that Kuching was but a muddy village when Charles Brooke became the second rajah in 1868. He was reputed to have been a practical and successful administrator who made Sarawak viable and profitable without seriously disturbing the status quo of the people who inhabited the 50,000-odd square miles of jungles and rivers.

On his first trip through, the previous September, Tubby had seen how wonderfully unspoilt the colony was out in the jungles and the upper rivers, and it was quite fascinating to see the nurses from the hospital uniformly dressed but of different tribes. The Keyans and the Kenyahs from the high reaches of the Upper Rejang have beautiful smooth round faces with no eyebrows, while those who are Kelabits from the high interior plateau areas of the fourth division round Bario have their elongated ear lobes and the dangling brass rings within them.

The influences and eccentricities of the family were all about

266

the place, and indeed when Charles Vyner Brooke succeeded as the third rajah in 1917 he even inherited a railway line, ten miles of which can be seen on maps of the area. There appeared to be no official record of the opening, but folklore had it that it was ill-fated from the start in that the inaugural eight coach train bearing dignitaries killed a child on a level crossing with the result that the driver and the fireman had to go into exile for many years.

There are arguments as to whether the railway ever went more than ten miles inland, though some public works department records indicate that when the road was being constructed towards Serian they had to lift some railway track from the tenth to the thirteenth mile. No less a figure than the widow of the third rajah – the Rané Sylvia – stated that the railway line went no more than ten miles. Many years later, back in the UK, Tubby saw a Michael Parkinson chat show which was to climax with the American film star Shirley Maclaine. As a fill-in interview before the grand finale, the Rané Sylvia appeared dressed in Far East style batik sarong and pinned-up Malay style hair, no doubt as a plug for her book about the white rajahs. She brought the house down in full flight with comments and stories about her childhood with nasty little princes in Queen Victoria's court, her 'arranged' marriage to the third rajah of Sarawak and her first impressions and experiences as a young lady from England in the *Astana* across the river from Kuching. One episode referred to her early attendance at a dinner for dignitaries on the verandah when she thought she heard the rain starting to come down. On suggesting to the butler that the rollers should be let down because of the rain she was gently informed that the noise was not rain but her husband, the rajah, relieving himself over the edge of the verandah. After more such hilarious tales, very frankly told, the audience had to come back down to earth for the big star Shirley Maclaine, who had the sense to come on with a laugh and say: 'How do you follow an act like that?'

The delay caused by the flight to Sibu and back had reduced the day, but after all it was New Year's Day, so Tubby was dropped in at the rest house for a wash and brush up before attending the party of the White Russian couple. Tubby was to meet other White Russians in other parts of the world and they always seemed to have a certain charisma about them, similar to the Poles. He remembered Michael Bentine once describing how he went into the RAF in the war and how he was posted to a Polish Squadron because he was a foreign Peruvian 'wog' – even though an Etonian one. He described the charm of these characters who had managed to escape from Poland to join together to fight for their country, but with a total disregard for any sort of conventions and orders and rules.

This couple were striking of appearance and of a similar charm and detachment which perhaps comes from adversity and having everything against one, which they had experienced as on-going supporters of the Czar in post-revolution Russia. Their tribulations in revolutionary Russia ended with their coming out via China and ending up in the fabled financial centre of Shanghai. Their stories of life in Shanghai before Chairman Mao were quite incredible with the signal for leaving parties being when the eggs began to be thrown up to the spinning ceiling fans, with obvious results. Like so many others they had become involved in the commerce of Shanghai, but they had had to move on down to Indochina and on again when that whole area broke up into disarray after the collapse of French colonialism after their defeat by Communists at Dien Bien Phu.

Anyone who was anything in the Kuching area seemed to be there and Tubby even met the organist of the cathedral with the promise of an impromptu Bach recital if he should still be about. The other couple who stood out among the others were a very short, very fair British colonial type, and his rather dark, taller than himself, wife. They were a real swinging couple and it turned out he was none other than a district officer in the interior, and she was the daughter of a Land Dyak Chief. Besides being tall and thin, she was not exactly pretty about the face, rather resembling the face on the sail of the Kon Tiki craft sailed across the South Seas. They told with much hilarity of their experiences courting when he used to creep into the hospital where she was a nurse and having to hide under the covers of a bed one night only to be discovered by no less than the matron, and expelled from the premises.

At that time the Kuching area had the most miles of roadway and Tubby was determined to see all places which could be reached by road transport. The next morning after attending to essentials at the office, they set off in the Morris 1000 to the interior in the direction taken by the ten miles of railway track, and then turned off right to follow the valley of the Sarawak River to the last village before the Indonesian border which was called Krokong. It was a journey of some 20 miles from Kuching.

As they walked up and down the shop houses on either side of the one street, Tubby was fascinated to come across one of the shop houses which was completely fitted out as a billiard room with a full pukka competition-class table from the UK with a slate bed. Down the sides were wall seats from which to spectate and cues were clipped along the walls, the score board screwed up on the end wall. While Tubby was trying to take in the scene by watching some of the locals at play it was explained to him that it was a tradition with the Rajah Brookes that when they did their periodic visits to all the five divisions and district officers with their entourage, they always had a game of snooker or billiards with the local head man, and to facilitate this there had to be the necessary equipment on site in one of the nearest shop houses.

For tracks in this outpost of empire, there are lines drawn on the maps between Sarawak and Indonesia, so they set off on foot for about two miles along a jungle track in this hill area until they came to a river. For crossing there was a footbridge of bamboo and vine in a triangular design, which allowed one to walk across, one foot over the other, while holding the vines at arm's length at either side. This was known locally as the border crossing into Indonesia and while they were there two Land Dyak ladies came across with their legs metal-bangled from ankles to knees, carrying high on their backs enormously heavy loads of large durian fruit, much enjoyed throughout these tropical regions and therefore readily saleable.

The durian fruit are about the size of a huge coconut with a great horny outer shell like a horse chestnut, and they have a similar pithy inside with smooth nuts. They are very nutritious and very satisfying to eat, provided you can stand the smell, which makes most Europeans want to run a mile. They are quite heavy, and these ladies had about 20 in large baskets which they carried high up on their shoulders by having a broad band draped over the top of their heads, allowing them to walk upright while carrying such a load. Apparently, trading with Indonesia using this type of human bearer was quite common among the Land Dyaks who occupy these upper reaches of the first division in particular, as opposed to the Ibans, or Sea Dyaks, who are more prominent in the second and third divisions particularly.

On the way back they turned off the road at a place called Bau where they came to what looked like a rock wall until Tubby realised that the old Morris 1000 was heading towards a tunnel in the rock face which was just about the width of the car. They slowly edged their way through and came out into the light again to find themselves in the middle of a circle of rock about the size of a stadium and this was the rich gold mine at Bau.

Graham was able to converse with the Chinese in Hokkien. Most of them were Hakkas who had come here in the early years because of the mining. They had got to speaking Hokkien as well since most of the commercial Chinese in these parts were Hokkien or Teochew. The Chinese, of course, just love gold and the high quality 22 carat gold available was being mined high in the rock face where various caverns had been blasted out.

After a most interesting day they returned towards Kuching, crossing the river again at Batu Kitang by the slow but sure pontoon ferry. Tubby had experienced the cable pontoon ferry crossing on the celebrated trip round Malaya and back from Malacca, but this was an oblong self-propelled custom-built raft with proper drop ramp at either end and metal-roofed areas on either side for foot passengers. At a push the pontoon ferry took three standard saloon cars. It all added to the

270

pleasant easy pace of life – you simply could not rush about anywhere.

The next day was Saturday, and they set off in the Morris 1000 to travel the longest stretch of road which was over 40 miles south-east along the edge of the highlands to a reasonable sized place called Serian, and then inland following the Sadong River Valley through the last outpost of Tebakang. As they drove along and past numerous pepper groves it reminded Tubby that these islands, together with the Dutch East Indies, were known as the Spice Islands because of these crops which were taken back to Europe. With the pepper plants being trained up huge poles it looked like ordered ranks of green yeti as they were in leaf. This was Iban/Land Dyak country, and once again in Serian one of the shop houses was fitted out with the snooker/billiard table.

The pepper groves, and indeed anything commercial, were usually run by Chinese, and, with Malays, they were concentrated in places like Serian and stood out as being quite 'dressed' up compared with the minimal jungle attire of the Ibans, who lived out in the *ulu* in their long houses, coming in only to trade their wares, fruits and wild boar which they gathered from out in the jungle.

When they came to the end of the road, Tubby was intrigued to find that to reach Tebakang they had to be ferried across a narrow stretch of the river. It was like the old days of the level crossings on the railways back home, in that the elderly Chinese ferryman had his dwelling place amongst the jungle trees on which lovely orchids were growing out of hollows where rain water collected. As in the Noel Coward song, *Mad Dogs and Englishmen*, the old ferryman had his huge hat like an upturned plate as an umbrella against sun and rain and, as was the custom in the east, he stood and propelled his boat across by pushing against his crossed oars, with his passengers standing together in the body of his boat as it progressed slowly at an angle against the current of the river water.

The crossing on the ferry boat was in silence and they paid by simply leaving their coins on the board seat of his open boat. Tubby had a feeling he was back in Greek mythology paying the dark and sinister ferryman who rowed departed souls across the River Styx to the place of the dead. However as they landed, the old ferryman's weathered face lit up as Graham Wood made some exchange with him in Chinese about his orchids. From the animated and voluble Chinese he was obviously very proud of his orchids, which in these parts of the world were equivalent to summer flowers in a country cottage garden in England.

It was late afternoon when they headed back on the very secondary road from the Tebakang ferry and they came across a party of Iban men and boys who had been hunting and gathering in the jungle.

With the very limited contact with Europeans within these parts, the Ibans readily responded when they stopped the car and got out to have a look at what they had been gathering. They had all manner of fruits and other items used as vegetables, and Tubby readily accepted a rambutan, which is a most succulent fruit with a red horny exterior, about the size of a plum when ready for eating. They had been successful in hunting in that one of the men had a rather large wild boar trussed up in vines for carrying high up on his back, for better balance as Tubby had noticed with the ladies with their huge loads of the durian fruit. It turned out that they were heading back to their long house which they said was not far away, and they readily invited the pair to come and have a look. Tubby was in his colonial shorts and white socks and began to feel like the veritable district officer on one of his visits.

With a mixture of Malay and Iban words Graham had been picking up, he seemed to be in communication and there was much laughter and banter as they made their way through the semi-open jungle. Tubby began to realise that over a mile would easily be a short distance as far as they were concerned and he was noticing that the children seemed to have that bit more boundless energy as they went on ahead, until he suddenly realised they seemed to be leaping about and shouting with some purpose. It was then that he was informed that they had become aware of snakes in the undergrowth and the best strategy was to make lots of noise and leap about since this encouraged the snakes to move off to another part rather than stay put and be trodden upon and thereby strike at the thing which had trodden upon them.

Eventually they reached a clearing and the long house, and there was much hilarity and hugging and talking in loud voices as they were greeted by the women and younger children who had remained at home while the men and older boys were away in the jungle. Tubby noticed that these Ibans had built a complex of long houses for their jungle settlement as opposed to the one long single Iban long house he had visited the previous September on his way up the Rejang River on Abe le Roux's farewell trip.

It was fascinating to feel a sort of timeless rhythm about this scene with their dwellings up on high stilts so that the waste could easily come down to be recycled by pigs and dogs as it had been with early man in Europe when life was totally related to nature and the things it could provide. It was an incredible experience, and indeed a kind of privilege, to be able to stand with his camera to observe the excitement at the return of the gathering party settle down, as the women began to move on with their end-of-the-day routine which was to gather the children and move down to their water facility which was a pond, or lake, fed by a small rivulet.

For this exercise the women had a one piece cloth tied over their bosoms and they carried with them huge nests of bamboo poles tied together which turned out to be for their water supply for the evening. After they had washed and splashed and had fun with the children they filled these nests of bamboo to the top with water and laid them on their backs as they went back up towards the long houses to store them upstairs near the cooking pots and the fires.

Like the bushmen in Africa and the Aborigines in Australia, they were people living so utterly in communion with nature that they were living examples of Christ's words, 'Take no thought for the morrow what you shall eat and what you shall drink.' Who was to argue whether these people, totally at ease and reliant with simple faith on the things of creation, might well have a deep understanding of 'He who is uncreated' – as

273

Mother Julian of Norwich describes God in her *Divine Revelations* in 1373.

It made Tubby wonder what had become of the great dynamic civilisation of Europe when it began to blossom from 800 under Emperor Charlemagne. Though illiterate himself, he brought Europe out of the terrible dark ages which looked like being the end in 700, to establish a climate where peoples were not known by nationalities but rather by which parish they belonged to for the blossoming of the most incredible 200 years of writing and learning and art, to bring about the confidence and imagination for the great buildings which were to blossom from A.D. 1000 onwards. Had the word 'civilisation', which got its meaning from those times, become a mask or a front for rampant materialism? Timber was being extracted at that time, as in Ceylon, at a pace not too different from nature itself, which struck down big trees with lightning, which in turn made a clearance in the jungle for sunlight to generate a wealth of growth. He shuddered at the thought of what might become of this happy scene when modern 'civilisation' might arrive with monster machines incapable of being selective, because their worth would be in that they could clear a whole square mile of jungle in a matter of days.

These thoughts were still uppermost in his mind as he attended worship at the Kuching Cathedral the next day and particularly as he later sat in the organ loft with his organist friend from the party, reeling off Bach preludes and fugues. What had become of the 'civilisation' of the Europe which had produced people capable of playing and writing such music and would one day stoop to exporting barbarism to places like this in the name of progress.

Alas, mankind is the paradox, since in the afternoon he decided to go and see where the Ibans and Dyaks partook of their favourite sport – cock fighting. The place was not difficult to find since on the outskirts of town there were plenty of them to be seen on foot – heading one way with an enormous ferocious looking cockerel under one arm and in many cases a baby suspended in a cloth under the other arm.

The actual cock-pit was a fairly large hexagonal wood structure with an *atap* roof with terraced seats around the inside for the gamblers, who were mainly Chinese with some Malays. It was a bit like being by the bookie stands at a race meeting at home with them holding wads of Straits dollars in their hands, and all the others standing around peering over the shoulders of those in the seats who were there for the 'sport', making knowledgeable comments about each ferocious pair of birds as they were brought into the ring.

Outside the cock-pit building, the match-making was taking place between those who had walked miles with their cockerels. The main criteria for the match seemed to be the birds reactions to one another in that they seemed set to launch off at one another while still under the arms of their owner. When this animosity was noticed the birds would be usually held and put down facing one another and when all their neck feathers shot out and stood up it was a signal for finalisation between the owners for a match and the officials would then book them in.

Tubby had never seen anything like this but he did remember that when he was selling soap in the sedate county town of Chester, an unofficial cock fighting ring had been discovered operating in a sweet little village called Christleton, outside Chester. This was in 1956, and the police had made a raid on the place one Sunday morning to find a proper cock-pit, and white-coated veterinarians in attendance. Those partaking had taken off across the fields to get away from the police, and there was a story that went round that some tried to dive into haystacks without realising that their feet were still sticking out, which the police duly took hold of to pull them out into the open.

The cock fighting which he witnessed that day in Kuching involved the fitting of blades to the legs of the birds once matched, and quite frankly Tubby couldn't quite see what it was all about because nearly always with the initial flurry when they went up in the air and lashed out at one another with their feet, one would fall mortally wounded from the slash of blades. It just seemed to be an utter waste of breeding cockerels.

On the Monday morning they had an intense time going over all the points he had compiled for his report before finalising the likely figures by product category for the year ahead as a basis for the orders to go back to his export department in London, via Harpers' co-ordinating facility for the Colgate Agency in Singapore. After lunch it was a quick clear up at the Rest House and then down to the docks for getting on board the *MV Rejang* for departure in the late afternoon.

The vessel was about the size of what was known as a tramp steamer, compared with the full ocean-going boats of Blue Funnel and Ben Line, but it was the layout of the vessel which intrigued Tubby most. His traditional idea of boats growing up in a place like Merseyside was to have a funnel and a bridge in the middle, with the fo'castle over the bow, and astern quarters for the crew with the holds in between fore and aft of the bridge.

In contrast the *Rejang* was more like a large scale ocean-going tug, since all the superstructure was at the front, with a wheelhouse at the top of the pyramid of cabin quarters and mast and funnel not far behind. The remaining two thirds to aft were the cargo holds, which, once covered, became a whole area for deck passengers. He was assured that the vessel was 'A1 at Lloyds' as it was made ready to leave at about 4.30 p.m. in order to get down through the twists and turns of the lower river before dark when it would sail out into the South China Sea to enter the wide estuary of the Rejang River at daylight again to navigate even more twists and turns on the way up to Sarikei and Binatang.

The sight at the docks took Tubby quite by surprise since it resembled the departure of a liner on a transatlantic crossing. There were a large number of passengers going to sail on the deck who were getting settled in with their *barang* (luggage) and their eating supplies for the night, and all their relatives seemed to have come to see them off to the 'new world' of the third division!

Tubby was checked into a cabin about two down from the wheelhouse and the only other *Puteh* was an elderly ex-planter who now had a commercial job. As Tubby looked down from his elevated level at the incredible scene of tears and waving of the relatives, the ropes were cast off and they began to draw away from the dock and make their way out to head down the lower river reaches. All that was missing was a band playing to see them off.

He stayed on deck almost until it went dark because it was simply so absorbing to observe all the comings and goings down the river. Silhouetted in the gathering evening light were numerous shallow local boats being propelled by a single oarsman at the front leaning against his long crossed oars with his plate-like hat. There was an *atap* roof over the rest of the boat since in many cases these were houseboats. Others were longer with a great stack of *nipah* palms in the middle of the boat and two oarsmen, front and back, rhythmically rocking on their feet as they pushed forward and backwards against their upright oars. As the river widened towards the open sea, under the wide sky in the fading light he could see the fishing boats of the Melanaus people of the coast, their angled square sails heading out towards the open sea and the horizon highlighted with monsoon clouds.

With nothing more to see now the light had gone, they came in for their evening meal and over several *stengahs* (Scotch) he heard that his fellow passenger had been a planter at the time of the Japanese occupation and, though now happily married again, he had lived through the sad experience of being parted from wife and children, never to see them alive again. When he heard that Tubby was once more heading for the Upper Rejang and the Kapit area, he recalled the legendary Iban chief Temenggong Koh.

The renowned Temenggong Koh reached back to before the early 1930s when the Ibans' favourite sport of head-hunting was finally eradicated. Chief Koh already had his fingers and toes tattooed with blue circles for each head collected, and when the country was occupied by the Japanese, he and the other tribes living in the interior took it as a personal insult to the white rajah and rationalised it as their duty to take revenge by collecting the invaders' heads.

Next morning he was up early for breakfast so he could go outside on his perch below the wheelhouse as they came up the mighty Rejang River. It was then that he realised why the boat had been thus designed compared with the traditional layout of ships because the pilot had to swing the boat this way and that as he lined up navigation markings on the banks before each bend, until they eventually arrived at Sarikei where the boat became surrounded by activity of unloading and disembarking passengers.

It was about 11 a.m. when they reached Binatang and there was big Frank and the jet boat as arranged. The new boat with its movable jet stream at the back was highly manoeuvrable and soon they were bashing away upstream against the current with Tubby totally absorbed in all that was going on while Frank, who had seen it all before, sat quietly catching up on his reading.

It was most interesting to arrive at Sibu by water this time instead of by air and he was able to see exactly the importance of this great river as an artery, and the strategic location of Sibu, the point where the lowlands of the estuary ended and the great river reached inward to the Upper Highland as an almost straight roadway. After the flying visit in the September with Abe le Roux, going up and down to Kapit in one day, Tubby had resolved to visit Kanowit on the way up, stop the night at Kapit, and on the way back call in at the small place called Song so that on the Thursday the 9th he could fly on to Kuala Belait and Seria in Brunei Sultanate.

Big Frank had been with them upstream to Kapit on the last visit and had enjoyed witnessing the excitement of the illipe nut season and Tubby did not want to bore him again with another trip.

It was resolved that a young Chinese clerk in the office would come with Tubby on the trip. He was a locally bred Chinese, son of a rubber planting family, and he had grown up not only with the all-purpose Malay language but also with the Iban dialect which would be most useful.

This time they were in a long boat made to order rather than the dug-out, with a designed cabin top against sun and rain rather than a nailed-on tin roof. It also had a proper stern on to which the big outboard motor was attached. This made it a bit more streamlined and speedier than the dug-out monster they had used last September and the impression of speed against the flow of the river was even more hair-raising.

The stop over at Kanowit was straightforward, the usual shop houses on either side with one of them having a billiard table for the visits of the big white chief and his district officers. Tubby always noticed at these out of the way places that even when there was a limited Chinese community, they always seemed to have the priority of setting up a school with financing for a school teacher, by fair means or foul. It was little wonder that they soon progressed against the other races together with their in-bred ability for commerce. However, as with the Jews throughout the world, there were often backlashes against the Chinese and indeed over the border and throughout the many islands of Indonesia where Sukarno ruled in chaos, there was a horrific pogrom going on against the Chinese. Unfortunately they were always a visible, prosperous and successful minority at which to point the finger when the real problem was the dictator's own idiotic way of running the country.

The long run to Kapit was as fascinating as ever to Tubby, though at times the sky was overcast with the monsoon season. The overpowering and pervading greenness of the jungle on either side of the river surface reflected the colours, so that at times it felt that they were being propelled along one vast green funnel, since the upper reaches of this great river to interior headwaters were very straight indeed.

Although Kapit was an important bazaar and administrative centre for the Ibans in the area of the great Chief Koh, there wasn't very much to it. As might be expected at this outpost the police station was a fair-sized wooden establishment near the landing but well up the grassy banks of the river, but to his astonishment Tubby found that on the wall of the police station and just below it, there were two white boards marking levels to which the Rejang River had risen on two occasions of tremendous flooding and heavy rain. The boss man at the police station, whom they met later in what could be called the

279

bar of the Chinese shake-down hotel they had booked into, was very typical of ex-pat colonial police officers who had often moved on to another colonial police service as each previous one had eventually changed with independence. He thought that some of them must have ended up with about three pensions by the time they came to retire. A most peculiar and standard thing about their colonial uniforms seemed to be the stiff, creased shorts, which always stood up when they sat on a bar stool to resemble an appendage of Sydney Opera House.

Kapit was indeed a very quiet backwater compared with the palpable excitement which had prevailed the previous September when the ocean boat was anticipated for the illipe nuts. The big pens which had been along the banks of the river had all gone and so had all the remarkable variety from those colourful but seldom seen tribes from the deep interiors whom he had been most fortunate to meet when they had gathered together in this place from the far reaches of inland jungles and highland plateaus with the illipe harvest.

While the sun was still up Tubby took time to look at the rapids where the navigable water ended up above Kapit and saw some Ibans manoeuvring one of their long boats over the rapids which was quite a hair-raising experience. After a far from comfortable night in the Chinese shake-down, where he had had to resort to his old trick of keeping the mosquitoes at bay by having a fan blow a mosquito coil's smoke across him, he was quite glad to be down next morning and on to the boat again for the run down the river. As their boat was still facing upstream, they had to take a swing round and then come back down for a final look up at the police station with its marker boards indicating where the river water could reach when in flood from the equatorial rainforests across the vast uplands of Borneo. Once again the seaward flow of the river and the big outboard took them along at an electrifying pace and they had to swing out wide and come round against the stream to make a landing at Song, some 30 miles straight downstream.

It was near to Song that he had seen the twin towers of the Methodist Church sticking up above the jungle and he was surprised to find that the town was more spread out than two rows of shop houses on either side of one street. Though the reason for Song could be that it was just more than halfway upstream from Sibu towards Kapit, it stood at the place where the Sungei Katibas river flowed in as a tributary from the high reaches up to the Indonesian border – ideal for a trading post.

Tubby had emerged from the one and only Chinese trader in Song after a successful visit with the young Chinese clerk from Harpers office. They were walking back towards the river when whom should they meet coming towards them but none other than the man from Union Carbide whom Tubby had last met pedalling his Ever-ready batteries away in the interior of Ceylon. They greeted one another like Dr Livingstone and Mr Stanley at the celebrated meeting in the African Bush in 1871. After a good laugh and an exchange of views on the prospect of trade in this outpost of the empire they parted company wondering when they might meet yet again out in the boon-docks, as the Americans say, for out of the way places.

They were back in the Harpers office before closing time and were able to round off details like the ordering for the first half-year so that Tubby could get off on his scheduled Borneo Airways flight first thing in the morning. Since Frank had to go downstream again to Sarikei, Tubby was quite glad to be able to see himself off. When he reached the Resthouse for the evening he found that the only other person booked in was Roy, the Borneo Airways pilot, who was to fly the Scottish Aviation Twin Pioneer tomorrow back east on a local flight to Bintulu, the Shell strip at Anduki for the Sarawak Oilfields Ltd, the oil export port of Lutong, then Brunei Town and the island of Labuan which was the headquarters point for the local Borneo Airways.

They dined together and it turned out that Roy was indeed one of these phlegmatic ex-bomber command pilots with a trim moustache and a half-closed eyelid look which highlighted his laid-back manner. Putting this character together with Tubby, a frustrated flyer, they soon got on very well together and Roy made mention of the regular approaches he and his colleagues received from various mean and monied rebels against Sukarno in Indonesia. They offered pilots such as himself vast sums to

281

fly missions against Sukarno as mercenaries using Mitchell bombers and Mustangs they had secreted in various places for these bombing and strafing missions. The benign tempo of life in Sarawak concealed the reality of what was going on in the rest of this huge island of Borneo and the very many islands which made up this scattered country which was originally the Dutch East Indies. As Tubby progressed on his journey to North Borneo he was to come in more direct contact with these mercenary activities Roy had been talking about.

By the time they met over breakfast in the morning they both recognised by one another's faces that they had had a fairly heavy night. As Roy went off for his pre-flight checks he muttered something to Tubby about looking in on him if there was no one else on the flight. After the bursts of monsoon weather which had been coming across the South China Sea, it was a lovely morning when Tubby got to Sibu Airport and they took off at nine o'clock for the angled flight north-east, which would take them directly to the coastal town of Bintulu.

Once the plane had levelled off and was going steadily, and since Tubby was the only passenger, he took up the offer to join Roy in the cockpit and carefully opened the door and stepped in. Roy was sitting at ease cross-legged in the left-hand pilot's seat with the *Straits Times* opened up before him, and with the benign weather conditions and his hungover state from the night before, he was not aware of Tubby until he had turned back from having a look out of the side window, and threw up the paper in reflex fright. With the noise of the engines conversation wasn't possible except by shout, and he motioned Tubby to the co-pilot's unused seat since there were no more crew other than the pilot.

From his limited flying experience at Liverpool Flying Club, Tubby made sure not to tangle with any of the controls as the two-handed stick was moving gently on auto in tandem with the other, since Roy had resumed his paper reading with periodic glances out of the window to check on which rivers he had crossed. The flight took them across the great green nipah palm area to the coast, where Mukah was the main export town for the quantities of sago which the Melanaus peoples of these areas grew as a second occupation to fishing out in the China Sea. Tubby was enthralled just to look down through the large window area of the Pioneer cockpit, watching the changing scenes made by the rivers running to and fro across this area, and every now and again the sun flashed back from the waters as the plane just passed through an angle of reflection for a few seconds.

The landing strip for Bintulu was an all-weather grass strip of 3,090 feet by 240 feet within the 500 feet contour to the north of the town, therefore Roy made noises to Tubby that he had better go back into the passenger area since they were to take on more passengers here, and he was about to start his swing out over the sea to turn and come in on to the grass strip from the north. The flight was about half full and while Tubby was heading for Kuala Belait, in the state of the Sultan of Brunei, the plane would actually fly up the coast past the great oilfields at Miri to land at the Shell strip at Anduki which is 1,080 feet by 150 feet of grass and which lay between shore line and a row of trees, just within the colony of Sarawak.

As they got within sight of the Miri oilfield area, where a number of oil tankers were anchored at the loading buoys offshore, there were signs of an almighty monsoon squall coming through that area with all sorts of things going on within it. Roy came on to the intercom and told the passengers to belt up while he would take the plane away out to sea round the storm and then come in behind it into Anduki. With the monsoon drift coming from the north-west, he banked the plane in sunshine behind the storm and levelled out for the descent on to the narrow length of grass betwixt the sea and the rows of trees. Tubby was keeping watch on the trees through the long telescopic arms of the fixed wheels, fully extended from the engine casings on the high wings waiting to take the impact of touch down, when all of a sudden they got caught by a tail end of down draught from the storm and the plane was thrown straight down on to the grass while Tubby watched the telescopics of the undercarriage go right up to maximum with jarring impact. The plane rebounded back up into the air again some 40 feet above the tree tops and then descended in a series of diminishing kangaroo hops to come to a halt at the very end of the 1,080 feet available without having been impaled into the grass by the force of any further down draught.

To put it mildly, there were some fairly wobbly passengers who emerged from the flight and even those who were going on to Brunei Town and Labuan felt it prudent to get out on to the grass so that Roy could give the plane a thorough check over before he decided to take it on to the other two stops. He had shown the value of his undoubted flying experience by holding the twin-engined plane level and steady during the diminishing hops.

32

BRUNEI: LABUAN ISLAND; BORNEO PIRATES

Tubby had now switched agents from Harper Gilfillan to the North Borneo Trading Company which had the main offices in Jesselton and Sandakan with lesser offices in Seria and Brunei Town. They had booked him into the Rest House at Kuala Belait, some ten miles from Seria and just over the border into Brunei state. It was a modern Rest House built of two storeys, with the accommodation for the guests on the top floor with the staff down below. However, it was most pleasantly situated near the sea shore and that evening before his meal he had a most pleasant walk in the glow of the setting sun, watching the little crabs scurrying about the beach ahead of the waves, with the only other humans being a father and a son who were walking into the sea with a net stretched between them which they drew round in an arc to pull in some fishes to take home for their evening meal – fresh from the sea.

By coming into the state of Brunei by the 'back door' from the landing strip, which was actually in Sarawak, his passport would not be stamped for entry into the sultanate until he reached Brunei Town on Monday, since it was planned that he would spend the weekend on the lovely island of Labuan which was actually in North Borneo territory. Before he left Singapore there had been messages about the free port of Labuan Island receiving abundant supplies of Palmolive soap from Chinese sources, and he had this on his agenda for Labuan.

The next day was hot and sunny so Tubby was in his shorts and white socks again for a drive back into Sarawak along the coast road to the oil town of Miri, since Abe had told him to have the agents organise a vehicle and this he had done. Tubby was rather tickled pink to find that the vehicle for his drive through to Miri was an original open Toyota Land Cruiser which in appearance was very much the Japanese Army's version of the American jeep, only bigger. It had a blunt nose, big tyres on big wheels, a crude metal body with cut out places where you got in and out, a spare tyre bolted on the back, and the upturned exhaust for going through floodwaters. With the windscreen secured flat on the bonnet, Tubby was raring to go and after initiation into the multi-speed gear box with secondary system for four wheel drive, he was off on his way along the shoreline road to the Shell Pontoon ferry which operated across the mouth of the great Baram River.

Once across the ferry he let the power loose and was soon bombing along with the wind through his hair and he couldn't help wondering what an incredible year it had been since his 27th birthday, his only previous venture outside the UK being an eventful weekend in Dublin. Already he had been through a revolution in Baghdad; driven through deserts and all round the north of Iraq; had a whistle stop tour of the federation of Malaya from Singapore; been to Burma, Thailand and Ceylon; and here he was totally alone driving along a sandy track in a four-wheel-drive Japanese jeep amongst the original oil rigs of the Miri Field with their wooden frames still intact. It was quite an incredible experience, driving along the dust track parallel to lines of oil pipes on the left, with the sea on his right, looking at oil tankers out in the sunlit sea at the offshore loading points.

As anticipated, the town of Miri was quite a bustling commercial centre and was obviously good for business, which would be handled by the North Borneo agent's office just over the border in Brunei because there were no other means of transport into the interior of the fourth division, other than the Baram River and the coastal roads associated with oil fields.

After lunch in Miri, Tubby thought he would make the most of his day with the big Land Cruiser by driving to the end of the road beyond Miri which went right along the coastline for just over ten miles before turning inland where the area of higher land from Miri ended at the great Baram River basin to the interior, where annual rainfall was well in excess of 200 inches.

On the way back, weaving in and out round the various lagoons and inlets, Tubby stopped in his tracks as he saw before him in a lagoon amongst the nipah palms, the great bulk of a Blue Funnel Line steam ship from his childhood days in Birkenhead he knew exactly their docking berth in the north end of the dock system where there were usually at least two of them loading before setting off for the Far East again.

Tubby stopped the big vehicle and got out with cine-camera in hand to appreciate fully that here he was seeing one of these ships at the very outpost of its journeying in a lagoon in Sarawak, putting on board with its own winches logs which had been floated alongside, and great loads of copra from the numerous coconut palms which grew in abundance in these places.

As Tubby revved up the great monster engine and accelerated away from the thundering noise of the exhaust, he thought that when he was home again in his parents' house and heard the sirens of the ships, and the tugs moving them through the docks at Birkenhead, seeing the distinctive blue funnels above the warehouses, he would be able to say to himself that he had been to where they sail to, and where they gather cargoes to bring home to replace those they have taken out to the far corners of the world. That night he wrote in his notes that this was another day which would go down in the annals.

He had arranged his schedule so that he would be taken back to the Anduki airstrip on Friday for the last Twin Pioneer flight into Labuan Island, where the new Borneo Airways Ltd for local routes was based, as from November 1957. It turned out that the chief captain of Borneo Airways, a man called Robbie, was himself piloting the plane, and they went straight to the bar where a session was developing by the time young Alan from the North Borneo Trading island office came to take Tubby to his house for the weekend. Robbie was in great form and confirmed all Roy's tales about the offers they kept receiving, as ex-wartime pilots, to fly clandestine missions for the Indonesian rebels. As the banter progressed Tubby realised just why they had established their base on this beautiful island, because it was the unwritten orders that the last to fly in on Saturday morning was to swing round the island and spot where the shoals of fish were, so that they could all then dive into their boats and get out amongst them.

When they eventually got away to Alan's home he found that this plum posting also carried with it a very pleasant house and garden with a local resident 'slow loris'. They went out to see it in the dark as it moved terribly slowly along the branches with the distinctive big eyes of the lemur genus for maximum night vision. It turned out that Alan was a frustrated cricketer, having spent some time on the ground staff of no less than Surrey County Cricket Club at the Oval. However he had realised he was not going to make the big time and here he was in this plum post at the outpost of the empire on Labuan Island off North Borneo. Anyway, like it or not, Tubby was booked to make up a cricket eleven on the Sunday so that Alan could keep his hand in at the game he obviously loved passionately.

On the Saturday morning at the office the top priority was to sort out the Palmolive soap problem. Apparently, on the last trip through in September Abe had acted on a London clearance to increase the price of the Far East Palmolive soap and as the higher selling price potential filtered through, the Chinese network had got to work and Palmolive soap had started to move to the free port of Labuan Island by sampans from other parts with unchanged buying prices, to take advantage of wider differential.

This was to be Tubby's first introduction to the workings of the Chinese network, which operated between the Towkays wholesalers, who in the main were Hokkiens or Teochews. Since they are into buying and selling throughout the Far East and since there are numerous Chinese junks and motorised sampans carrying goods all round the Far East, and since they use goods as money, it does not take them long to spot where they can shift a good high-demand commodity and make some quick money on it. Tubby restored the price accordingly and then sent some cables and messages round to confirm the situation.

The island of Labuan was a very charming and peaceful place in those days, being sufficiently off the mainland to be cooled by sea breezes. It was a glorious morning on Sunday and Tubby took himself off for a walk. After some distance he came across what appeared to be a very well-kept, almost English garden in a hollow below a wall, and on descending into it he found that it was a British war grave area. He had seen the large war cemetery at Kranji in Singapore towards the north of the island and his generation were well aware of the huge cemeteries in France and Belgium from World War One, but they had always been too much to take on board.

He found it was a most beautiful and moving experience to be in this quiet place, beautifully maintained by the War Graves Commission. The stories were that this area had seen much activity in the Pacific War with the Japanese and Jesselton, the main town of North Borneo further up the coast, had been heavily bombed. Tubby moved slowly round reading the names and ranks of those who lay peacefully here in this far post of the empire and felt like a child of the peace, who was living and enjoying what they had died for turning back naked aggression on a massive scale. He stayed a good time in that place on that Sunday morning thinking only on the moving words of the Rupert Brooke poem *The Soldier*:

> If I should die, think only this of me:
> That there's some corner of a foreign field
> That is for ever England. There shall be
> In that rich earth a richer dust concealed;
> A dust whom England bore, shaped, made aware . . .

After a curry tiffin lunch he went off with Alan and his family to his beloved cricket match, and it was all very much like being at home with the knock of the ball against the sacred willow. Alan was in his element even at this level of cricket and it is when one faces someone bowling of his like, who had been at county level cricket that you realise that lesser mortals play at a significantly lower level of gamesmanship. Tubby remembered having a contemporary at school who was school boy county level at golf and to be near this chap when he hit a golf ball was to witness a tremendous degree of controlled power.

On Monday he flew on to Brunei Town and once again as they came in over Brunei Bay he could see that the lovely mosque at the end of the lagoon had come nearer to being completed. As they banked round for the landing he was again fascinated at the number of dwelling houses on stilts out in the water from the main town.

On this second trip through he was beginning to think that there was no other aviation activity in these parts, so he was most interested to see as he crossed the tarmac from his plane that there was a twin engine Percival Prince operated by the Shell Company in Brunei taxiing away for take off. It seemed to be the day that he would be proved wrong, since before he left on his way into Brunei Town, a Red Bell helicopter, with floats instead of wheels, came in from the oilfields and dropped down by the single airport building with its glass control tower atop. Nevertheless, it was all part of the rather sleepy back-water tempo which prevailed when he compared it with other airports he had been through in various parts of the world.

Once he got his business work under way he was determined on this visit to Brunei Town that he would have a good look at the beautiful mosque, and when the opportunity came on the second day he found there a friendly Imam who was obviously very proud of his mosque, and who had been on the Hadj at Mecca too. In these situations he was beginning to find that with followers of Islam in these Far Eastern parts, who were usually Sunni Moslems, it impressed them no end when he could count in Arabic and speak some Arabic words from his days in Baghdad. It was not particularly politic to mention the fact that Iraq was a hot bed of Shi'ite Muslims to the less fanatical Sunnis and Ismaili Moslems, who were the followers of the Aga Khan and mainly Indian shopkeepers from northern parts of that Continent. The Malays would usually respond to Tubby's Arabic words with wide eyed admiration saying, '*Tuan boleh cha kap Arab*' (White boss man can speak Arabic.)

Anyway, Tubby spoke his Arabic to the friendly Muezzin at the Brunei Mosque and got taken on a grand tour from the lavery, where the faithful wash and leave their shoes outside, then into the beautiful interior with magnificent mosaic work in gold, and on to where he called the faithful to prayers at the top of the high minaret for a breath-taking view of the lagoon and Brunei Town to the higher ground beyond. It was indeed a most wonderful experience and he thanked the Muezzin profusely as he took his leave after retrieving his shoes. It was general knowledge round the place that even this magnificent mosque had not taken too much out of the oil revenues of the Sultan of Brunei and he hoped that any building programme to follow would not ruin the charm of this place.

Tubby had been back to hotel dwelling in Brunei Town after the colonial elegance of the government Rest Houses, and he found it was wonderful in the evening after a meal to walk across in the dark to where the town streets ended in a broad area for landing across from all the stilt dwellings which lay out in the lagoon with twinkling lights.

As he was coming along to what was obviously one of Brunei Town's prominent eating establishments, he was aware that there was an unusual gathering of taxis and trishaw men, and a commotion developing from inside which made Tubby hasten along to see what was happening. He arrived at the edge of the onlookers and, being a *puteh*, he was tall enough to see over the top of most of them. He was delighted and highly amused to find that it was none other than Mr Hennessey himself, busily working his way through Sarawak and the Borneo territories, just as Tubby was, and sure enough he must have just finished one of his celebrated attendances at a Chinese dealers' *makan*. It was now the week since Christmas but now there was the brandy consumption time of Chinese New Year to come and here he was, exactly as Tubby had seen him coming out of the events in Singapore, acknowledging the cheers and admiration of all the Chinese and waving them a

291

farewell as he got into his taxi at the end of another good day promoting his family's famous spirit.

It was too late for Mr Hennessey to be heading for another event and perhaps that was his second of the evening anyway. As the cavalcade went on its way Tubby continued his evening stroll down to the water's edge across from the dwellings out in the water on their stilts. Tubby could see at least two cinemas from where he was standing above the dark waters which lapped some feet below, and he was musing as to the commercial size of the cinema industry in the east, which had vast amounts of material being pumped out by studios in Hong Kong and in India for their respective races, on top of all the Hollywood stuff. The shows ended as though synchronised, and people began to pour out of the cinemas to head for home.

Tubby had not actually looked over the edge down into the water since he had strolled down, but he stood absolutely fascinated as many of the people coming out of the cinemas simply ran straight across the open space to the edge of the quay area and disappeared over the edge. His in-built reaction, from having done life saving and even beach patrol part-time at Wallasey beaches, was to look for a pole with a red life belt on it and a bit of rope to throw after them. It must have been a really bad horror film, he thought, but then looked over the edge and to his surprise realised that all the people who had come running out of the cinema and jumped over the edge were on their way to the homes out on the stilts in the water. He then witnessed a positive armada of all kinds of personal crafts or boats being rowed, poled and propelled by hand, as they gradually fanned out heading for their respective dwellings and disappeared into the darkness. With yet another abiding memory of Brunei, he headed back to the hotel for a nightcap and bed.

It wasn't possible to drive from Brunei Town into North Borneo and on to Jesselton, so it was back to Brunei airport to pick up the Malayan Airways Dakota for the one hop to Jesselton as it went on east to the end of its journey at Sandakan. While he was waiting on the tarmac for the DC3 to come through, he found yet another private aircraft standing there. This was the single engine high-wing Auster, the type of plane in which Tubby had started to have lessons at Liverpool airport before he was sent overseas. This was one of two Austers owned and operated by Borneo Evangelical Mission based at Lawas in the fifth division of Sarawak, which was not far from the frontier town of Merapok, and was just over 30 miles from Brunei Town by direct flight across the swamps and numerous rivulets edging Brunei Bay.

While Tubby was showing interest in the Auster the missionary pilot came out with some mail to take back to Lawas, and Tubby was able to have a chat with him. While he was British and part of the Wycliffe Organization doing translation work, he got the impression that the mission was American-financed since from what the pilot was saying it seemed to be a fairly extensive operation, and there were other grass strips they operated into the high interiors of the fifth division from the base at Lawas. It disturbed Tubby, the extent to which they seemed to have to bring with them a heavy presence of the materialism of their home comforts for large-scale operations such as this, with aircraft and goodness knows what. This could bring a negative result if the natives developed an increasing reliance on the mission station's resources, with the success of the mission work becoming measured in the numbers who began to attend meetings dressed more and more in the clothing of the ex-pats. Tubby could not help comparing this sophisticated and high-powered operation with the witnessing of Agnes and Joyce, the two missionaries living in the new village in Kulai in Johore.

Tubby pondered on the way of life of those natives from the interior he had been privileged to meet up with at Kapit in the previous September. They had brought in their bumper crops of illipe nuts for export via the ocean steamer which had come up the Rejang River. For aeons they had lived a lifestyle in total faith and rhythm with the abundance of natural resources and wealth in the jungle, and thereby lived their whole beings in communion with the One who is Uncreated, the Mastermind behind all that is created and the fantastic interrelated rhythms whereby the whole of creation reproduces itself. What they

293

must think of a faith which was brought to them 'in love' by those with a total reliance on a materialism which would in turn require destruction of the world within which they lived in harmony, was anyone's guess.

The flight on from Brunei Town to Jesselton was uneventful and he was met there by the manager of the major branch of the NBT for an intensive three days, before flying due east to Sandakan where they had their other major office. This was the capital of what was then British North Borneo and it had struck Tubby as being a rather characterless place on his first trip through, and nothing occurred to change that opinion this time. This was the main commercial and developed area of North Borneo with lots of paddy fields along the coastal flat areas between the sea and the start of the great mountain ranges to the interior. The only stretch of what could be called proper roadway went for over 100 miles due north to the tip of North Borneo which was a great plantation area for rubber, copra and even tobacco.

When they reached the end of the road at Kudat he was enthralled to see a twin engined de Havilland Dragon Rapide bi-plane, in the silver and blue livery of Borneo Airways, circle as it came in to land on the strip. He was delighted to find that this unique passenger bi-plane of the 1930s was still being used for a twice daily bus service up and down the north coast of North Borneo from Kudat, on Northern tip, to Sandakan and then on to a place called Tawau which was the last outpost of British North Borneo on the coast due south of Sandakan, across the water of an inlet from Indonesia. The prospect of being a scheduled fare-paying passenger on this lovely old plane meant that nothing would divert him from a trip down to Tawau when he reached Sandakan.

After a very busy and intense three days, Tubby was quite glad to fly on on the DC3 Dakota to Sandakan where he had an invitation to stay at the local manager's house as guests of Jim and Heni Mayhook. For some historic reason which he had not yet been able to clarify, the Colgate Palmolive agency for the geographically isolated eastern corner of British North Borneo, centred on Sandakan, was in the hands of a very capable Chinese Towkay – the redoubtable Mr Wong. Tubby had felt the pressure building up at the Jesselton office with regard to North Borneo Trading handling their agency for the whole of North Borneo, and Tubby could feel another Ceylon situation developing. Jim Mayhook (with his charming Danish wife Heni) was regarded as the senior European manager on the spot for this London global import/export house and it was obvious that Tubby was going to get the treatment for the transfer of the Colgate Palmolive agency from Mr Wong.

It was going to be a most interesting visit to Sandakan and besides, Tubby had liked the place very much on the short visit last September – there seemed to be something very British about the town. It was late on Friday, since Tubby had come in on the Dakota on its last hop at the end of its day long journey from Singapore, and it had been arranged that Tubby would come round to the North Borneo Trading offices after he had been seen in by Mr Wong. From NBT he would be taken back by Jim Mayhook to his house for the weekend, which would be a welcome break after what had been a very intense and busy tour so far.

Tubby came off the plane with his bag and typewriter to be greeted by the smiling Mr Wong, who was a tough-looking, stocky character, with thinning hair on top which seemed to be the norm for Chinese in their fifties. Tubby was not sure whether it was for the occasion of his visit, but Mr Wong was in a European suit, looking very smart and projecting that air of power and authority which was usually evident in Chinese Towkays who had made it good and were determined to see that it stayed that way. There, in his shadow, was his faithful clerk and interpreter, he of the black hair, the white face and the large adam's apple which bobbed up and down as he came towards them. They were indeed a sight to behold , Mr Wong in his suit and the Clerk in his too long colonial shorts. Tubby was just glad it was good normal practice to laugh and smile in exaggerated form when meeting up with Chinese associates, because it set everybody at ease and it certainly saved Tubby from having to try to keep a straight face when he met the welcoming pair.

Mr Wong had his big car laid on with a driver, so they were soon at the hotel and Tubby again watched in quiet amusement as he went through the routine, Tubby answering questions to the clerk as he signed in at reception, while out of the corner of his eye he could see Mr Wong disappearing with his product samples ready to decorate Tubby's room and shower room with his beloved Colgate products. After Tubby had dropped in his things and freshened up, they went along to Mr Wong's office so that Tubby could look over the latest figures for the products across the range and resolve what he might like to do on Monday and Tuesday.

Tubby was quite delighted at the way the turnover of his products had improved, even more so that Mr Wong was now putting through more products and a wider range than North Borneo Trading were doing in the whole of the rest of the territory. The huge mountain ranges in the interior from Mount Kinabalu southwards made the eastern corner of the territory an economic unit on its own so Tubby was even more determined to find out how Mr Wong could do better than NBT. He announced his intention to fly down to Tawau on the Monday on the Rapide since he had found he could fly on a 10 a.m. flight and return when the Rapide came back in the late afternoon to return to its base at Sandakan for the night on the last of the day flights.

The poor little clerk was pretty white of face under his black raven hair already, but at the announcement of a visit to Tawau by Tubby, any vestige of yellow in his colour disappeared and Tubby watched intently as he interpreted to Mr Wong in Chinese. The reaction of Mr Wong to the translation about Tubby's intention to go to Tawau was almost volcanic, in that he went into a high-pitched outpouring of voluble animated Chinese which had the poor little clerk leaning back against the desk. Tubby realised he had found the touchstone and listened carefully with much sympathetic smiling all round since the whole office staff sat transfixed at the outburst. It took the poor little clerk some time before he could pull himself together to pass on Mr Wong's reply in level English – that this visit might be a waste of Tubby's time since Tawau was but a small isolated fishing village across from a very swampy and uninhabited area of Indonesia.

As it happened, Tubby had studied his maps and had noticed little oil rig symbols on an island some 70 miles south of Tawau on the Indonesian coast which were the same sort of symbols they had on the map of Sarawak at Miri and at Seria in Brunei. So he stuck to his guns by showing to Mr Wong that he had the timetable for the flights of the Rapide to facilitate spending a good day in Tawau. It was highly amusing that the words interpreted back to Tubby by the clerk were but a fraction of the outpourings in Chinese which had come from Mr Wong. Therefore, Tubby turned on all the charm at his possession to convince Mr Wong that it was no different from what he had been doing all the way along from Kuching in Sarawak. He was here to visit every part of his territory in order to get the feel of the market and the channels of distribution at the start of a new year in order to get his figures correct for his big boss in London.

There were more animated exchanges between Mr Wong and his clerk (the tempo of which Tubby picked up from watching the faces of the various other employees who were obviously pretending to work but were finding the whole situation somewhat exciting) and the poor little clerk's adam's apple was rapidly bobbing up and down. He turned once more to Tubby and with great difficulty translated that Mr Wong had understood his intentions and had decreed that he, the faithful clerk, would accompany Tubby on his visit to Tawau. For someone who had never been on a plane in his life and probably never out of Sandakan in his life, the whole prospect was obviously extremely daunting to the poor little clerk. Tubby immediately responded favourably to the proposition and said that since they were going to be fellow travellers he should get to know him better by starting with his name. This helped to put Mr Wong more at ease and there was much laughter as he apologised for not having done this earlier, so Tubby was formally introduced to Lee Cheong.

With a flourish Mr Wong said that his organisation would make the bookings for Tubby and Lee Cheong to fly down at

10 a.m. on the Rapide to Tawau and return on the late afternoon flight. Tubby then went out of his way to follow Lee Cheong to his desk and sit down with him and spend some time on the pretext of looking at the figures for the year ahead when in fact he was really hoping to set the poor little fellow at ease at the shock of finding that on Monday he was going to be travelling in an aeroplane.

Having achieved his first objective he took his leave from Mr Wong as he took in the scene typical of a Chinese business: the warehouse staff coming in and out in singlets and blue shorts, the staff at the desks making out invoices in Chinese characters, writing beautifully and swiftly with the brush between thumb and second finger while the first finger held the top steady; the clatter of the beads on the abacus as they added up the bills, the smells of spices, and the ever-present level of noise where Chinese are congregated.

From there he walked into the contrast of the European ordered style of office for the British agency house, with Jim Mayhook presiding over all from his glass office in the corner. Jim Mayhook was stocky and middle-aged, of hale and hearty manner very typical of the post-war British types who had made it to positions in such out-station offices of these companies. After a demonstration tour of their offices and facilities they set off for a drink at the club.

When they arrived at the Mayhook house, Tubby was extremely impressed since it was very well appointed by UK standards, with a lovely garden and a large swing on the lawn, since they had a boy and a girl of school age. The problem for these colonial top level European managers, was that they lived a lifestyle which could not be matched in the UK without an extremely high-powered top executive job with quite a large company, which in all sincerity most of them would be unlikely to achieve.

He had heard stories around the Jesselton office about Heni, the Dane, being an animal lover, and there were various dogs including a Rottweiler and several cats, but he simply hadn't been prepared for the monkey. Tubby and Jim were standing in the middle of the lawn taking in the lovely garden and flower

298

beds when the charming and pretty Heni appeared down the steps from the house walking hand in hand with an eight month old Orang Utang female called Olivia. By then it was equal to a fair sized child, but of different proportions, and since Heni seemed to be treating it as just another member of the family Tubby, being fairly friendly towards animals, bent down to shake Olivia's free hand only for the other long hairy orange arm with which they are endowed to reach out swiftly round the back of his neck and propel it into a head butting greeting, wrapping her legs round his waist.

Because there was a feeling going abroad about that time in British North Borneo that these apes might become an endangered species, there was a reward paid out to those who came across, and indeed then rescued from the jungle, an orphaned orang utang baby for safe keeping by the authorities. There were comments beginning to fly around that numbers of orphaned orang utangs being found were increasing, and it was wondered if mothers might be getting bumped off by Malays and others anxious to get their hands on the reward money for the young ones. Be that as it may, these baby orang utangs were then fostered out to animal lovers, such as Heni Mayhook, who were happy to bottle feed them and bring them on until they were a year old and ready to go on, which meant that dear Olivia was destined for Sydney Zoo in Australia.

Tubby began to wonder if Jim Mayhook, in his keenness to smother him with hospitality in order to gain the transfer of the agency from Mr Wong, might have enquired whether this new Far East rep for London export was indeed an animal lover. It could hardly be assumed that everyone might readily accept the embrace of a powerful orange hairy ape at first meeting.

As the weekend progressed in this lively and friendly household it was indeed obvious that Olivia had been adopted into the family to the extent that she was playing a major role. She picked up the cats and carried them round, she occupied chairs and joined them at the meals, so Tubby decided he had better be a poor man's David Attenborough and join the zoo. He helped feed Olivia with a bottle, which was quite an experience because the extra-elongated arms seemed to get all round the place while the bottle was being readily sucked dry. Olivia didn't wear a nappy and they never really went into detail about what happened to the other end, so he remained apprehensive about that for the whole of his stay.

Anyway, it was another weekend to go down in the annals and he did come away with some footage of cine-film of himself and Olivia on the big garden swing where she demonstrated to him that there were different ways in which the swing might be enjoyed. He later got the reel of film copied and sent it on to Jim and Heni in Sandakan a few months later. In return he received back an acknowledgement together with a photograph of Olivia, then one year old, in the Purser's office of the ship taking her to Sydney Zoo, with a mug of tea in her hand. A footnote said that she did not take kindly to the ways of the seafarers and bit the Purser to make her point. Tubby thought to himself that he probably had a good idea where she would end up suitably encaged for the voyage once the Mayhooks were out of the way, no doubt looking for the next baby orang utang to foster.

On Monday it was back to the hard-nosed business of trying to find out where Mr Wong drummed up all his business for Tubby's soap, toothpaste and detergent, and even shaving cream and shampoos which Mr Wong seemed to shift in good numbers. He got to Mr Wong's establishment in good time to help set Lee Cheong at ease and Tubby noticed that he was still dressed in his normal clerical rig out which was his open necked shirt and his knee length white shorts, three quarter black socks and black shoes, but he did have a shoulder bag with him. Tubby was in his shorts to make him feel more at ease, and his bush type shirt with multi pockets and his piece of towelling round his neck.

The old Rapide, with its lovely double wings was sitting on the tarmac and a New Zealand pilot in short sleeves and shorts took the passengers out like a coach party. It was a bit like a coach inside too, in that the pilot and co-pilot's seats and indeed the wide-windowed cockpit was all visible and Tubby was fascinated by the tubular metal and canvas seats for the passengers, duly bolted into the floor. Like the Dakotas the plane sat at a high angle on the tarmac, having just a small tail wheel at the back, and the passengers climbed up the steep slope of the centre passage to get to front seats. He wanted to be up front near the pilot, but he made sure to shepherd Lee Cheong alongside him with himself at the window seat in case Lee took fright as the ground disappeared from underneath them as the plane climbed.

Lee Cheong was a bit quiet and withdrawn as might be expected, but since he was very pale naturally it was difficult to tell whether he was in deep fright or just being normal. Tubby was too absorbed to take much notice since he was revelling in every moment of this flight in which he could see all that the pilot was doing, as both engines got started up and they taxied off to drive down the runway with the tail coming up for a graceful lift off, no doubt due to the biplane's double wing area surfaces. Tubby had noticed that the pilot had been carrying a paperback in his hand and sure enough he noticed that once they got up on level flight and set fair, nose due south, he was settling down to a good read of his book. The journey was quite long since it was almost the same distance as the flight from Jesselton across to Sandakan, and there were similar high mountain ranges below. Tubby noticed that the double surface of the biplane wings also gave it a heightened sensitivity to lifts and downturns since they did go through some grey cloud patches before they began to come down and across a fairly extensive water area to a promontory of land before they banked and came along for approach into Tawau from the sea. As they came in Tubby couldn't help but notice that there was a tremendous amount of activity going on at various landings, with most of the ships being motorised sampans.

It wasn't an easy landing place to negotiate since the town, while down by the water, was backed by fairly high ground, and they would have to travel down into the town to see what was going on. The scene that Tubby found in Tawau was just utterly fantastic and he soon realised that it was most useful to have Lee Cheong with him as he would have been much more suspiciously regarded as a European looking around on his own. It was the biggest barter centre he had ever seen. It was a centre for those Indonesian rebels opposed to Sukarno who organised the twin-engined Mitchell bombers and Mustang fighters which the Borneo Airways pilots were continually being asked to fly on sorties down the coast from here. It made Tubby wonder if the continued use of the old Rapide planes for this service was because they were not likely to be heisted and used for strafing missions since they were hardly war planes. It was also a pirate centre since the many islands of the Philippines were not far away from these parts. The Pirates and the smugglers from that notoriously unruly country were known for their high powered sampans with half inch machine guns of American origin, or bigger weapons, up front to be used in tight situations. Tawau harbour was ideal for access to the great Celebes Sea which stretched up to the large Philippine island of Mindanao of second world war fame.

The oil installations down the coast seemed to be an obvious target for bombers flown by mercenaries to reduce Sukarno's oil revenues, and Tubby remembered an incident related by an ex-pat with Shell during the session they had had in the bar with Robbie after the last flight into Labuan just over a week ago. This chap had been the Shell man at an island in the Philippines called Cebu, minding his own business in his office on the one and only airstrip when certain characters of no definable nationality entered. After placing bags of gold dust on his desk they asked if they might have their three planes filled up with petrol. He went outside with these characters and they pointed to three unmarked Mitchell bombers parked away in the far reaches, semi-camouflaged against the jungle background. He swallowed and thought he had better check with the Filipino in the official office with the control tower on top, who was responsible for things around the airstrip. As a precaution he left the visitors in his office with their bags of gold dust while he walked over to see the Filipino in charge to find out how he felt about the planes. The Filipino had looked up from his desk, with that expressionless poker face that people in the East can adopt, and simply responded by saying 'What planes?' This immediately indicated to our Shell man that the Filipino already had his bags of gold dust, so he returned to his office and put his bags of gold dust in the safe and organised the fuel for the three unmarked Mitchell bombers which duly took off. He knew not where, though he hoped that he might not hear that a Shell tanker had been damaged sailing away from the Celebes Sea.

As they made their way amongst the hustle and bustle of the commercial area, Tubby became aware that the presence of Lee Cheong as his companion seemed to act as a pass for entry into all sorts of places since in various godowns they saw not only plenty of his own products, but nearly all the other products of the multi-national organisations which were marketable and useful for currency conversion as he had found in Burma. There were people there out to buy weapons, of which there was an abundance of all kinds and which required ammunition to go with them. In one place he even saw bales of the cloth from which American army uniforms are made.

As they had first come down into the town from the higher ground, which gave a panoramic view, he did notice that there were two smaller godown sites which had been burned down, and later he was to find out that these burnings had been an act of retribution. Considering the abundance of strange characters around the place and the high stakes involved, it was not surprising that such things could happen.

Tubby began to get the feeling that Lee Cheong was doing business at some of the places and at lunchtime he followed Lee's lead into a well-patronised Chinese eating establishment in buildings near the water front. As they lunched with chop sticks from a bowl of rice and some meat, fish and vegetable side dishes, various characters would join them at the table and talk with Lee Cheong and it seemed highly likely that Mr Wong himself was a regular visitor to this hive of activity. Gradually he began to perceive that Lee Cheong was warming to his role as Mr Wong's man even though he had never been down here before, and Tubby let him develop in his role so that he could be the quiet observer and not the initiator of where they should go and who they should see since he was seeing enough anyway.

As they made their way back to the airport he could not

help noticing the strategically placed and well-appointed branch of the Hong Kong Shanghai Bank in this centre of activity and remembered how this organisation and the likes of Jardine Matheson in Hong Kong and China over many centuries had been involved in commerce related to such nasty events as the Opium Wars. Lee Cheong was beginning to enjoy his day and as they walked out to the old Rapide for the flight back he actually asked if he might sit at the window over which they both had a good hearty laugh, which was a Chinese signal that all was going well. Tubby had made the point of not mentioning to Jim Mayhook anything about his visit down to Tawau and he resolved that this was going to be his secret and in no way was he going to recommend to his export manager that their agency be changed over to anyone other than Mr Wong in this part of North Borneo.

The next day at Mr Wong's establishment the atmosphere was pure magic since Lee Cheong had obviously made a good report and perhaps was now going to be landed with a monthly visit to Tawau as he had been such a success. The three of them were huddled together in Mr Wong's office for a three-way exchange via Lee Cheong, the interpreter, who seemed to have grown in stature and confidence after the visit to Tawau. Tubby assured Mr Wong that he had seen nothing out of the ordinary which might undermine the position of Mr Wong's organisation as the on-going agents for this Eastern corner of the North Borneo territory.

On the first day Tubby had noticed out of the corner of his eye that Mr Wong's right hand would readily reach out to the abacus on his desk and use it like a desk calculator. As another way of further cementing the relationship established he asked through Lee Cheong that he might have a demonstration of Mr Wong's dexterity with the abacus. As this was translated, Mr Wong threw his head back and laughed showing all his gold tooth fillings and proceeded to rattle through all sorts of equations and calculations which Tubby threw at him. Always he would repeat the calculation on the other half of the abacus and exclaim in triumph as the bead pattern turned out the same, as proof that the answer had checked out correctly.

304

That night all three of them had a very good Chinese *makan* together. Tubby related his tale of Mr Hennessey drumming up business from the European Christmas festivities and the Chinese New Year and said that he had seen him in Brunei. Mr Wong threw up his arms and said he had been through Sandakan too. Tubby could just see Mr Wong enjoying a good *yamsing* at the visit of Mr Hennessey promoting his celebrated brandy. It had been a strenuous three weeks, but most rewarding.

33

THE VIP VISIT

On the long flight back on the DC3 to Singapore, Tubby enjoyed circling and dropping down again into Jesselton, Brunei, Sibu and Kuching, which helped him draw his thoughts together, using the long haul to Singapore to finalise his notes and report for sending to London. He had qualms about what he was going to come back to, as he switched back to his other brief of handing over Singapore and Malaya Export to the new subsidiary under Jim Kevlin.

Back at Amber Mansions the greeting from Cookie made him feel like returning royalty, as ever having to restrain the old soul from the shoe treatment on his knees. Van Marken, with his Dutch love of good food, had kept Cookie producing a good variety at the meals and it was very welcome indeed to feel at home at his own table, as it were, after three weeks of living out of a suitcase in a wide variety of hostelry.

Tubby still had the little wire tape recording equipment which the revolutionary authorities in Baghdad had listened to and cleared before he was able to leave for Cyprus, so it was fortunate that Tubby had got his notes taped for London export before hitting the office because Kevlin was in a state of excitement and wild apprehension. This stemmed from the fact that during Tubby's absence over the last three weeks, Sears Wilson-Ingraham had been emitting all sorts of messages from the second floor in New York concerning his so-called responsibilities for the three new subsidiaries in Hong Kong, Thailand and here in Singapore/Malaya. Apparently the formidable George Lesch had succeeded Bill Miller as president of Colgate Palmolive International and he had intimated that one of his first overseas trips would be a visit to these three new subsidiaries, accompanied by Ed Spika, vice president of international manufacture, and Fergy Ferguson, the vice president of international advertising.

Jim Kevlin seemed still to be having problems establishing a working relationship with the very English top brass at Harper Gilfillan and having noticed Jim's jumpy reaction to this prospective visit by the very top VIPs, Tubby had a creeping suspicion that Bill Bailey, the urbane top man of Harper Gilfillan, would make a play for the new president of the international corporation to make sure that, even with the manufacturing facility, Harpers would continue to be part of the Colgate Palmolive scene for a good number of profitable years to come.

Whether it was his age, together with lack of direct experience with American top brass, Tubby could readily feel the tension which was building up at the prospect, but could not come to terms with the obvious apprehension in Jim at the prospect of this VIP visitation. It was apparent that he was having serious problems with the other British colonial civil servant types who were still in charge of the Foreign Exchange departments of the Federation and Singapore governments so Jim had been soliciting the help of the lawyer introduced by Harper Gilfillan, who was a Scot, operating from offices in Kuala Lumpur where he lived, and in Singapore. He was in his fifties and was the undiluted version of the very special and inbred law fraternity of Edinburgh, with their built-in requirement to foster and uphold the mystique of Scottish Law as being different from and thereby superior to any other variety. The post-colonial legal scene in Malaya and Singapore suited his background since it involved advocacy, though barristers were flown out from the UK if particular specialised expertise or personality was felt to be necessary and the money was available to pay.

With all this heavy atmosphere prevailing and the anticipated build-up into the beginning of March, Tubby was delighted to find out when he got in amongst the cricket club gang around the bar that night that Scoops Urquhart and other Tankard team players were finalising arrangements for a Chinese New

Year tour up in the federation. The tour would involve a match in Kuala Lumpur, on the *padang* at the Selangor Club and, with the extended weekend at the start of Chinese New Year, a second game against the Klang Club, also in the state of Selangor, but away to the west towards the main sea port for the area which was called Port Swettenham.

Tubby was asked if he might be available and was counted in, which was great for a break since London had decreed that his presence was required for the forthcoming top brass visit as their man in Singapore. This would give him a stretch for getting in some good hard rugger and getting really fit again, with the addition that it would give him the opportunity to have a good look round the Kuala Lumpur scene since he had not been there other than on the through trip with Sears and the initial visiting party last September.

Even though Jim didn't seem to have got his act together yet, there were certainly indications that their future would be in the Federation. It could well be in his best interests to investigate aspects of registration, work permits and identity cards which he understood were an essential part of the scene in the Federation because of the Emergency against the Communists in the jungle. The scene in Singapore looked like being fluid for some years to come since the election was hotting up, with anti-British rhetoric going down quite well.

Scoops Urquhart had invited quite an interesting bunch for the Tankards' touring team when they all congregated together on the Saturday before the game in the long bar at the far end of the Selangor Club, affectionately known as 'The Dog'. This was short for 'Spotted Dog' because as you came in through the wide-stepped entrance from the front parking area and looked up to the timber framework you would see a wooden carving of two spotty dogs. Legend had it that the early colonial ladies in their long flowing dresses would walk their spotted dogs on the *padang* as was the fashion of that time, but to the KL ex-pats it was now the equivalent of the Singapore Cricket Club, the main homing-in and meeting point for drinking and socialising. A walk across from the town offices for a club sandwich at lunch on the verandah dining area along the side of the *padang* was the order for the day for many of the ex-pats.

The beautiful green *padang* stretched along the main roadway across from the magnificent Moorish style GPO and the municipal buildings with the domes of the Masjid Jamak Mosque behind, and on the same grand style was Kuala Lumpur railway station on Victory Road. A slip road turned off this main highway in the town to pass the very archetypal Church of England parish church which lay along the end of the *padang* and then there was the beloved Selangor Club, of timbered construction as opposed to the imposing edifice of the Singapore Cricket Club.

It was beautifully custom built for socialising and sporting by the ex-pats over the years with a dance floor as you went in from the secretary's office with tables round the sides. Alongside the cricket area of the *padang* there was a long, side verandah area with tables and the usual green and white striped 'chicks' to be rolled down for rain, or the heat of the day.

To Tubby this really was a colonial clubland, especially the long bar some steps down at the far end of the club where the rugby field started. Changing rooms stretched through to the far end of the club where entry could be made from another car park beyond the hairdresser's shop which was by the rear entrance.

With the Emergency on (even Ampang Village not far beyond the Racecourse was a black area still), this far end of the club had had bunks installed for the rubber planter fraternity who came in for a weekend away from the tensions of unexpected ambushes. A strange variety of vehicles could be seen at weekends with personalised armour plating to their own design and requirements, as the planters would come in at this end of the club on Fridays and throw their carbines, gun belts, ammunition and other personalised weaponry over the bar to be stowed until they were heading back again for another fortnight or three weeks in the front line out on their isolated plantations.

This was the tremendous, almost wild west atmosphere in

which they gathered, and like their visit down into the back-woods of Johore to the Ladang Geddes Dunlop estate, the visit of this Tankards invitation side to play the Selangor Club was all adding up to a great social event over the extended Chinese New Year weekend. Unfortunately, in the Federation the coming advent of the year of the Pig would be a subdued event for the Chinese compared with Singapore, since the Emergency regulations banned Chinese from having their particularly noisy fire crackers.

Scoops was in his element at the centre of things with all his chaps around him. There were two Naval Base types, one of whom was an enormous red-headed seaman from the engine room for the scrum, and a fleet-footed Maori from the New Zealand brigade up in Perak. Of the two RAF types, one was a diminutive, extremely jovial navigator type, who would not disclose his age and made no bones of the fact that he was totally reliant upon the thug forwards Scoops had brought together to complete the pack. There were two planter types and the rest were made up from the nucleus of commercials such as Tubby, Derry Fraser from Harpers' KL office, John Marriot from Singapore Cold Storage, Stuart Dalgleish, who had come out to Sandilands Buttery Limited from playing with London Scottish. Since his flashes of darting brilliance at stand off were spaced between periods of apparent idleness, he was affectionately known as 'Tired Tim.' Two of the regular big men were there in the form of Big Bob Catford of Pirelli Tyres, who had had a spell in Iraq just ahead of Tubby, and the redoubtable 'Sports and Chaps' Mark Chilton of William Jacks (M) Limited on the Philips Agency.

As usual, Scoops led his impressive Tankards in their touring white rig with black socks and black Tankards on the jerseys out on to the beautiful green sward of the Kuala Lumpur *padang*, with a great crowd for the occasion all round filling every seat on the small uncovered five level seating stand, which was along from the clubhouse. With KL being capital of the country and the main commercial centre, the Selangor Club had a large spread of ex-patriates to call upon, so that their first team was quite formidable. However, the Tankards, having a nucleus of regulars and the fellows from the Forces of very high calibre, came out winners from a very hard and fast game.

Always after playing a hard game in such hot and humid conditions, Tubby found it was a long time before he cooled down to some semblance of normality, but the long bar at 'The Dog' was the ideal place to be, and it turned into a whale of an evening with drink, food and dancing all there to be enjoyed.

Since Derry Fraser at Harpers was of Scottish parentage like himself, Tubby was stacked up with them over the weekend, and fortunately they had Sunday before the next big game on the Monday down at the more planter-type club at Klang, formally known as the 'Klang Club'.

Kuala Lumpur was a very pleasant capital city and very sedate and orderly to those up from Singapore, used to the overwhelming wild, noisy Chinese population, the mad free for all traffic, the half drugged taxi men driving on their hooters in amongst the pedal trishaws, and the lively nightlife round Bugis Street, where the clatter of mah-jong pieces was a constant noise coming from the upper rooms as the gambling went on through the night.

Tubby was taken for a very sedate curry lunch on the Sunday at the Lake Club which had affiliations with the lovely Nuwera Eliya Club in the high tea country of Ceylon. It was genteel colonial in ambience, with a slightly faded look outwardly, but with its own swimming pool it was a gathering point for ex-pat wives with their little ones too young yet to be shipped off back to the UK for schooling. It had accommodation for ex-pat visitors along Rest House lines. Once inside it was very well appointed and had a magnificent air-conditioned dining room with inset glass cabinets on the walls for the display of orchids against black velvet, hence it was called the Orchid Room.

It had been agreed that they would gather again down at the Klang Club in this second town of the State of Selangor, which was some 23 miles down from Kuala Lumpur and centred in a great rubber area, with the final stretch of road running down to the inlet which was known as Port Swettenham. This was certainly not dockland though it was the main sea port for

311

Kuala Lumpur and all ships had to anchor to be off-loaded from lighters alongside. Port Swettenham was rather an unpleasant, swampy sort of area, with many rather dreadful looking houseboats amongst the muddy inlets and nipah palms. Having had a look at Port Swettenham, Tubby was quite glad to get back to the Tankards gang at the timbered Klang Club on the great green *padang* at Klang, with the very dominant presence nearby of the magnificent gold-domed new dwelling of the Sultan of Selangor.

On his way down to Klang, Tubby had been driven through an area where the railway passed along and it was obvious that this was being prepared as a potential industrial area to which the new Federation would seek to attract new industries. Tubby was not to know then that by his next tour he would be presiding at the opening ceremonies of a new Colgate Palmolive toothpaste factory in this very place.

They all gathered again at the Klang Club and got kitted up in their white gear, all newly laundered since the last match. Already Tubby was entering the dangerous state of taking for granted the ever-present and willing servant facilities in these parts of the world, since with all his tripping around laundry was simply not a problem; the stuff was always back there the next day, washed, dried in the sun, ironed out and neatly back on one's bed. So, here they were after one day off all back ready to go for the next rugger match, their shirts and shorts and jerseys all immaculate again. The Klang Club did not have such a wealth of talent to draw upon so it was a fairly easy match for the Tankards – luckily, as they had not fully recovered from the night after the great first game at 'The Dog' on Saturday.

Having been so busy flying off round his vast export territories and having only knowledge of the federation via the great initial tour round with Sears Wilson-Ingraham and Abe le Roux before his departure, Tubby thought it would do no harm to stay on up in Kuala Lumpur for the rest of the week to gain some working knowledge of Harper Gilfillan's facilities and the market in this important central area of the mainland in preparation for this frightening VIP visit pending. He was acutely aware of his delicate manoeuvring to maintain his

312

stateless person status and therefore not resident anywhere for tax purposes, so he took the opportunity of being in Kuala Lumpur to take soundings on the uncertainties resulting from the Federation's entering its third year, with the whole matter of Singapore being in, or out of, the Federation after the elections as a great unknown factor.

He was very pleased by the end of the week to head back to Singapore with an entry permit stamp from the Immigration Department of the Federation of Malaya in Kuala Lumpur, which could subsequently be produced to the Registration Office at some future date for the object and purpose of obtaining an identity card. The last visitors entry 'chop' he had in his passport from the Immigration Department of Singapore, from his return on the 21st January, took him through to the 20th February. Now he could return to Singapore over the Causeway from the Federation with this stamp of credence from the Federation Immigration Office, which would give him the status of being down in Singapore from the Federation.

The atmosphere on his return back to Singapore indicated that this visit of the new President himself, with his two Vice-Presidents, was going to be a crunch visit totally concentrated on the three new subsidiaries, with Frank Hill in Hong Kong being his first stop. Sears was not going to be able to manage an advance visit to check the three incumbent general managers, though they had received a long list of things he wanted set up, which included promotion activity to date, which would be interesting to Tubby anyway. Side tables were laid out in the big meeting room with all competitive products and the Colgate-Palmolive products all marked at comparative retail prices and respective market shares as far as they could be worked out.

Tom Glaze of Grant Advertising was also getting worked up since they were a branch of an American-based agency and he claimed to have had first-hand working experience with Fergy, the Vice-President of International Advertising. The presence of Ed Spika, Vice-President of Manufacture, confirmed that these subsidiaries were set up with local manufacture as a centre point of their financial viability and investment.

313

It was soon into March and the tempo and tension was heightening as arrival day for the VIP party got nearer. Tubby was not as much in Harper Gilfillan offices as when he had first had a room after Abe left, but they were summoned to a meeting in Big Bill Bailey's personal office where Desmond Brown, almost hypermanic in his obsessional concern for detail and his beloved office manual, had drafted out a programme in which they featured particularly on the social side. This indicated that the tension was fairly flying around Harper Gilfillan as well, in their keenness to be part of the next phase of development from being agents for the export territory, dealing with London. On the way in, Tubby had bumped into the urbane Californian Howard Frey of the patrician Heinz organization, to whom this type of big boss US visit pressure was completely alien. He announced that this was the time to take himself to the Hong Kong part of his domain, since his visit would coincide with the party leaving Frank Hill and heading towards Singapore. As the gathering progressed, Jim Kevlin didn't particularly add anything to the proceedings, so Bill Bailey and Desmond considered they had things organised their way. Little did they know what George Lesch would be like.

Tubby was young enough and completely innocent enough of the ways of New York and the second floor politics through which the aspirants like Kevlin had come to understand just how Jim was feeling. At least he had established himself with his first overseas general management post – albeit it the small domain of Panama which was almost an American satellite colonial situation for that land on either side of the Panama ship canal, until such time as it had been agreed to hand over the canal to the locals, some time at the turn of the century.

Singapore/Malaya was to be Jimmy Kevlin's next big jump up, but in the still very British colonial atmosphere of Singapore, his American accent and short stature were not conducive to an imposing presence. Further unnerving factors were the electrifying rumours coming out of New York as to the more powerful position of George Lesch, because the Colgate International company had overtaken for the first time the huge

314

domestic Colgate Palmolive Company of the USA over which the aging Ed Little still held sway, holding the three titles of Chairman, President and Chief Executive Officer. The things that George Lesch had done in Mexico, and which had got him to where he was now, still reverberated round the 44 subsidiaries worldwide, and there were tales filtering through from Hong Kong, where the VIP party had arrived, indicating that Sears was having difficulties.

Nothing but the best would do, and their accommodation had been booked at the most modern hotel – the Prince's Hotel Garni in Orchard Road, with its advanced air-conditioning throughout, and individual accommodation being virtually suites with luxuriously equipped private bathrooms attached to each room. The accommodation had been the prime consideration, since the a là carte menu and wine list was excellent, while the size of the dance floor and the reception area off the pavement were very economical. Tubby went out with Jim Kevlin to the airport to find that Bill Bailey and Desmond were already there, with his large Austin Princess limousine and Malay *sais* (driver) in attendance to carry bags out to the car.

They arrived at mid-afternoon and even though Paya Labar was the new large Singapore airport, the handling of the passengers was all still somewhat *laissez faire*, and soon the VIPs emerged into the milling crowd with hand shakes and greetings all round. The visitors must have wondered quite who was who, but eventually it was worked out and they did at least know Jimmy Kevlin by sight. To a 27-year-old, they all looked like old men, but what a diversity of characters they were.

Fergy, Vice President of Advertising, still had a polished Scottish voice and, while dapper as regarded his appearance, the style reflected years in an American or Latin American environment laid over his origins in Scotland. He looked as though he had taken the opportunity to get another lightweight suit made in Hong Kong, which is possible in 24 hours, and any nervousness, or holding back, was covered up by a lively, though droll sense of humour and banter.

By contrast, Ed Spika was a very large booming presence and though much of his blond fair hair was going and he wore glasses, it was almost possible to visualise him in youthful Scandinavian form with horned helmet and an axe in his hand, except that his features and the name Spika were not quite Norse, so he might have been of Finnish or Hungarian origin from way back. Being Vice President of Manufacturing for the International operation, he was constantly on the move round the world and Tubby didn't think he needed to stock up with a lightweight suit since he seemed well-dressed from his 'on the move' lifestyle.

George Lesch did look very much the Accountant of German extraction from Milwaukee, and was in the suit which you might expect him to be wearing in New York office. In size he was midway between Ed Spika and Fergy and totally different being quite middle-of-the-road and ordinary with dark black hair, greying at the sides, and he exuded quiet authority and a steely awareness of what he was about and therefore did not need to pretend anything. He seemed shrewd enough to have sussed out who needed flannelling first and said that he would go in the big limousine, and Ed Spika quickly stepped in by saying he would follow in Jimmy's car and so the convoy set off for the Prince's Garni.

They all got out at the Prince's Garni and were soon inside reception, which although cramped, was a welcome haven with its air conditioning. The Harpers brigade stood around for a moment, keen to hang on and wag the ears a bit, but it did sound as though George had made the point in the car to Bill Bailey that this was going to be very much a working visit as far as he was concerned. He had 'accepted' for a big lunchtime session on the Sunday at Bill Bailey's palatial house, so he politely, but very firmly, bade them farewell which left just the Colgate gang together with their big new boss. The three travellers seemed keen to retire to their rooms and settle in and wee Fergy had already gone off to do just that.

Jim Kevlin was invited to join them at night for a meal at the Prince's Garni and, after running over a few details for the programme with George Lesch, it appeared that Ed Spika was

going to be out and about on his own checking on the manufacturing facilities, availability and throughput of materials,
gleaned from the list of contacts he had built up from his
involvement with installations round the world. Before they
left, George Lesch mentioned one or two other things they
would be interested in having available for the meetings to
start in the morning first thing, which touched upon accounting
and the big black volume from New York called the Accounts
Department Instructions, which had been delegated to Tubby
to sort through with Price Waterhouse. Back at the office they
checked that the big table in the meeting room was set up with
seats, pads, pencils and pens and Tubby, for the umpteenth
time, checked the array of known and competitive products, all
laid out and priced and labelled for the big day.

For some reason Sears Wilson-Ingraham was coming down
from Hong Kong on a later plane and with Jimmy going to join
them at the Prince's Garni for the evening meal and Rita and
the kids still in the Ocean Park Hotel near the sea, Tubby was
delegated to go out to Singapore airport and bring Sears in, so
as to avoid any episode again with him bargaining with taxi
men in US dollars. Sears was certainly not as loud as he was
the first time, nor did he have his great portable radio for
picking up the broadcasts on the Americas Cup races as on his
first visit. He was a bit shell shocked and indeed psyched up
for what was to be his second round on the visits to the new
subsidiaries for which he had been given responsibility – before
George Lesch became the new boss of the International
operation.

When Tubby had bought the green Zephyr motorcar, he
remembered that Abe had given him the name of a small
Chinese car man round at the back of some industrial area in
Singapore as the only one to go to when the front wheels got
out of balance. The main Ford dealers seemed not able to cope
with their new machines. Tubby had begun to feel manifestations of being off-balance in the form of a shudder coming up
the steering column and being accentuated by the big white
steering wheel and column gear stick, to give an impression of
going through the sound barrier in an aeroplane. Indeed, as in

the film *The Sound Barrier*, Tubby found that by pressing his foot on the accelerator and driving quickly through the speed band from 40 to over 60, the Zephyr went into a smooth passage again and all was well.

They were on their way in from the airport, with Sears spread out on the far corner of the bench seat and door, when the sound barrier occurrence began. He developed all sorts of panics not knowing what to exactly get hold of with the long smooth dashboard layout of the Zephyr and the bench seat particularly, as he felt impact of Tubby stepping his foot down on the accelerator since there was a good stretch of road before they got into the congestion of Singapore's bustling, bouncing taxi traffic. However, he collapsed with a big sigh of relief as they sped through the sound barrier to 60 mph and into the smooth flight again. Once they were into the busier part of town and getting through the traffic to the Prince's Garni in Orchard Road there was not the opportunity for the Zephyr to get up to 40 and over, so all was well. As Tubby took his leave of him and shifted his bags into the hotel, Sears made Tubby swear on the book that he would get the car attended to before he would ride in it again.

Tubby went back to Amber Mansions to mull over his first impressions of the three visitors. He had found all three most agreeable, with George coming over as a very warm person, but with a quite powerful and authoritative undertone.

Fergy was the most intriguing since the UK company's main advertising agents were an ad agency called Masius and Ferguson. This was the Ferguson of the Masius and Ferguson, so he was a founder member. Mike Masius, the other partner, had been a contemporary and American friend of Bob Foster, who was the American athlete who had come to Britain as a competitor in the 1920s Olympics and liked the place so much that he had got the agency to establish the Colgate Palmolive company in the UK. His son, David Foster, was currently coming up to being boss man of the UK company, having been at public school in the UK and served in the British Navy Fleet Air Arm as a pilot during the war. The story had it round the UK office that he had been married for a short period to the film actress Glynis Johns and had ended up with too much of her tax debts.

Anyway, Mike Masius and Fergy Ferguson had built up quite an ad agency on the back of Colgate products as the UK subsidiary developed into a major force in the UK, with great export territories. From subsequent conversations and from other stories Tubby had picked up since being elevated to export, these two had made their money in the gung-ho days of the early 1930s down in Argentina and round Buenos Aires, when Aristotle Onassis was also there in his younger days, building up the capital base for his ultimate fortune from shipping.

Tubby had been over to Masius and Ferguson for some high pressure and concentrated advertising and media experience under the guiding hand of Alan Monroe, who was much loved and highly regarded in his role as Personnel Director of the agency. From his own overseas and military experiences Alan Monroe had given Tubby some very useful and helpful hints which he had found to be invaluable once he got into overseas situations which had already been quite hairy. At that time, in the late 1950s, the adertising agency scene was quite fascinating with likes of David Ogilvy using his personality to make a great name and agency in the States, but amongst all the mayhem and cant which does exist in the ad agency world, the likes of J. Walter Thompson always remained very big, steady and aloof from those with gimmicks. While not in McCann Erickson league, Masius and Ferguson had developed a very pukka image by having as account executives elegant public school types in well tailored suits, bowler hats, very white collars above striped shirts and rolled brollies, sheathed as in the manner of the best of the Guards Officers seen in civvies walking through St James's Park. Many had double-barrelled names and they were all tall, so that there was a legend about that Alan Monroe had on the wall inside his office a measuring line such as parents use for children growing up. The story went that as the candidate for interview came into the room and Alan asked for their coat, he would gently move them back against the wall and if they didn't measure up to six feet, their interview could be quite cursory.

During his spell at Masius and Ferguson, Tubby was in a team led by a particularly presentable and well turned-out character called Peter Gwyn, with whom he became very friendly. One day they had been in a particular session on a cat food, and were going over the first attempts by the visual chaps at putting it into storyboard form when Tubby involuntarily exclaimed that a cat in one picture looked particularly 'manky'. The response was a rather puzzled reaction by those present except for Peter Gwyn, who almost fell off his chair laughing. The others obviously did not understand the adjective, but Peter Gwyn, as it turned out, had had a spell in Merseyside in his youth when his father was the Woolworths boss in Liverpool and so knew exactly what 'manky' meant as regards cats likely to be seen round those rather terrible areas of Liverpool, the Dingle or Scotland Road. It was then explained to the others that it was to be hoped that when the storyboards turned into film the cat's appearance would be much improved since 'manky' cats were so moth-eaten that there· was often a gap in their furry tails where just the vertebrae showed.

That night before the big meetings, Tubby had a really good meal with van Marken on Cookie's fare at its best, which set him up no end for the next day. He was innocently open-minded, but intensely interested in watching, listening and participating in whatever was going to happen. The great day arrived and since George Lesch had left Harpers quite firmly with the message 'don't ring us, we'll ring you, otherwise see you for lunch on Sunday', it was Jimmy who went to the Prince's Garni Hotel to pick up the entourage for a 9 a.m. start. With his delayed arrival, Sears grabbed Tubby to run over the bits and pieces prepared round the meeting room on products, maps of the country with background and write-up of promotional activity up to the date.

Fergy had come into the room to choose where he was going to sit, while Tubby noticed that George Lesch took time to go round, meet and shake hands with each of the staff recruited so far to date. Surprisingly, there seemed to be no particular messages for him, but there was a list of calls for big Ed Spika to attend to and, remembering the episode with the great Bill Miller, Tubby wondered if there were any other General managers round the world seeking permission to dismiss someone.

They were soon sitting down in shirt sleeves, with George at the head of the table, while Ed Spika was outside in the general office attending to his phone calls and his schedule of visiting and contacting as regarded contractors, engineering and raw materials. Jimmy Kevlin was at the other end of the table, with Sears to his left obviously psyched up to dominate and lead proceedings while Tubby sat beside Fergy on the other side to the left of George Lesch.

Sears launched into an explanatory run in of the product ranges and their order of size and turnover in the new subsidiary and then moved into distribution patterns and logistics as related to the seven branches of Harper Gilfillan about the country already distributing all manner of products across the eleven states, including Singapore.

Before he got much further, Tubby could sense increasing agitation developing in George Lesch by his hands and noisy clearing of air through his nasal tubes, until eventually he said with a gesture with both hands, 'Where's the budgets?' Fergy, on Tubby's left, began to twitch and shuffle in his chair, while Sears in a rather exasperated manner said he wanted to take the meeting through the marketing background. Sears soldiered on in his upstate drawl, with what Tubby regarded as his rather flamboyant Ivy league mannerisms, until George once again said, 'Where's the budgets?'

It seemed as though they must have had other stops in Japan and Manila on the way to Hong Kong before coming down to this second new subsidiary in Singapore, because Sears threw up his arms and exclaimed, 'God dammit he's been like this all the way down the line!' Tubby felt under his breath that perhaps Sears might have got the message by now that George preferred another way, perhaps an agenda? Ever since the state of apprehension which prevailed from the time the visit was announced, Jim Kevlin had not come up with an agenda, and it was obvious that neither had Sears, or perhaps he had his own agenda but hadn't realised yet it was not to George's liking.

Like a dog which has had a bucket of water thrown at it, Sears shook off the interruption and aroused himself to come back for more by launching into details of promotional activities and what sort of advertising had been done so far. Jimmy was on to his third cigarette by then, and Fergy was studiously involved with his notes and papers when George again interrupted proceedings with his now established words, 'Where are the budgets?'

Sears threw down his pen, and with a half turn to Jim Kevlin, but really making his comment to all and sundry in the room, 'What can you do with this man? He's done this all down the line.' From then on George Lesch took control, and looking Jimmy firmly in the face at the other end of the table, he related that Colgate Palmolive (Malaya) Limited had been given the go ahead as from the 1st March and as such was scheduled to cable the first month's accounts to New York International for tabulation with those from the other 44 subsidiaries, with a pro forma balance sheet to follow in 28 days. Tubby had noted this down when going over the ADI's with the guy from Price Waterhouse.

Jimmy wasn't very big anyway, but he seemed to lower himself even more behind the cover of the table and pronounced that the budgets were not done yet. George, the President himself of C P International, in that firm but level manner of his asked, 'Why not?' Jimmy then went into long rambling explanations about all the problems he had been having with these rather toffee-nosed British colonial Foreign Exchange controllers within Singapore and the Federation of Malaya who had been ganging up in order to proposition him as the new general manager regarding the location of the proposed Registered Office for Colgate Palmolive (Malaya) Ltd – Singapore, or the Federation of Malaya as the name suggested.

George Lesch had been made most recently general manager of the large Mexican subsidiary over the border from the USA and his experience was that you retained a local law firm, usually a long established family concern, on the basis of their involvement in Latin American politics and ability to fix things with whoever happened to be the Minister for Commerce. It followed that half the family involved in the law firm would be in exile or in the mountains, while a certain regime may be in charge so that they could change over with the family currently running the business as and when the regime might change. It was therefore perfectly logical to George that he should ask, 'Where's your lawyer?' At this he was told that Maurice Edgar, the Edinburgh Scot with the big eyebrows, had made a point of being down from Kuala Lumpur where he lived, to be at the Singapore office of his firm for possible discussions concerning the on-going situation of where to incorporate the new subsidiary. Messages went out hastily to summon him to attend.

To the consternation of all around except Tubby, George Lesch positively beamed as he spread his hands out and said, 'Well, then. Let's do the budgets.' Now, Tubby had had a thorough going over with his export manager in London on the export turnover figures for all the products to Singapore and Malaya, as the prized export territory of the UK subsidiary for the calendar year. Additionally, he had had his sessions with the Account Department Instructions, so he asked George Lesch if he might explain what he was about to do. Being of German extraction, George Lesch had been quite interested to note that Tubby and Fergy had a common Scottish background and took to calling him 'Forby', mentioning that he had known and been impressed by many Scottish accountants encountered over the years.

While lawyers originally wrote the American constitution and thereby maintained themselves as top dogs ever since over accountants and all others, George obviously prided himself in being an accountant, and proceeded to explain to Tubby like some gentle professor how they were going to cost each product right the way down against shipping costs, with above and below the line promotion budgets, local and international overhead factors. With that base done and with Ed Spika's figures, they were to do a direct comparison against local

323

manufacture, existing and depreciation write-off, to see what improved significant profit margin there might be to be remitted back to the States. Tubby was quite in awe to be privileged with a personal demonstration by the President of C P International himself on how to do the budgets, which would hold him in good stead for the rest of his commercial life. From that point on there started one of the most intense ten days of application in terms of mind, body and spirit for all involved.

Big spreadsheets of accounting paper were summoned and Tubby was delegated to go off with Fergy to see Tom Glaze and bring back the above and below the line budgets for presentation, but before they left, the door opened and Maurice Edgar was ushered in – the lawyer himself, looking every bit the senior partner in a firm of British solicitors back home in the UK.

Maurice, the immaculate, was seated to the right of George at the side of the table and proceeded to listen attentively with a masked expression initially. However, as George Lesch went on to relate how and why they retained lawyers in the Latin American arena, particularly in shifting political and government situations, and as the picture came to Maurice of himself scampering off into the hills or jungles, while another legal partner took over, there started a great pulling and curling up of his eyebrows, as was his wont in times of stress.

There was a silence round the table as he started to speak in a very measured way in his best Fettes College, Edinburgh advocate's accent, 'You know, George, it always has been and still is very British here. We just do not do these things that way here.' There were two things working in his favour as he pressed on, using various tactics, to enlarge on how things were done here after years of rule under empire. Firstly, George Lesch – with Fergy in his entourage and his respect for Scottish accountants he had done business with – was inclined towards Scots. Secondly, and most thankfully, he did not have any idea as to how rarefied Maurice's Edinburgh accent was, and Tubby was acutely aware out of the corner of his eye that Fergy, on his left, was biting his bottom lip to stop having a fit of the giggles.

When he had done a convincing job on George Lesch as regarded not being able to put monies into Politicians hands, or the back pockets of ex-pat civil servants for Foreign Exchange favours, he went on to give a masterly summary of the Foreign Exchange Control situation together with the developing situation between the Federation of Malaya and the abundantly Chinese colony of Singapore, which Kevlin had not yet come to terms with, nor Sears.

It became abundantly clear that an industrial site somewhere near Kuala Lumpur might be best for Colgate's local manufacture installations since the free port advantages of Singapore were being heavily outweighed by the Independence elections build up. The future political scenarios being thrown up for years to come were quite alarming in 1959, with such anti-colonial men out after the voters as Lee Quan Yew, Ong Eng Guan and David Marshall – all potential bogeymen as Head of State! It was lunchtime by then and George delegated that Tubby go off with Fergy to Grant Advertising and get to work with Tom Glaze, while George set to on the budgets with Jimmy Kevlin and Sears. The target was given that after the big lunch at Bill Bailey's palatial establishment on the Sunday, they would have a get together to see how far they had got.

It was suggested that they walk along the quay and to the famous Change Alley where anything could be bought at a price, provided you were adept at the Eastern tradition of haggling. This alley would bring them through to the famous Raffles Place, which on one side was flanked by the large and imposing ex-patriates European department store of Robinsons. At the far end was the Sikh department store of Gian Singh's which was almost as famous and had the extra of a glittering array of eastern goods. Tubby fitted himself with an excellent double opening wardrobe type case for his hectic travelling at a lot less than he would have paid in Robinsons.

For the rest of the week Tubby had an absolutely fascinating time at Grant Advertising listening to Fergy and Tom Glaze, since they had put in a lot of living between them in various parts of the world and were of similar lively temperaments so that the ideas were fairly crackling. Also, there was the matter of getting to grips with the diverse, but limited, media facilities available. There was no TV in those days and commercial radio, though highly developed, had to span a complete diversity of languages.

The Chinese in Singapore were mixed up together, though predominantly Cantonese, whereas in the Federation there tended to be pockets, or enclaves, of Chinese like the Cantonese round Ipoh in the tin state, Hokkiens up in Penang, and Teochews mixed up between there and Kota Baru, but Chinese written was the same across all dialects. The cinema was a tremendous industry but a specialised media. The radio was diversified across English, Chinese (in several dialects), Malay and Hindi or Urdu for the Indians. Tubby had already come across the fiasco of the metal posters produced in the UK using a Burmese girl. The prime newspaper was the *Straits Times* (in English) on the mainland and the island, and its circulation, though good, hardly gave it national paper status, since there were Chinese, Malay and Indian papers with similar circulations.

This fragmentation of media emphasised the successful cornerstone already established with the promotional vans and teams which went to the consumer to stimulate interest through the trade, which caused the wholesalers to stock up and keep pace with the throughput. Fortunately, there was abundantly available, very high class and proficient production capability available in Singapore and Malaya, for making up their own tapes and jingles for their own promotional vans with their loudspeakers as a very successful marketing operation.

The once-a-year Gold Ring promotion had their detergent FAB as the dominant market leader, and with the Palmolive and the Colgate toothpaste being also market leaders it was agreed they could risk pretty low cost media and promotion budgets.

The big day came when all were to gather for curry tiffin lunch at Bill Bailey's house, prime perk to incumbent boss man of Harper Gilfillan. Both the big Princess and the big Humber limousine were in use with chauffeurs up front as they all gathered on the lovely terrace from which they moved easily into the lovely garden, or into the house. When summoned, they all settled round the big table which, to Tubby's amazement, actually incorporated a built-in goldfish pond and fountain in the centre. He felt very tempted as a starter to reach out and pick one little fishy out by the tail and put his head back and drop it down, if only he had been up to it.

Harper's people were absolutely bursting to get in amongst the action having been kept at a distance while George had his team's heads down and working like the very devil. Bill Bailey was a little taken aback when George asked if they might have an upstairs room to retire to afterwards, since he and the team had all arrived with bulging briefcases. Over coffee, George was observed huddled with Desmond Brown and Bill Bailey and it transpired that he had very carefully taken the opportunity to assure them that they were going to be very much in the action with the new subsidiary, since it was simply going to sell on the stuff as before to Harper Gilfillan, who would then handle it and distribute it as before. This would maintain prices and income to the new subsidiary, while it would buy at intercompany cost and eventually, with its own local manufacturing costs, boost profits further. The whole marketing function would be developed and supervised by the new subsidiary via Harpers with ongoing management at most of their branches working, or allocated for, 100% on Colgate products. This seemed to spread calm upon the waters and by mid-afternoon the Colgate team had withdrawn to an upstairs room for a fantastic budget session with George Lesch as the ringmaster.

The fiendish application of his business mind and ability was quite awe-inspiring to Tubby, and it was quite revealing to him to watch how the great man and Fergy interreacted with one another. Jimmy and Sears got quite rattled at times as George would get very forceful, until one realised that it was very cleverly staged. Fergy would counter this with delightful humour and asides and comebacks, which Tom Glaze was adept at too. It became abundantly clear that George Lesch was going to go on to the next stop in Thailand with a set of papers and plans in his pocket for C P (Malaya) Ltd which had his seal upon them and which Jimmy would do his damnedest to carry out – or else! From the very over the top character Tubby and Abe had met up with back in the September, Sears was becoming more and more subdued, which was understandable with such a powerful character as George Lesch around. Quite simply, it did not work to go at him head on and Sears had started but rather to humour him and probe along with him as Fergy was doing. Tubby was quite happy to be the spectator, fully appreciating the incredible experience at his age to be involved first-hand in this level of management and decision-making.

The team eventually joined the others downstairs where Ed Spika had been left since he had been busy doing his own production homework without having to be involved in the marketing. George would fill him in on the quantities set for the first budget as a basis for him to work out the countdown on manufacture, if at all, and if so, which products would come first in order of simplicity and profitability.

It came to departure time, and with Harpers being privy to the fact that the centre of operations was most likely to be in Kuala Lumpur in the Federation, it was resolved that Tubby and Jimmy Kevlin would go with Desmond up to Kuala Lumpur on the internal DC3 flight, after seeing the others off at Singapore Airport. George and Ed Spika were going for a very brief look at Indonesia before joining Sears in Bangkok to meet with Ken Page at his subsidiary which was up and running. The accountant in the Bangkok team, was from a UK Company, and there was comment that toothpaste production was going better since Tubby's visit to Rangoon and Burma. Everybody was very proud of the Comet 4 coming to the Far East in BOAC livery and Sears went off on it to the delight of all and sundry. It was therefore with some consternation that they noticed the Comet sitting on the tarmac at KL airport as they swung round on the slow circle the Dakota usually took to get a clear fix on the railway line on the embankment at the approach end to the main runway.

As they walked out of the Dakota there were ground staff and other engineering people in overalls round under one of the places where the two engines on either side of Comet were built into the wing roots. As they went through the airport building they all cringed when they heard that ever familiar voice shouting, 'Hi fellahs!' Yes, it was Sears somewhat restored to his larger than life self now that he was clear of George Lesch, so he came with them to an hotel. While they were at the hotel in KL, they got a message from BOAC which really set them back. Apparently one of the engines had a major problem and it would probably be two days at least for RAF Hastings transport to fly out from the UK with a spare engine for the Comet which would then have to be fitted in. By the time they saw Sears on his way March 1959 was rapidly disappearing.

34

NEW BEGINNINGS

After living on a pumped-up state of adrenalin hype over the VIP visit which had come rapidly after his return from the detailed trip through the Borneo territories, Tubby felt that he must catch up on his Singapore social life, and there were two events which turned out to be very special – one quite wild and the other relaxing.

Back in the swing of the cricket club after work, where his car automatically drove to, Eddie Flannigan reminded Tubby that there was the sailing date for Tony Pitt, the rubber planter with whom they had stayed on the rugger tour, and as it happened an old friend of Flannigan's parents would be leaving on the same ship for extended leave in the UK. This friend of the Flannigan family was a roly-poly French abbé who was finishing a prolonged tour in a leper colony. It was still daylight when they set off and down Anson Road to Keppel Harbour where the liner was tied up preparing for departure, and they were soon on board where Tony Pitt and the roly-poly abbé had set up court in the bar for all their friends and well wishers.

It developed into quite an evening and at the third and final call the crew were still getting the likes of Tubby and Flannigan down the gangplank at the last minute to join the others on the quay, catching the streamers and ribbons which were falling down from the decks in festoons. In those days when long leaves of six months, or possibly more, followed tours of three years at least, the leisurely sail home on a liner was very much part of the leave and the send off parties on the ships down at the docks were events which just had to be experienced.

The night was still young, or at least they felt as though it was, when after much hooting and shouting and waving, the great boat eventually slipped away into the night. So, it was not surprising that a gang of the well wishers should end up in a notorious drinking spot in the dock area called Toby's Paradise. Tubby had heard of the place, but as yet had not had the dubious pleasure of a visit. It was indeed a very unique drinking place and Tubby took note of the huge Sikh doorman as they went in and entered the nearest thing to a film set from *The Life of Susie Wong*.

There were all sorts there, including planters out for a wild night in Singapore with hands half up the *cheong sams* of the many delectable girls available, while presiding over it all from behind the bar was Toby and his very striking Chinese wife from Shanghai. In stark contrast, Toby was as black as the ace of spades and probably from some original slave stock like the wealthy blacks Tubby had met up with in Baghdad up from the Gulf. What made Toby utterly unique was the fact that one eye looked slightly inwards and the other one slightly upwards, which made having a conversation somewhat disconcerting. They were indeed a fascinating couple and had been running places like this originally in Shanghai and then down the coast as Chairman Mao and his hoards bounced back from the long march. Then they went on into Indo-China until the Viet-Minh Communists moved them on from there, and so to Singapore, while it remained wild and free for all as it was in those days.

In spite of the huge Sikh doormen, their departure was eventually precipitated by the outbreak of a fight which Tubby and Flannigan did not feel inclined to become involved in, as an assortment of weaponry was produced as the fracas escalated. From the Baghdad experience with Charlie the barman in similar circumstances, he had always checked out escape routes in such places of ill-repute, so he pulled Flannigan out to the rear via the kitchens.

The other event, which was most relaxing, was a leisurely lunch on a large Blue Funnel boat called the *Tyndareus* lying at anchor in the Outer Roads. Out from the wharfs, godowns and dock areas of Singapore there were two wonderful large safe anchorages for ships called the Inner and Outer Roads, and Tubby had been down with his cine-camera to a vantage point a week or so earlier to film the Royal Yacht Britannia as it sailed from the Inner Road. This was the place where some tourist boats stayed without actually tying up alongside while their passengers were brought to and fro by launch tender, or sampan, to the steps at Clifford Pier for immediate access into Raffles Place and all the interesting parts of the city.

The lunch had been arranged by Scoops and Tom Lough-head because of their shipping agency responsibilities for the Blue Funnel vessels of the privately owned Alfred Holt line of Liverpool. Since Tom Loughhead was from Liverpool he thought Tubby would be interested to see over this Blue Funnel vessel since it was rather special. It was immaculately turned out, as all Blue Funnel vessels were, but on being taken on a tour round by the skipper, their host, he found to his amazement that it was totally adapted and fitted out for taking thousands of Moslems up the Red Sea and on to Mecca on the annual pilgrimage of the Hadj in July, which is about the hottest time you can get in the Red Sea.

The decks were marked out in white lines reminiscent of pictures and drawings Tubby had seen in old books of the slave ships, only this time the demarcations were actually marking out the deck allocation paid for by each pilgrim for the sail from Indonesia into the heat inferno of the Gulf. Having seen the deck passengers on the Rejang River boat from Kuching to Sibu in Sarawak, Tubby could understand how the pilgrims/passengers would accept this as the norm, against a hot stuffy cabin and they would bring all their own stuff for feeding during the journey and back again. The unique extra fitting was on the top deck astride the stern, a padded cell, no less! The skipper explained that hard experience had shown it was not unusual for pilgrims to become a bit mad and deranged in the appalling heat during the sail up the Red Sea to Jidda, the port Mecca, and so they had found that this extra room facility was a good thing to have.

Over lunch the skipper explained that the *Tyndareus* had been doing this trip for many years now, with re-fits as and when required at the excellent repair facilities available at

Suez, and once its trips for the pilgrimage season were over it would return to its anchorage here in the Outer Roads at Singapore. Afterwards the skipper showed them the ship's manifest and the bills of lading for the ship's ballast which was actually a cargo of ore and sulphates, which the bills stated were to be delivered as, when, and if, the ship should reach the UK eventually. Otherwise the *Tyndareus* was more than earning its keep for Alfred Holt and Son transporting Sunni Moslem pilgrims each July.

When Tubby had been on his trip through Sarawak and Borneo he had picked up stories circulating about a group of pilgrims who had returned by air to Indonesia with their white hadji hats as the symbol of their attendance and their walk round the Kaaba, the black stone at Mecca, when in effect they had actually stopped at Singapore having a high old time with the funds accumulated for their trip and had returned home in great style having bought their white skull caps across in Singapore before coming back. It therefore made their trip more credible if they went with a very well known and respected shipping line like Blue Funnel which would take them there and back without any diversions to any other attractive places.

It had been most interesting to eat and drink well on this boat, watching all the comings and goings of this tremendous crossing point of the world's major shipping routes, and by late afternoon their launch appeared again to take them back to the great city of Singapore.

One day shortly after the visit, Tubby had been over in Harpers big office by the Bank of China talking to Howard Frey of the Heinz Company who was listening in horror to the antics of the Colgate VIPs who had come amongst them, when Desmond Brown came along and asked him into his office. Tubby felt himself becoming defensive, anticipating a back door attempt as one British ex-pat to another, in order to find out what had been going on and if there was more to what Lesch had told them, but it turned out that Desmond was being effusive because he wanted a personal favour.

Desmond was a mad keen horseman and before he ever

reached the office in the morning, early as it was, he had already been at the stables and exercised his horses, and himself for that matter. He explained to Tubby that once a year they were allowed to have an amateur day at the great and famous Bukit Timah race course. He and his keen horse folk would ride their horses adorned in racing silks with all the facilities of the Singapore Turf Club's race course. Desmond had got to hear about Tubby and his cine-camera and he asked if Tubby might attend as his guest and take films of him in his races, from the parade ring through to the winners enclosure. Horsey people and the racing fraternity were not Tubby's scene, but he said he would have a go, much to Desmond's delight.

When the day came he felt like the Aga Khan since Desmond had arranged for him the full facilities of the Owners' Enclosure with all the necessary owners' badges, identities and everything else hanging from the lapel of his new swish lightweight Singapore suit in beige by Chee Fatt, his Northbridge Road tailor. It really was all rather pukka with the Gurkha pipe band to play and march between the races and, with the Chinese being the most frenzied gamblers in the world, there was a good crowd of punters to complete the whole atmosphere and razzmatazz of a full race day.

It was a totally new experience for Tubby to come into racing at the top as it were. The sun shone and he was wined and dined like a lord within the facilities befitting the sport of kings. Desmond won two of his races and he got them down on film to pay for his day out.

On the new subsidiary front, things seemed to be looking up since the departure of the VIPs. Although it was now over six months since he had first met with Jim, he still wasn't sure what the real Jim Kevlin was like. Tubby's first hand experience of Americans person to person could not be regarded as being normal, ranging so far from American soldiers who came to England in the war and from whom as a child he badgered chewing gum, through to rather unpleasant 'ugly' Americans in Baghdad and Iraq, who kept very much to themselves and their PX Stores.

Indeed, the Americans Tubby had met in Baghdad helped to endorse the unfortunate image currently around at that time from a book known as *The Ugly American* which highlighted rackets and the way with which American aid to Indo China got diverted off to the benefit of local spivs who were supposed to be involved in the process for helping nations, or peoples with problems.

He had come to like and respect Rita and found the three children good fun, particularly little Gita and her Spanish, which was translated by the other two. Jim, on the other hand, seemed to be holding himself back which gave the impression of being unsure of himself, so Tubby satisfied himself that Jim was playing himself in, particularly since his general manager experience was limited to the small Panamanian operation. It was more likely that Sears Wilson-Ingraham was the problem and, while the experience of not having budgets ready for George Lesch had been pretty traumatic, it probably reflected more on Sears than on Jimmy, and Tubby had a creeping suspicion that he may have left things to drift that way on purpose. Certainly things were an awful lot better after the VIP visit and it had certainly helped his standing that Harpers were put in place to some extent. As far as Tubby was concerned, they at least now had a set of figures for the year to come, or at least what was left of it, and they could apply the ADI manual by getting all the accounting books set up to produce the figures which they could cable off at the end of each month to New York.

Soon they had had their first ratings on how they stood against the 44 other subsidiaries around the world, nevertheless, he still had an underlying feeling that not all was being communicated through. On top of all this, Tubby did have his export responsibilities to London and the shipments set in motion by his positive Ceylon visit would soon be on their way to Rajandrams for the drive into the market in that glorious island to support possibly another overseas subsidiary, with local manufacture. It was from communications with London export on Ceylon and their reactions to his Sarawak/Borneo reports that he got some inkling that something was afoot.

There were some veiled remarks about 'our man in the Far East putting the UK company big on the international scene' and, showing this to Jim Kevlin, he was handed a communication out of New York.

The communication concerned Tubby's own ongoing status in that he was to be the second ex-patriate to Jim Kevlin in the new subsidiary operations for Singapore-Malaya, which meant that he would be part of New York International personnel and no longer the Far East export rep for the UK subsidiary. His simplistic first reaction was that it now rationalised his position since he was finding it increasingly difficult to control his involvement in the escalating activities of this high potential new International operation in Singapore and Malaya which was proving to be far from a simple matter of handing over on behalf of UK export. He welcomed the announcement as just this, and in his naivete began to rabbit on to Jim about what he had set in motion in Ceylon and who was going to handle it now.

At this Jim Kevlin abandoned some of his secretiveness and tried to get over to Tubby the enormity of this appointment out of New York. He did this by telling how, back from the war in the Navy, he had fought his way up the trainee ladder and the second floor in New York to be boss in one of the 44 Colgate subsidiaries round the world. He then waxed strong about the level of profit sharing which went with such a position in an overseas subsidiary and used terms such as 'making a killing' when fortunate enough to get in on the ground floor of a new subsidiary such as this one which they were both going to be involved with.

It was all a bit too much for Tubby as some of this sank in, because it was little more than twelve months since he had left the UK as the first pioneer long-stay export rep to be in Iraq for two to three years. The implications of this new beginning were to gradually sink in and as and when they did, the realisation thereof was somewhat overwhelming. However, both agreed the major priority was to get himself off his UK export responsibilities and there followed a series of rapid exchanges with London export and John Steele who came back fairly smartly from London with the name of one Kevin Wood, who would be flying out to Singapore shortly to take over Tubby's files and notes. Additionally, there was a request that he be initiated into the highly successful marketing strategies which had been developed with Harpers and the advertising agents for the Malayan marketing programme which was so profitable.

When they had done the whistle-stop tour last September as the new team, Abe le Roux had made special mention during their stopover in Ipoh, in the great tin mining state of Perak, about a painting competition promotion for children related to Colgate toothpaste. The top prizes were to be brand new bicycles and Tubby had been in touch with Stuart Robertson at the Ipoh branch concerning the afternoon tea party and presentations to the winners. Tubby decided that this would be an ideal occasion to introduce Kevin Wood into the ways in which high levels of exposure and public relations could be achieved at very low cost for maximum benefits to the product, the company's name, and their locally placed agents.

As it happened it would work out very well with the rugger front since Tubby had been getting some first team exposure during this prolonged period of time in Singapore. He had found that towards end of games the extreme temperature and humidity began to take its toll, but the climate seemed to keep muscles in trim without the stiffening one gets in colder climates. He was getting in some good hard games as a fighting fit, two hundred pound plus, prop forward and with the end of season coming up, the club had a game up in Perak.

The day came when Kevin Wood arrived at Singapore airport and Tubby was quite looking forward to getting some first hand news and an update on how some of the others were getting on. He was still in touch with Dick Malyan (the Reeve) but only occasionally – he was apparently doing great things in Greece, while Patrick Bresnan, a very French looking and French speaking graduate was doing well and enjoying himself to the full in the Congo where the old colonial names of Stanleyville and Leopoldville were still being used and remembered. However, there were signs that troubles were brewing

337

up in the former Belgium Congo with increasing United Nations involvement.

With memory of these former larger than life colleagues buzzing round in his mind he was a bit taken aback when he was confronted with a stocky, clean as a button, dour and rather earnest Yorkshireman. Tubby could just visualise him laying down the law to a district meeting of front line sub-salesmen with whom Tubby had worked when he was on the road. It turned out that this indeed was the case, Kevin had been a district manager when called in to export for this posting.

He carried his North-country bluntness and competence to a degree that he sometimes gave the impression of knowing it all, which made Tubby feel it was going to be difficult to try and get him to understand that the sort of things they were doing in this market situation were abundantly sensible and right, because it just simply was not a UK marketing situation.

Colgate Palmolive were very unique round the world in operating on a minimum level of ex-pats, and Nestlé, with their mass market tinned milk products, were not far behind, and nor was Shell since beyond the glamour image of oil production, they had a very big hold on the consumer market for paraffin, which was a prime requirement for light and heat. ICI and Unilever tended to be a bit heavy on ex-pats and the latter had started sending Chinese graduates back to the UK to Port Sunlight and Unilever House for indoctrination. There had been creeping signs of this UK indoctrination showing up here and there in the form of tests of 'banded packs' and 'money off' packs – the curse of the UK market. If only they could get over the reality that both Colgate and Unilever had many years of highly profitable throughput of products at prices the market could sustain, without resorting to such offers which throw profits away. While FAB, Colgate and Palmolive were leaders, there was still tremendous scope for simple, well-thought-out promotions to get more of everyone's products into the market for those millions who hadn't even tried them yet to become regular users. Against this background Tubby did his best to give Kevin an intensive few weeks and Harpers were very co-operative, though he did seem to keep himself a bit of a distance apart, though after all he was from Yorkshire.

The visit up to Ipoh on the Malayan Airways Dakota was very successful and Alan Pitt, the Ipoh branch manager and Stuart Robertson had really maximised on the Colgate sponsored school colouring competition and Tubby found that the whole presentation was to be in a big school hall, with tea and refreshments to follow the big presentation. He found that the wife of the Mayor of Ipoh, a princess in her own right – Tengku Abrijah – was to present the prizes. There was a top table, and a raised stage with all the prizes neatly displayed and Tubby found he had to address the gathering at a microphone to which they had attached a Colgate box.

Alan Pitt was a great character, having been on small boats in the navy in the war and had quite a rough time on convoy duty. The whole level of the presentation was superb PR for image building since it had brought lots of children and proud parents, all potential toothpaste users for the better health of the nation. Being a Moslem state, there were no heavy drinks about and after all it was an afternoon do and tea and goodies would be most welcome by all and sundry. They didn't really get much socialising in and Tubby looked forward to future visits to Ipoh when he might get to know everyone a lot better.

Tubby did get his rugger match in, although Kevin Wood did hold that it would never match up to Rugby League. Little did he know what it had been like on the pitch since Tubby had been facing a ferocious Maori prop with a great scar down one side of his face who came into the scrums with his head swinging two and fro like a bell clapper. The concentration of military from all other Commonwealth countries, helping out fellow member Malaya against the Insurgents meant that there was a tremendous range of rugby talent for the Perak team to call upon. John Marriott, at loose forward for Singapore, started by darting under the arm of the big Fijian opposite to pin the scrum half until the third time when a big brown knee met his face head on like a humane killer at an abattoir. At the third line out, big Tom Loughhead was felled and all 18 stone

339

of him went down, which turned out for the best since, once revived, he became somewhat fighting mad throwing his 18 stone around to good effect. Tubby had never really experienced this level of rugby before as everyone stepped up a gear. He had a taste of what it might be like at international level since he felt himself go through a barrier into another level of adrenalin, and the pain and exhaustion didn't seem a factor any more. It was indeed a very hard and exhilarating experience even as losers by a short head, and in the get together afterwards he found his big, brown, scarred opposite prop, Rangi Christie, to be a very friendly New Zealander!

Kevin was much more relaxed and genial by the time Tubby saw him off to Ceylon with a suggestion that Colombo might be a suitable base from which to cover his future Far East export responsibilities without Singapore and Malaya, and possibly Sarawak and North Borneo since there were indications that these territories would become part of an enlarged Federation of Malaya. Kevin took with him personal letters and gifts from Tubby for Mr Rajandram and Tim Horshington in appreciation of their help and hospitality. Later he was to keep in touch with Tim Horshington and hear that Kevin was getting to grips with things and working well with Maharajah, John Fernando and others in Colombo.

With Kevin on his way he was able to have a proper read of a copy of the latest issue of the UK company's *Ra! Ra! Ra!* house magazine. Tubby was taken aback to read about himself and the kudos to the subsidiary from his being the first UK employee to move on to the International scene for many years. The reading of this write-up about himself helped to attune his mind to the new potential Jim Kevlin spoke about and what might be the situation over the next year or so.

Singapore's part in his whole market was highly significant and out of all proportion to the rest, in terms of 1.5 million consumer-orientated Chinese concentrated in one small island, with money to spend, by Far East standards, and built-in attitude for improved levels of hygiene and cleanliness. Singapore was much more developed and concentrated in terms of wholesale retail functioning and within Harpers organisation it was much more developed with a nucleus of established sales-men who were 100% Colgate. Tubby thought this could be the place to apply initial thinkings as a blueprint for the whole marketing for the new subsidiary, both here and across the Federation. It could be the testing place to see just how far and at what speed one might bring in UK style innovation. But over and above these matters were the developments of the subsidiary and its operations towards local manufacture, which were more exciting since the visit of the Vice President of Manufacture – Ed Spika – had set in motion lines of investi-gation and actions to resolve the best factory site which might be in the Federation.

George Lesch, the accountant, had in turn set in motion actions to resolve the financing for the new subsidiary oper-ation and the expected return thereon. They were told that they might expect a visit from an American called Ray Crearan of a lesser merchant bank called White Weld & Co, apparently much used and respected by George Lesch. All the subsidiaries round the world had their own very varied situations, politics and goodness knows what, which had to be analyzed and weighed up before the great Colgate company put any money in, with the aim of getting more out. Local manufacture might even be arranged with minimal input of money since the Federation of Malaya was offering pioneer industry status, with tax advantages over five years for new manufacturing ventures. In advance of this visit, Tubby was delegated to go along to Price Waterhouse again in order get something down on paper about these Pioneer Industry inducements being offered and he got in touch with Maurice Edgar since he had touched upon this in his masterly address to George Lesch at the start of the celebrated visit.

Tubby realised that he had indeed done the right thing back on the February Tankards tour at KL by getting himself registered in the Federation. Once he knew more about likely time schedule, and if he played his cards carefully not to expose himself to Singapore Authorities, as Jim Kevlin had done, he could probably stretch out his non-existent tax status for another twelve months at least. This, together with his enhanced financial situation as one of the international operation, pushed at his inbred caution on financial matters to wonder if he might go a bit mad as one of the up and running young blades of the Singapore set.

He couldn't understand the chaps whom Abe had pointed out as having no savings who yet would blow any windfall, from a tip-off, on a rubber or tin share deal, on buying a Jaguar. He did think he had accumulated more than enough for any future tax liability, particularly over twelve months away, and he had started buying stocks and shares via a stockbroker back in Liverpool. Why not invest in a real sports car like those some of Tankards gang turned up with?

One evening over Cookie's lovely food, he raised the subject with van Marken to see how his canny Dutch friend might react, because they both came from backgrounds where nothing had been easy, in terms of money or handouts. Sander responded by saying that there was a fellow Dutchman who only that day had mentioned he was having to leave Singapore and did Sander know of anyone who might be interested in his sports car. It seemed to be the pat on the shoulder Tubby had been hoping for, with a little voice telling him to go for it. When he did go out with Sander to see the vehicle there was no question but to go for it. It was a sleek, low, red MGA projectile, with its chrome glistening in the sunshine, white walled tyres on spoked wheels, with a copper hammer for tapping loose the wheel bosses emblazoned with the MGA emblem.

Against Tubby's bulk it seemed to have been tailor-made since on stepping over the door to get in he seemed to slip into the glove of the lovely black upholstery. The highly practical little stubby gear stick was in exactly the right place for reflex speed control and he had never had a car with a rev counter and speedo before.

They had a demonstration of how the hood was brought out from under the tonneau cover and the side windows clipped in place, which was not very practical. However, this was to be for fun driving in this lovely climate, with the tonneau cover half in place, with the other half zipped up once out of the car and parked. SS3547 was duly purchased from Sander's Dutch friend and Tubby felt he had completed the picture with his red bullet of a sports car.

With his new 'two car status', he found out that there was a lock-up garage at the back of the block of the Amber Mansions building which no-one had bothered to mention since Sander had always parked his Fiat out front and Tubby just carried on doing the same with the Zephyr as Abe had. There was a paved entry-way round to the lock-up at the back which was just over a car's width and went in straight from the road at the end of the buildings, with a 90 degree sharp corner for the run in along the back to the garage door. Tubby began driving his red flash very gingerly since he found that it was a highly sensitive thoroughbred which could leap from a standing start at traffic lights yet extremely sure in its handling. In his second week of ownership, as he was becoming a bit cocky, Tubby was to find out just how sure when, changing down to slot the MGA into the back passage of the flats, his foot hit the accelerator instead of the brake and somehow the red flash seemed to steer itself round the 90 degree corner with him just managing to hit the brake in time to prevent going into the garage, without the doors being opened. It took him a few minutes just sitting there in the little cockpit breathing steadily before he felt confident that his legs would support him in wriggling out, but it proved to be the breakthrough he needed, since from then on he knew exactly just how well this car could corner when pushed to order.

Another incentive to take the plunge with a sports car was the suggestion from Jim Kevlin that, with himself now permanently part of the new subsidiary operation, he should endeavour to make a detailed tour of all the branches right up through the Federation on a programme of familiarisation, as he had been doing on his export territory visits so far. The idea was that his fact finding trip would concentrate on the populated areas along the main north/south road which went from Singapore straight up towards Seremban, on to Kuala Lumpur then to the rest of the country to the north-west of the great central highland range. Since Malacca and the region south of there into Johore was to the west of the main road, he decided to do a run up this west coast from Singapore, which would give him further familiarisation with his red flash automobile.

Tubby had found that wind coming over the low windscreen of the MGA seemed to make his hair stand on end, so his old cord flat hat from the UK, with the stitched-down peak, became part of his sports car attire. One morning, he jumped into the cockpit, slid under the steering wheel, flung on his flat hat and started backing out, when he became aware of movements inside the cap and on snatching it off two horrible big cockroaches fell out and down between his legs. They really are the most horrible things with their two long antennae out in front, and the very thought of their getting down into the well of the car cockpit and possibly getting up his trouser legs was powerful motivation to grab at them with his bare hands, while they were still as surprised as he was, and toss them out. Even so, as soon as he backed the car out sufficient for plenty of daylight about he leapt out to make a thorough inspection of the whole area down from his seat towards the pedals and under the floor mats. From that day onwards the dear old flat hat was always carefully lifted out and shaken in case there were any more horrible night visitors.

Having not long purchased the red car, he double checked that his tax disc was all in order before crossing the Causeway into Johore. As he began to open up this speed machine out of the town of Johore Bahru, he was glad that he didn't have to look in the mirror as in yesteryears in case the old Sultan of Johore was after him with his pistol, as he did to those who overtook him. This was real driving and living, thought Tubby, as he sped along the metal roads, and even when he turned off on to the minor red road on his faithful Shell map which led down to Pontian Kechil, it was also well-metalled though narrower and quite twisty.

Many of the gang in the cricket club had been asking if he had done the ton in his red car, but 100 mph, was not the real pleasure and point of this splendid machine. Tubby was finding that it excelled on these twisty minor roads with good surfaces and he found that he could keep pushing up the average using

344

the gears and the rev counter until the car just ran as on rails through all the bends with not the slightest feel or fear of breaking loose. It was a glorious sunny day and he found this whole stretch along the west coast on the southern tip of the Malay peninsular mainland up towards Muar very untouched, with great stretches of palm swamps to the seaside and plantations on the land side.

As he went further north he came into the lower part of the paddy growing areas and pulled up at the sight of two enormous black water buffalo having a head-on confrontation, which was the nearest thing he had seen to Sumo wrestling in terms of the bulk of the contestants and the minimal movements. Tubby couldn't stand too much of it since the banging together of the heads made him feel sore, even just watching. While he had been watching he had not been fully aware that other water buffalo had emerged from the paddy along the road like keen spectators of the event. When Tubby came to move off from amongst them, he leaned out and took a whack at the flank of the nearest one as one might do with cows at home heading in for milking down a country lane. He did think that the hides of these big beasts might be a bit more impenetrable than a cow, so he put a bit more of bite into his slap and wished to goodness he hadn't. From the moment his flat palm made impact it caused a tingling pain which shot back up his arm to be almost unbearable. It brought back memories of a chemistry master who used to produce a sizable piece of rhino hide as his ultimate deterrent, beating down on the bench top to demonstrate how it might be administered to a miscreant pupil.

On his way back into Singapore in the late afternoon Tubby had noticed the odd thunderhead clouds building up as he crossed the Causeway. He wondered if he might stop and unfold the hood from behind the seats before the downpours came, but he decided to chance it and head on into Singapore. It was as he reched the outskirts where bus routes petered out that he heard the noise of the rain coming up behind as it began to pitter patter down on the abundant leaf growth present in the tropics. He headed off the main highway and found himself going down a one way road with houses on one side until he came to what looked like gates to a cemetery, with a bus shelter at the end at which a few Chinese stood.

They watched with fascination as Tubby screamed to a halt near the gates, leapt out of his car and zipped up his tonneau cover over the steering wheel and the driving area to dash across to join them under the bus shelter just as the rain came down in large lumps. He had found that these late afternoon build ups to thunderous outbursts could be very localised, but the rain does come down very hard to bounce back up about six inches off the ground. Tubby soon followed the example of the other Chinese in the bus shelter by climbing up onto the lowest bar of the rails round the bus shelter to keep one's feet just above the splashback level. This caused no end of amusement and cross chatter amongst his fellow shelterers. After about twenty minutes the sun was out again, and while Tubby had to brush off two minor lakes with the palm of his hand before turning the tonneau cover back, he noticed that the rain soaked car was beginning to dry off already with visible steam from the heat of the tropical sun. The arrival of such a volume of water into the tropical heat steps up the humidity factor and Tubby was very glad to get the MGA under way again with the breeze flowing around him as a great cooling presence.

On very short notice, George Lesch's international banker Ray Crearan arrived in Singapore from White Weld & Co. In appearance, he was certainly not of the smooth suave pin-striped suit brigade Tubby had in mind from the City of London scene. Indeed, he really did appear to have been living out of a suitcase for a while, being about the age of George Lesch, but with untidy dull grey hair, rather than silver, so that his overall presence was not very impressive.

His general manner did not win friends, nor his adverse comments about his hotel, and nor did his direct questioning, without giving anything away from his end. Jimmy Kevlin was so irked that he delegated Tubby to wine and dine Ray on the second night before his departure for Hong Kong. This proved to be just right for Tubby since with no third party, it turned into one of the most fascinating and informative evenings in his life.

After a buzz round Singapore in his red speed machine, Tubby took him to a place he favoured, specialising in Szechuan cuisine, since he had noted that Ray Crearan was quite cosmopolitan on food, which was not usually the case with Americans. The buzz round Singapore had been appreciated because, after playing things very close to his chest in the formal meetings, Ray began to enlarge on how he operated in putting together finance and related currency deals for international operators and multi-nationals by being constantly on the move round his offices which were located in the main money centres of the world – New York, Caracas, London, Zurich and Hong Kong.

Tubby was content just to listen as this merchant banker related how his grandfather had been in vaudeville management way back and could work out the likely takings, cost and then profit by just standing on the stage in any vaudeville house, taking in the auditorium without having to count the seats. Ray felt that this sort of intuitive business sense was a very powerful ingredient within the other family folk like himself who were this tightly run White Weld & Co banking concern. Within the scale of banking and finance in those days in the late 1950s, companies like this could still operate and were much respected by the likes of George Lesch for ideas on financing for his great range of diverse overseas subsidiaries.

The meal was very relaxed as Ray related examples of his day to day working round the money centres of the world, such as having approaches from a Jewish organisation with vast sums locked in Poland. How could they get it out or working for them and their various causes? This could be carried in his head as he went on his rounds until a matching need should come to hand such as an emigré Polish group desperate for money to be available to them in Poland behind the Iron Curtain. Put the two together and both parties are delighted. The Jewish organisation suddenly had their locked away Polish funds available to them in US dollars in New York, while the emigré Poles found in return that they had at their disposal much needed funds right there in their homeland, in exchange for their Yankee dollars, and White Weld & Co had their percentage!

Tubby learned that the prestigious Shell building, which dominated the Singapore skyline with that of the Bank of China, was not owned by them at all. As soon as building was completed, the capital outlay had been recouped for other projects by a lease back arrangement. This and many other bigger business finance ideas were learned that night for possible use in later years, and particularly he began understanding how they eventually ended up with three separate companies to handle the Malayan venture into local manufacture. Later, all three of the subsidiaries would become a subsidiary of the large Canadian subsidiary, with its historic remittance advantages across the 49th parallel to return profits into the parent company in New York. He knew now that for any future personal trip to Ceylon, where the poor exchange rates prevailed, he would make his money arrangements via the local *chattiars* (Indian money men) for the Straits dollars he paid here to be made available to him in Colombo in local rupees, at much better rates since by this means the Ceylonese were getting money out of Ceylon.

There was one event he had to attend before he was to get away on his fact-finding federation trip over the next few weeks. It was the huge retirement *makan* to be held at the Chinese swimming club for the retirement of the much respected and long serving Eurasian Office Manager of Harpers Singapore.

This was the first Chinese *makan* Tubby had attended on this scale since everyone was there, from the top brass, the expat agency people like himself, Jim Kevlin, Howard Frey of Heinz, and so on all the way down to the promotion team girls and Bah Seng of Havelock Road godown. In proper Chinese style the whole gathering was split up into groups at round tables spread throughout the great hall of the swimming club. Chinese *makans* of this scale could be 13 courses or more, some of which can be indulged in and some can be left as each course dish is placed centrally in the middle of the round table for all to reach out with chop sticks and keep replenishing their eating bowls. All the food and drink was on the house so it was not surprising that the noise of voices began to rise imperceptibly.

Tubby then noticed that big Bah Seng, the huge buddha-like boss of the godown, started to go the rounds of each table with his charged brandy glass issuing a challenging shout of: *Yam Seng*, which meant that all at the table had to down their glasses as well. In tandem with him, and of totally contrasting build and appearance, was one of the chief clerks from the main office who was very thin, semi-stooped and wore large glasses. Like Mr Hennessey, these two seemed to be completely unaffected by what they were consuming, then Tubby noticed that a newly arrived young ex-pat of Harpers was following the pair around thinking this was great sport.

There had been a buzz round Singapore in the business community that the likely change to independence in one form or another under those competing in the elections, might well result in a restriction on ex-pats with the introduction of work permits. So, this young chap had been shipped out in haste from Plantation House in London to get him into Singapore before he was actually ready. None of the established Harpers chaps seemed to take him in hand and he got more and more ragged trying to keep up with the very seasoned Bah Seng and Chow Wan who went on, table by table. When it came to going home time and the whole affair breaking up, the poor young chap was found in one of the toilets willing himself to die.

With Tubby's commitment now to Colgate Palmolive (Malaya) Limited, he was able to turn his total attention to the sales marketing processes whereby the goods got shifted out from Harpers' godown to the retail and wholesale trade, the stimulus then to the consumers being to buy it off through these distribution channels and thereby maintain their market leadership in toothpaste, soap and detergent. Before setting off on his Federation trip he was determined to put certain activities in motion in Singapore to assess for future operations, and remembering how he had begun the territories and van operations with salesmen in Baghdad and Iraq before the revolution killed everything off, he wondered how things might be arranged better in Singapore.

The main volume of the products went out into the market via the wholesale trade who were visited by three very good Chinese salesmen employed by Harpers with the names of Voon (the fixer), Little Tann (who looked as though he was born in the year of the rat) and Big Wong – genial and round and easy going. With the trade dominated by the Chinese and to a lesser extent Indians. The up-market shops tended to be Islamic North Indians who were Ismaili Muslims – followers of the Aga Khan. The rest were South Indians from Bombay and round Madras and the Tamil south. Tubby worked out that with all going on in China under Chairman Mao, the Chinese had nowhere to run off to, while the Indians could disappear back to India if there were any money problems for the non-payment of bills. Taking these factors into account, he put up the proposition of introducing credit selling to the better end of the trade at least, as was standard system in the UK, but in Singapore and Malaya there were no sophisticated Neilsen shop audits with their in depth market research data, classifying all the outlets, as was available in the UK.

The strategy was to make Messrs Voon, Tann and Wong into potential supervisors by setting them the task of doing a trade census of Singapore. Desmond at Harpers was convinced of the idea and in his usual meticulous method for detail put together very good and detailed manual of road maps then available of all the streets in Singapore, blocked into areas. The Three Musketeers of Tann, Voon and Wong were sent out with clipboards to set about taking a census of the wholesale and retail outlets of Singapore by block, recording their ideas of potential turnover in any year, with their credit rating. With no organized banking system as in UK, these chaps could ferret out from local gossip as good an idea as anyone as to credit rating; anyway, these were going to be their territories to manage and supervise, so it was in their own interest to get the details as accurate as possible.

He felt good that he had set something of this magnitude in motion before his departure through the Federation west side from the Causeway to the Thai border. Additionally, his fact-finding trip was given heightened urgency during his final briefing with Jim by a cryptic cable from New York simply informing that George Lesch was now President, Chief Executive and Chairman of the International operation. No Mr Ed Little, they both exclaimed, and with his first hand knowledge of the politics and infighting at the top at 300 Park Avenue, Jim gave the opinion that George had most likely gone off on his Far East tour to be out of New York while the knives were out, to return to step over the wounded and pick up all three titles. Jim began now to plan for a move of family to KL for a future there with local manufacture in the Federation.

35

DRIVE OF A LIFETIME THROUGH AMBUSH COUNTRY

Tubby's flashy red speed machine had been checked over, filled up and pumped up for the trip, and while his out and about gear was shorts and double-pocketed bush shirts from Africa, with his neck towel for the perspiration, he realised there would be much wining and dining at the Harpers offices and centres on route. So Cookie had got all his clothes geared up in his all-purpose travel bag which fitted into the boot at the back with the lid shut, while his briefcase, typewriter and sports gear went down behind the seats. An early start was not needed since he was going to go straight up the main road north, by-passing Malacca which he would visit on the way south, for a first stop at Seremban, the seat of government and authority of the Yam Tuan of Negri Sembilan, not a Sultan as in the other States.

The little two seater car was fairly purring as he swept north past Kulai where the two dear lady missionaries lived and worked in the big New Village, then on to the fast level road through the big fertile flat lands of the state of Johore where the British had planted their commercial rubber plantations. Once clear of the main centres, there was hardly any other traffic which meant that the width of the road didn't matter that much. The surface of the roads was well-metalled and maintained since the war and into the Emergency to enable fast movement for heavy military traffic, therefore the driving was shear exhilaration and had to be experienced to be believed. In an open car, with the wind to keep him cool from tropical heat and humidity, and with next to no traffic and only isolated *kampongs* to worry about, he could concentrate on the pure unadulterated fun of driving this machine, stepping up his competence mile by mile as to how far he could go with safety, which with the MGA seemed to be limitless.

Before long he crossed the first main junction at Ayer Hitam and went on into the notorious black bandit country around Yong Peng. With warnings to be constantly alert for signs of ambush, Tubby was pleased that the road along that stretch was extremely straight for very fast driving and the jungle in many parts alongside the road had been replaced by oil palms which meant less dense cover. Oil palm plantations were becoming almost as numerous as rubber plantations, but rubber was the dominant factor in this area.

Soon he was driving alongside the great massive estates at Cha'Ah which were along the east side of the road for about 15 miles with the high wire of the New Villages on the left, within which were the *kampongs* for the Chinese rubber tappers, shut in at night curfew. Being a very notorious area for bandits, it was not surprising that the forces arrayed against them were the two most feared by the Communists, the Ghurkas and a brigade from South Korea who likewise followed the same policy of taking no prisoners.

After Labis, where the railway crossed, the road then turned to be heading west instead of north and Tubby pulled in at Segamat Rest House for a lovely fresh lime drink and some *makan*. From there on and through Gemas there was virtually nothing but rubber and he noticed the turn off by the Gemas New Village where he had shot off on to the army laterite road with the Tankards, heading for the great Ladang Geddes estate on that great hairy rugby weekend.

After Gemas the road was very much due west and began to wind and climb as they began to follow the foothills of the great central massive range down the spine of the Federation to touch the railway again at a place called Tampin which was another notorious black spot. From then on the road interlaced with the railway which had come away west with the road because of the Central Highlands. The other main railway, going due north to the east coast via the King George V

National Park on the eastern side of the Central Highlands, separated at Gemas.

Since way back in the late 1920s and into the 1930s, Seremban had been a great junction town with the line running down to Port Dickson at the coast from a place called Bahau away inland near the big Dunlop rubber estate. Indeed the whole area back in the 1930s had become a big Dunlop area, with some tin mining too, but it was the traditional dominance as the seat of the Sultans of the State of Negri Sembilan which gave the town a special atmosphere. In the height of the Emergency both rail and road ambushes were common, therefore it had been a heavily fortified area and still was, judging by the abundance of services people about the town.

Centuries earlier the Sultan's family had originated from the great island of Sumatra and the old *Istana* was remembered as being in the same style as buildings at Menangkabau in Sumatra. The traditional establishment of the Sultans of Negri Sembilan was similar to those in Malacca in that they had had a British Advisor to the ruler into the 1930s. The Sultan of that State had been in the running to be first *Yang di-Pertuan Agong* (paramount ruler) of the Federation of Malaya.

Tubby checked into the Rest House and then went on to the office to meet the manager, Goh Hean Chye, Harpers first and only non-ex-pat office manager of a major branch, other than Kota Bharu, way up on the north-east tip in what Tubby referred to as monsoon country. He soon struck up a very good relationship with Hean Chye and that night they dined together for Tubby to be introduced to the great Chinese eating event – the steam boat. This great metal pot device sits in the middle of the table, with openings from which one can dip in and spoon out soup and dip in with one's chopsticks and take out vegetables. Throughout the meal the great machine cooks up marvellous soup which seems to get better as the meal goes on. The enjoyable thing about this Chinese meal was that as other courses came along one could indulge while still dipping at the soup, thus it was always a great fun eating event.

Tubby had rapidly reached the point whereby Chinese food tasted better with chopsticks, and although he was at home with them and held them in the classic fashion, it always annoyed him to see the easy way in which Chinese youngsters wielded them with great speed and dexterity with the sticks hanging loosely from their fingers in a variety of ways.

After a short session with the manager the next morning, Tubby set off on a 40 mile journey to Kuala Lumpur. This was to be the first time Tubby was to experience mountainous roads and there was an immediate steep climb out of Seremban which required holding third gear towards the summit, when he noticed the temperature gauge shoot straight round to boiling and felt an eruption under the bonnet. He was able to just freewheel off the road and an examination showed that the hose to the top of the radiator had ruptured. Fortunately, it was a simple matter to push the car round pointing back down the hill to Seremban and jump into the cockpit before it gained too much momentum. The climb out had been such that it was a fast roll back down the hill into Seremban which helped to cool the engine and there was a garage nicely placed for him to freewheel into, after slowing down with the levelling off of the road on entering into the town again.

Tubby felt all the hang-ups going through his mind about buying second hand cars, even from a Dutch friend of a Dutch friend, but it was a very simple matter of just fitting on a new piece of hose and clamping it all up again and in no time he was away back up the same hill again to top the crest in third gear. Soon he found himself enjoying the exhilaration of gear changing with the little stubby stick in his left hand, as he hurtled in and out of the bends with very close rockwalls on either side in places. He was fairly high in the mountains as he held the car hard left round one corner to find that the road entered a square 'U' section with 90 degree corners as it gradually went down the valley side. To his horror he realised that two Chinese rubber lorries were ascending the other way side by side into the bottom edge of the square 'U' against the cliff edge. In no way could Tubby stop, reverse and shoot back again so he had to take the only option available which was to hurtle on down to a small triangle of road at the apex of the first 90 degree turn in the hope that he would scream to a halt without embedding his car into the cliff wall. He got the braking just right as the lorries shaved his offside rear wing – he still carries the vision of the near driver, in his lorry man's blue shorts and sleeveless singlet, grinning down at him in admiration.

The rest of the drive to Kuala Lumpur was thankfully uneventful and he was able to meet up with John Bell at the Harpers office by lunchtime. Tubby realised that he would not need to spend much time in Kuala Lumpur, since John Bell had been appointed full time on to the Colgate account on a national basis through until his leave in the following year, after which he would be coming back at senior management level. There was mutual ground in that John came from Wallasey in the Wirral which is on the other side of the Birkenhead docks, facing Liverpool across the River Mersey. John had gone on to Cambridge and read history and with his reputation for detail, things would be kept moving and allow Tubby to press on with his tour to the north.

In the large office Harpers had in Mountbatten Road in Kuala Lumpur he met up with Derry Frazer again who had played for the Tankards on the tour game at the Klang Club. It was a most pleasant stroll once again from the office across the *padang* of green grass to the 'Dog' (the Selangor club) for a club sandwich lunch on the verandah looking across at the marvellous municipal buildings on the far side of the roadway from the *padang*. After lunch the whole idea of credit selling underway in Singapore was reviewed for development in Kuala Lumpur too, starting with a census. However, there were no immediate Chinese salesmen of supervisor potential since Kuala Lumpur was not such a concentrated or intense market as Singapore.

Since it was certainly on the cards that the factory site would be in this central region, Tubby took the time to motor round the areas set aside for industrial development and pioneer industries down the road towards Klang in an area called Petaling Jaya, where ground was being broken already for some new factories. While Tubby had made moves towards registration in the Federation when he was up on the rugby

356

tour in February, he made certain enquiries about any other requirements to enable him to carry on with his stateless, taxless status, until he actually moved to the Federation.

There was a developing enclave for the up-market ex-pats called Kenny Hill and while the development was in progress there was a piece of road winding up through into the hills which was ideal for a hill climb competition for the motoring enthusiasts in the area. The event was on over the weekend Tubby was there before shooting off north, and wishing to show off his MGA he went along and met up with a renowned character called Paul Gibbs Pancheri, who was a director of Harper Gilfillan Shipping whom Tubby did not meet up with at the office because he was mainly down at Port Swettenham. He had heard about Paul but still couldn't believe the sight when, with the roar of thundering exhausts, he appeared in his magnificent vintage open Bentley to a great cheer from his fellow club members. With old style racing leather head gear, scarf round neck and his black eye patch from an accident many years ago, he was without doubt a larger than life throwback to the 1920s era of 'Tim' Birkin and the 'Bentley Boys' winning at Le Mans.

The next day Tubby was on his way north from Kuala Lumpur and soon passing the famous Batu caves high up in the huge limestone outcrops which border the road from here on. These caves with their 395 steps had become a holy shrine for the Hindus who gathered there in great numbers once a year at the great festival of Thaiapusam.

At Rawang the road followed the contours of the central ranges with the railway line through the town of KKB (Kuala Kubu Bahru) where the main road into the central highlands branched off to the hill station of Frazers Hill to end eventually at a place called Kuala Lipis, to connect with the railway line which had branched off to the other side of the central highlands and on to the north-east coast. These were black bandit areas, so Tubby took a stop at a place called Tanjong Malim in order to set himself up for the next 30 miles or so, since the road went inland from the railway, and after some 20 miles came back out again to join up with the railway line heading north at a place called Slim River. This next thirty miles was a stretch of road well known for its twists and turns, which he was anticipating could be the ultimate experience for himself and his red machine.

He had been getting more and more into tune with this wonderful sports car which was built in such a way that the driver simply became part of it. Once again with traffic being almost non-existent, he experienced 30 miles of complete bliss and exhilaration, at one with his red racing-wheeled speed machine as he maintained a high average through all the twists and turns using the gears with the rev counter to position the car at the right entry to get the right line of exit. Soon he passed the other main road to Telok Anson where he hoped to return for a working visit with the Miss FAB Promotion Team. He carried on north and he soon passed the road off up to the main hill station of Cameron Highlands. Soon he was seeing once again the evidence of the tin workings on either side of the great tin town of Gopeng, the many large tin dredgers sitting in their own special lake of water from which they dredged ore bearing soil for washing. The little car slid into Ipoh after a most exhilarating drive.

At Ipoh the place to stay was the magnificent huge colonial railway station hotel which once again was pure empire. At the office it was good to renew acquaintances again with the manager, Alan Pitt and big Stuart Robertson, whom he had met when he came up to speechify at the Colgate painting competition prize giving. After an intensive morning getting to grips with the figures and the plans laid for the FAB gold ring promotion, he went off to his favourite up-country Ipoh Club for lunch. This club had a tremendous atmosphere with tin prices and rubber prices posted on the board in the entrance hall beneath a huge buffalo head, or *sladang*, as the beast is called in these parts. All the ingredients of past colonialism were evident, symbols relating to Caledonian societies and many regimental emblems since the state of Perak had a high concentration of armed forces from all over the Common-wealth co-operating against the Insurgents. The club was a great meeting place for the commercials as well as a kind of unofficial officers' mess, which had been upgraded, as far as some were concerned, with the arrival of a detachment from the Hussars Cavalry Regiment. While rapid pursuit, scout cars and other light armoured vehicles were order of the day now, they were still a very horsey lot with many flying back to UK for point-to-point meetings, and so on. They became evident round the cocktail circuit in their narrow dress trousers with spurs at the heels. With his wartime naval experience on small boats on very rough convoy duties, Alan Pitt of Harpers was not one to enthuse too much about them and there was a story going about of him being asked at some drinks event by a lofty Hussar gentleman as to what he might do for a living. Since Harpers had the agency for Colgate, Heinz, and Reckitt & Colman, he looked up at the cavalry gentleman with a poker face and said quite solemnly, 'I sell soap and beans' which was just too appalling for him to comprehend.

With a goodly number of Scottish voices round him, Tubby felt quite at home at this club and while he had gathered something from the rubber planters as to how they carried on in the Emergency, it was interesting to hear how the tin company's executives had kept going amongst all the ambushing and shootings from the governor general downwards, in this area particularly. One very laid-back tin ex-pat related how he had handed over the presidency of a local tin association to a big Chinese dealer for the next year and had been asked by him to look after his Chinese wife at subsequent dinners and functions. He had been appalled at the prospect, then absolutely delighted to find at the first dinner that the new president turned up with the most delightful Chinese woman. On noting his reaction, the Chinese president had commented that this was his 'going out wife' while his 'child bearing wife', born in the year of the Pig, was at home with the many children.

After such a marvellous lunchtime session, it took a certain amount of will power, but he did manage somehow a busy afternoon followed by a good bash at squash at a Gurkha Camp with a South African he had met through rugby. The long and high traditions of British Ghurka regiments meant that they were very often the first choice for young fellows from the Commonwealth countries bent on having an army career.

Tubby had been most pleased to find that they had a salesman at Ipoh branch who was very much a candidate for a supervisor to get started on doing a census of the trade first in Ipoh, then Telok Anson and then in Taiping, as the three main towns for this central area. His name was Fung Swee Seng and looked a hard customer and had a fairly uncompromising manner but thankfully, like most Chinese, a sense of humour. He was of a Chinese tin mining family and from an early age had been daily carrying the takings from the business to the bank in an ordinary school bag to avoid attracting the attention of any Triad members who had designs on taking the money.

It was arranged that Tubby and Swee Seng were going to go in the sports car round to Telok Anson at terminus of a branch railway line from Tapah where the mighty Sungai Perak (Perak River) turned towards the sea to meander through the flat coastlands after coming from the north down through the state from the highlands.

Heading south out of Ipoh through Gopeng and Tapah they soon turned right at Bidor to get to Telok Anson by mid-morning which allowed them to have a good look round at the town and surrounding area before lunch. This was quite difficult country and from what Tubby could gather, this had been the area where Sir Gerald Templar started to turn the tide against the Communist Insurgents by making the new village system work. There had been a shooting of two policeman in this area and he had insisted on a strict curfew with only one hour a day for replenishing until the local population came up with information on the perpetrators.

When it came to lunchtime, Tubby had been somewhat bemused that the tough-looking Chinese chap should suggest that they went to an Indian place for lunch. They went up a staircase in one of the buildings in the centre of town and found himself looking at a large area of tables across the second floor which was certainly an Indian restaurant by the marvellous smells of curry. He began to realise that this place probably appealed to Swee Seng's business mind because it was the ultimate Tubby had ever seen in cost effectiveness. The whole area was set out with trestle tables and benches which took six to eight people, with tops completely bare. In the corner was a huge trough-like white sink with one big tap at which everybody cleaned and freshened up from the tropical heat outside. The place was certainly not air-conditioned, being open all along the sides, and being on the second floor there was a bit of a breeze passing through.

The Indian waiters in white dhotis and bare feet came along and placed a huge green banana leaf in front of each diner from a bunch they carried folded over their left arms, then simply asked 'chicken or meat?' Soon another one came along with huge bowls on a tray, out of which he ladled the rice, then the meat dishes into heaps on the banana leaf. Tubby was hungry and the curry looked and smelt good, so he soon rolled up his sleeves more, and dug in with his right hand as he had in Iraq. While Indians seemed to be the only ones gifted with bent back fingers suitably adapted for this way of eating, it was not difficult to make a go of it if one observed carefully how the food was being manipulated all round. The food was indeed superb, with lots of iced tea to wash it down, and at the end they sat back and picked their teeth while the waiters came round and simply scooped up the big banana leaves with any bones and left overs and away went everything for re-cycling as compost. It was a most delightful experience and later Tubby was to find that there was a similar establishment in Kuala Lumur to frequent because the low prices charged certainly reflected the cost saving from the simple banana leaves with no washing up of utensils, plates or whatever. Before leaving, they went back to the big white trough at the big tap for a good clean up and cold splash against the sun and the tropical heat for the afternoon.

Their prime task was to meet up with Mrs Yong and her sales promotion team in the sound van with its gaudy artwork of all the products on the sides. Having worked out for that day where she was most likely to be along the back roads amongst the tin valleys, they had hoped that the sound of the promotion jingles from the loudspeakers would help them to pin down where the van was. The other prime reason for meeting up with the sales promotion team calling on consumers direct was the testing of a new comic, which was the brainchild of Tom Glaze of Grant Advertising. Because there was no national media and because there were distinct Chinese, Malay and Indian papers, and because the reading of Chinese characters was a single unifying factor across the various dialects spoken, Tom Glaze had thought of the idea of having a comic with stories written by locals that would appeal to average consumers by having words in Chinese and romanized Malay in the blips from the mouths of the characters in the pictures telling the stories.

There were two other main operators who went for the consumers direct because of the wide usage and appeal of their products. These were Shell, with their paraffin, and Nestlé, with their condensed milk, and the motivation behind Tom Glaze's idea for this comic was that it would get him and Grant Advertising into Shell and Nestlé, with the potential spin-off of some of their business as extra to the Colgate Palmolive business. In fact the meetings together with the Shell and Nestlé people had been quite a fascinating pool of ideas, particularly when the Nestlé man related his experiences in West Africa where the tin product which sold best was their skimmed milk as opposed to the thick condensed milk in the Far East. He related how in West Africa he had a promotion demonstrator (like the manic Negro-Arab Tubby had had in Baghdad) who would grovel on the ground to attract a big gathering round him wondering what was going on only to jump up and start giving his sales patter on the Nestlé skimmed milk. Like the dominant Dutch Unilever NV with their margarines and fats, Nestlé had fighting brands they could swing into action to swamp anybody who tried to get in on their market. The comic turned out to be a most clever combination, with Shell particularly pressing in at the *kampongs* with their paraffin, in demand for increasing numbers of cooking stoves, while Nestlé were much like Colgate, going after the consumer with a food related product which did not compete with their oothpaste, Palmolive soap and detergent. With all three major companies pooling the costs, they were going to be able to produce thousands of these comics twice a year, so Tubby was keen to find their team in this part of Perak because they were doing a test run to gauge consumer reaction.

The first sign that Swee Seng and Tubby had of getting near to the Miss FAB team was the sight of some Chinese women reading the comic as they sat not far from the perimeter fence of a New Village for tin workers at the local mine. This was not actually a true *kampong*, in that the barrack-type huts were really company employee dwellings and the women were sitting on the steps down to the ground since all dwellings like this and in the *kampongs* were on stilts for obvious reasons of the creepy-crawlies. Swee Seng went over to the fence and started to have a very loud conversation with the women who were swarthy, flat nosed, and sun-blackened since they probably spent their working hours up to their knees in the run-off water from the tin run with their huge wooden *dulongs* panning for tin ore. Tubby always felt completely ignorant alongside these Chinese who were to be his potential supervisors because they spoke English, but also Malay, and then at least four major Chinese dialects.

He was therefore most surprised and somewhat amused at watching the exasperation of Swee Seng when he had to announce that he could not communicate with these women since they were Hakkas. With their whole lives centred in their place of work within their own clan, they could not speak anything else, nor had any need to. However, because of the marvellous unifying factor of the Chinese characters they were sitting reading avidly from the new comic books and when Swee Seng had finished trying to communicate with them, they were back chatting amongst themselves and comparing the pages which was as good an evidence as anything to Tubby that this comic book idea was going to be successful, with every other page featuring a large advert for Shell, Colgate and Nestlé products.

They eventually caught up with Mrs Yong and her team of Miss FAB girls and they sat around in the back of the van as the girls chatted away confirming that the comic books were going to be a winner. One or two even suggested we might get away with selling them instead of just giving them away, a good Chinese commercial instinct.

Tubby was to find these experiences of being out and about with these promotion teams were quite unique to the general experience of Europeans or ex-patriates, who seldom had any opportunity actually to see how the other half lived. Depending on the time of the day, there could be all sorts of things going on in some of the *kampongs* depending if they were predominantly Malay or predominantly Chinese, and sometimes they were Indian, particularly so in areas with plantations which had traditionally been staffed by Tamils who way back had been brought over in slave conditions from South India and Ceylon. Because of the noises made by their leg chains when they came initially as slaves, there were many Malays who still referred to Tamil workers on rubber estates as 'Klings'.

In the Chinese areas he had noticed that houses all had an altar, or small shrine, in the living area, with joss sticks smouldering away. In many places he saw some most fascinating posters which he would have liked to have taken away. One had shown what he understood to be the original eight Chinese characters which were often featured on the edges of those hexagonal mirrors often strategically placed at doors and windows to drive the spirits away. One of these posters in one house showed these original characters with their evolution through to the elaborate ones currently in use, together with drawings alongside the earlier primitive characters to show how they had originated as simple brush pictures of the object they represented.

The only other ex-pats he could think of who had similar access, or cause, to enter these *kampongs* where the majority population lived were of course the likes of the missionary midwives he knew down in Kulai and out-station GPs who were much respected, especially those who readily went into the *kampongs* as they were called upon when the local cures were not doing the trick. Very many years later Scoops posted to Tubby a piece which had appeared in a Perth newspaper in

Western Australia by a Scot, Dr Ballantyne, who had practiced in these parts of Malaya in the late 1950s. There must have been some previous correspondence concerning another's experiences of Singapore *kampong* Chinese and their disappearing penile problems.

In response, the good Dr. Ballantyne threw in his contribution:

'When I was working as a GP in Malaysia in the 1950s, it was not uncommon to receive a panic phone call about midnight to treat a patient with a retracting penis and thus save his life. There was no difficulty in identifying the house in the *kampong*, even in the pitch darkness, due to the large number of people milling around outside. Someone grabbed your medical bag and you pushed your way through the throng upstairs to a bedroom. The patient lay on the bed with his penis secured with a complex arrangement of pencils, chop sticks, string and elastic bands to prevent it from disappearing into his abdomen which would have resulted in immediate death.

'The room itself was packed to capacity with family, neighbours and the inevitable crowd of small children. Experience had reduced therapy to three simple procedures. Firstly, expel everyone except one female attendant, the wife or mother, from the room regardless of sex, age or relationship. Naturally this was done only after much argument and constant appeals for an exception to be made. Secondly, inform the patient honestly that you have treated many successful similar cases with 100% rate of recovery. Thirdly, inject the patient with a sedative and give the female attendant a mild sleeping tablet – using a euphemism – to ensure a trouble-free night for everyone. You could then return home with the unusual certainty of a job very well done.

'Following up professionally next morning was always most unsatisfactory as the patient had left for work, the wife or mother was out shopping and the only inhabitants of a Chinese household during working hours were ancients who spoke no known language. I never found the cause for this hysterical symbolism even from the people involved. Strangely enough the patient was always a young Chinese – no other nationality seemed to be affected.'

This was indeed a wonderful anecdote on how Tubby found the ebb and flow of life amongst these Kampong dwellers people in the late 1950s in Singapore and Malaysia. Indeed, he often watched Chinese women out shopping stop by a temple to light up a few joss sticks to placate the spirits, since it reminded him of women he used to see in Liverpool out shopping going up into any Catholic church to light a candle to Mary, or St Peter and then carry on with the shopping, removing their head scarf as they came out.

Since Tubby was next heading north out of Ipoh with the object of getting to Butterworth for the ferry crossing to Penang, it was agreed that John Bell, on the Colgate account, would come up by car with Swee Seng as far as Taiping, the last major town in what was regarded as the valley's commercial area centred on Ipoh. The sports car was still performing superbly as he drove off in bright sunshine through the rest of the great Kinta tin valley in which Ipoh lay. The road followed the railway line as it went north through the valley between the massive central highlands to the right and the lesser range of mountains around which the road and railway took a great sweep and literally turned south again to the great Malay town of Kuala Kangsar. This was the old capital of the State of Perak, with the Sultan's *Istana* (or one of them) and the unique large yellow mosque with great twin domes.

Once again the driving was superbly demanding and rewarding as he raced through that stretch immediately out of Ipoh where the valley floor resembled a lunar landscape with the great sugar-loaf outcrops of limestone dispersed amongst the lakes created by the huge tin dredgers. As always he looked out for Lion Rock, which really did look very like a sphinx or a lion *couchant* in heraldic terms. This stretch of road right through to Taiping was through black bandit country and had a long history of ambushes which, though much diminished,

366

were still happening from time to time, particularly the stretch from Kuala Kangsar through to Taiping, because of the dense jungle on either side and the bends to slow down the target of a vehicle.

When things got too hot, or the Communist Insurgents needed replenishment, it was well known that they retreated towards the Thai border, so there was a well-maintained road which went off right after Kuala Kangsar away up to Grik near the Thai border for use by the Forces.

After visits to the main Chinese wholesalers in Taiping, and comparing notes over lunch about things to be done before Tubby's return, he took his leave and headed off almost due north away from the hills and into the flatlands cultivated all the way up the west coast to the Thai border. It was again hot tropical sunshine with no particular build up of thunderheads, so with the road straightening out once clear of the mountains and hills it was a case of letting the car show how it could maintain a speed which ate up the mileage.

With his destination of Penang Island in sight across the sunlit waters, it was good to stretch the legs while waiting for the ferry at Butterworth and then enjoy the cool sea breezes on the crossing. It was even better to be in, parked and unloaded for a lovely Sundowner, sitting out by the canons on the water front of the marvellous E & O Hotel in Georgetown. The old E & O had been there since the 1880s and was said to have had the longest sea front of any hotel in the world.

The front entrance of the hotel was in old Georgetown and he could drive the car in down the side and park in the grounds at the back where the whole place was open to the Straits of Malacca and the Andaman Sea. He was delighted to find that he had one of the rooms which opened out to the sea for the cool breezes to come right in and through the room and across the bed to dispel the tropical heat. This was real old colonial living.

As he went down into the bar to get his gin and tonic to take out by the canons on the sea front he could hear Albert Yeoh on the piano, and on entering found that there had been some sort of high-powered gathering going on about border

367

matters, since he recognised big General Sarit, the power in Thailand behind the almost divine status of the King and Queen. The general had his scotch in his hand, having no scruples as the Islamic Malays did about being seen with a glass of the hard stuff. The real surprise came when Tubby turned to the bar and found standing there one of the chaps he had known in Baghdad who was with New Zealand Insurance, who had stayed on when Tubby and the Brits had eventually left ten days after the Revolution the previous July. This meeting called for a few drinks and a recall of all they had been through almost a year previously and Tubby felt particularly justified that he had taken the decision to leave with Dick Malyan when they did, because this New Zealand chap had stayed on for almost another six months. With all the influx of the Eastern Europeans and isolation of the place with Colonel Nassar in ascendancy with his United Arab Republic of Syria and Egypt, it had all been rather pointless as regarded business potential. His departure had been sudden and at twelve hours notice when some military heavies came to his dwelling place and gave him an ultimatum to go. Listening to this experience and taking account of the possible imprisonment of his Iraqi friends and agents, it had certainly been the correct decision not to stay in Baghdad, though he had grudged having to pay his government the price of the airfare to escape on the MEA Viscount to Cyprus. After a great night of reminiscences over a good meal, he returned to the lovely room which was to be his home for the next week, and once General Sarit and the other high officials from Thailand had gone on their way, the easy pace of life in the E & O began to prevail again.

He was pleased to find that Mark Chilton of the Singapore Tankards mob was on the island on business too, which meant there would be a good week of socialising with the crowd at the Penang Club. However, on the Friday evening there was a great excitement about the place which he found centred around the arrival of two celebrated Indian film stars on a publicity stop in Georgetown. The cinemas were tremendously big business throughout Singapore and Malaya and indeed the whole of the Far East. There were cinemas all over the place being fed by very active studios in Hong Kong and in Bombay – hence the excitement. Cinema was a great pastime for expatriates too, because with no preparation and no washing up after meals it was a regular habit suddenly to decide to go to a late show at the cinema, since as well as the outpourings from Hong Kong and Bombay studios, there were outpourings from Hollywood and the UK cinema industry, which in those days was quite buoyant. The posh seats at the cinemas were occupied by the ex-pat brigade with a pervading smell of Old Spice about them. Tubby remembered one classic night when a popular Ealing comedy was doing the rounds and the ex-pats were there in large numbers. There was consternation when there appeared in the sharp beam of light from the projection room the enormous shape of one of the great moths common in the tropics. These moths were pretty huge by insect standards anyway, but as the thing flitted in and out of the projection lights the shadow would get enlarged so that at times it appeared as if there were two sizes of giant moth let loose from a horror film. As the thing swooped and dipped out of the projection beams there would almost be a stampede accompanied by great shrieks so that the rows of audience in the darkness flowed to and fro like the waves of the sea until the thing had either been bopped or disappeared out of a vent hole. Those who had stayed settled down to enjoy the film once again.

By Saturday the E & O was besieged round the front by a throng of black faces, since all Indian ex-pats and locally borns were mainly South Indian and there to catch a glimpse of their favourite film stars from the Bombay studio. As a precaution, the great white doors at the side of the E & O for entry and exit to the car park were closed, and when Tubby and Mark in the open sports car came to leave for sport on the Saturday afternoon, they were advised to make a dash for it as both doors were swung open together and closed behind them. Immediately, they were the focus of a great wash of adulation which turned to shrieks of laughter and great waves of cheers as they went on their way through the throng of black faces and white dhotis, with Mark sitting up out of the cockpit on the back, waving in recognition of the adulation.

On the Sunday morning it was the done thing to drive way out along the marvellous beach through rows of palms to the swimming club which was up above the beach and back from the sea. This rather puzzled Tubby until it was explained to him that there were nasty poisonous sea snakes in the waters round this most beautiful island whose bite was fatal to white people. Well, that was the story, but it was probably the case that when one of the locals or Indian fishermen who hauled in their great nets to rhythmic stamping died from the bite of a sea snake it went unrecorded.

After Saturday's activities, and particularly those into the night, Tubby was ready for a stretch out in a good lounge chair at the swimming club with a nice large fresh lime to drink. The hair of the dog would come later with the curry tiffin, but alas his wish was to be in vain. He had hardly got settled when there were shouts from the pool for him to make up number for a water polo game, which had never really been his scene. He remembered one particular big gangling lad in Liverpool in Chalmers Wade, the accountants, who played water polo at a highly competitive level. He would often appear with rainbow-coloured bruised eyes from back-heel kicks when attempting to get the ball from an opponent, and there were memories of the blood bath in the 1956 Olympics when the Hungarian polo team set about the Russians.

Tubby was a reasonable swimmer and had done some helping out on beach patrols at Wallasey since he had some life saving medals, but water polo was like playing rugby with the added dimension of drowning in the attempt. He vowed there and then never ever to be dragged into a water polo game again and only began to recover over some beers and a marvellous curry tiffin from one of the numerous Indian stall holders along the beach road amongst the palm trees. It was all rather idyllic under the shade of these great bending palms with the noise of the waves on the beach not far away, the sunshine dancing on the sea, until one of the great coconut husks fell down with an enormous thud too near one of the chaps to be of comfort. Back home in UK, one's knowledge of coconuts goes as far as those hairy things one sees on stands at fun fairs, but these nuts come out of great green husk pods of a huge size which provide valuable coconut fibre which is extensively used by locals for matting.

Penang Island and Georgetown were a free port so much of Harpers business here was related to shipping, therefore Gerry Moxon, the head man, had come up through that side of the business and Tubby also understood he was related to senior family names back at Plantation House, London. On the next management level down, Jim Coates was ex-pat on the Colgate account. The main salesman who worked on the account was a tall Hokkien called Goh Boo Cheng. After a day out in the Georgetown market with Boo Cheng, Tubby was of the opinion that he could be the one to do the census of trade in this branch area, as potential supervisor material. Tubby decided to take him on his exploration of the mainland territories covered from this branch on Penang Island.

As they crossed on the ferry in the early morning to the mainland again with the cool breezes on the sparkling sea, Tubby decided that Penang Island was understandably a favoured retirement spot for those who had come to like the life in the east. As they neared the landing he watched Canberras from RAF Butterworth taking off to fly operations up round the Thai border to support troops on jungle patrols. Soon the sports car was eating up the mileage, and not long after entering the northern state of Kedah the road ran parallel with the railway again, and after a town called Gurun they were on straight road eating up the miles through fields and fields of rice. This was the rice bowl of the Federation after the Malacca area and at the main town of Alor Star they touched the railway again. This was the home town of the Prime Minister and father of independent Malaya – Tunku Abdul Rahman, known affectionately as 'the Tunku'. This was a very Malay state and while seeming very Islamic the general atmosphere and feel of the way of life seemed to reflect that of their favourite son the Tunku, the urbane Cambridge graduate of princely status.

After a good look round the market in Alor Star as the prime town of Kedah, the road crossed the railway and went inland because of the extensive wet paddy areas along the wide coastal plain with irrigation canals, until it turned towards the coast again at the next town called Kangar, which was the capital town of the smallest northern state of the Federation, called Perlis. This was very similar in character to Alor Star, but on a smaller scale with a dominant mosque as a centre of the way of life. From there on they headed north to the last town on the Thai border called Padang Besar, where the last railway station was situated on the great line north.

The country here was very similar to the great tin mining valley round Ipoh with flat ground and then great limestone outcrops like Sugarloaf Mountain in Brazil. The hills to the west were actually on the Thai border. Padang Besar really was an end-of-the-road town and seemed to resemble those early wild west frontier towns seen in Hollywood westerns. There was a row of shops and dwellings on either side of the road on low level stilts, with the railway station slap on the border as the main feature, where the train arrived from Thailand pulled in on one side and the train all the way from Singapore pulled up on the other platform so that the signs of the middle platform had letters all in Thai script on one side and in English and Romanized Malay on the other. Tubby was most pleased to have been there to film when both trains arriving from opposite directions came to a halt side by side. The atmosphere up in these parts did not have much evidence of Communist insurgency – probably because of the railway crossing and the Thais' desire to ensure that the border on their side hereabouts was clear of any Communists, while on the federation side it was extremely clear that it was a Malay State, with not many Chinese in evidence.

They drove back from the high Thai border area down to Kangar to stay the night at the small idyllic village on the coast called Kuala Perlis. Tubby had wanted to come and explore this area because this was the place from which one could hire a boat to be taken out to the little inhabited and lovely island of Langkawi. Abe le Roux had told Tubby about his long weekend out there, when he was taken by the locals on Langkawi by fishing boat from Kuala Perlis to see the giant monitor lizards which throughout the East are known as the Komodo Dragons from their being first found in 1912 on the Dutch East Indies island of that name. They had the heads and bodies of lizards, but the size of alligators and the local fishermen on Langkawi tied up a goat carcass for Abe in order to bring the lizards out for observation as they tore at the carcass with their great claws and took bites out of it, trying to drag it away. This was something Tubby marked down to do since, after his brief episode with his cine-camera meeting the similar big lizard in Ceylon, Langkawi could be the ideal location for some cine-filming of a Komodo Dragon. That evening with Boo Cheng they checked out with local fishermen as to likely cost and timing for being taken out to the island, which was not much over ten miles away from Kuala Perlis.

The next day they went and explored the interior country on a minor road through to the main north road heading to the Thai border and came down this road to Jitra and back into Alor Star. There was a road heading east right into the interior fertile flat valley area where the road forked at a place called Pokok Sena. This was real bandit country since both roads from here on ended abruptly some ten miles or more from the actual Thai border. With them tearing along at speed in the sports car, Tubby had lent Boo Cheng an American style cap he had found left in the car by the Dutchman, and only after they had been stopped by several patrols did he realise that Boo Cheng with this cap on needed only a red star on the front of his cap to be taken as a Chinese Communist from the jungle. They managed to get by because of Tubby looking so terribly British with his old UK rugger stitched-down corduroy flat hat, nevertheless, they did have their papers examined by each patrol they came across. When they reached a place called Naka, at the end of the other road, there was a large wire-fenced New Village for Chinese working on the rubber estates which existed in these jungle areas nearer the foothills. While the road did go on further east and south on a minor level, he thought better than trying to explore other areas after their meetings with several patrols already. This whole inland area was dotted with Malay *kampongs*, but these Malays were different from those on the coastal plain and there seemed to be evidence of Thai buddhist influences as opposed to the pronounced evidence of Islam into Alor Star and Kangar.

Just before they left Naka they noticed a high-posted timber building with an *atap* roof like the more substantial buildings seen in Thailand with the beautiful fluted roofs in the temple areas, where there would be schools for young girls to learn Thai dancing. Indeed, something similar seemed to be going on here since there was a kind of orchestra with the Malay men in sarongs sitting cross-legged with the leader playing a three stringed *rebab*, while others played gongs and a *gendang* (a double faced gong and double faced drums) and dancers, who were performing a *Ma'yong*, which is a mixture of drama, opera and ballet. While these people involved were certainly Malays in this very rural outback area, he was able to catch on his cine-film the movements of the bodies and the hands which very much related to the Thai dancing he had seen in Bangkok with the beautiful subtle movements and bent back fingers. Judging by reactions from people and the various patrols they had met to their appearance these back country areas were not frequented by tourists coming to see the local amateur dramatic society rehearsing a *Ma'yong*.

Back on Penang Island and round Georgetown, Tubby spent a most entertaining day with Mother Lim and her Miss FAB girls who were in the middle of the annual gold ring promotion. Mother Lim was a seasoned campaigner who had now handled many gold ring promotions and knowing all the tricks the consumers could get up to, and knowing the whole areas like the back of her hand, she knew how to pick new areas for gold ring visits each year. While they had made great noise with the loudspeakers over the early years to whip up excitement, the promotion was now such that in some places when the van and the girls appeared, they would try and drag the Miss FAB into the house to claim the gold ring. There was one sweetie called Julia Koh in her team who was quite good at the whole act of suddenly appearing in a housing area blindfolded, and moving off feeling her way towards a dwelling house while the others kept people at bay from influencing her.

The ideal was to have the unsuspecting mother, or housewife, come to the door of the flat, or dwelling, and on seeing who was at the door, rush away inside and come back with their packet of FAB, to which Julia Koh would be unmasked and produce the gold ring and slip it on to the finger of the winning lady with great cheers and jingles from the van. Mother Lim would then present the winner with the goldsmith's certificate of its gold purity and value. Tubby's presence as the big boss man had warranted a camera man in the form of Goh Boo Cheng.

Before departing there was an action plan agreed with Jim Coates and Goh Boo Cheng for getting the census of wholesale and retail trade done for Penang, Georgetown and the mainland towns as soon as possible to catch up with the other areas for ongoing planning and the introduction of credit selling, in addition to the limited van sales which existed from Georgetown.

Tubby bid them farewell and was once more on the ferry across to Butterworth, tingling at the prospect of a great drive right down through the Federation on these well-surfaced roads, with limited traffic to intrude on the fun of driving the MGA. He went fast down a straight road to northern Perak which was uneventful except for a local *kampong* hen which took off in almost the same direction but couldn't match his speed and eventually got a bump on the backside which sent burst of feathers across the windscreen and over Tubby's head. The other fright was on a very fast straight section and the sudden realisation that a different coloured patch of roadway ahead was actually water running off a paddy field. With no time for breaking, he simply gripped the wheel with all might and main so that the direction of the wheels didn't vary with the impact as he went through the wall of water, which shot out but fortunately had no depth.

With a stop at the lovely old colonial outpost of the Taiping Club for a fresh lime, Tubby got on his way again, and as he was leaving and driving away down a heavily jungle-clad area, he passed a group of Sakai, native trackers with some of the men carrying their 6 foot long blow pipes on their shoulders, their main hunting weapon for projecting their poison darts.

After the long straight roads in Kedah, Tubby had geared himself up to the high-rev fast gear-change driving through the bends of this jungle-clad section of road, and it was fortunate that he was thus sharpened up as he came round a bend only to be confronted by the aftermath of an ambush situation. He thought all the Fijian troops had left for home, but the scene he took in was of an odd body on the road, army trucks off the road and into the jungle, and big brown athletic soldiers bounding off into undergrowth like kangaroos, some carrying bren-guns and shooting off as though they were light automatic weapons. He started to slow down rapidly in a series of four wheel drifts to left and right in between the action as one big soldier bounding alongside shouted: 'You go man.' Tubby was already down into second gear and he didn't take any second bidding amongst the noise of gunfire, his foot slamming full down until the rev counter was up to the red marker. The MGA cleared the mayhem leaving a series of black rubber streaks on the road and he didn't stop until he turned off to the sanctuary of the very Malay town of Kuala Kangsar and pulled up near a mosque.

This was the most unlikely place for any Communist insurgents to be about, and he could check over the car and take stock of himself. Compared to Ipoh with the high tensions of the emergency and the driving energies of Chinese and Europeans in commerce and business, Kuala Kangsar was almost the perfect example of that gracious quality of the Malays to take life as it comes and say 'Tidak Apa' – or 'so be it.' Tubby had not experienced combat situations during National Service since he had been given Grade 3: 'Wanted only in emergencies.' However, at the age of 2½ he had fallen on the fire and a pan of boiling fish, and cried for two days and carried burn marks since. At the age of 16 he had been in the Valley of the Shadow of Death again for two to three days with general peritonitis. In the Baghdad revolution he had seen at first hand a mob's inclination for killing anything and anybody – but particularly the British on that occasion. Then he had had the nightmare bus journey in the dark from Rangoon Airport with Ne Win's revolutionary troops out and about, and now he had just come through a gunfire situation in daylight. How many lives left?

From any early age via his parents and others he had grasped the intensely personal nature of a Christian faith and taken on board the Holy Trinity as a mystery he could live with. He tried to keep to a daily 'time out' with a book of scriptures ever present in his toilet bag in order to keep the spiritual leg of his proverbial stool the same length as the body and the mind legs for balance. Having checked that his dear little car was still all in order he just sat in it in the shade in the quiet of Kuala Kangsar and had a 'time out'. This was just as well since before he left Ipoh he was to experience another situation which demonstrated mankind's penchant for killing one another.

It had been agreed that on his way back he would go out with Swee Seng, his potential supervisor, to meet up with Mrs Yong and her Miss FAB girls doing the gold ring promotion. Ipoh is not unlike Singapore with a high concentration of voluble Cantonese, and they caught up with Mrs Yong in a bustling busy market area on the outskirts. There was a high police presence and a heightened level of noise and activity, from which Mrs Yong was anxious to depart with her team. While Tubby was having a word with Mrs Yong, Swee Seng took a look over near the centre of excitement and came back to say that there had been a Triad killing and someone had been knifed in broad daylight. When they got away to another area and stopped, Mrs Yong explained that they had seen it take place as they had been sitting at a stall having some seaweed drink. While the newspaper reports of these incidents usually mentioned that the killers had disappeared into the market throngs, Mrs Yong explained that those who had done the killing were actually sitting at another stall since this made sure that, out of fear, all present explained to the police that they had all been extremely busy serving customers and had not actually seen what had gone on. The assailants had then gone off among the crowds.

While Tubby had been north in Penang territory, John Bell and Swee Seng had got the census well under way and John was impressed – which was an accolade indeed. Tubby ran over all the action plans left with Jim Coates since John would be following up the progress under his Federation responsibilities for Colgate. This was done at his stop over in Kuala Lumpur after another simply scintillating drive in the MGA, in the opposite direction through the miles and miles of bends of the Slim River stretch north of KKB Town where Frazer's Hill traffic joined.

With only a brief stop at Malacca remaining to confirm the need and potential for a trade census Tubby was able to switch off and escape into the sheer pleasure of the drive south from KL to sleepy Malacca and race through Johore after overnight stop because of a night curfew on driving through that area. He had one worry at the rickety pontoon ferry at Muar, but the low slung sports car managed to get on and off with exhaust pipes intact.

36

JULY 14TH CELEBRATION –
ONE YEAR ON

On his return to Singapore, Tubby felt as if he had been away for an eternity, and after getting all his notes and reports done on his fact finding tour up through the Federation, he had to wind himself back into the Singapore scene. His census of distribution and wholesale trades was very advanced and he found Desmond and the other people at Harpers quite excited about it since, for the first time ever, by blocked areas, they had typed lists of existing and potential outlets. Tubby had called into Malacca on the way down, and since Big Wong had shown an interest in possibly being located there, he was despatched off to start doing a census of Malacca Town and the area spreading out therefrom.

Cookie was delighted to have him back in the fold, as it were, at Amber Mansions, and whether inspired or not by Tubby's red sports car, he found that Van Marken had splashed out on the ultimate in two wheel speed machines – a BMW motorcycle. Sander explained that his four year stint for Mirandolle-Voûte would be coming to an end in 1960 and he had been plotting the idea of sailing as far as Colombo in Ceylon and then using his new machine to go up through the Indian continent and across into Europe and home. On the excuse of wanting to check out his speedometer, they went for a bash one Saturday afternoon out to the Causeway and back where there were stretches on the Bukit Timah and Woodlands Roads where they could really open up. Tubby was out front in the car waving prearranged signals for each ten mile an hour step-up in speed, while the goggled Van Marken slip-streamed in the BMW behind.

On the social front he got back into the rhythm of the Singapore Cricket Club and the writing of letters home on a Sunday morning at the table on the verandah of the flat. Once again, it became a race to get it done before Eddie Flannigan would surface and ring him up to say, 'Brian Boru – I'll see you in the club in half an hour.'

With the 14th July not far away, Tubby felt he should commemorate the revolution in Baghdad on that day in 1958, and the stand he and the Reeve had taken in the Hotel Khayam under the leadership of Colonel Nimmo, and their escape to Cyprus. He put up the idea to Sander and then Cookie who positively beamed at the prospect of having a party in the flat, which had never been done before.

Tubby started the preparation of invitations which asked people to come and celebrate his escape from Baghdad, and those symbols of the empire – Colonel Nimmo and the gunboat. They thought the best way to deal with the other residents in Amber Mansions was to give them an invitation which would warn them that it was going to happen and give them time to object, if so inclined. After talking to Tom Glaze, he thought of the idea of doing a tape which would tell of all the happenings which had taken place in the ten days or so they were trapped in the Hotel Khayam in Baghdad as the revolution unfolded, and how they had wished that Colonel Nimmo might conjure up a gunboat to come up the Tigris River as in days of old. Tubby wanted some good Arab music which Tom was able to get on tape out of Radio Singapore which was actually Indian in origin, but it sounded near enough for the uninitiated ears which were to listen.

While he was taping one night he got a call out of the blue from big Tom Loughead to say that he and Mark Chilton were in the 'Cockpit' bar of the lovely Hotel de l'Europe at Oxley Rise. This truly magnificent pillared building was not far from the centre of Singapore and since Ronny, the daughter of the owners, was one of the Singapore, gang at that time, Tom and Mark had gone there for a drink to restore themselves after being in an overturned car episode on the way back through Johore. Quite a number of the Tankards and the cricket club gang appeared and it turned into quite an evening with a magnificent meal in the 'Cockpit' restaurant.

These impromptu events and happenings were part of the spontaneity of the work hard, play hard life Tubby was enjoying in Singapore. Another great joy was to drive out on impulse at any time of the night to Bedok Point where the east coast road along the water's edge turned at ninety degrees inland to Changi Road. There was always a line of Chinese food stalls along the water's edge for any range of foods – a bowl of Hokkien Mee, Fu Yung Hi, rice, soup or whatever, and diners sat on the benches and enjoyed the cool breeze, the lapping of the water and the lights of the tripod fishermen away out in the shallow water with their nets at the end of their long trestles of criss-crossed bamboo.

As the day of the party got nearer, dear Cookie really got into the swing of things as they got down to working out what food and so on they might have to hand around, and it was obvious that he had had experience of these things before. The week before the event Cookie produced a big galvanised bath and an enormous Aladdin earthenware vessel to be filled with ice for keeping the beer and other drinks cold.

For the night itself Tubby had done some sketch drawings to hang round the wall of gunboats and Colonel Nimmo in his pith helmet, but pride of place went to his letter from Her Britannic Majesty's Government with her lion and unicorn embossed into best quality parchment. It had been sent on by his parents and was at Amber Mansions on his return from his New Year travels through to North Borneo.

(XF19/18425)

C.D. Forbes, Esq,
12 Tulip Avenue,
Birkenhead,
Cheshire.

The Under-Secretary of State for Foreign Affairs presents his compliments to Mr. Forbes and with reference to his recent repatriation from Iraq, is directed by Mr. Macmillan to inform him that the cost in this connexion amounted to £55 details of which are as follows:-

1   Air fare from Baghdad to United Kingdom
      at £55   =   £55
    Advance for subsistence   -
    Total   £55

Taking into account the deposit of £91 paid by Mr. Forbes in Baghdad, a refund of £36 is due, and before remitting a payable order for this sum Mr. Forbes is requested to confirm that he is still living at the above address.

Further correspondence on this subject should be addressed to the Under-Secretary of State, Foreign Office, London, S.W.1., *and the above number quoted.*

FOREIGN OFFICE,
LONDON, S.W.1.

January 16, 1959

At 11 p.m. silence was called for the tape, which brought a great cheer at the end and an excuse to fill up the glasses all round again. Cookie seemed to enjoy the proceedings as much as anyone and was congratulated on his food. The events of 14th July 1958 were truly celebrated and a good night was had by one and all.

Shortly after that there was another gathering of the gang at Singapore airport to see off Jean Tierney, who was one of the girls at the Foreign Office mess for those attached to the governor general's staff. Once the plane had gone, the crowd repaired to the mess of Sandilands buttery where 'Tired Tim' Dalgleish had his abode. There was a droll Doberman dog as part of the establishment with similar sense of humour to Dalgleish in that it would carry ice cubes and lay them on the bare feet of those wearing flip-flops which were common off duty attire in the heat and humidity of Singapore.

After a while, when a fair amount of beer had been consumed, 'Tired Tim' announced with abject apologies that the Anchor beer had run out and only the plebeian Tiger beer, as drunk by NCOs and other ranks, was left. Before long, comments began to be voiced about the beer and the need to move off or switch to something else. As everyone was finally leaving it was revealed that it was the same beer and the switch to Tiger had been mentioned just to see how all present might react! Via Sander, Tubby had met a few of the Dutch brewers who were responsible for the output, and they had confirmed that only one brew was produced by Malayan Breweries. If they could get ex-pats to pay more for bottle labelled 'Anchor Beer' on snob value – so be it! There was certainly never a dull moment to life in Singapore.

However, things were certainly hotting up on the new subsidiary front and Tubby began to think in terms of being based in Kuala Lumpur from the start of 1960. With the impending timetable, it was possible he might be in Kuala Lumpur in the Federation even by the end of the year, and so Tubby set himself two particular priorities. One was to get Singapore up and running, sales and marketing wise, with the credit selling according to the census divisions and with salesmen in place being supervised by little Tan, with Voon Kim Chua marked for being the supervisory boss of the Kuala Lumpur area of the federation.

The extensive trip through the Federation really brought home to Tubby the concentrated and exaggerated nature of Chinese life-style on the island which was probably now more traditional than China itself under the strange antics of Chairman Mao with his uniformally dressed legions waving their red books. Even that wonderful Chinese authoress Han Suyin was making favourable noises about the improvements to the masses in China which we were supposed to believe were happening under the great Mao Tse-Tung, but Singapore was still rip-roaring Chinese, with all its good and bad traditions.

One day shortly after his return, Tubby was out with one of the new credit salesmen who did not seem to be a particularly forceful outgoing salesman type. They had just walked into a square surrounded by well-established buildings when a wedding party emerged to be greeted by the lighting of enormous traditional Chinese fire crackers hanging from each side of the door, resembling enormous rip-raps made up of gaudy red sticks of dynamite. Once ignited at the bottom they began to explode with a noise resembling a high velocity half inch machine gun. Having just been in the Federation, where this sort of thing was not allowed because of the emergency, and with his recent ambush experience and his memories of Baghdad, Tubby's reflex action was to dive behind the nearest car on the side away from the explosive noises. He felt like a complete fool as he raised his head above the level of the car to find that everybody else was cheering madly and clapping the newly married couple as they went off through an ankle deep carpet of the red remnants of exploded fire crackers.

The episode was related with much mirth around the sales force which all helped towards the goal of building up the best and first ever credit selling operation on the island, with a bond of trust and loyalty between himself and the Chinese in general. Besides the rather withdrawn salesman he had been out with, the others recruited were younger. One studious·tall lad with big glasses had been withdrawn from the very Malay north-east of the Federation. On the very first trip up there with Sears, Desmond and co the previous September, Abe had been warned quietly that there was talk of the lad possibly being axed – literally. While there were Chinese communities up in the north-east states of Kelantan and Trengganu, it was a real fact of life that an axe in the back of the head was the way Chinese were dealt with if something went wrong in the eyes of the traditional Islamic Malay population.

Another young salesman was an extremely jovial and smiling young chap called Yeo, who had a broad face and very smiling eyes, though half closed and slanting at the edges of the eyebrows. Poor young Yeo got jaundice rather badly and Tubby went to see him in the big general hospital in Singapore, which was run exactly as any hospital back at home in the UK, except it was all very open because of the tropical heat and humidity, and patients and staff were not British. He eventually found the ward where young Yeo was confined for the initial stages, and found him sitting on the bed with his feet dangling over the edge, with his large face resembling a cartoon 'lemon person' in an advert, or a comic. The Chinese are yellow to start with, but young Yeo was just unbelievably yellow, and with slightly pocky face skin, he really did resemble the outer peel of a lemon. Tubby just could not control himself from laughing until tears ran from both their eyes because young Yeo had seen himself in the mirror and he too felt that he could play the part of the original cartoon 'lemon man', or offer his services to Tom Glaze and Grant Advertising for a poster advertising lemon juice.

The impositions against traditional Chinese life both back in China and across the Causeway seemed to have the effect of stimulating the people in Singapore to throw everything into their traditional festivals such as the event of the next Chinese New Year around February. Besides being out and about in the streets with the Chinese and dining with the salesmen whenever possible, Tubby used to like to go up to the top of the great concrete tower which was the Cathay hotel and look out over the vast array of twinkling lights across the great city of Singapore. At New Year the explosions, noises and bursts of light from the crackers and fireworks went on all through the night to give an unbroken blanket of noise, and with the wild level at which life was lived in Singapore, these festivals went on for days and nights.

Against their great drive for business, the Chinese main downside was their weakness for gambling, and while the credit selling did not seem to be creating great loss situations, it was a fact of life in Singapore that apparently quite well-established *towkays* would suddenly go bust. Tubby was absolutely fascinated at how they rolled money over because he found, through the reliance and confidence of his supervisors, that they could receive sudden orders for excess amounts of detergent, toothpaste or soap which the *towkays* would sell off at discount for fast turnover and cash intake so that they could run down to the docks to buy in sugar, or some other commodity which was being landed at a very advantageous price. Having found out by close contact with the Chinese community

385

how they used money this way on a thin capital asset base, he set up strict veto procedure when any *towkays* started to go over the top on the credit selling.

With the success of the introduction of the credit selling manifesting itself in increased turnover and throughput of the products, Harpers had introduced the process for their other high profile consumer goods under the Heinz and Reckitt and Colman agencies, and for the booze products Vat 69 and Courvoisier brandy, certainly a high-volume product with the Chinese. However, their tidy British bookkeeping and accounting methods resulted in their presenting some of the major Chinese *towkays* with a combined monthly invoice on all their agency products together. Little Tan and his salesmen had come in to Tubby in consternation complaining that *towkays* could not cope with one bill for all products all at once. They had to take counsel with Harpers in order to establish a rolling system of invoices on a weekly basis so that the wholesale trade, particularly, would receive an invoice at the end of the first week for the Heinz products and then the Reckitts products at the end of the next week with the Colgate products at the end of the month.

The other more serious downside of the Chinese character was the drug habits of certain sections of the population, and the totally integrated activities of the Triads. From their origins as benevolent clan institutions for the poor, based on temples, their clan loyalty ran deep and over-shadowed any conventions which had evolved over the years, with involvement in commerce and then extortion. It had always puzzled Tubby why Chairman Mao with his comeback and sweeping take-over of China after the retreat of the Long March, had not completed the job by taking over Taiwan where Chiang Kai-Shek with his Kuomintang remnant retreated and were hanging on. On voicing his puzzlement about this situation on several occasions, he had received rather old-fashioned looks from senior Chinese, who shrugged and commented that both leaders, way back, had roots in the same Triad.

It was quite evident that the extortions and the killings were always amongst Chinese and never involved or threatened other races, therefore it was a surprise one day when it was reported to him that one of Colgate's two cash-sales vans had been chased by a threatening vehicle, but had got away. It was a pity that it had not been the other cash van, or perhaps it was significant that it had been left alone, because Tubby understood on good authority that the very tough looking Chinese who operated the other van was known to be a Black Panther, which in Triad terminology was one who would carry out the disposing of undesirable or threatening elements.

Fortuitously, it had come to Tubby's attention that the rather 'reserved' salesman he had been out with recently, together with another credit salesman, were of much higher status in a Triad. Tubby remembered Batch in the Khayam who had been responsible during the war for recruits into the King's African Rifles. He had related how the first task was always to identify the *juju* man in each intake from the bush and immediately make him a corporal. It was then left to the *juju* men to exert their 'influence' on any unruly recruits. Following the same line of approach, Tubby invited the two high up Triad salesmen to his room and without speaking directly to them he brought into the discourse the episode of the threatened van and suggested that it might be better for everybody all round if this sort of thing never happened again to one of his cash-vans, or indeed, to any of his sales personnel. The faces were inscrutably oriental, but as they backed out, their faces broke out into those lovely toothy smiles – all gold teeth, and they assured him that they would continue to do their best for him personally, the company and its revered products. There never was another such episode, and in a creepy way it strengthened Tubby's conviction that you simply can't be an aloof ex-pat when you need to get under the skin of the people you are working with and enjoy their loyalty and trust, with mutual respect for one another in spite of vastly different cultural backgrounds.

The Chinese are an incredible people and without doubt a dominant factor in the east, and Tubby found it fascinating to try and identify which were Hakkas, Cantonese, Foochows, Hockiens from Fukien province, Teochews from Swatow, or lowly Hainanese. The Hainanese were one of the lowest in the pecking order and he later found that one of his best salesmen in Kuala Lumpur was a Hainanese, but had worked very hard to pass himself off as totally Cantonese. Tubby always started from the basis that the Chinese would try and pull one over on him, so he would carefully watch for the right moment to jump in and call their bluff which would always trigger off the gold toothed smiles which indicated that negotiations could then proceed on basis of mutual respect for good business deals together.

While Desmond Brown in Singapore was highly involved in the Colgate Account, he was getting higher up the Harpers executive ladder, so a new recruit was introduced on to the Colgate account for the Singapore and Johore areas, called Garry MacDonald, who did not need to be shipped out from the UK, since he had been in the Borneo territories for some years away in the middle of nowhere west from Kudat, which was the main outpost on the northern tip of British North Borneo.

Garry was finding life in Singapore somewhat overwhelming since his isolation had been such that he only ever saw another white person once a month when he either had an air drop with the wages or had a four-wheel-drive visit. A rush of blood after the isolated existence he had followed for some years, plus his enthusiasm for motoring and competing, resulted in his buying a rather splendid Citroen Light-15 two door version, which had a marvellous varnished wooden racing steering wheel. He was absolutely delighted when Tubby suggested that a good run out into the outbacks of Johore to Mersing was long overdue and he suggested that they might go in his new Light-15 to see just what it could do for the 200 miles or so.

On the way out Garry was obviously feeling his way along in his new pride and joy, and since Tubby was probing into his life as an isolated tobacco planter, concentration was not 100% on the driving. It was fascinating to hear about his lone bachelor's dwelling, an *atap* building on high stilts in the corner of the estate, with a mynah bird and a civet cat as household companions. In the middle of the night he had found out to his horror that the mynah bird could wind up to a large noisy impression of someone spitting loudly. One day he had occasion to go to an all purpose workshop place with a broken implement, and found that this was where the bird had originated, and noticed that one of the Chinese fitters had the habit of spitting large mouthfuls into the glowing embers of the blacksmith's furnace.

The estate workers for whom he was responsible also lived in houses on stilts, and one evening before darkness fell he had been summoned by a crowd of the workers to come with all haste to the far side of the estate, where someone was running amok with a large, very sharp *panga*, hacking at the stilts of one dwelling place to bring it down. As so often in these circumstances, a sea of anxious faces surrounded the ex-pat *tuan besar* anticipating the solution for stopping the man, who was having great success with his chipping away at the house stilts. Remembering the pictures of the gladiators in Ancient Rome where one always had a net and trident, Garry related how he eventually threw a great twined net over the man and everyone jumped on the edges to pin him down before he could swing the *panga* to cut a hole in the net. Once disarmed he was strung up in the net and hung from a tree to cool off overnight.

Like the natives he lived amongst, Garry had chickens below his house on the ground level for eggs and poultry, and a garden of sorts which he could survey from his hammock slung on the verandah where the other two parts of his menagerie were allowed, a pie dog and a gibbon monkey. They were apparently such pals that the gibbon would ride on the dog like a jockey on a race track as the pair would have sport chasing the hens, often to where the gibbon would be waiting in ambush to grab them by the neck as they went through. While this life of a planter could seem to be idyllic, it was equally understandable how Garry was revelling being back in the 'gung ho' life of Singapore, as it was at that time for young ex-pats. Having miles and miles of metal roads for him to bat along in his Light-15 was beyond his dreams after North Borneo in 1950s.

As it happened, the day was the birthday of the prophet Mohammed, but living in the predominantly Chinese Singapore, these festivals didn't particularly register. However, they were over in the very Malay State of Johore where it was a national holiday, and as they passed through places like Ulu Tiram and then Kota Tinggi on the road to Mersing, they saw processions of Malay school children and adults all dressed in their best *baju* or *kabayas*, with the men in their black *sonkohs*, with their very colourful sarongs round their middles. At a bridge crossing the great Sungei Jahore River they stopped the car by a flood notice label for the legendary great 1923 flood, which showed that the car would have been well under water.

As they got further on, where estates of various kinds had become more isolated they felt like some refreshment and Garry decided to investigate a track into the *ulu*. After a short distance they stopped the car and he got out as though following some deep instinct, muttering something about there being a Club somewhere round here. To Tubby's astonishment they came to a clearing and there was a Club, of sorts, made from local materials and resembling, but much smaller than, the Taiping Club. It did have the essential of a bar and at the shout of 'Boy' a Chinese appeared from the back and soon made them an excellent fresh lime drink with ice from somewhere. There is no doubt that the ex-pats of the empire first established a Club and bar of sorts, so that wherever you found some rubber, palm oil estates or whatever, Garry reckoned you would always find a Club of sorts if you knew the type of tracks to look for.

On the long drive back Garry got into his element with his Light-15, and the position he seemed to favour was with the seat fairly far back so that his arms were virtually out straight in front to grip the wheel and with his face set in concentration, Tubby sat tight ready to take what came. Fortunately, the road from Mersing down into Singapore was pretty steady with just some bends here and there and as Garry was set on going through these without diminishing speed Tubby became more and more impressed with the engineering and layout of these wonderful Citroen Light-15s, the French police cars seen regularly in continental films. It seemed that the continentals knew a thing or two since with the front wheel drive he seemed to claw the thing through the bends, and with its low slung centre of gravity, and wheels placed well out, Tubby became more relaxed as it seemed increasingly unlikely it would be able to turn over.

As they got more and more amongst the Estates and the New Villages, the usual afternoon downpour happened. Garry saw this as the opportunity to test his long dormant skills of handling a car in the wet, and they were coming down one particular straight in the rain, with a New Village on one side and a rubber estate on the other, when a *kampong* pie dog was seen running at great speed a way ahead of them diagonally on its way across to the left side where Tubby was sitting as the passenger. He watched out through the windscreen between the big headlamps and the great sweep of the big front mud guards on the Light 15, with Garry muttering between his teeth that he was not going to chance crashing the car because of a dog. The poor dog seemed to get wind of the charging car coming up behind, but even with extra acceleration there was a bump as the big front fender made impact. Since there was no follow up bump of the wheel going over it, Tubby looked out of his side window and there in the luxurious, very wet tropical grass along the roadwide was the dog, with four legs up in the air and a bemused look on its face. It must have got caught neatly on its backside at that moment when its back legs were in front of its front legs for more speed and it had been projected forward by the bumper to the same speed as the car for a few seconds. Tubby looked out of the back window to watch it bounce up on to its four legs once it had slowed down enough, and take off into the *kampong* with its tail between its legs, and no damage apparent other than shock.

As they crossed the causeway back on to Singapore Island, Tubby felt quite relieved that they had come through this trial run of Garry's Light-15, and Garry was obviously as pleased as punch and ready to share his experiences with the many other motoring enthusiasts there were in Singapore amongst the young ex-pat blades. Tubby commented on how impressed he had been with the holding and the performance of this French motor car, muttering something about how the continentals, and particularly the Italians with their small cars, seemed to be streets ahead. This was then September and Garry made remarks about hearing through the motoring grapevine about a mini motor car which had been launched back in the UK by Morris Motors of Lord Nuffield fame. The lovely big Austins designed by the Italian, Farina, had been a massive export success and indeed all the taxis round Singapore were these Austin Morris cars because they had great load capacity to engine size, and reliability, but the funniest thing was the big high steering wheel through which all the small Chinese taxi men seemed to peer, rather than be above, when seen from behind. Now there was to be this Mini at about £500, designed by someone called Issigonis.

When they started to appear in the autumn of 1959 they were a sensation with their little ten inch chubby-tyred wheels stuck on the four corners, like a brick on wheels. No one could believe that there was an engine under the bonnet until it was opened up to see the transverse wonder with the drive shafts seemingly direct on to the front wheels. The impact on the lads in Singapore was quite alarming since, as they became available, everyone became convinced that they simply couldn't be rolled over, or break off at a bend, and all the car mad brigade particularly were trying to do just that. Tubby was most pleased that his continental flat partner was also hugely impressed with the Mini, and Tubby has never really forgotten the first sit and drive in one.

In Iraq, Tubby had had up and down Volkswagen vans where you sat right up front on top of the front wheels with the steering wheel coming up between your legs. The 'sit' in the Mini was much the same, since one felt one was all round the steering wheel and capable of seeing the four corners of the vehicle. The sliding windows were ideal for the tropics to bring in the breeze which went out through the side rear windows out on the clips, while the long gear lever coming up from the floor by the pedals reminded him of a Ford Popular he bashed about UK in. The push button floor starter for the engine was a hoot. While just sitting in it and feeling the controls, the way the thing fitted all round was a new experience in itself. Moving off and driving it was just another dimension again. Because of this, one experienced hesitation until one got the totally new feel of this thing, and once confident in its very sensitive responses to being driven, it became an absolute sensation to experience just how far this magic machine could be pushed. The motoring club enthusiasts went for them a bundle and as time went on their eyes positively glazed at talk coming through of there possibly being high performance Mini Coopers for the sporty rally types.

With Tubby highly occupied in Singapore before the likely move to KL and the Federation at the end of the month, involvement in rugger was quite intensive playing, occasional bigger games against services teams, and keeping up his games with the beloved Tankards since Scoops was getting responses to invites from some very good players. Rikki Braybrook, a sergeant in the engineers, was so keen to get games of rugger he used to pedal round on a bike with his rugger kit seeing where he could find games, and one Saturday found the Tankards. He turned out to be an absolutely cracking scrum half and in later years when back in UK played for the army in the big services matches at Twickenham. Tubby reckoned his style of play would have been ideal for Rugby League.

The other character who came in to the Tankards circle as a class winger was a Dr O'Brien, who was at the army hospital in Alexander Barracks. Doc had played at high levels of rugby in Ireland, being in the Queens University side and Ulster, within the marvellous rugby scene of Ireland which knew no boundaries between north and south. With the usual Irish flair for words, he recalled many incidents such as his first confrontation with the 18 stone England and Wasps winger called Woodward. He claimed that on the first confrontation when he tackled this man, he was actually trying to crawl out of his way and Woodward fell over his legs. He recalled the first international game of a contemporary called Macarthy, a loose forward for Ireland, against the Welsh of all people, who had a frightening trio on the front row of that time made up of Billy Williams, the steelworker, and the two Meredith brothers – Courtenay and Bryn. As he lined up at the back of the line, as was his wont as a loose forward, he found standing next to him the huge knobbly form of Courtenay Meredith, with a grin of intermittent teeth. (In those days gum shields had not come into vogue.) The ball was of no particular consequence to Meredith since he was really there to give young Macarthy an idea of how things stood at international level amongst the fraternity of the forwards, and particularly the fellowship of the front row. In the 1950s the language of the Welsh pack was Welsh, and indeed Tubby knew of one local player back home in The Wirral who had won a Welsh cap via playing in the Varsity match for Cambridge, only to find himself at a great disadvantage not having grown up speaking the native language of Wales. On the Irish side, particularly amongst the hard heathen forwards from Leinster and Munster who usually played Gaelic football and hurling, as well as the rugby, they could confound the Welsh in turn by speaking Gaelic, or Erse, as it is sometimes called, though it is almost identical to the Scottish Gaelic.

On this subject, Doc O'Brien related how once they were all in full dress rig for the big army medical dinner, being presided over by the formidable chief surgeon and Scot – Brigadier McKenzie. Matters had got really wound up even at the pre-dinner drinks, and the chief Chinese steward at the barracks had asked Doc what the Irish said for 'bottoms up' before throwing a drink back. Doc had said in the Irish *pug – mahone* which was sort of the same thing, but in a more uncouth lewd vein. He had not thought any more about it until he was hauled in before Brigadier McKenzie the next morning because apparently the Chinese head steward was going around Brigadier McKenzie's table with the liqueurs and malt whiskies after the dinner, and delivered the Brigadier's celebrated malt with the words *pug – mahone* and a great Chinese grin, bowing as he took his leave. The Brigadier's monocle fell out as he asked the Chinese steward: 'In the name of God – who on earth taught you to say that?'

While Scottish ex-pats were predominant and the Irish were not too far behind, it was only very seldom one came across a

Welshman. One evening after a rugger game, Flannigan and the others were all together in the Cricket Club when he was aware that there was a small Welshman in their midst with a very pronounced accent. He was an academic, as might be expected, down at Singapore University on a visit from his regular post as a Professor of History at the University of Malaya in Kuala Lumpur. Like the New Zealand tea merchant Tubby had met on the plane from Ceylon, Dai Jones had moved round top circles in Welsh rugby and had as many anecdotes about top players as Doc O'Brien had on the Irish side. Since the Welshmen are usually loners in these far away places, and possibly because Tubby was a reasonable listener, he was to find that once he moved to Kuala Lumpur he would get calls from Dai at the most unusual times to meet up and have a drink and a chat over rugby, which seemed to be his escape from the trials of the academic life.

As the year drew on they saw off at the docks another of the gang – Liz Graham, who had been secretary to the High Commissioner. She had been very much one of the Tankards-related gang since Scoops had had a great yen for Liz, which manifested itself in a self-elected responsibility for her well being – which was a great source of banter all round. The send off down on the boat at the docks was once again a night to be remembered, but this time they thought it better not to go to Tobi's Paradise and risk getting involved in another fracas.

The departure of Liz, and hints that Mark and Tom Loughead and some of the then gang might be moving on, brought home to Tubby that the great ex-pat life in these places was transitory. As he made plans to depart for life in Kuala Lumpur at the end of November 1959, there was to be another event which was to bring home to him rather sharply that the great and wonderful gung-ho of his initial Far East experience was coming to an end, and there would be quite a significant gear change to his life in its new phase in Kuala Lumpur with the new companies moving on to local manufacture.

The whole prospect of leaving Cookie and the Amber Mansions flat and Sander, his Dutch friend, was much relieved in that a rowing club member out with a German company had recently come down from Penang and could take over Tubby's room. Against the growing tempo for reductions in ex-pats from Europe, Charlie Fell, the director at Harpers who looked over the various mess properties, was quite happy for Sander to continue with Peter Hutz in place, as Harpers tenants for the on-going occupation of Amber Mansions, which meant dear old Cookie and his wife could continue with unbroken service.

In the intense tropical humidity, the three-quarter horse-power air-conditioner bolted into the bottom part of his room window would go with him, and he eventually set off for Kuala Lumpur in the Zephyr with the air conditioner sticking out of the boot. The red sports car remained in the garage to be picked up on his first business flight to Singapore from his new base in Kuala Lumpur.

He was only into his second week in the third floor office they had taken in office block in Ampang Road, KL, when he received a telephone call from Eddie Flannigan in Singapore which he could tell right away was bad news. Tubby's big friend Bob Catford, with whom he had played in the Tankards team in his last game before coming north, had been electrocuted in his home and was gone. Both Bob and Joy had become particular friends because of their previous placement with Pirelli tyres in Iraq. Apparently Bob had a towel wrapped round him after a shower and had simply picked up a metal standard lamp which had become live since the wire coverings can easily perish in the humid tropics. In the tropical humidity of Singapore, bodies cannot be kept around and Tubby was just not able to get down to Singapore in time for the crema-tion, so this whole episode really did bring his Singapore era to its end and helped him switch to the new phase in the Federation.

37

ADJUSTING TO LIFE IN KUALA LUMPUR AND THE FEDERATION

Tubby's new beginnings and the heightened commercial stakes were brought sharply into focus with the go ahead from New York to make application for Pioneer Industry Status for a Colgate Toothpaste factory and the need for another new subsidiary company called Colgate Palmolive (Far East) Limited, the vehicle for local manufacture on the five acre site they had applied for in the new industrial area of Petaling Jaya.

Maurice, the lawyer, had drawn up the Articles of Association for himself and Jim to be the original subscribers to the new subsidiary with one share each no less. Tubby could not help but be amused inwardly since only two years ago he was at the big annual sales convention in the Piccadilly Hotel, London at the end of his extended period as a UK soap salesman collecting his accolade for Salesman of the Year for the north-west district. Here he was being the original subscriber of yet another overseas subsidiary of Colgate Palmolive International and was already a director of Colgate Palmolive (Malaya) Limited, which was going to turn in a very profitable first year. Phew!

The adrenalin was fairly pumped up at prospects for the new year, and was boosted even more with the message of the 'second coming' of George Lesch on the 20th January. However, before Christmas they received a second message that his visit was likely to be delayed until the beginning of March, with stories filtering out of New York that his teenage daughter, Georgette, was quite seriously ill.

Jim and family had been up and settled into Kuala Lumpur

ahead of Tubby and had established an office within walking distance of Harper Gilfillan's office in Mountbatten Road, with a short lease in anticipation of having offices in their very own new factory, possibly within the year. The set back date for the Lesch visit meant that if they really got stuck in, they could get their second-half budgets completed and have more monthly results under their belts. Jim was showing signs of really popping at the prospect of the likely profits by the 30th June year-end, with his cut thereof as the big pay out for general managers of overseas subsidiaries being the dream of him and his contemporaries as they came up through the ranks from the second floor back in New York.

Having come out of George Lesch's first visit debâcle reasonably unscarred, Tubby began to nurture the thought that if this next visit went well, he too might get a cut, as the only other ex-pat in this international operation in Malaya. He could not help but compare the tightness of their operation, with locally recruited staff from the accountant downwards, against the heavy weight of ex-pats in British Company operations in this place. ICI, with many more ex-pats, occupied a whole floor above in the same building and the boss man conducted himself like the Queen's ambassador, arriving in splendour by Austin Princess limousine.

Waiting at the entrance of the office building would be the office *tamby* (messenger) also in full Malay rig-out, ready to open the door of the limousine and to collect the boss man's briefcase from the *sais* (Driver). The *tamby* would then lead the way into the lift to press the button for the lift door to close and ascend to the ICI floor. Tubby used to find it acutely embarrassing if he happened to arrive at the time this charade was happening since he always felt he was intruding by getting into the lift at the same time, which he did anyway to be perverse.

The occupants of another floor of the building were the Dutch Consulate. He envied these Foreign Office types, of whichever Country, as it seemed to be the norm that they started at 8 a.m. and then finished at about 2 p.m. with the rest of the day free, and regarding any contact after this hour as a gross intrusion. There was a Dutch Vice Consul who would appear from time to time from the university scene, where he was a highly regarded Chinese expert, speaking Mandarin fluently. He looked the part, with a goatee beard, and one day when they were going up in the lift together it had a hiccup which prompted Tubby to vent his feelings with a guttural Dutch expletive he had picked up from living with van Marken in Singapore. He hadn't the slightest idea what it actually meant and over the years he got the impression that it had better remain that way. He had come to use the word having heard Sander utter it during moments of frustration, because its sound alone expressed one's feelings. In the situation in the lift he had not even started to think in terms of having uttered Dutch words in the presence of the learned scholar from the Netherlands, until the Vice-Consul began to shake his shoulders and chuckle, and looking at the ceiling of the lift he said quietly, 'Now that is the language!'

Tubby's intensifying application to the demands and urgency of the developing business situation was helped in a perverse way by the first game he had for the Selangor Club after his arrival in mid-December, which had resulted in a heavily bruised shoulder, thus curtailing his rugby activities. Furthermore, the 'Dog' (the Selangor club) was not situated on the same through-way traffic situation as the Singapore Cricket Club had been on his route from place of work to place of residence, which meant that there wasn't the same gung-ho post-work socialising.

However, he did get going again before the rugger season petered out for another year and was able to join the Tankards for a tour of rubber estates down in Negri Sembilan where they had another great weekend hosted by planters. The pre-Christmas death of big Bob Catford made it difficult to enter into the weekend with the same zest as the first tour he had experienced up to the big Dunlop estate at Lading Geddes in Johore. Still, it gave him an opportunity for another super drive in the sports car, particularly over the top of the hills to Seremban where he had had his confrontation with the two Chinese rubber lorries – never to be forgotten. He even got out at the spot where he had managed to bring the MGA to a halt up against the rock face as the lorries went past and pondered again how he had ever managed to do it in the time available.

He never thought life would ever be quite the same after leaving Amber Mansions in Singapore, and with his new mess-mate in Kuala Lumpur being in stark relief to van Marken it certainly was not. Harpers had renovated a lovely old house on two stories out off the Ampang Road past the Race Course and just beyond the site where the wealthy Sultan of Brunei was having an *Istana* built for when he should stop over in the Federation of Malaya. There was no expense being spared on this magnificent *Istana* and Tubby got a preview while it was going up via the electrician retained for the factory develop-ment, a roly-poly Anglo-Indian. He had found that his hobby of 16mm cine-filming brought an income, as films of such interesting places as this *Istana* were in demand in the USA for fill-in time on the schedules of many TV station networks developing there.

This Harper mess was very well appointed indeed with its own grounds and with garages for his Zephyr and the sports car and he was installed on the top floor with Malcolm, a young Aussie accountant in the Harpers empire. Harpers in Kuala Lumpur had a very big engineering division, being agents for Rushton-Bucyrus, the manufacturers of the big heavy plant drag machines used in the tin industry. The ground floor was occupied by a very presentable, up and coming executive who was thought to be a protégé of Bill Bailey, the boss man in Singapore. However, there were senior and powerful directors in Kuala Lumpur such as the very tall, ascetic John Sibree, who looked and behaved sometimes as though he might be better suited to being archdeacon in some Cathedral Close back home. Gordon had brought back his new bride to set up house downstairs in this renovated mess with the apparent object of having everything 'as it should be'.

This included having an Alsatian dog which was introduced to them as a pedigree – of course – and being a bitch, it was christened Trudi. It never struck Tubby as being capable of progressing from being a rather floppy puppy to becoming an imposing guard dog, the very appearance of which would scare people away. The poor beast had a floppy ear which couldn't stand up to appear very alert, as a German Shepherd should. One day Tubby had a look at the bitch as it flopped over to him as he was getting out of his car. On examining inside of its mouth he saw that it was rather multi-coloured which to his limited knowledge indicated that the pup was far from being a pedigree. Gordon had informed him in very knowledgeable manner that it would be duly spayed as and when it had had a litter, sired by the right pedigree dog, but poor Trudi came on heat rather earlier than anticipated.

One night Tubby had been aroused from his bed (even through the noise of the air conditioner) to come out to the large balcony on the top flat, and there was Trudi, backed in against a corner with every blade of grass covered by a legion of pie dogs which had assembled from every corner of the immediate and further Kampong regions in response to her being on heat. Gordon was throwing things from the windows downstairs as they both shouted for the pack animals to go away. Pie dogs were not usually evident in these neighbour-hoods, but at the sniff of a bitch in season they would appear from all over the place. Tubby remembered an incident whereby a couple with a very special springer spaniel had locked it away in an upstairs toilet when in season. Somehow, the pie dogs had managed to make a pyramid, or whatever, so that one of them got up and into the window of this upstairs toilet for the owners to find on their return their springer spaniel and pie-dog happily together after a successful mating.

Tubby went off and shut himself in his air conditioned bedroom away from the hullabaloo and took solace in the recollection of a very amusing incident in Singapore when he had been out with one of the Miss FAB teams in a special housing area for PWD employees. The area was near the back of the runway for Paya Lebar Airport with rows of identical houses along a block pattern of roads on low stilts resulting in a semi-dark area under the houses. Alongside each of the roadways of this block living complex were concrete monsoon drains, and on walking round looking for the girls, Tubby could not help notice that there seemed to be an absence of pie dogs, normally fairly numerous in housing areas of this type. Crouching slightly, he noticed that all the resident pie dogs were crouched deep into the shadow under the houses and peering out demonstrating a mutual feeling amongst them that there was some danger afoot.

As Tubby rounded the corner into the next roadway, he noticed coming towards him a Tamil PWD dog man carrying a huge double-barrelled shotgun. He had on his loose khaki Public Works Department uniform, a big handle-bar moustache often seen on Tamil workmen, and his van was parked further down the roadway as part of his equipment for shooting and removing surplus pie dogs. His arrival on this estate had been transmitted around the pie dogs by their own bush telegraph, so that wherever this dog man walked there were none of them in sight.

Malcolm had been in the mess ahead of Tubby coming up from Singapore and he found that a *kebun* (gardener) had been organised to keep the grounds in order, while for washing and cooking there was a Malay amah called Abibah. She was a far cry from Cookie, the dear old slave in Amber Mansions, but she turned out to be quite a gem and introduced Tubby to the marvellous wonders and tastes of Malay curries. They were mild by comparison with the Indian curries Tubby had grown up with and relished, but they had a far greater subtlety of taste since they were marinated when prepared with the curry powders selected according to the meat to be cooked. To complete the experience, they were served with a range of delicacies called sambals which were arrayed round in various dishes. There was of course Malay satay which can be out of this world. This is delicate chunks of meat marinated and put on thin wood skewers and cooked over charcoal, much favoured for cocktail parties and finger buffets. All these came from the skills of Abibah in the kitchen, together with the now expected daily laundry!

Malcolm was quite a pain, being almost the archetypal abrasive Aussie, not only in tone of voice, but also in picking

402

points to argue and emphasise until one day he turned up at breakfast looking like a prize hamster. Tubby's mother, having come from an isolated fishing village in Highlands with limited medical resources, was a sort of amateur medicine woman, so Tubby knew enough of signs and symptoms to prevail on Malcolm to get back to bed while he got the GP in to confirm that it was indeed the mumps. In an adult male this can be quite disastrous unless you get a rope and tie the ankles from the ceiling to try and prevent certain things descendings into the vital organs. At the same time Tubby sent a hasty communication back home to his mother to consult with a little black book of dates and occasions when he and his brother had gone through all the gambit of childhood plagues. He was soon relieved to receive the anticipated communication back from UK that he had indeed had the mumps, together with his brother as per dates recorded. Poor old Malcolm's mumps were quite severe and this episode helped to mellow relationships as it unfolded that dear Malcolm had not exactly had the happiest of childhoods having spent many of his early years in a Jesuit orphanage. Tubby came to the conclusion that much of his abrasiveness possibly stemmed from the need to get some response from others, albeit not necessarily one of endearment.

In addition to the mumps, two other factors helped to prevent tensions heightening. One was the fact that the Kevlins were now planning for Jim's first leave from the 1st July, to come back in September, which meant that Tubby could think in terms of going off on leave back to the UK some time in September, and would be getting clear of Malcolm earlier since the Kevlins were keen that he move into their house from the 1st July. The other factor which helped was that since his coming to Kuala Lumpur he was working more closely with John Bell, the full time Harpers national co-ordinator on the Colgate account, who was well involved in the local St Andrew's Kirk which turned out to be a much more lively proposition than the much larger one in Singapore.

Additionally, there was a great couple whom he knew from Singapore called Ray and Margaret Honey, and there was the

Reverend Tommy Scott and his dear Welsh wife who would throw their house open for coffee after the church services, which helped everyone to get to know one another. Reverend Tommy was an ex-RAF Padre from the war and a Scot, which was rather necessary since the church of St Andrew's in Kuala Lumpur was very much on kirk lines. This helped with his other responsibilities which were the monthly tour down into the Caledonian enclaves of planters in Negri Sembilan and on to Malacca and back again, which he enjoyed immensely.

The Honeys were very much involved in the life of the church and were there because Ray was an architect from New Zealand, who had settled into exercising his professional skills within the Public Works Departments of Singapore, and then the Federation. He was very much in amongst the powers that be, and related how Tun Razak, who was a very go-ahead Government Minister from National Development, quietly told all his staff that they could ignore all the emphasis for use of Malay as the national language in order to get on with the projects he had programmed without trying to do things in a language which, with all due respect, could not cope with modern vocabularies, particularly technical ones. Though Margaret Honey came over as a very superior and almost archetypal colonial *mem besar*, she really had a heart of gold and was a great motivator. She was from Orpington in Kent which meant that to Tubby, as a northerner, she came over as quite an overpowering southerner. The two had met up in Singapore through Margaret having come out to be a school teacher in a very well appointed Presbyterian Mission school, and had therefore been sent forth from England with all the trappings of a missionary going out into the bush.

A third factor that helped Tubby endure things at the mess was the pure pressure of work which was building with regard to the increasing research required for the essentials for manufacture and the setting up of the factory, all on top of continuing work to achieve growth potential on volume and profits for the marketing company of Colgate Palmolive (Malaya) Limited. Both he and Jim were charging round the country on their

404

field trips and when Jim was away on his first trip of the New Year he had to cope with a communication from Ed Spika's manufacturing department for the acquisition of a further five acres before they had finally clinched the site dimensions at Petaling Jaya. This meant his getting down to the architects because New York were now thinking even further ahead beyond the toothpaste factory to the really major project, the local manufacture of their market leading detergent FAB. New York's requirement was that the extra five acres simply must not be 'fill' land, but 'cut' land because of the anticipated weight of plant for manufacturing detergent, involving the huge tall blowing tower.

At the same time, in anticipation of more technical visits, they were given a shopping list of oleum and other chemicals likely to be used in detergent manufacture. An American called George Shroll stopped by in Kuala Lumpur on his way home to the States with his wife and two girls after a stint in Australia setting up a detergent plant. Rather than going home by the Pacific they had decided to try BOAC's Comet 4 which was a flying experience way ahead of anything as yet from Boeing, and besides the Americans liked to take in the UK on their way back home.

While Tubby was at the architects Booty & Edwards, going over this whole problem of getting the new site extended from five to ten acres with extra 'cut' land, the architect, Francis Bailey, discovered that Tubby was from the Merseyside area and this prompted him to go away into his office and produce great rolls of drawings from a special drawer and laying them out for Tubby who was absolutely fascinated to find that Francis had come second in the competition for the design of the Roman Catholic cathedral in Liverpool. With Liverpool having the highest ratio of Roman Catholics in the population, the vision before the war was for a cathedral to match St Peter's in Rome itself. Indeed, the crypt for something of this dimension had been laid to a large extent before it became obvious that the necessary money to continue was just not going to be forthcoming. After the war there had been momentum to have a Catholic cathedral to match the magnificent red

405

stone Anglican one, but it was to be of revolutionary circular design. On examining the drawings with the architect, Tubby could not help feeling that his would have been a much more classical design than the 'Paddy's Wigwam' which was eventually built instead and has been plagued with leaks and maintenance problems ever since.

With Jim back from his run round some of the Harpers branches, it was the end of January and Tubby was ready to go off on his long delayed trip up to the north east corner of the Federation centred on Kota Bharu, in the State of Kelantan, which he had only previously visited on the celebrated tour with Sears & Abe in September 1958.

As a frustrated flyer with only a few lesson flights in his log book, Tubby had enjoyed the 'seat of the pants' flying in Borneo and Sarawak and to his great delight he found that because Dakota flights were not commercially viable along the east coast, nor were there the required standard of landing facilities, Malayan Airways operated a single-engined Beaver plane. This left Kuala Lumpur each day to fly straight over the top of the mountain spine of Malaya, virtually due east to the first main town on the coast called Kuantan, before going due north to Kota Bharu. Twenty miles south of Kuantan there was the mouth of the huge Kuala Pahang River with no road from there southwards for almost 100 miles to Merseng, which Tubby visited from Singapore and Johore on the celebrated drive with Garry MacDonald.

The Beaver was a very chunky, high powered single radial engined four-seater which left quite early in the morning from KL, and Tubby was the only passenger with the Aussie pilot, so he was up front in the right-hand seat. He was absolutely in his element since he was all but flying the damn thing himself and was able to use his cine-camera to capture the sensation when they were coming down through banks of cloud to break out into the sunshine again. He then captured the sensation of landing as the plane swept out over the sea, banked and came in over the shore with the landing area in his sights until the plane rapidly settled down on its tail wheel after the first touch down, with the camera then pointing to the sky.

Tubby was on for the full flight up to Kota Bharu, and while mailbags were changed at Kuantan they talked about the terrible episode in December 1941 when the great battleships *The Prince of Wales* and *The Repulse* had been sunk by Japanese planes just off the coast from Kuantan. The episode was still very much in the people's memories and the pilot knew that they had gone down quite close together in only 250 feet of water, and he related that in good conditions their bulks could be made out from the air. Since no other passenger had boarded, he took the Beaver straight out for an eventual left hand banking turn over the site to head due north towards Dungun which was to be their next landing. It was an utterly incredible experience to look down on the water where this vividly remembered episode from the war had taken place.

As they swung in low over the sea towards Dungun, Tubby took note that this was a stretch of shore he must come to in, mid to late May, to witness that incredible phenomenon of the giant turtles on their annual visitation from the vast oceans to lay their eggs above the tide line on this remote stretch of the east coast of Malaya. From skipping along almost on the surface of the water, the pilot eased the nose up and then dropped the Beaver on to the grass above the shore, which was the extent of the facilities at Dungun. They dropped off some mail and then headed north along the coast, looking down on the Malay fishermen coming back in their unique boats with the single sails from their night long labours in the South China Sea, until the Beaver came in sight of Trengganu, banked and came in low over the shoreline and on to the grass for a perfect touchdown.

At Dungun there had been simply nothing but the stretch of grass, but here at Trengganu Tubby was amused to note that they had an 'airport building' which was no more than a large timber bus shelter covered with *atap* leaves. In this glorious post-monsoon weather with the sun shining brilliantly on the dazzling sand of the east coast, the plane followed the road, only out over the sea parallel to the coastline until they turned in over the famous Beach of Passionate Love, which was not really safe for swimming because of its steepness and the undertow of the waves which washed these beaches from the vast South China Sea. The Beaver seemed to enjoy the smooth touchdown and taxi along the metalled runway at Kota Bharu, which was necessary for Dakotas and military aircraft active along the jungle areas to the border. Tubby bade farewell to the Aussie pilot and said he would see him later in the week when he was scheduled to join the plane at Trengganu for a hop back down the coast to Kuantan.

He was met by Mr Majeed, who was the manager at this Harpers branch, with a young Chinese salesman, Ong Eam Teck, who later wrote Tubby with photos he had taken of his visit to the branch. They had one van salesman with a driver, loudspeakers and vibrant paintings of the products on the van, plus one Miss FAB operation which was very special for two reasons. Firstly, it was an all Malay team led by a very attractive and charming Malay Princess Tengku Maimunah. Secondly, because of the severe climatic conditions, their vehicle was a long-base, four-wheel-drive Landrover, with a winch fitted at the front and back so that the vehicle could pull itself out of monsoon floods and severe off-road conditions into *kampongs*, which could otherwise bog it down – even with four-wheel drive.

The days in Kota Bharu were beautiful and balmy after the onslaught of the monsoon. Even the full heat of the day was tempered by a gentle breeze coming off the China Sea and reaching well inland with all the coastal area being extremely flat. Since the salesman was going to take him by road visiting all the places down to Trengganu, Tubby concentrated on seeing the other main road which climbed directly inland, though heading south, keeping east to the great Sungie Kelantan, the main river flowing north through the State. The place was totally Malay and Islamic, except of course for the traders, shop keepers and the wholesalers he was taken to see. However, once they got beyond Machang and on to Kuala Krai, some 40 miles up, they were really in bandit country in the hills where the railway emerged from the central mountains of the King George V National Park. Here was the first, fenced New Village he had seen in this region for night curfew on chinese.

408

Where the railway reached the high central mountains there were tunnels as the descent was started through Kelantan, and it was a favoured place for ambushing the railway trains during the height of the Emergency. The many bends as the line went to and fro down the gradients were ideal places for ambush, so there were special armoured jeeps going up and down the railway track with railway carriage wheels instead of normal tyred motor wheels. There were plantations, and many Chinese were into timber, going into the *ulu* with their crane lorries to extract huge trees at a rate atuned to the natural cycle of rapid new growth in the jungle clearings vacated by felled trees. All the logging was done by small Chinese firms with do-it-yourself lifting and dragging gear, and with the same for transporting the logs once they were out to any sort of road surface. They somehow attached one end to a front articulated unit while the far end of the logs was lashed on to a two wheel unit so that the logs tended to sway to and fro, as the two wheels behind did not follow the front through the bends of the road. Tubby had been following one of these log lorries and as it slowed down for a *kampong* area he watched with impotent horror a Chinese lady up ahead with a child on the crossbar of her bicycle, blissfully unaware of the fact that the rear end two wheel unit was about to demolish her from behind. At the last minute it bounced and swayed back out into the middle of the road and passed her. Both she, and the driver away up front were blissfully unaware of what had almost happened. These log transporting contraptions were one of the worst road hazards to negotiate since they used to shift at a fair pace along roads, and with no decent stretch of straight it took some fine gear changing and acceleration to get past.

The whole of this State and area had a character of its own and it was most difficult to picture the *kampongs* visited being all flooded just a few weeks previously with bridges under ten feet of water. After branching off away back in Negri Sembilan for the east coast via the central highlands, the railway ended at a small place called Tumpat right on the coast beyond Kota Bharu. Before Kota Bharu, at a place called Mas, there was a line which headed off into Thailand, but there was no road to the station at the border crossing as there was at Padang Besar over in the west.

It was round Pasir Amas that they met up with Princess Maimunah with her team of Malay girls in their white uniforms, while jingles in Islamic style sounded out from the big Landrover. It was pristine white, adorned with paintings of the Colgate, the Palmolive soap and the FAB detergent. The girls were obviously very proud of the fact that they were in the team of a Princess and it gave them a certain kudos and status in introducing the products round the *kampongs* door-to-door. The old firm certainly had a winner in this area. The driver demonstrated to Tubby how they managed to get around in the monsoon times which confirmed it had been absolutely essential to invest in this unique personnel wagon with powered winches on the front and the back.

On the way south the next day, with salesman Yem Teck, there were two places about 20 miles out of Kota Bharu where they had to turn off out to the beautiful coast because the road went well inland until it reached Trengganu at the mouth of the great Sungei Trengganu River. Here there was a large primitive pontoon ferry on which cars were towed across by a great chain. While Trengganu State was pretty vast with the usual myriad Malay *kampongs* along the Sungei Trengganu River and its tributaries, there was only one road into the interior, with the main coast road south to Dungun and Kuantan following the shore line. Before looking round the town of Trengganu, they went off south down the 20 miles of better road, shown in red on the Shell map, which turned right to meet the great river at Kuala Brang where a tributary joined and the main river turned west to the watershed of the central highlands.

It was the only place of town status in the area and could support one *towkay*'s business. As they drove into the centre by the bus terminus there was a voluble excited throng not far from a recently arrived bus. Being taller than most locals, Tubby was able to wriggle in close enough to see that the centre of attraction was the body of a large reptile – almost of Komodo dragon proportions. It was common to see these big reptiles cross roads near rivers or swamps and hair-raising to see a lorry or bus being driven at them before they made it to the other side, with the object of hitting, but not squashing, them, as squashing reduced their commercial value for medicinal purposes. The driver of the recently arrived bus to Kuala Brang must have had the fortune to hit this one and pull it on board, and was now auctioning off outer and inner specialities with help of a *panga* knife, and the local *bomo* – medicine man!

Everything around Trengganu seemed to have something to do with fish, and out on the tip of the lagoon which sheltered the wide mouth of the river, beyond the narrow part where the ferry had been installed, there were dwelling places right out under the bending palm trees with vast areas of timbered surface, about two feet off the ground, covered with fish drying on mats for fast dry preservation using the hot tropical sun.

At the lagoon edges at the mouth of the river there were rows and rows of the very uniquely decorated east coast fishing boats with their carved high prows and lesser beam at stern. Other numerous little boats went in and out and up and down the river with single square sails on an angle, with company names on the sugar or flour bags from which they had been made. One proud boatman noticed Tubby's cine-camera and assumed a proud pose holding his oar, shouting for his picture to be taken.

Tubby had noted on the way up in the Beaver that the landing for Trengganu was well out of the town on a grassy patch above the sea shore, so he had the salesmen leave him at the funny *atap* covered 'bus shelter' to listen for the plane, about 20 minutes ahead of estimated time which did not matter much in a dreamy place where the folk rarely bothered to keep time. Instead, he heard the noise of a Landrover engine, and a Police Landrover came into view. It was of the long wheel-base variety with a metal hooped open back with rolled-up canvas sides, and as it came to a halt he noticed that there were two big wooden boxes in the back, between two policemen sitting on either side on bench seats, with their rifles between their knees. The driver got out and from the passenger side a tall British bank official came round to Tubby as the only other

411

person in sight, and introduced himself. The Malay policemen with the rifles got off and stood at the back and it was a bit like a scene from these war films as they scanned the sky, all waiting for the first faint sound of the aeroplane engine returning from a raid. After his experience of the trip up, Tubby remembered that the pilot would swing the plane out over the sea, except that there was a bit of a breeze that afternoon so that he actually touched down coming from the land direction so as to be against the breeze for take off out over sea.

The Beaver sat quite high up with its big propeller on the radial engine out of reach once it was in its three point position, so Tubby helped to heave the boxes up through the back passenger doors and on to the two rear seats since once again Tubby was to be the only passenger with the Pilot. He climbed up beside the Pilot and they waved out through the windows as the *puteh* bank clerk went on his way in the Police Land-rover. They bounced along as the revved-up Beaver taxied along the grass a sufficient distance inland for the brief rush out into the wind and out over the sea. As the Pilot swung the plane into a beautiful climbing, banking turn for the flight down to Kuantan, he was able to look down on the waves which broke along this silvery shoreline to which the great turtles return each year. Once the big radial engine was throttled back to normal cruising and the Pilot was setting the trim he shouted across to Tubby, 'You notice I was never asked to sign for the boxes.' Since he had been running late he barely stopped the plane on the ground at Kuantan for Tubby to lower his bag down, leap down after it and wave him a farewell as the radial roared on again and he was off.

On the next Friday night he came across the Aussie Pilot in the bar of the new Merlin hotel in Kuala Lumpur and over drinks he related to Tubby how they had both missed a chance of sharing the two million used Straits dollar notes which were in the two boxes. He had mentioned to Tubby in the plane that he had not been asked to sign for the boxes so quite easily they could have touched down at Dungun grass patch and dug a hole for the two boxes for collection later. This sounded a bit far fetched, until he went on to relate how he had reached KL as the tropical darkness rapidly descended, to find that no one knew, or seemed to want to know, about the two boxes they had loaded on to the back seat. From the control tower where he had checked in at KL, they found the bank had closed and all staff gone so eventually they had got hold of the bank manager at home, who nearly had a heart attack and soon had officials running down to KL airport with armed guards to take the boxes away to the lock-up.

At Kuantan, Gordon, who had come over from KL by road, already had the hotel arranged and the next morning they visited various *towkays* with whom Harpers had business with their other products as well as the Colgate products. It was quite fascinating to hear one old *towkay* relating how he had come to Kuantan as a very young fellow as crew of a junk which carried cargoes from Singapore up the coast. He had liked the place and jumped ship and, like so many industrious Chinese, he had hired himself out to the Chinese who had started businesses in Kuantan. Here he was now with his own wholesale business in this busy sea port of the State of Pahang which was nothing like as Islamic and Malay-dominated as at Kota Bharu.

The drive back was yet another first for Tubby as they went straight through due west, skirting a minor ridge about 20 miles out of Kuantan, and then went across the densely clad jungle valley of the great Sungei Pahang River, to cross at the central towns of Temerloh-Mentekab. The river was flowing fast from the monsoons and they saw that the central span of a new road bridge across this great river had been demolished by great tree trunks and logs which had come down on flood waters. After crossing the railway line about ten miles further west, they began the great climb up into the central highlands, first to Karak and then on to Bentong, to straddle the highlands at Bukit Tinggi, after which the road fairly hurtled down through great bends and twists and hair pins amongst the heavily-clad jungle hills to come out at Batu Caves, north of Kuala Lumpur. Tubby had not as yet visited one of the high hill stations, and he found it like being at home in the cool of these high mountains. He noted that he must try and get a break at

413

Cameron Highlands, but judging by the papers on his desk it was not likely to be this side of his return to the UK on leave, which looked like now being towards the end of September, since Jim and Rita looked like coming back from the USA about the tenth of that month.

In the meantime, there was far too much going on even to think about details of leave. On the day to day front, Tubby had dreamt up and set in motion a big promotion aimed at the wholesalers, as a balance to the great consumer annual gold ring promotion, which always came late in the year. This, together with the continuous work of the Miss FAB promotion teams, helped the building up of consumer awareness and the habit of using these products, so that it was necessary to try and stick some extra volume into the trade pipeline. The census of trade for the credit selling was going extremely well, and his potential supervisors who had conducted the census to establish credit ratings for the various outlets were now in place as supervisors. The no nonsense Fung Swee Seng had been brought down from Ipoh to be in KL with the future intention that he could be the local sales force boss nationally.

Tubby began to look upon his inner gang of Chinese supervisors as his Tong and, like the great informative session he had had with them finalising their Chinese New Year card for the trade, he had gathered his Tong back in January for a similar session for ideas on a promotion for the wholesale trade.

It was always best to try and forget all about UK marketing tactics and focus totally on the local situation, so they started by putting down on paper suggestions as to gifts or prizes the *towkays* could get for free, according to the amount of extra volume of the products they purchased during the month of February. They ended up with things like cash registers, tape recorders, radio appliances and even calculating machines and typewriters. The most popular large item agreed was a three-wheel delivery bicycle based on the design of the trishaw *towkays* could get for free, according to the amount of extra volume of the products they purchased during the month of February. They ended up with things like cash registers, tape

414

recorders, radio appliances and even calculating machines and typewriters. The most popular large item agreed was a three-wheel delivery bicycle based on the design of the trishaw taxis. The Chinese *towkays* liked having photographs around their work places, so Tubby was quite in demand going out with Swee Seng for the presentations of prizes, with a photographer in attendance. In the end the whole promotion pushed more than a whole month's extra turnover into the trade pipeline which would help no end their figures for the second coming of George Lesch, which was now scheduled for the 2nd March.

However, it was the new manufacturing which required immediate attention, and on his return from his east coast trip, he found there was a summons for Jim Kevlin to appear before the Secretary to the Minister of Commerce and Industry, concerning their application for a Pioneer Industry Status Certificate.

After the setting up of Colgate Palmolive (Far East) Limited with Jim and Tubby as original subscribers, they had been able to make the formal application to the government of the Federation for the Pioneer Industry Status for the toothpaste factory, and this was their first response. It was scheduled for the Saturday morning and since the Secretary to the Minister was still an ex-pat colonial civil service-type, Jim insisted that Tubby went along too because the strong post-colonial atmosphere in Malaya still prevailing made him feel very much like a foreigner in a strange land, particularly with his American voice. Jim once asked Tubby in all sincerity and truth why there was such a feeling of distrust of the Americans, since his own wartime experience in the US Navy had been totally within the Pacific area.

He was aghast when told in no uncertain terms about the anti-British feelings which prevailed within American isolationist policies, reinforced when Pearl Harbor focused their whole attention West to the Pacific. Jim was further taken aback to hear that, as far as Europe was concerned, it was Hitler's mad declaration of War on America to unite with Japan against the common foe, which brought America east into the European war as well.

Now, anti-American sentiments were on the up and up again in Far East, with books like *The Ugly American* popular reading about the gross abuse of so-called aid distributed in Laos and Vietnam by USOM.

They duly attended as bidden one Saturday morning, and after a formal check through of the details on their application for Pioneer Industry Status, the deadpan civil service-type raised for consideration the matter of possible local capital participation, together with the training of locals, particularly Malay nationals. It was a historic fact that the wonderfully take-it-as-it-comes, happy go lucky Malays, while essentially highly intelligent, were handicapped by their limited Islamic education system. With no inclination to the rough and tumble of the commercial life, they had not advanced economically and had a willingness to live on the credit that was readily available from financially astute Chinese and Tamils. Certain details were incorporated into the Constitution of the Federation to address this imbalance by 'suggesting' that Malays have a seat on the boards of companies, and that they have assisted entry into places of higher education. As half of the population, it was important in 1956 that they be happy with the Constitution and be won over against Communism, about which they simply couldn't care less.

It was gently pointed out to the civil servant that in nearly 50 overseas subsidiaries, in countries of every nationality throughout the world, Colgate International simply did not get involved in local participation and would not do so now. It was understood that his prime concern was for another new pioneer industry to start in this emerging country of barely two years. On the matter of local staff, he was reminded of the staffing of the Colgate operation with only the two ex-pats sitting before him, backed up by a local accountant, and with the rest of staff reflecting the demographic break-down of the population as near as possible. It was suggested, in the nicest sort of way, that he might like to compare this with the staffing of other multi-nationals, such as ICI, in the same office building. By his gulp and the changing direction of the meeting to other matters, it appeared that he had got the message.

38

THE SECOND COMING

It had now become firm fact that George Lesch would be back again with them on 2nd March 1960 in his supreme position as lord of lords and boss of bosses of Colgate International. Mrs Lesch was coming too, plus the 16-year-old Georgette, whom they understood had had major surgery. Sears was coming too and they understood he would join the party after a few days in Singapore. It was said that his in-laws would be passing through at that time.

From their previous experience in Singapore when Budgets had not been ready, they were certainly going to prepare for George Lesch this time and not for Sears, particularly since there were whispers coming out of New York that Sears might well be on the wane, and no longer the rising star they had first met in 1958 who was going to be responsible for the three new subsidiaries in Hong Kong, Thailand and Malaya. The final run-in of preparation included an all-day session with Desmond Brown up from Singapore with all his manuals and his books on the admin. for the running of the Colgate agency. Another all-day session was with Tom Glaze from Grant Advertising, who was in the process of establishing a Kuala Lumpur office in addition to the one in Singapore which he had founded some years earlier. Suites of rooms had been booked in the new Merlin hotel which was still very much a novelty in Kuala Lumpur, being the first multi-storey hotel in the grand manner of European places, with a Swiss manager who, like most of the Swiss managers Tubby had come across around the world, was immaculate and charming, but totally unsmiling.

It had been hinted that a large reception party should be

417

avoided, so Jim and Tubby went to KL airport with no Harper officials on hand. With Sears down in Singapore meeting his in-laws, it was just the Lesch family who arrived. They were both taken aback at the sight of young Georgette minus one leg doing very well on lightweight crutches. It unfolded that the amputation had been necessary almost to the hip and she and her mother had come along on the trip primarily to keep them together as a family, with first time visits to fabled countries around the Far East as a rehabilitation factor. This lovely 16-year-old was certainly brave and coping extremely well, while Mrs Lesch seemed to have worked out an extremely delicate balance between motherly concern and encouragement towards normality, as far as might be possible in the circumstances. It was most interesting to see this great man, George Lesch, as the real father in this situation, but once the meetings got started he was very much the same George the accountant as he had been on the first visit in Singapore.

Sears was with them again for the start of the second meeting and it became apparent from snippets of conversation and comments that, so far, they had 'done' Japan, Hong Kong and the Philippines, and they were to be in Singapore by the 13th for a quick visit by the pair of them across to Indonesia and then back before going on to Thailand. Whether it was having been with his in-laws in Singapore, or being alongside the Lesch family in their current circumstances, he was much toned down. However, on the marketing and returns to date, and the progress in the foreseeable future of the Malayan operation, he developed again into being at variance with George and the local management who had really got things together for this visit.

On the toothpaste manufacturing front, they were able to report on their recent meeting with the Commerce and Industry department, which meant there would soon be visitations by Manufacturing Executives from New York, and in advance of this they were to anticipate help in the form of the manager of the plant in the Philippines, Pablo Soriano, with an advance meeting with the architects and further shopping lists for materials and ingredients. Much of the time in the meetings was taken up with the next phase which would be the detergent manufacture, a much larger and more detailed operation. Following Tubby's report and details sent to New York on the availability of an additional five acres of cut land, there were visits to the site and the architects, with a go-ahead given for documentation and contracts to be prepared for purchase of a ten acre factory site for toothpaste initially, and then for the detergent plant on the rest of the site. It was all very exciting stuff taking priority on their day to day work schedules since they had moved to KL.

With the weekend coming up, George intimated that the family would like to go down to the seaside on the Sunday which meant a motor trip down to Port Dickson, where Tubby went water skiing. George announced this at a social gathering organised by Harpers with the, tall, very English John Sibree as the host. Straight away, a limousine with a *sais* was promised for 10 a.m. on the Sunday morning outside the Merlin, and George announced that Tubby was to go with them for the day. This set up panic reactions in Tubby, even more so in Jim at the thought of not being there to hear what was being asked by George, and prospect of being alone with Sears for the day, since he had been excluded from the trip to Port Dickson too!

All the meetings on this visit were extremely high-powered and detailed as before, but George did retreat to be with his family as much as possible which gave Tubby and Jim the opportunity for detailed cram sessions on their figures and everything else they could think of to anticipate what the old man might spring on Tubby as captive over the whole of the forthcoming Sunday, from 10 a.m. to goodness knows when.

It was bright, sunny and hot as usual as he met up with them at the Merlin hotel and, while Georgette had been making great efforts with her artificial leg, she decided to have a day off from her struggles. Since the road out of KL towards Port Dickson passed through Petaling Jaya, they turned off to the ten acre site on the industrial estate development so that the ladies could see something of Dad's International empire in the making, though it was then just a patch of red laterite soil, but definitely all cut ground.

Once they got going again and were clear of the turn off to Klang and the road to the shipping port of Port Swettenhan, Tubby was ruminating on his head full of data, up front with the *sais*, when he heard George's voice say, 'Hey, Forbee!' and found that George had leaned forward and was holding alongside Tubby's head a card for him to take and look at. Tubby recognised it as one of the pocket information cards he had seen George writing on a year ago in Singapore once they had finalised the forecasts and budgets for the new Colgate Palmolive (Malaya) Limited, and, sure enough, there were all the figures they had worked out together. Here we go thought Tubby, and sure enough the grilling started: 'What about this? What about that?' and so it went, through the products, until Tubby felt quite drained and George settled back, seemingly in some form of satisfaction, to take in the view of the beautiful blue sea and the dazzling beaches.

They had a marvellous curry tiffin lunch with all the delightful Malay extras, including the favourite ex-pat's pudding called 'Gula-Malacca', which was like white sago made with cream and coconut. It was certainly not Tubby's favourite from vivid memories of sago at school dinners in the war, but George and the others seemed to lap it up. It was a very relaxed and fun meal and Tubby could not help but admire the family banter considering the stresses they had all been through together and were continuing to do so. If this trip was meant to be therapeutic, it certainly seemed to be working.

The journey back was quiet with no grilling since after the meal, the sea air, the sun and the humidity, they seemed content to relax and enjoy the drive back, commenting with questions now and again on the various items of interest along the way.

They were about into the last third of the journey when Tubby began to feel that not all was well with the *sais* and he noticed that his eyelids were drooping and his head was beginning to give the odd nod forward to the extent that he became extremely alert and had his hand ready to grab the wheel if necessary. Fortunately the family in the back were blissfully unaware of what was happening, but Tubby remembered that it was the month-long feast of Ramadan, when Moslem Malays abstained from food and drink through the hours of daylight. Fortunately Tubby was able to talk the matter through with the *sais* in Malay without the others in the back having the slightest idea of what was going on. The immediate effect was that the body of the *sais* straightened up from the slightly slumped position he had drooped into gradually, and after a few blinks his eyes were alert again and his fingers were gripping the wheel. He replied '*Ada baik*,' (All is well) and when Tubby had suggested he might take over the driving, it was doubly confirmed that he was '*Ada baik, dua.*' From then on until they reached the Merlin, to ensure that he remained *Ada baik*, Tubby maintained intermittent conversation in Malay about his family, children or whatever.

It had certainly been a wonderful and most interesting day and after seeing the family safely back into the Merlin he drove round to see Jimmy at home so that he could have a good night's sleep after hearing all that had been raised, and that all seemed to be well with the boss. Tubby thought that a visit to the long bar and the 'Dog' was required before retiring totally drained.

By mid-week they were all down in Singapore for final combined meetings with Harpers, and for the family to take in the sights, while George, Sears and an engineer from Hong Kong went away for a few days over at Djakarta on the island of Java. Details Jim had picked up from conversations were confirmed by Desmond Brown, that George had given Harpers' associates in Hong Kong a rough time on his stop over there with Frank Hill. The anxieties this raised meant that at the big do by Harpers for the Lesch family, Bill Bailey went a bit over the top in his desperation to know what might be the implications from the events in Hong Kong. The awareness of all the activities on the factory front within the new subsidiaries were wrongly interpreted and Harpers were assured of a long term future – with any local manufacture.

As soon as Lesch and Sears had gone off on the Saturday morning it was a scatter to get off back to KL that day in order to start getting all the minutes of meetings written up, and umpteen other things prepared for approval, as it would be so much easier to nail the big boss man down while he was here and thereby avoid the long process of writing to New York and waiting for replies. It was then down to Singapore once again for the final set of meetings and to see them off before collapsing for the weekend. It was the end of the feast of Ramadan, and after the great month of fasting there was the great celebration day of Hari Raya which meant a public holiday on the Monday. Jim went back to the family in KL and Tubby decided to stay on in Singapore with his old mates. Although Tubby had only moved 250 miles or so up north to Kuala Lumpur, he was always amazed to find on these quick business visits the impact of the heat and humidity in Singapore, as the door of the aeroplane would be flung open and he would step out into the atmosphere of a steam laundry. He used to wonder that he had ever actually lived in this atmosphere and had thoroughly enjoyed life, too.

The long weekend in Singapore gave him the opportunity to write to his dear Penelope who was totally occupied over these years of separation applying herself to six years of study extending and heightening her medical skills in various hospitals round Merseyside. Apparently, at each location it would get around that she was in the habit of receiving envelopes from far away places with red, white and blue edges, and she related an occasion when she was in an operating theatre and looked up at the observation window to see a friend at a glass waving an air mail envelope so that she would know to look in the mail pigeon-holes in the porter's lodge. In order to cheer him up on one occasion she had written to relate how, on starting as a surgical houseman, she had had a confrontation over a patient on the operating table when assisting her supervising surgeon for the first time. In situations of high intensity she had not been aware of her habit of drawing air through her teeth, which happened every time the surgeon made an incision with his scalpel. He had to stop, look up, and ask her to stop or leave, since every time he heard the air intake he was convinced that he had severed a main blood vessel which she had noticed and he hadn't. So, in their separate ways, they were both highly active, which helped the time to fly along until they would be together again.

With all the excitement going on at his end, a letter was certainly due, particularly with regard to items which had been resolved during the visit of the great man. Firstly, he had taken the opportunity to float in the idea of his going back to the UK on leave via New York, which would allow him to see the States at company cost. As anticipated, George did not approve, but at an unexpected moment he did take him aside and said, 'Forbee! Once we've gone I want you to go up to Vietnam and Cambodia and take a look for me.' Wow, thought Tubby, this could be exciting and hairy, since these places were hardly quiet back-water areas at that time. It was explained that with all their developments going on in the Far East, and taking account of other information he had picked up on this trip starting in Japan, George felt that someone should visit for an up-to-date look at these two countries, which were export territories of Colgate Palmolive Français. Subsequently this was confirmed by Sears later in writing, with Jim Kevlin equally as puzzled as Tubby as to why it was to be him.

In Tubby's mind this really did confirm that he was now one of the International gang, and as such he had confirmed during this second coming that he could bring back his Penelope to Malaya as his wife after his leave, which was to start in September for two months. With his idea of a New York visit on the long way home declared a no-go, he could think in terms of actual dates, so he was able to write asking if she would be his 'lawful wedded wife' and be willing to come back to these equatorial climes. Also, when should he write to her father for her hand in marriage, if she said yes? Over rapid exchanges of correspondence which followed, the letter did go off to his father-in-law to be, some 6,000 miles away, since by mutual understanding her birthday on the 18th July might be the occasion for an engagement to be announced, to be followed by a wedding on the 15th October, her sister's birthday. However, in stock exchange terminology, events had been discounted in advance by a wave of approvals all round, to the extent that the purchasing of the ring was well in hand by the month of May.

Against this unfolding background, Tubby's involvement at the Kirk of St Andrews had been such that on Easter Day, the 10th April, he was ordained an Elder of the Kirk, thereby enhancing the status back home of the bridegroom-to-be with all and sundry in the Presbyterian Church in which they had both grown up and were now to be wed. On that Easter Day after church he had gone back to the home of Margaret and Ray Honey for lunch, and on telling them of the pending engagement and return with his wife towards the end of the year, dear Margaret just about took off at the prospect of introducing a new ex-pat wife into the ways of how things were done in Kuala Lumpur.

39

VIETNAM AND CAMBODIA

Once back in KL, and with confirmation that the French Colgate company in Paris and their agents in Cambodia and Vietnam were informed, Tubby sent off letters to Monsieur Vattaire, as the only English-speaking Frenchman there, at Companie Technique et Commerciale Du Cambodge, in Phnom-Penh. By the 4th April he had had no response, but was totally involved in local happenings, with the arrival of Pablo again from Manila in the Philippines, and an American called Bill Van Nostrand who was from New York and with the accent to match, but who was fair-skinned with tremendously blue Scandinavian eyes. He was not great of stature, and had a crew cut, and what there was of his hair was red, or possibly titian.

Bill had been the Project Manager at the building of the Colgate factory in Manila, so he and Pablo were old colleagues and certainly did get on very well together. On hearing Tubby was from the UK company, Bill related his journey home with his wife and two children after finishing their two years in Manila, when they stopped in London on the way through and were put up for a night in none less than the Savoy Hotel. In the morning, before he and his wife realised what was happening, the two children had run along ahead into the great palatial dining room. The very superior head waiter was there in his penguin suit to greet people, only to be addressed by the two children as 'Boy', which was natural to them from living in the Far East. Bill and his wife wished that the floor would open up and swallow them and accepted his response when the head waiter escorted them to a table in a corner with a screen round it to isolate them from the other guests at breakfast.

425

Bill was fascinating to listen to, since he had been involved in manufacturing operations and the building of factories in very many locations, particularly down into the Latin American countries. He got going with Jim Kevlin once about a particular Vice President in the southern hemisphere, who was a Latino, with the name of Rabazza. He had such a notorious reputation that Tubby had heard of him and indeed nearly made contact in London once. Abe le Roux related how Rabazza had reached South Africa once and on the long road journey from Johannesburg down towards Durban with the bosses of the South African subsidiary, Rabazza had suddenly shouted in a loud voice for the car to be stopped since he wished to 'squeeze his lemon'.

In Argentina and Brazil and other places in South America, he had favoured rooms in hotels, and would go to great lengths to have others thrown out if he arrived and found his special room was occupied. Bill related that at breakfast Rabazza had once asked the waiter if the half-grapefruit in front of him was the bottom half. When the waiter wavered with uncertainty, it was demanded that he take the half-grapefruit back and return with a half grapefruit which was assured to be the bottom half, since that would have more juice in it than the top half. On another occasion, in another well-appointed establishment in Rio, Rabazza had asked for a glass of milk which was duly brought. He then announced that he wanted it hot and it was taken away and brought back again only to be asked if it was boiling. The glass of milk was then taken away and brought back by the waiter wearing a pair of asbestos gloves to place the bubbling glass of milk in front of Vice-President Rabazza. By this time Bill said it was already quite embarrassing enough, with the attention of other guests and waiters riveted on this man who was going to drink boiling milk, when he looked round belligerently, and said in a loud voice, 'I wait till it cool.' It was quite a natural precaution in these places to ask for drinks to be boiled for one's own health safety, but it was the wonderful Latino way in which Rabazza went about ensuring this fairly straightforward precaution, which sparked off the other Latin temperaments into frenzied responses in voluble Portugese.

With Jim thinking very much about his hoped-for departure at the beginning of July, he was very keen to use the visit of Bill van Nostrand with Pablo to move things on as much as possible on Colgate Palmolive (Far East) Limited and the toothpaste factory. Tubby was only too glad to leave them to it so that he could get his work up-to-date before his departure to Saigon.

He began to get concerned when the only responses to his letters to Monsieur Vattaire in Phnom-Penh were cables from un-named persons at the agent which said, 'Don't come.' Tubby had been thrilled to find out that the best flights to get him to Saigon were on Pan-Am's old Boeing Strato Cruiser planes, on which Rita and Jim's kids came out from USA across the Pacific and down from Saigon to Singapore. These were the bulbous four-engined petrol planes adapted from the war-time bomber, with the downstairs lounge and spiral staircase connecting with upstairs, still being used because Djakarta Airport had not yet been equipped to take the new jets. With the negatives coming out of Phnom-Penh, he asked Pan-Am about hotels when he was making his 1st May flight booking, and they were able to book him into Hotel Majestic in Saigon and another hotel in Phnom-Penh, as well as on a flight with Royal Cambodge Airline from Saigon.

When the day for departure came he had to rush to KL Airport with about 20 minutes to spare for the 8 a.m. flight down to Singapore, only to find that, due to uncompleted work, it was three seats short and he had to wait around until the 11 a.m. flight. This meant that he had just three-quarters of an hour to get to the Cricket Club in Singapore to pick up some cine-films he had organised to be there for him, and then out to Singapore airport, which somehow he managed to do.

Once on the huge great Pan-Am Strato Cruiser with the blue on white livery, he was amazed at the space, and sat himself down to read the copious literature about Pan-Am's being the most experienced airline in the world, as the huge plane lumbered away down the runway and up into one of those great storms again, as it crossed the Causeway with the four engines at full pitch. After reading all about the experience of this famous airline, he went for a walk about and down the stairs to the lounge. He noticed that the back view of the captain and co-pilot up front confirmed the point about experience, since both had balding patches at the back and greying temples, which was not unexpected since these lovely old planes were soon going to be stood down, hence no likelihood of younger pilots being trained up to fly them. While still musing about the apparent age of the guys up-front flying this big plane, he had his first confrontation with the Purser. This was a term he had not come across before on aeroplanes and apparently the person in charge of the cabin crew on Pan-Am was known as the Purser. On this flight they were 'privileged' to have the only female Purser in the Pan-Am fleet, and she was a battle-axe. She was like one of those elderly female army sergeants in the American TV comedy series *Sergeant Bilko*, since her blue Pan-Am jacket was adorned with silver bars down the sleeves from above the elbow, denoting her long years of service in the fleet.

Her pet hate seemed to be passengers, and before long several started running battles as she seemed hell-bent on not letting anyone have the free drinks. Tubby got in an absolute panic when the call came out about the approach to Saigon, since it was requested that passports be ready for dropping into a bag which would come round, to facilitate clearance once they were grounded. Tubby had suddenly realised that, in his panic at KL airport, he had somehow left his passport within his baggage at Singapore which was in the luggage compartment, and he was filled with dread with the prospect of explaining to this female dragon of a Purser that his passport was not readily available.

With all the military activity across Vietnam, the regulations for Saigon airport were that civilian planes would fly in at 1000 feet, and with Saigon being some 40 miles in, the flight across the delta took quite a while. It was amazing and a bit hairy to look down out of the window at the paddy fields and walkways of the delta growing areas, and wonder if someone down there with anti-American feelings might have an ground-to-air missile launcher to hand, or just take a shot at such bulk flying at below 1000 feet.

With all the problems of arranging his flight at Pan-Am, and with their booking the onward flight on Royal Cambodge Airlines to Phnom-Penh, he was quite taken aback to be met at Saigon airport by none other than Monsieur Vattaire himself. Without any explanation he announced imperiously that he was now *Directeur* in Saigon as of the week before. Tubby was left at the Hotel Majestic on the waterfront to be picked up later, which gave him a little time to explore on his own. The Hotel Majestic was well placed on the river front and from his verandah, some five floors up, he had a magnificent view out across the river and the flat delta area disappearing into the distance. It was incredible just to see the funnels and masts and top decks of ocean-going ships above the green of the delta, as they wended their way up through the twists and turns of the waterways to anchor just across in the wide loop from the hotel. The flow of the river was used to turn the boats round for facing out to sea again, having anchored the sterns against the wharf where they were to unload.

It was a strange feeling to hear the noise of planes and the odd gunfire in the distance, and look down on the streets with their daytime normality as the ladies seemed to float along in their beautiful *ao dai*. Saigon was indeed the Paris of the east, with beautiful boulevards and a Roman Catholic cathedral in the centre. It was here that Tubby was able to ask for the car to be stopped to catch with his cine-camera a beautiful shot of a lady in her flowing *ao dai* strolling in the dappled sunshine amongst the trees by the cathedral.

The traffic was quite chaotic with numerous motor-driven pedi-cabs, legions of little blue and white Renault taxis, and the traffic police in white on their raised island stands in the middle of the road junctions. With the other side of the river and certain areas being Vietcong territory by night, he took the opportunity in late siesta time to walk out of the hotel and down the front to the piers and then up by the bridges across the Rach Ben Nghe Canal, which linked the river with the vast Cho Lon Chinese District with its huge pagodas, temples and vast warren-like market areas.

The Noel Coward song about 'Mad Dogs and Englishmen'

rang in his ears as he walked through Tu Do Street past people stretched out asleep under the trees with their plate-like hats over their faces for shade. The only activity he came across for filming were two pedi-cab men on their haunches with their topee hats on, using lunchtime siesta time for playing noughts and crosses, with chalk on the little squares of the sidewalk pavings, which were ideal for this passtime. A little further on he found himself facing the Continental Palace bar, and realised he was in the square where, in the early 1950s, a massive car bomb had exploded, causing such carnage that what had been a covert CIA operation became world news, and the Vietnam saga really started. It reminded Tubby to be alert because any passing cyclist could be a potential grenade thrower, since one had been tossed into the doorway of the residence of a USOM expert recently, inflicting unpleasant injuries.

There were anti-communist slogans posted prominently, and while Saigon and Vietnam as a whole were in a peculiar lull period with President Ngo Dinh Diem and his archbishop brother Ngo Dinh Thuc propped up by the Americans, visitors were advised not to travel too far out of Saigon, even in daytime. Therefore, Tubby's business activities were confined to visits with Monsieur Vattaire to prominent Chinese dealers whom he considered worthy of his attentions. From one of these Tubby did pick up some information with regard to a local entrepreneur who had a West German engineer in town who was from a manufacturer of machinery for producing toothpaste. He wondered if George Lesch had picked up the same sort of information, and his visit here was to come back to New York with an opinion as to long term prospects, since any local manufacture would need a long period of ongoing stability to recoup the financing.

He noticed that the Chinese *towkays* on Monsieur Vattaire's visiting list were all very patrician and wore old French colonial style tunics, and the one they were visiting just before lunch had a prominent picture of anti-Communist Chinese General Chiang Kai Shek on the wall of his office and reception area. Within the anti-Communist climate prevailing in Saigon, it was abundantly sensible to demonstrate in every way possible that you were not a Communist. As they went off for lunch the elderly *towkey* put on his colonial topee against the rigours of the sun. The superb lunch confirmed that amongst the Chinese, wherever in the Far East, one common factor is their excellent food, and the shark's fin soup, to which he had become addicted, was as good as ever, as was the rest of the meal.

In the evening he was in his best suit since Monsieur Vattaire was inclined to dine in a small but very chic French restaurant at which he must have had something going, judging by the attentions of Madame. When she was out of earshot Monsieur Vattaire explained in low tones that unfortunately her husband was the proprietor, but he was so idle and something of a wheeler-dealer. Then, throwing back his hands up and outwardly in a gesture of despair, he said to Tubby, '*Il est Corse.*' To those who knew anything about the French, the fact that he was from the island of Corsica explained everything. This was always an amusing paradox to Tubby, since the celebrated Napoleon Bonaparte was himself a little man from the island of Corsica. It was possible that the same thing could be said about the Germans, since Adolf Hitler was a little house painter from Austria.

Tubby had noticed that the American 'round-the-world-sight-see' types were in good number in the Hotel Majestic. Apparently, in this relatively quiet phase in the Vietnam cycle, and in spite of nasty things that might happen out and about in the country, Saigon was considered all clear for a stop-over from which they could fly direct to the north of Cambodia for a landing at Siemréap, which had the well appointed Grand Hotel d'Angkor for the many visitors to the world-famous ruins and temples at Angkor-Wat. After doing Angkor they could then board the plane to Bangkok where the Yankee dollar was supreme, and all was well and truly safe from the big bad Communist bogeymen in Phnom-Penh.

Even at the airport to see him off, Monsieur Vattaire, George Lesch's named speaker of English who was to have been in Phnom-Penh, had not really given a valid explanation as to why Tubby had been receiving cables to stay away. His manner was almost aristocratic in his disdain of commerce and having to work for a living, and Tubby noted that his business card indicated that he was a *Directeur* of the Companie Technique et Commerciale, and the 'Cambodge' had been crossed out in ink and 'Vietnam' written in, as was his new address in Saigon instead of Phnom-Penh. Though he did not say it directly, he indicated that Robert Guerin and his number two were certainly not of the same status as he, and he mumbled something about Monsieur Bouet, the number two, having been a legionnaire.

It was getting on in the afternoon when Tubby walked out to the green and gold DC3 Dakota of Royal Cambodge Airlines which had been sitting on the tarmac in the direct sun since it arrived in the morning. Thankfully he was in his usual bush shirt with his sweat towel round his neck, since the plane was like a humid oven. Most of the American tourists he had seen in the Hotel Majestic seemed to be there, so he had made a dive to get on quickly and got placed up front at a window seat while the horde of ancient and not very presentable American widows were herded on board by their tour leader, who had a big round badge on his lapel denoting that he was, indeed, the tour leader. His voice boomed above everything else, probably because most of his flock were deaf anyway, and on what they regarded as the most dangerous part of their overseas trip across the Pacific seeing the sights. These women were probably spending the vast amounts of money their husbands had made dying in the attempt, but the other passenger who flopped down in the seat beside Tubby turned out to be an exception, he was a male in his fifties. He was immediately complaining about the suffocating state of the cabin and the pile of his wife's clothes he had on top of him, to prevent them being crushed in the bag, did not help. Soon Tubby was aware of the abrasive American voice of his wife in the seat across the aisle, confirming that he was Mr Henpecked indeed. Every seat was occupied when the Dakota trundled down the runway and got airborne with a bit of a struggle, and with the usual flow of air which manages to come in through various holes and cracks in Dakotas the

432

passenger cabin soon began to cool down to a reasonable temperature.

Tubby spent the first half hour simply taking in the incredible scenes down below as they gained height over endless cultivated areas of this extremely fertile delta area which meant that shortage of food was never a problem in this part of the world, except as the results of war and fighting and insurrections. It was the end of the dry season, and between them and the ground were the first signs of the monsoons to come down from the high Himalayas, in the form of white clouds scurrying along almost in an opposite direction to the plane, which doubled their rate of passing. For the rest of the journey Tubby got to turning over in his mind all the background details he had tried to pull together on the country of Cambodia.

Following the final breakdown of the great French Far East territories of Indochina from 1953, Cambodia had developed into a kind of buffer state between Thailand and the Communist insurgents in Laos and North Vietnam, who were rapidly infiltrating down and round South Vietnam like the arc of a great sickle. Even as late as October 1964, Cambodia was referred to as Indochina's 'neutral' corner, and without doubt this was because of the mercurial Prince Sihanouk who was of the Royal line, restored in 1949 at age of 19 into this French protectorate, a remnant of the Khmer empire which at its zenith in the twelfth and thirteenth centuries reached from Burma to the South China Sea.

The prince was a great one for the dramatic gesture, going into exile and coming back, supposedly renouncing his position as royal ruler in the mid-1950s to be involved in politics. He ran the country balanced slightly to left of centre by which means he played off Russia, China, France and America, to benefit from great projects such as the new sea port called Sihanoukville on the south of Chhung Kompong Som Bay, which in turn was served by a railway line and a new big motor highway from Phnom-Penh to Kampot and on to the port. Each was supplied by one of the major powers in the East/ West stand-off situation prevailing in the world at that time. In the name of the United Nations (goodness knows who was financing) a great project was underway to dam and harness the great lake – Tonle-Sap – dominating the centre of Cambodia by increasing its size enormously in the wet season. At these times the volume of water was such that the river flowing in from the north would flow out again and to the south, and the great Mekong River would come up some 30 feet. On the food side it provided more fish than the country of 6 million people could eat, and the water from it ensured vast growing regions for paddy as well as the great rubber plantations established by the French, who after being defeated at Dien Bien Phu were all living happily as before, managing the estates and much of local industry.

With the prince's balancing act being left of the centre, this was certainly regarded as Communist country compared with the hyper anti-Communist situation in South Vietnam. As Tubby sat on the plane he wondered just how on earth he was going to get on in this country, which as far as the Americans were concerned was Communist, and where he was to deal with two long-established Indochina hands speaking only colonial French.

As the engines were throttled back for descent and touchdown, the American designation of Cambodia as Communist territory compared with Saigon and Bangkok was emphatically reinforced by the voice of the tour leader. As the door of the Dakota opened for passengers to disembark at Phnom-Penh airport, the tour leader announced in a very loud and threatening voice that nobody, but nobody, belonging to his tour party was to step out of the plane here. They were to stay seated exactly where they were. There were only two other commercials out of the full passenger complement besides Tubby to disembark at this capital of Cambodia and, being up front, he had the furthest walk down the long sloping passageway between the two rows of seats on either side as the looks on all the faces said quite clearly, 'Commie sympathiser!'

After all the cables warning him not to come and having had no inkling from Vattaire as to what Guerin and Bouet might be like, Tubby was glad there were only two other passengers ahead. Hopefully they would make contact with whoever had

434

come for them which would leave someone else with an expectant look in his direction. As it turned out there were two left looking for him, being the last of the three to cross the tarmac. One was a quite large, untidy figure with fair crew-cut hair, a bit longer at the front, with a little fair moustache and a semblance of what might pass as a tiny front beard which helped to cover a slight impediment of his bottom lip and speech. This, thought Tubby, must be the number two, and indeed it was, Bouet the ex-legionnaire, who did indeed look as though he could tell of many bloody experiences from Dien Bien Phu and years in Indochina. The meeting was very low key and he was introduced to the other chap, a Vietnamese Chinese who, though casually dressed, was certainly more smooth and sophisticated than Bouet. Tubby gathered that his name was Cheng, and the word *compradore* was all that Tubby could grasp.

The airport was miles from town and Tubby was glad that they were in a small CV2 with the canvas half back top, since the road was potholes most of the way and this vehicle was built for that sort of thing. Tubby was given the back seat with his luggage. Cheng drove the car, and Bouet spread himself over the seat with one arm over the back so that he could give Tubby a look over and make any exchanges that might be forthcoming. He was quite glad when they reached paved roads on entering the edge of Phnom-Penh, which appeared to be very well appointed, clean and with abundant evidence of the French colonial past. Towards the centre of this capital city of Cambodia, they came out of a tree-lined boulevard into a resplendent section of road with a great wall on one side, above which Tubby could see the magnificent pointed roofs of a temple-like building, and he was informed that this was the Royal Palace compound.

Within walking distance of this they turned into the grounds of the hotel, which appeared to have been adapted from a two-storey well-appointed colonial house. The boisterous entry of Bouet brought a similar response from all and sundry, and he was obviously on very good terms with the mistress of the establishment who happened to be at the reception as they swept in. Madame was very well turned-out and probably towards her late forties with that rather weathered, sunburnt look colonials develop after many years of living in these parts of the Far East. Tubby was handed a pen for entering his details in the hotel book which had been turned round to face him, and by the look on Madame's face as she glanced slightly past Tubby's head, he suspected that Bouet was making some sort of gesture behind him.

The lack of conversation on the journey in from the airport was understandable considering the language problem, though Tubby had made an effort with his dictionary to hand for certain tested greetings. But over and above that there was another indefinable barrier between them – not hostility but certainly a kind of stand-off situation. As Tubby bent over to fill in his details in the register, he was aware that the heads of Cheng on one side and Bouet on the other were strained for a better look over his shoulder as finally he completed the last column by putting in his nationality, which of course was British. As he straightened up he was taken aback by Bouet turning him around and almost shouting '*non Américain.*' He had a very puzzled yet expectant look on his face, and Tubby, remembering his Scottish parentage and the Auld Alliance from the days of Bonnie Prince Charlie replied '*Ecosse, c'est moi!*' Bouet gripped him by both shoulders beaming all over his face and shouted, '*Ecosse et Français – tres bien – alors!*' Tubby then felt he was being presented with the legion of honour because Bouet proceeded to give him a great embrace with a kiss towards each ear. With arms flung up and wide, he turned to Cheng, Madame and anybody who happened to be nearby, and in voluble French repeated: '*Ecosse et Français.*' This was the real hyper-manic Bouet, and from then on the whole trip became quite fantastic and wild.

It is always amazing what can be dragged up from the recesses of the mind, particularly in a language situation such as this as Bouet, his little bottom lip quivering, launched into a great exhortation to him, the gist of which was that if he was to go on up into Laos and Vientiane he was to put a prominent Union Jack on his chest and on the middle of his back, because

Americans – and he drew his hand across his throat to signify what happenned to them. He went on in some detail to tell of a Dutchman who recently had been mistaken for an American, and had ended up with his throat cut. It all became clear now to Tubby as to why George Lesch had asked him to go up for a personal look at Vietnam and Cambodia for New York.

This lovable big ex-legionnaire survivor of the final colonial battle of Dien Bien Phu had decided that he was going to look after Tubby, '*Mon ami Ecossais*' as he became. When they entered the office of Compagnie Technique et Commerciale du Cambodge, at number 18 Boulevard Preah Bat Norodom, Bouet walked him straight into the office of Robert Guerin, with his arm round his shoulder, shouting the great news that he was 'Non Américain.'

As part of Prince Sihanouk's ongoing balancing act between the great powers, they were to have a visit during Tubby's stay from no less than Chou En-Lai, the Prime Minister of Communist China, that great man who managed to keep the economics of China going somehow in the face of the grand gestures of Chairman Mao, the excesses of the Red Guards and the great staged marches of legions in drab tunics, with their little red books. Ahead of his visit they had had the head of the Chinese secret police in Phnom-Penh and elsewhere checking out all the places Chou would be visiting and staying, so the reasons were obvious for all the cables telling Tubby the Yank in Kuala Lumpur to stay away! However, he was here now, he was *Ecossais*, therefore a friend, and they were going to help him as much as they could. Bouet and Robert Guerin had really no English at all and Cheng, the Chinese *compradore*, educated in Paris, had about as much English as Tubby had of French, so it was agreed they would all save everything up for a periodic conference, when they would get an architect friend along as interpreter, called Monsieur Pettigura, who was half-English, half-Indian and born in China. These gatherings became quite hilarious occasions.

At that time it was obvious that Phnom-Penh was a pleasant comfortable place to be in, since there weren't the stresses of Vietnam and Laos, and there was still a lot of money to be made from all the big projects Prince Sihanouk was bringing in from all of the major world powers through his 'neutrality'. As in most colonial places of the world when they break up, there is a state of anarchy when numerous international wheeler-dealers come in and make lots of money, and when taken out dining in the evenings to the 'right places' in this clean and happy-go-lucky city, Tubby noticed there was a high incidence of these very smooth-tongued, urbane, confident, dubious background people about like Monsieur Pettigura, the multilingual 'architect'. The French have a much less uptight attitude once their former colonies have broken up, and so they were still very much running things in this place, the commercial areas and out in the estates. The land was fertile and the climate pleasant, though the rainy season was about to start in the next month of June and likely to continue for five months. With the entrenched French habit of the siesta, evenings out wining and dining in the pleasant warmth of the climate would get going quite late and were a very leisurely experience.

There were to be public holidays during Tubby's stay, and on one of these Bouet said he would drive him down the new dual highway, financed by one of the great powers, to the great new port laid on by the Chinese called Sihanoukville. For Tubby's business trip up country for several days it was agreed that Cheng would accompany him in a car with a driver for a two night stay at Siemréap, at the Grand Hotel D'Angkor.

Before setting off, Tubby wanted to call on the British Embassy for a session with the commercial secretary, and with Colgate using the Hong Kong Shanghai Bank in Malaya and Hong Kong, he had an appointment with Blair Allan at the branch in Phnom-Penh. Additionally, one of the chaps from the Singapore Cricket Club was now here with the Chartered Bank, and Tubby had been asked by friends of others here in Phnom-Penh to look him up. He was able to make contact at quarters provided by the bank for the young, single males, which, as in Singapore, they referred to as the mess. Later they went out for a night on the town, but at the end of it Tubby was somewhat taken aback by the general attitude they seemed to share about being stuck in this awful place, and counting the days before they could move on. He could not help feeling that it was really a splendid opportunity for a young person to come away from a spell in this place bilingual in French and English, albeit possibly colonial and Legionnaire French. It would be another major European and extensively-used language with any overtones or the peculiarities picked up from the colonial and Legionnaire influences giving their French a certain kudos.

Normally the fabulous royal compound of incredible buildings which he had passed on the way to the hotel was open to the public. However, he had noticed as they passed the entrance that instead of the national flag being on the flag posts, there were long trailing white cloths which moved in the light wind, resembling cut-outs of great white fish. Tubby was informed that these were funereal, or mourning, hangings since a distant aunt of the prince had died and the palace was in mourning, so the grounds were not open to the public. Having seen Tubby's cine-camera, and since the ebullient Bouet seemed to be known everywhere they went, and particularly among the various 'fixers' they met up with day to day in commerce or at evening meals, he put out hints that it would be wonderful if entry into the compound could be 'fixed' for some filming one morning.

The hotel was very friendly and very charming, but poor Tubby found the breakfast a bit of a trial, and even when he asked for his eggs to be cooked for twice the normal time they still arrived on his plate in a transparent form. He found the answer one morning when Bouet bounced in to have breakfast with him while telling with great gestures how he had arranged for Tubby to get inside the royal compound after all. Tubby watched, fascinated, as he broke off pieces of his French roll and used them as a sort of scoop to transmit his transparent egg mix into his mouth.

With a black tie on out of respect, Tubby had a fascinating hour or so, moving round the immaculately manicured and gardened royal compound, from the ornate Royal Ballet building, to the reception halls and the fabulous Preah Morokot Pagoda with the four faces high up on the spire and the great and beautiful pink steps up, edged with balustrades rounded with ornate snake heads, which he was to see again among ruins at Angkor. Further on there was the Veal Men, or Royal Plain for the National Congress, with the format of meeting twice a year, and finally the beautiful royal residence beyond with its saffron roof, like all the others immaculate in the sunlight.

The officially published 1957 *Year Book* for Sarawak had been invaluable for his business trip up through the Borneo Territories. Here it was through his visit to the British Embassy, with the help of Terry Empson, second commercial secretary, that he was able to put together a solid grounding of statistics on Cambodia for his final report. Blair Allan at the Hong Kong Shanghai Bank had also been useful with statistics and a list of things to look out for in the up-country situation as he was to drive to the east of the Great Lake of Tonle Sap.

Their early start from Phnom-Penh with Cheng and the driver meant that they reached Kompong Cham for the ferry crossing over the Great Mekong River while there was still some semblance of morning freshness in the bright sunshine. This was the area of the great Chup rubber plantation established by the French, and it was extremely dry and dusty, almost like Baghdad, being the end of the dry season, and the level of the Mekong River was very far down. The place they took breakfast in, near the ferry, was pretty grubby and Tubby did not feel inclined to have much in the way of food. As the Khmer driver placed the car in the queue on the slope down to the ferry, he took a walk on the road which came up from the border with South Vietnam, some ten miles or so away. When he had studied the maps before coming, he thought it might be possible to drive from Saigon through into Cambodia, but when he met the real situation of Saigon and the killings going on not far out into the delta area and beyond, it was out of the question, and indeed Monsieur Vattaire in Saigon had thrown up his hands in horror at the thought of anyone having such an idea.

When he came back to join Cheng at the car, most of the other car occupants were talking in groups squatting down on their haunches having a smoke, or a bowl of something from the various stalls, their arms extended beyond their bent up knees, as was the custom throughout the east. Tubby had found from his many experiences of being out and about with salesmen, the Miss FAB promotion teams and the black man he had in Baghdad demonstrating the FAB detergent, that mirth and laughter was one of the easiest and simplest ways of establishing some sort of contact, then communication. He found that settling down into the same knee squat position as the locals would immediately create smiles and start comments going amongst the various others. Because of his bulky body, he found that he carefully surveyed in advance where there might be a slight pavement edge or a stone that he could settle his heels on to ensure that he didn't make a complete fool of himself by falling over backwards. Their Khmer driver did not quite know what to do about this, or what to make of it, and had a bemused look on his face, but Cheng joined Tubby in the squat. He wished for his kilt in the Forbes tartan to stimulate further on-going exchanges and banter with the others, since Tubby was aware that it was being explained that he was certainly not American, nor French, but Ecossais, and he endeavoured to make the right sort of gestures and responses with smiles and nods while asking questions back through Cheng. As ever in these situations, he wondered how much we had lost with our materialism and 'developed' way of life, totally detached from the rhythms of nature for our needs. There seemed to be a freeness and openness about these peoples of the east, related to an anchor point of some in-built form of philosophy because of their total dependence on what the land produced – watered by monsoons in their season.

Squatting and having great fun passing the time as cars crept down with each ferry crossing he could never have imagined that this place of Kompong Cham would be visited with such death and destruction in years to come as the Vietnamese would advance up this road as their armies had done many centuries ago for the destruction of the great Khmer Empire.

They hadn't been going very long on the road when the pain started in Tubby's belly, and it became obvious that something he had eaten was going give to him a short sharp attack of the upset stomach he had last experienced on his great drive in northern Iraq through the fabled walled city of Erbil of the Kurds. Every now and again he had to stop the car and dive off into the *ulu* where he would always have this ridiculous notion that, with the abundance of insects, he was being watched by thousands of eyes. He had a potion from Cheng, plus the famous Tiger Balm from Singapore's famous Chinese medicine establishment applied liberally. Whether it was his faith in this magic Chinese balm or Cheng's potion, he was certainly on the mend by the time they drove into Siem Riap in the late afternoon and checked into the well-appointed French colonial hotel – the Grand Hotel D'Angkor. This was the place where the Americans were allowed to come, such as those on the plane from which Tubby had disembarked in Phnom-Penh, and certainly they were very much in evidence in the hotel as he signed the register with Cheng, the Chinese *compradore*.

He had intended to spend an hour or so first thing in the morning to get some cine-film footage of the fabulous ruins of Angkor, but since they had daylight still, they set off down the road as soon as they'd finished checking-in. They had soon covered the five miles, and stopped entranced, at the sight of the incredible towers at each corner and the one large towering centre-piece of this impressive *wat*, with its array of outer buildings for the Buddhist monks. The Angkor Wat building is but one dramatic element in a vast area of ruins across several square miles of what was the capital city of the great kingdom and empire of Kambuja.

When they had arrived from Siem Riap it had become totally overcast with a low cloud layer, therefore the stonework looked rather dull as they drove on to turn at right angles north to what was the main gateway to the temple and the great causeway across the outer moat, with another causeway to the great towered temple itself. With it being the end of the dry season, these moats were not filled up with water which would make the scene even more spectacular. About a mile down the road towards main city, the fantastic Angkor Thom, there was a ziggurat type ruin sticking out of the jungle trees, very similar to the pyramid-like buildings to be seen in Mexico and in Ur, Lower Iraq, from where Abraham first set out. While much clearing has been done over the century since Henri Mouhot, the French naturalist, came across this place 'more fabulous than the ruins of Ancient Greece', the view from this high ruin, called Phnom Bakheng, gave one a feeling of what it must have been like at the discovery, with just the high parts of the building showing above the great jungle canopy.

Having gained this feel of the place for the next morning, they set off back along the road, past the gateway of Angkor Wat itself, when miraculously the descending sun broke clear of the low shroud of clouds and the whole magnificent temple turned gold in the horizontal light from the setting sun. Even the occasional tall cabbage palms were burnished gold, and Tubby ran from the car like someone demented to get this incredible sight on film, since it was likely to last for only a few minutes. After getting a shot with the full area across the two causeways he ran as fast as he could along the first outer causeway and moat to capture this magnificent spectacle of burnished gold through the archway of the next gate. It was almost dark when they got back to the hotel, and he hoped he had managed to get a decent record of this most incredible and fortunate display of Angkor Wat bathed in gold light, so that it appeared to be gold plated.

As he showered and got dressed to go down for a drink and meal he could not believe how the dreaded upset belly had subsided, and began to believe like millions of others through-out the Far East, who can't be wrong, that Tiger Balm can cure an attack of the runs even by being applied externally. Or was it Cheng's potion?

The Grand Hotel was wonderfully French colonial, with a large ground floor area in from the reception to a long bar with tables and chairs and walled seats across the floor, and the high ceiling had slowly turning fans to circulate the air. The Yanks were everywhere, and Tubby sat near to a table of particularly ancient looking female tourists with one fifty-year-old man in blazer and slacks, which wasn't exactly the usual American tourist attire – even when down for drinks before dinner. While in his fifties, he still looked positively young compared with his companions round the table, and having heard that Tubby was neither French nor exactly American, he was called upon to join them at their table to close the ranks as it were.

With great enthusiasm the American explained that he and Mom were fulfilling a lifetime ambition, in that Mom wanted to see Angkor before she died, and here he was bringing his Mom to the very place. However, the conversation soon changed and turned to the fact that this was 'Commie country', though it was wonderful how they could fly into this place, see the fabulous ruins and then be safely off to Bangkok without being contaminated.

After looking round the other dear ladies at the table, as though for assurance, he leaned over very earnestly and confidentially to Tubby and said through his teeth, 'Do you know who's come into Phnom-Penh today?' Then with a quick look round the others again to see if there were any other Yanks within hearing, he leaned forward again and said very menacingly, 'Chou en Lai from China.' The American then leaned back and kind of shuddered, and showed his pleasure at being more than 200 miles away. Tubby could see above his head in a sort of cloud, a picture of this little chain-smoking man from China in his Mao tunic, with the devil's horns coming out of his head and a red-pointed tail, and a three-pronged fork in his hand, so he had to bury himself in his glass to hide his mirth. Alas, his perverse sense of humour once again came to the fore, and he lowered his glass and in a very deadpan best English voice threw in: 'I believe so, and I am travelling back to Phnom-Penh with my Chinese *compradore* tomorrow.' When what he had said had sunk in, a shudder went through the ranks, so he thought he had better not add that he was here as an employee of the good old USA company which gave them their famous and finest toothpaste. They would have probably reacted by getting rid of any shares in Colgate on returning home, but their immediate reaction to Tubby's stated intention to return to Phnom-Penh with big boss from Communist China was to start edging away, so that there was a visible gap between himself and them. No longer could it be

444

seen that he was part of their party and drinking with them, and he thought they were going to stampede when Cheng finally came down and sat with him for a drink.

The next morning was brilliantly sunny when Tubby woke up early, as was his usual habit. He went and stood at the lovely big open window high up in the building, taking in the scene of Siem Riap coming to life, and this was literally the case for a group of taxi men with their vehicles bunched under a huge tree across from the hotel. Instead of the three-wheeled pedi-cabs he had seen in Phnom-Penh and Saigon, with the seat for two passengers out front, the pedal taxi men of Siem Riap had a thing which resembled a domestic bath tub on two wheels, hooked by a bar just behind the saddle on a normal two wheel bicycle. Passengers would recline in the bathtub while being towed around to their destination. As Tubby observed the circle of bicycles, he realised that their two wheel bath tubs were the night rest for the taxi men to sleep in, and it looked so funny to see feet sticking out at one end and a head out of the other, and then a pair of arms would appear as they stretched, before they sat up rubbing their eyes prior to going off for something to sustain them during the day.

After an early breakfast and signing out, they shot off down the road again to Angkor, and already the sun was high and getting very hot as though wishing to parch the earth before the imminent rainy season. In the high sun the stones had a totally different appearance from the evening before; however, the intense downward light did show up the incredible carvings. How spectacular it would be to see this whole fantastic area with all the reservoirs and moats filled with water. Nevertheless, from high up in the great central tower of the Wat it was a spectacular vista through the delicate stone tracery from the high openings, or windows, and Tubby could see the other incredible buildings which made up this capital city of the great empire that was.

They drove on again passed the high ziggurat of Phnom Bakheng which they had climbed the night before, and entered the great city of Angkor Thom through the south gate under the triple-towered carvings of large faces, which paled into insignificance when they came on the multiple towers of the Bayon. Each of the four-sided towers had enormous carved faces with inscrutable oriental calmness, as reflected on a small scale on the high spire of the temple in the royal palace in Phnom-Penh.

Beyond the Bayon was the royal palace, and the main gateway was flanked on either side by rows of huge carved warriors behind one another as though engaged in a great tug of war, with the 'rope' being a continuous stone balustrade ending in the form of a great snake-head carving. All over the stonework were incredible carvings of battle scenes done to very high standard and detail, whereas Preah Khàn, the next building with a moat beyond Angkor Thom city, was almost Grecian in its style, with pillars and numerous free-standing carved stone figures.

A car was certainly necessary to cover the vastness of this place in the time available, and the next turn-off was to Neak Pean which was the pool for cooling off in the heat of the day. It was almost the size of a dry dock for repairing ships back home, with terraced-in steps at the sides for the bathers to sit around on or down which to descend leisurely into the waters, which alas were not there.

The two places further on which were most impressive were Ta Som and Ta Prohm, because these buildings were still twined in vines, banyans and huge silk-cotton trees grown right up through the buildings over the centuries. This was how the vast array of buildings were found by Henri Mouhot before the clearing and restoration started on the other buildings allowed them to be seen in their full glory. Ta Som had a particular stillness and timelessness about it, with the high canopy above supported by the huge white barked silk-cotton trees resembling rockets standing on tail vanes. Into the strange stillness of this shaded scene came a boy with his family's few head of cattle, making a distinctive clacking noise from their peculiarly small cattle bells which were actually carved from bone or horn. The young lad carried spares to sell to tourists and Tubby bought one since he always tried to take some small special object away with him from these incredible places he had been so fortunate to visit.

As they drove back up the road to Siem Riap to get on with the business part of the visit to these northern regions, Tubby could not help comparing the architecture with the incredible areas of ruins he had been fortunate to see in Ceylon; these were certainly more spectacular.

Siem Reap was certainly a thriving, bustling place with good business structures through to all levels of the trade. The bustling market-places for produce confirmed yet again that the people of this land did not have problems with regard to hunger. Fertile land, irrigated by the presence of the great Tonle-Sap Lake, dominated the western half, while the great Mekong River and its tributaries irrigated the eastern side of Cambodia. Add to the crops the great source of fish, and it was not difficult to understand why these people seemed to be so easy-going, particularly when compared with what was going on in Laos to the north, and Vietnam to the east and south. Prince Sihanouk was sustaining a very clever balancing act betwixt the great powers, and it was a matter of how long he could keep this up.

On the return journey south, Tubby sat back in the car trying to assimilate all he had seen against other great wonders about the world. His mind's eye brought up the beautiful, vertical stone traceries in the openings at each level in Giotto's fabulous bell tower in Florence, since they were almost identical to the vertical stone supports of the openings in the walls of the great tower of Angkor Wat. The great development in the high period of the fabulous buildings of the Khmer empire had almost paralleled the incredible Renaissance in the same years in Italy. Indeed, many of the great surges of progress in mankind's history had been almost global, without modern means of communication. The period around 3,000 B.C. had seen great developments in the Indus Valley, Egypt and in Mesopotamia – all with waters from great rivers. Later there were the surges of development to a high point in Greece in about 500 B.C., with similar things happening in Peru, and Central America. However, there were the awful slaughters and convulsions such as the Hyksos swarming into Egypt to the Valley of the Kings, while the Greeks descended from the high points of Socrates and Plato to become the slaves of Rome.

In Russia, the convulsions of Communism resulted in over 8 million dead even before the second German invasion to the gates of Moscow, as far as Bonaparte had reached, too. Even that dynamic race of Europe – the Spaniards – had their appalling 'killing fields' experience of the Civil War in the 1930s, then sat out the all-consuming horror of World War Two throughout Europe while cities and societies were devastated.

In the years to come, the little cow bell bought from the lad with his cattle in the shade at Ta Som was to become a touch point with the freedom of movement, and the contact with the people up and down this country in May 1960, when later Tubby tried to come to terms with the phenomenon of the 'killing fields' which came to pass in this most pleasant land. Was it the result of the input of the totally alien culture of Communism which had already resulted in deaths of millions from famine and killings in Russia?

Back in Phnom-Penh, the presence of Chou en Lai from Communist China certainly heightened the atmosphere, if only in terms of higher police presence on the streets and awareness of the military being about in the wings and on the alert. Driving back late, tired and in the dark didn't help either. The next day in the office they had one of their hilarious conferences with Monsieur Pettigura as central interpreter to go over impressions of the interior, with Cheng throwing in his comments too. As *compradore* – the in-house 'Mr Fix-it', he had found the occasion of the trip with Tubby to be most helpful in terms of maintaining relationships with the agencies' activities up-country, no doubt establishing new contacts for further dealings on which he could make some percentage on the side.

A public holiday had been declared for the visit of the great man from China, and Bouet announced in great triumph that he was going to take *mon ami Ecossais* for a day out to Kampot and Sihanoukville on the coast with a meal at Le

Golfe, which sounded like the place to go to on a day off. Early the next morning Bouet blew in for a breakfast with Tubby, and soon they were bashing down the new highway the Russians or Americans had built for free, to the new great port of Sihanoukville which the Chinese had built as their gesture of friendship. Bouet was no slowcoach when he got on a big highway as good as this, and soon they were eating up the miles between the jungle and plantations to hit the sea of the Gulf of Siam at Kampot.

Between the great lake to the west of the centre and the Gulf Coast, there was the great range of the Cardamom Mountains and the Elephant Range, which was why the new highway went south and then turned north again to hit the coast at Kampot. From there on it was about another 20 miles out to the headland above Sihanoukville where they drove up to the hotel and eating place called Le Golfe, which Bouet had built up as the best place to visit. All the way down, Bouet had kept up his usual patter, with Tubby thumbing through his dictionary to keep up the conversation. As they swept into the place, with Bouet to the fore, it was obvious that he was just as well known to all and sundry here too, with many shouts of '*Ça va! Eh, bien?*' all round.

They immediately settled on to high stools at the bar and Bouet introduced him to the proprietor, who was a very frightening-looking hard-case. He just looked like the American actor Ernest Borgnine in one of his baddy roles, such as the sergeant in *From Here to Eternity* and once he was out of earshot Bouet gave the hunched shoulder blank-faced look and muttered, '*Il est Corse*' in order to explain why the proprietor looked like he did, just as Monsieur Vattaire had done in Saigon.

Indeed, looking round the gathering it seemed to Tubby that the Indochina section of the *Union Corse*, the French equivalent of the Mafia, were having a day out together at Le Golfe. Since the *Union Corse* controlled all rackets and drugs in Marseilles and beyond, it would seem natural that they had a chapter out here where the main sources of heroin were to be found in the Golden Triangle.

449

As they left and went part way down towards the car, they were suddenly enveloped in a phalanx of soldiers with rifles at the ready and there was the little man Chou en Lai himself about to walk past. Tubby couldn't get his cine-camera out quickly enough, but was soon confronted with two military on either side who indicated that he, or the cine-camera, or both, would be the subject of sharp blows from rifle butts, so he did not get his shot of the man from China.

After that, all was anti-climax and routine pulling together of all the details to go into his report. Bouet and Cheng took him back out by the potholed road to the airport in the CV2, in an atmosphere completely opposite that which had prevailed on the strained journey into Phnom-Penh on his arrival. Before he left to go off for the Royal Camboge DC3 to Saigon, he received the 'Legion of Honnaire' farewell on both cheeks. After withdrawing from the bear-hug of Bouet, he bid them *au revoir* in the fond hope that they might meet again.

450

40

THE RUN-IN TO HOME LEAVE

It was a very strange feeling coming off the Pan Am flight from Saigon at Singapore after two manic weeks in what was left of French Indochina, having been in a totally French-speaking situation with the larger than life Bouet as guardian and friend. On the DC3 flight up to Kuala Lumpur he was able to get in touch again with the outside world, with the media all worked up about Kruschev threatening America with rockets, and Princess Margaret getting married. It was nice to be back in the mess in Ampang Road, even with Malcolm, and the food of dear Bibah, their Malay Amah, acted as a balm to his inner self.

The reality of what it was going to be like over the next few months, prior to the hoped-for departure of the Kevlin family by the 2nd July and himself in September, was highlighted by the amount of work on his desk in addition to his report for New York on the trip, which he had started to some extent on the plane back. He had made a large note not to mention nearly shaking hands with Chou En Lai after the reaction of the Americans in the hotel in Siem Reap. The week he got back he went round the northern branches of Harpers to keep everything moving regarding establishment of the sales forces and the supervisors, which didn't allow much opportunity to get on with the report.

On the non-business front, the mail from dear Penelope continued the excitement towards their future nuptials with blow-by-blow accounts of the purchase of the engagement ring, as assisted by mother and sister, and pieces cut out of the *Liverpool Echo* and *Birkenhead News* with typical provincial journalist hype about the local doctor's future life in Malaya.

Poor Penelope was weaving away at the build-up of her medical experiences doing obstetrics and gynaecology at Broad Green in Liverpool and was working about the same hours as Tubby, which meant that at least both were finding time passed very quickly. With his life progressing at a hyper-manic level on two fronts it was a huge effort to keep them in balance.

On the business side, the Treasury Department of the Federation government turned down the finance deal worked out by New York for the much bigger detergent plant project on the extra five acres of purchased land and as the executives-on-the-spot Jim and Tubby couldn't help feeling a bit as though they'd 'told them so' concerning the concept of borrowing sterling and rolling up future profits in dollars. Cables were sent off to New York accordingly, but the feeling of euphoria from being proven right was balanced by the consternation at the idea of planned leave dates of the 2nd July and September being postponed. This would be particularly galling to the Kevlins since, with three kids, summer was certainly the best time to go back on leave to the States and thus avoid having to buy the kids winter clothing for a few weeks when they were in the quick growing years.

This had all happened before the end of May, and somehow he got off his report to New York as well, which enabled him to get back out in the field with a trip to Ipoh in the state of Perak. Harpers had had a change round of executives, which was usually the case when people had been off on leave and come back again, since all concerned were conscious that they must be seen to be creeping up the ladder within Harper Gilfillan by attaining more responsibility.

Before he took off again in his red sports car, they got a message that a big meeting was scheduled in New York for the 31st May, with George Lesch himself presiding for the putting together of a new finance deal for the detergent plant. Even thoughts of any local leave in the present climate had gone out of the window and after another marvellous shunt with the little MGA through the twists and turns of Slim River, he looked fondly up the road to Cameron Highlands at Tapah.

452

He did manage to turn off into the big new village at Tapah to see David Priston, whom he had met at Crusader Camp away back in 1953 down at Polzeath in Cornwall. Like Joyce and Agnes down in Kulai in Johore, the Pristons (David and Ruth plus children) lived in a Cantonese community as missionaries, totally integrated since they were both fluent in Cantonese and much-loved by the community.

On his return he found that Pablo was back from Manila with the final schedule of documents and staff recruitments to be done before the signing of the building contract by the end of the month. Again Tubby was involved on top of his other work, because all the big insurance companies were from the UK, with UK ex-pats who did not have broad enough experience to cope with all the aspects which International Manufacturing required from the establishment of manufacturing plant in a variety of locations around the world. The great bible of the ADI's was once more the basic guideline as they turned to the sections on new plant, machinery and so on, and in the end they were not satisfied with the respective insurance company presentations, which seemed to be an amalgam of specialised rates rather than the co-ordinated whole they sought.

It was like manna from heaven when someone out from London called Charles Rig came in to see them, announcing that he was a Lloyds broker from Hudig Làngeveldt, and asked if he could help. For the first time they felt they had in front of them someone who could talk their language and bring to their project his total broad knowledge and expertise in the insurance market, and then relate it to the ADI's and requirements therein. Within a few days he flew off to London to go into the Room at Lloyds with insurance package for the toothpaste factory. Within about a week he was back from London with rates established for the whole project which were significantly below those put together by the local offices of the big names in insurance. Without a murmur, the five selected insurers accepted the Lloyds rates at the prospect of getting a piece of the action, and particularly with the whiff of the bigger detergent plant project to come.

On the basis of this breakthrough into the high potential

market of the Far East, Charles Rig set up an office in Singapore which Tubby visited when he was next down concerning a problem they had been having with aerosol canisters of Palmolive foam shaving cream. Since these were pressure vessels they had concave bottoms, but obviously someone in R&D back at the factory had not really thought the design through for being in tropical heat. Particularly in Singapore, there were reports coming through of explosions in shops and display cabinets, which fortunately happened when people were not about and in the main were not too violent. However, one day Tubby went out with Swee Seng to reclaim one of these aerosol shaving cans which was embedded in the ceiling of a shop, having taken off from a counter display as perfectly as a V2 rocket from the violent kick as the can bottom changed from concave to convex. It became Charles Rig's gimmick in his Singapore office to have samples of these shaving cream aerosols in a corner behind sandbags waiting for one to actually perform in his office, which was not likely to happen because of the air-conditioning.

The month of June was becoming extremely intense with the Kevlin's 2nd July departure being in the balance almost daily. As the only Britisher amongst the Yanks, Tubby was particularly in demand for meetings with government officials, particularly when Ray Crearan, the merchant bank man arrived, almost straight from the meetings with George Lesch in New York. The Federation Treasury people required a particular amount of charm and delicate handling, being suspicious from the turn-down of the previous deal, and after one particular point raised, Ray asked for an adjournment. They retreated back to the office and from scrambled contacts with New York, they pinpointed a World Monetary Fund regulation which overcame the problem, and they were able to clinch the capitalisation deal with the Treasury Department. It was quite fantastic for Pablo to leave on schedule for return to Manila having got the contracts all signed for phase one building for the toothpaste factory.

They were able to see Pablo and Ray Crearan off to Singapore together in the first of the new Malayan Airways Vis-

454

counts – a four-engined prop jet – but alas, as seemed to be the habit in these parts, the engines wouldn't start and there was a two hour delay before a standby DC3 appeared. This breakthrough left them with just over a week before the Kevlins' departure, to get the application drawn up and signed for the pioneer status for the phase two detergent project, to do the half-year accounts for New York, and then make a start on the first half-year budgets for 1961. Accounts were not an onerous task now, since they had Rajah as their locally trained accountant/company secretary, who could make the staff jump through hoops and order them around in a manner any ex-pat wouldn't dare to.

From his visits to Ceylon, Tubby had high regard for the Tamils for their industry and business acumen, and Rajah was a natural wheeler-dealer for rolling money around using borrowings from numerous Tamil co-operatives, which were almost the equivalent of local Friendly or Trustee Societies in the UK. On one occasion he had come into Tubby's room when he was listening to a problem brought to him by Swee Seng and one of his credit salesmen concerning an Indian shopkeeper who was now three months behind with his account. On hearing the name of the shopkeeper, Rajah had become particularly attentive and when he heard the details he almost went pale under his dark Tamil skin. Tubby thought to himself that Rajah was going to sort the problem out without any race discrimination problems involving Chinese and ex-pats pressurising for the three months' credit to come to an end. However, he was completely thrown off guard when Rajah announced with some rage that he was indeed going to see this Indian shopkeeper, not concerning the repayment of outstanding account to Harpers, but because the shopkeeper was allowing Rajah only two months' credit on his personal grocery account while taking three months' credit from Harper Gilfillan. He was going to demand that he should have three months' credit too.

With the hectic schedule on the factory building and the financing and the pioneer status documentation, trips away round the branches had been abandoned and suddenly it was departure date for Jim, Rita and the kids and they were down at the airport to see them off. They were amused to find that the Unilever contingent were down at the airport to see their boss off on leave as well and, as with the ICI set-up on the higher floor of their office building, the two ex-pats of Colgate were heavily outnumbered by the ex-pats of the Unilever sending-off party.

That very day he got himself moved away from the mess and Malcolm, and into the arms of the Kevlin Cookie who helped Tubby unload his *barang* for him to take up residence for the next two months. He really did get waited on hand and foot.

The stark realisation that he was on his own came from being in the boss man's seat back at the office and the words of Harry Trueman became only too true; 'If you can't stand the heat, get out of the kitchen.' On the toothpaste factory front, work had actually started, and while Pablo was due back at the end of the month from Manila, he had left with Tubby a detailed check list which at this stage meant almost daily visits to the clerk of works on site, in tandem with the architect.

On chasing progress on the Pioneer Certificate for the phase two detergent project, he found that it had got onto the desk of Inche Khir Johari – the Minister of Commerce and Industry – but the parliament had dragged on and the minister had now gone on holiday for five days so he diaried it to check within ten days.

Before the ten days were up an official envelope arrived from the Commerce and Industry Department with the phase two approval, but to his horror he went on to read that it was 'in principle only'. After reference to a few of the remaining ex-pats in the ministry structure, and off-the-record chats with his friend, Ray Honey, at the church, who was a kind of 'insider', being within the Public Works Department and the designer of the new agricultural college, Tubby was able to cable New York with follow up letters indicating the requirement for a third subsidiary company. When gone into in detail it was fairly logical, since Colgate (Far East) had the toothpaste five year Pioneer status ahead of the detergent plant, which would then be wound up. Therefore, Tubby and Maurice, the awyer, put forward Colgate Palmolive (Asia) Limited for the phase two detergent project with start date in 1962, and it too would be wound up after its five year Pioneer Industry tax status to leave the original trading and marketing company Colgate Palmolive (Malaya) Limited. After not too long a time, a message came back from New York for the lawyer to work on another set of documents of incorporation for himself and Jim Kevlin once again to be the founder members of Colgate Palmolive (Asia) Limited.

In their first real full year, the sales and marketing side was going extremely well, since the free gift promotion at the beginning of the year had caused the wholesale *towkay* trade to take in more than a month's extra stock, while the gold rings and other activities had moved the stock out to consumers. With the whole credit and supervisory system beginning to work and John Bell back from leave with his bride, he was able to cope with these pressing matters on the corporate side, except that New York had cabled for legal action to be initiated by Maurice Edgar on the most recent rash of toothpaste imitations from Hong Kong and Taiwan.

Pablo duly arrived back from Manila for two weeks since it was quite electrifying to see how the factory site was developing. After a particularly intensive two days going over all parts of the works daily at the factory sites, checking against the ADIs, Tubby was particularly pleased at what he had been able to initiate on the insurance front with Charles Rig and, more importantly, it pleased Pablo no end too. Pablo's presence over the two weeks gave him a bit of scope for other work and after another two intensive days at the end, Pablo went off home expressing the opinion that by the time Tubby returned at the end of November with his new wife, the toothpaste plant and machinery would have arrived for installation.

Towards the end of August he heard from Jim Kevlin in New York that they were both to have company cars on return from leave. Tubby had never been able to work out at first the reluctance to push for company cars, which were a standard perk. Now that he was alongside general manager status he saw the whole scene in a different light, particularly the cut of the first twelve months' profits Jim was able to transfer to his bank account in Texas before going on leave. The cost of the cars would go into the next year, and with the toothpaste manufacture then on stream, with pioneer tax status, there would be a further significant jump in profits. The other news out of New York from big Ed Spika's Manufacturing Department was that a project manager was to be in KL for the big detergent project, a man by the name of George Boggs III, which conjured all kinds of images of American dynastic families in which his father and the second carrier of the name would be known as George Boggs Junior. Would there be such a person?

By the end of August, and with the Kevlin return date of 10th September becoming very real, Tubby found a creeping notion entering into his head which he tried to ignore until it became a sudden realisation that Pablo had not intimated a date for his next visit from Manila on the phase one toothpaste project, which was going ahead in leaps and bounds. There had been talk all along that a combined ten acre site and plant for toothpaste and detergent manufacture usually required an expat factory Production Manager, but nothing further had been mentioned. Suddenly, completely out the blue, a letter arrived from a Canadian calling himself Al Day who had been in Venezuela and was currently factory manager in the Dominican Republic, the country which occupied three-quarters of the island of Hispaniola, with Haiti occupying the rest. Both places were ruled by terrible dictators, with Papa Doc in Haiti, and Trujillo in Dominican Republic, who liked his people to refer to him as 'The Benefactor'. He ended up being assassinated in his car by a hail of bullets. Al was writing to say that he was going to be the next factory manager and was coming with his wife, Scottie, plus two boys, and could he have the low down on hotels and the housing situation. As parting action on the corporate front before his leave, Tubby was able to shoot off a reply and welcome, stating that the Days would most likely be in KL by the time he came back at the end of November with his new wife.

Running parallel to all the hectic demands of the corporate ront there had been a heightening action schedule focused on iis departure date of the 21st September. The posting of Immigration papers to Penelope for signature and return with photos for entry into the Federation as his wife, sharpened his mind as to getting over to his beloved something of the unusual happenings, habits and peoples of the Far East, since her travelling experience was limited to a few European continental trips.

There was also his day down at Ampang Village with his cine-camera for the all-day events at the temple or pagoda in that village named after the 'Nine Emperor Gods'. While Ampang Village was in what was still designated as a black area under the Emergency regulations, it was always open day for this annual event, The Festival of the Nine Emperor Gods. As the village was approached, the smoke could be seen rising above the trees from the huge bed of charcoal being prepared in front of the temple, which was adorned with great dragons and lanterns suspended from the turned up corners of the roof. Huge smoking joss sticks added to the atmosphere, and with smoke rising from the charcoal, and the incredible noises and rhythms from the gongs and cymbals from inside the temple, it was not difficult to imagine the Chinese mediums from this particular temple getting worked up into a deep trance.

The tension and atmosphere building up was palpable and with their backs to the temple walls were two elderly Chinese women in their black trouser suits with their hands together in an attitude of prayer, eyes closed, with their lined faces intense as they experienced a sense of innumerable demons around the place about to be placated by the mediums, who burst from the temple in a trance. Each had the long thin, tassled metal skewers through the cheek and the tongue and out through the other cheek, with yellow bands round their heads, bare chested above their coloured baggy pants. Two were carried on wooden thrones on poles by temple devotees, which made them rock like ships on a heavy sea, while the others on foot strutted around in most peculiar trance-induced movements. After parading once around the area before the temple under the canopy of smoke, sustained by the great noise of the cymbals and gongs and massive drums, some of them then strutted across the bed of charcoal with their bare feet. On entry back into the temple, Tubby was close enough to see them have the great skewers removed into a yellow sacred cloth without any gushing of blood. It was a tremendous experience to witness and once the mediums had done their bit and gone back into the temple, the great crowds who had gathered from far and wide with the little metal dishes from their domestic shrines almost fought one another to get pieces of the charcoal that had been walked upon. This they would carry back to stand on the domestic shrines and altars in the little bowls, since this charcoal was very special for warding off the demons for another year.

Demons appeared to play quite a role in the lives of the Chinese and often seen at windows were mirrors in the hexagonal set of original Chinese characters, which were also hung at doors to ward off any demons that tried to enter. Houses directly facing a 'T' junction, it was said, were avoided and gates to great cemeteries were often set at angles so demons entering therein might miss the graves. Once a year they seemed to have a great clean up day at the great shrines in the cemeteries and whole families could be seen as they covered the burial hillocks like ants, or sat in families for picnic.

One day his very down-to-earth, highly-regarded supervisor, Fung Swee Seng, asked that he might go back up to Ipoh since he had a message from the family that one of his sisters was in hospital and sinking away. This was most alarming news and Tubby had no hesitation in sending Swee Seng on his way as quickly as possible. On his return a week later he was glad to hear that sister was all well again, and sat transfixed as Swee Seng related what had happened. When he had got to Ipoh he had found the family in the big hospital round his sister's bed where she had been in a coma for several days by then.

Having confirmed from the medical staff in this fully up-to-date UK standard hospital that there was nothing more they could do, the family had asked if they might bring in a Thai Monk known in the district to have special powers. After an hour or so in the room with the sister out of communication, in a coma and sinking steadily, he had indicated that he was aware of what was going on and produced from his pack various leaves and tinctures which he set to smouldering in a special dish. Within two hours the sister had roused herself and sat up and indicated that she could do with some food and sustenance. From then on she was on a recovery pattern and the accepted explanation was that, since she and her Chinese husband lived in a government compound for civil servants, they were very much outnumbered by Malays and other nationals who had started to *suheil* them. This is emotive word in Malay language, of Arabic roots, for putting a hex, or spell, on someone – unto death. In some cases and certainly in other cultures, little figures are often left around to signal *suheil*. Coming to live and work amongst people from environments totally alien to one's own culture, it simply had to be accepted that people can have an influence put on them, even unto death.

The business side was continuing to run Tubby ragged, what with changing date lines as he went to and fro with the lawyer to the various government ministries. But this was all unbeknown and of little consequence to all at home, where Penelope's mother was beginning to run amok with the wedding preparations for October 15th – whether it might subsequently be changed or otherwise. Being a good Scottish family, there would have to be a present showing. All and sundry, and especially those who had come up with presents, would be expected to stop by at the bridal home to view a special room which would be set out with all the presents.

Since father-in-law was an invalid, they were used to visitors dropping in unannounced, and Tubby always reckoned they should have had in the kitchen something continuously on the brew, like a British Railways café tea urn. When Tubby had first come out to Malaya and found that Harper Gilfillan were the agents for the Boh tea plantations in the 6,000 foot Cameron Highlands, he had sent a volume bulk shipment home, and similarly when he had hit Ceylon for the first time, he fixed up through Rajandrams for a medium-sized tea chest to go to

461

the in-laws-to-be. On both occasions he had been dumb-founded to receive letters indicating that tea was much appreciated and almost finished. Anyway, the present showings would just step up this process a gear and with this, together with messages coming back about place for the Reception and so on, Tubby was beginning to understand that it might not be too bad after all to arrive back in the UK just a few weeks before the event on 15th October.

On top of this he had a letter from John Bell following his wedding to his Scottish lass in Innellan in Scotland, to say how he had been overwhelmed by the number of presents they had received and the unsuitability of many of them for life in tropics. This caused a flurry of letter exchanges concerning the lifestyles of wives of ex-pats, such as they hardly had need to go into the kitchens since they had servants! They needed lots of crockery and dishes and glasses suitable for mass entertaining and lots of suitable Marks and Spencer cottons, as recommended by other Harpers wives coming back from leave. In amongst all this there were letters to Reverend Poppa 'P' as the Minister of their Presbyterian Church was fondly referred to. This was the church which they had grown up in together and taught Sunday School together, and the Reverend wrote back confirming that the church was equipped with a 24-hour licence so they could have maximum flexibility for their day, which he began calling 'The Sunday School romance'!

Excitement was building up in the KL Church of St Andrew's as well with Margaret Honey being very imperious as concerned taking Penelope in hand once she came back as new ex-pat bride to be initiated. On the basis of this he began to refer to her in letters back home as Mother Honey, and related how she had been on a particular high during the months of June with the opening ceremony for the new agricultural college outside Kuala Lumpur, designed by Ray Honey himself. Because of his New Zealand origins, the opening ceremony was graced by the Prime Minister of New Zealand – then named Nash – and it proved to be a grand occasion all round.

After this great event for the Honey family, Tubby shot off

to get in a field trip to Ipoh and points north before the Kevlins' return, and while there he took the opportunity to go into the Harper Gilfillan Travel Department and ask them to work out a plane flight schedule for them to leave UK about the 10th November for Rhodesia in order to see his brother, the rest of the clans in that country, and the wonders thereof. The schedule was then to see a relation on Penelope's side in Nairobi, then another in Bombay, then Ceylon for a week of rest before hitting work schedules again by the end of November. Once this fell into place they really would have to try and hold to October 15th since he was to have a week in the London office to extend his leave, and a day at the factory in Salford, Manchester. The priority to him in Harper's Travel Department in Ipoh was to get his homeward bound ticket booked, first class, on the Comet for the 21st September, which would mean arriving in the UK on the morning of the next day, such was the new era of jet travel.

With the sending on of immigration documents for return with photos to allow her entry into Malaya, and with the excitement of coming out to Rhodesia for a visit on honeymoon on the way back to the Far East, Penelope's letters began to probe more urgently for unmentioned aspects of life in the tropics such as the heat, humidity, rain and the creepy crawlies!

While Singapore had intense humidity and great tropical downpourings of rain towards the end of the day, there were never any great experiences of thunder and lightning. Rumbles could be heard in the distance sometimes and at night time there were often distant flashings whereby the whole sky seemed to behave like a faulty fluorescent tube. Up in the Federation in Kuala Lumpur, though, the thunder and lightening could appear quite suddenly and be very intense indeed.

One day Tubby was returning to Kuala Lumpur by the high road above the valley through which the university campus was spread. It was very overcast and pouring down with rain when a great charge of lightning came down out of the sky and attached itself to the ornate dragon on the swept-up end of a very traditional Chinese building. He actually stopped the car

463

to watch this incredible sight since the lightning bolt did not just flash, but appeared to be channelling down out of the heavens and began to melt the dragon on the top corner of the roof end. On another occasion in the late afternoon when Tubby was walking along the landing from the lounge area towards his bedroom, there was a simultaneous deafening crack of thunder and the most blinding flash of lightning, and the stained glass window at the end of the landing became so brilliantly illuminated that Tubby found himself rolling over backwards along the landing, base over apex, exactly like Charlie Brown, Snoopy and others in the *Peanuts* cartoons getting bowled over backwards by some bolt from the blue. He understood this expression came from Africa where this sort of thing has been known to happen out of a blue sky, and as he picked himself up he fully understood.

On the matter of creepy crawlies and flying objects, life in Singapore and Malaya was certainly nothing like Thailand, Burma and Indochina, and indeed no room or household was felt to be complete unless it had the little chi-chahs, small cold-blooded lizards which ran across the ceiling and up the walls, at least one in each corner of the ceiling as its territory. In the evenings they darted round the lights gobbling up anything flying which came within range. The only problem came when they would drop off either in the act of lunging for something, or having periodic fights when they would get hold of the foot of another which would loosen the grip for them to drop off. They would readily scoot along the ceiling, their feet running in such a rhythm that there were always at least three of them attached at any one time. In the heat of the topics it was quite often a habit to lie on the settee reading in an evening wearing just a sarong and it would be a bit disconcerting when one of these little fellows fell off on to one's bare chest, causing an involuntary leap three feet into the air.

Nasty big fat cockroaches with their extended horns were attacked on sight and the odd praying mantis would appear at the windows. However, the thing that really made Tubby's hair stand on end was the great screeching beast. This was the great mutation of a bluebottle about the size of a man's finger which had appeared beside him in the airport lounge at Sibu in Sarawak which big Frank had picked up and thrown out of the window before it made any noise. One night in the big lounge of the KL mess, Tubby was again reclining deep in reading, wearing just his sarong before retiring when one of these things which he had not seen since Sarawak flew into the room.

As Tubby sat up to try and locate it, this greatly enlarged bluebottle thing started to try and get airborne again, like some overloaded helicopter as it went round bumping into chairs till it flopped down again towards the window. He went to the kitchen to obtain one of Bibah's floor sweeping devices, with the idea of swiping it straight out into the night again. His body came between it and bright light from the kitchen as he came through the door and it immediately let out the most piercing, blood-curdling, death throe kind of scream which sent Tubby on impulse straight along the landing and into his room with the door tightly shut. After finally convincing himself that, after all, it was just a flying insect, he made his way cautiously and slowly back into the lounge area to put off all the room lights and leave only the kitchen light on with the door partly open, then retreated to his room on the theory that the wretched thing would follow the light into the kitchen area.

About midnight he thought he had better just check to see if the strategy had worked, and as he cautiously peered through the glass window in the top part of the door into the kitchen, he saw that the huge bluebottle thing had settled in the middle of the kitchen floor. He then very carefully inched the door shut, except for reaching his arm in up to the elbow to press the light switch. The moment the light went out the thing screeched again and after nearly severing his arm in his haste to slam the door once more, he fled down the landing and into his bed for the night, under the sheet for even more security.

In the morning he made jolly well sure that he did not go bouncing along to the kitchen until he had heard Bibah in the kitchen getting breakfast. He sauntered along as nonchalantly as possible, all the time peering around the kitchen for any sight of the previous night's intruder, but all was clear as she had probably picked it up and thrown it out or given it to her cat to play with.

It was some weeks later that he was in a friend's house for drinks one evening when one of these oversized bluebottles flew in again and plopped on the floor, and the husband got one of his golf clubs to see it on its way. As he approached to take up his stand his body shadow came between the beast and the nearest strong light and again it let fly with its noise, but fortunately the golf swing was completed and away it went out into the night to the relief of all concerned.

While the episode of the screeching beast from the night was still very much on his mind, and the work level was almost impossible after one month running the show on his own, he received a call from a Dr Fallowfield – ships doctor on the Blue Funnel vessel *Peleus*, homeward bound from Japan and Hong Kong. Tubby had been tipped off from Singapore a few weeks earlier that Dr Fallowfield had called in to the Harpers offices at Collyer Quay looking for him when passing through on his outward bound journey.

Having had this tip off that the redoubtable Dr Fallowfield was out and about loose in the Far East, Tubby quickly resolved that he would come up from Port Swettenham for a day in Kuala Lumpur. Though Richard had been a form below Tubby at school in Birkenhead, they had shared the experience of being in school plays together. Subsequently, he had been in the same year at medical school in Liverpool as dear Penelope and was one of the 'inner core' in the medical year together with another girl from Penelope's school called Anne Jacques. Rather true to his larger than life character, Richard had decided to use his medical doctor's status to see the world and be paid by Blue Funnel Line for doing it, before he settled down to a strenuous mundane medical post back home. It was the first time Richard had ever been out into these parts of the Far East, and indeed all the other places on the way, and it was most refreshing to Tubby while taking him round Kuala Lumpur to feel his wide-eyed amazement and hear comments on things going on and sights about which Tubby had become quite blasé.

When they went into Selangor Club for lunch, Tubby had just called to the Boy for their drinks when ebullient Dickie Fallowfield seemed to have gone over the top, rushing over to another lady for big embraces and hugs all round and shrieks of, 'Fancy seeing you!' It turned out that she was Sheila Marsh – by then a Mrs Miller – working part-time in a medical practice in Kuala Lumpur since she had been about two years ahead of them at Liverpool Medical School. It turned out to be a right royal lunchtime session since Sheila Marsh produced a recent letter she had received from none other than Penelope's close friend Anne Jacques. From this she read out something about Penelope busying herself away at Broad Green while counting the days for the return of her Odysseus from his great adventure in the Far East.

Mrs Miller, as she then was, said that she was going back to the UK soon and would not be far behind Fallowfield when his ship, the *Peleus*, returned to Merseyside. Before they all parted, Tubby made them swear on the holy book that they would tell Penelope how utterly wonderful things were out here, with simply no mention of creepy-crawlies, cockroaches and least of all screeching beasts. In his follow-up letter home, reporting on this incredible meeting together in the Selangor Club, he again emphasised the lack of creepy-crawlies and related how Ray Crearan, the New Yorker, had said how pleasant it was compared even with Hong Kong, where some days it was necessary to change three times in certain seasons. In all innocence he was not to know that they would be hitting Rhodesia at the end of the long dry season when there were flying objects and creepy crawlies beyond all imagination and experience so far. Fortunately, his brother, his cousin, and his dear old Aunt Jean out there on the Lower Veld took all these flying objects as a part of the way of life and never thought to mention them.

It appeared that the marriage syndrome was spreading through the ranks of the Tankards rugby mob since John Marriott down in Singapore got married at the end of July. Big Tom Loughead from Liverpool was set to be hitched on the 10th September with a move to Mansfields Shipping in Penang, and Eddie Flannigan had asked Tubby to be his best man in

December when he would be back with his beloved Penelope after the great day on 15th October. Alas, Scoops still pined for his Liz who had gone away back to the UK.

With the hectic work schedule it seemed that the Kevlins were back sooner than expected, and with the demands of the last two months he had not been out and about in the open as much as normal.

So that he would at least appear bronzed at an October wedding as evidence that he was back from the hot tropics, he thought he had better get some sunshine on him at the Lake Club. However, with his fair skin it proved a bit disastrous particularly when on his return, he and Penelope went to see the Reverend Poppa 'P' in his rather immaculate study at the Manse to finalise wedding details. When Tubby stood up to take his leave he left heaps of peeled skin which had come down his trouser legs. Mrs Reverend was not amused.

Harper Gilfillan Travel in Ipoh had come up with the tickets for the great honeymoon trip back: London – Salisbury – Nairobi – Bombay – Colombo – Singapore – Kuala Lampur. On 21st September 1960, after two and a half years of non-stop living, Tubby was London bound on a BOAC Comet, with a business card in his pocket with Chinese on one side and English on the other, showing directorships of two international subsidiaries with one more to come.